SRA
REAL SCIENCE

William C. Kyle, Jr.   Joseph H. Rubinstein   Carolyn J. Vega

A Division of The McGraw-Hill Companies

Columbus, Ohio

Authors

William C. Kyle, Jr.
E. Desmond Lee Family
  Professor of Science Education
University of Missouri – St. Louis
St. Louis, Missouri

Joseph H. Rubinstein
Professor of Education
Coker College
Hartsville, South Carolina

Carolyn J. Vega
Classroom Teacher
Nye Elementary
San Diego Unified School District
San Diego, California

PHOTO CREDITS
Cover Photo: © Gary Vestal/Tony Stone Images

SRA/McGraw-Hill

*A Division of The **McGraw·Hill** Companies*

Copyright © 2000 by SRA/McGraw-Hill.

Send all inquiries to:
SRA/McGraw-Hill
8787 Orion Place
Columbus, Ohio 43240-4027

Printed in the United States of America.

ISBN 0-02-683806-0

3 4 5 6 7 8 9 RRW 05 04 03 02

Content Consultants

Gordon J. Aubrecht II
Professor of Physics
The Ohio State University
at Marion
Marion, Ohio

William I. Ausich
Professor of Geological
Sciences
The Ohio State University
Columbus, Ohio

**Linda A. Berne, Ed.D.,
CHES**
Professor/Health Promotion
The University of
North Carolina
Charlotte, North Carolina

Robert Burnham
Science Writer
Hales Corners, Wisconsin

Dr. Thomas A. Davies
Texas A&M University
College Station, Texas

Nerma Coats Henderson
Science Teacher
Pickerington Local
School District
Pickerington, Ohio

Dr. Tom Murphree
Naval Postgraduate School
Monterey, California

Harold Pratt
President, Educational
Consultants, Inc.
Littleton, Colorado

Mary Jane Roscoe
Teacher/Gifted And
Talented Program
Columbus, Ohio

Mark A. Seals
Assistant Professor
Alma College
Alma, Michigan

Sidney E. White
Professor Emeritus
of Geology
The Ohio State University
Columbus, Ohio

Ranae M. Wooley
Molecular Biologist
Riverside, California

Reviewers

Stacey M. Benson
Teacher
Clarksville Montgomery
County Schools
Clarksville, Tennessee

Mary Coppage
Teacher
Garden Grove Elementary
Winter Haven, Florida

Linda Cramer
Teacher
Huber Ridge Elementary
Westerville, Ohio

John Dodson
Teacher
West Clayton
Elementary School
Clayton, North Carolina

Cathy A. Flannery
Science Department
Chairperson/Biology
Instructor
LaSalle-Peru Township
High School
LaSalle, Illinois

Cynthia Gardner
Exceptional Children's
Teacher
Balls Creek Elementary
Conover, North Carolina

Laurie Gipson
Teacher
West Clayton
Elementary School
Clayton, North Carolina

Judythe M. Hazel
Principal and Science
Specialist
Evans Elementary
Tempe, Arizona

Melissa E. Hogan
Teacher
Milwaukee Spanish
Immersion School
Milwaukee, Wisconsin

David Kotkosky
Teacher
Fries Avenue School
Los Angeles, California

Sheryl Kurtin
Curriculum Coordinator, K-5
Sarasota County
School Board
Sarasota, Florida

Michelle Maresh
Teacher
Yucca Valley
Elementary School
Yucca Valley, California

Sherry V. Reynolds, Ed.D.
Teacher
Stillwater Public
School System
Stillwater, Oklahoma

Carol J. Skousen
Teacher
Twin Peaks Elementary
Salt Lake City, Utah

M. Kate Thiry
Teacher
Wright Elementary
Dublin, Ohio

UNIT A

Life Science

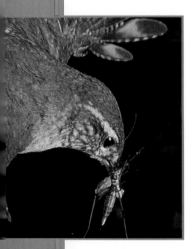

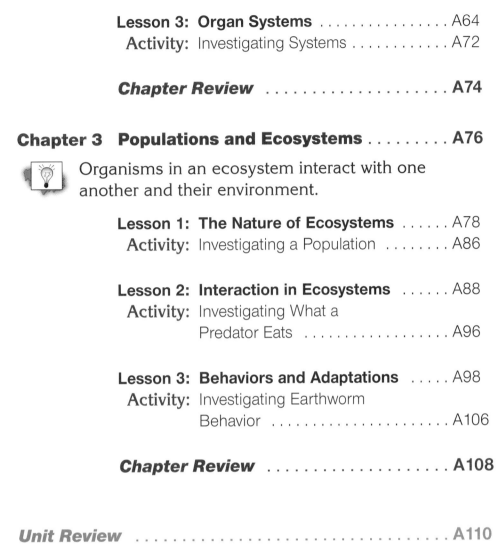

Organisms in an ecosystem interact with one another and their environment.

UNIT B

Earth Science

UNIT C

Physical Science

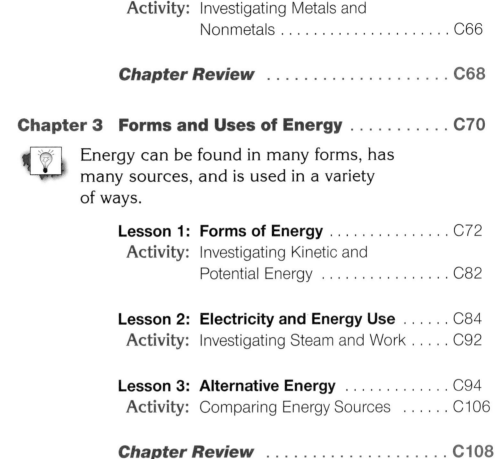

Energy can be found in many forms, has
many sources, and is used in a variety
of ways.

UNIT D

Health Science

Science Process Skills

Understanding and using scientific process skills is a very important part of learning in science. Successful scientists use these skills in their work. These skills help them with research and discovering new things.

Using these skills will help you to discover more about the world around you. You will have many opportunities to use these skills as you do each activity in the book. As you read, think about how you already use some of these skills every day. Did you have any idea that you were such a scientist?

OBSERVING

Use any of the five senses (seeing, hearing, tasting, smelling, or touching) to learn about objects or events that happen around you.

Looking at objects with the help of a microscope is one way to observe.

COMMUNICATING

Express thoughts, ideas, and information to others. Several methods of communication are used in science—speaking, writing, drawing graphs or charts, making models or diagrams, using numbers, and even body language.

Making a graph to show the rate of growth of a plant over time is communicating.

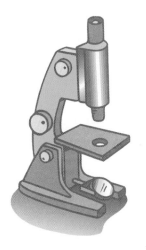

CLASSIFYING

Organize or sort objects, events, and things that happen around you into categories or groups. The classified objects should all be alike in some way.

Sorting students in the room into groups according to hair color is classifying.

Using Numbers

Use math skills to help understand and study the world around you. These skills include ordering, counting, adding, subtracting, multiplying, and dividing.

Comparing the temperatures of different locations around your home is using numbers.

Measuring

Use standard measures of time, distance, length, area, mass, volume, and temperature to compare objects or events. Measuring also includes estimating and using standard measurement tools to find reasonable answers.

Using a meterstick to find out how far you can jump is measuring.

Constructing Models

Draw pictures or build models to help tell about thoughts or ideas or to show how things happen.

Drawing the various undersea formations on the ocean floor is constructing a model.

Inferring

Use observations and what you already know to reach a conclusion about why something happened. Inferring is an attempt to explain a set of observations. Inferring is not the same as guessing because you must observe something before you can make an inference.

Imagine that you put a lettuce leaf in your pet turtle's aquarium. If the lettuce is gone the next day, then you can **infer** that the turtle ate the lettuce.

PREDICTING

Use earlier observations and inferences to forecast the outcome of an event or experiment. A prediction is something that you expect to happen in the future.

Stating how long it will take for an ice cube to melt if it is placed in sunlight is **predicting.**

INTERPRETING DATA

Identify patterns or explain the meaning of information that has been collected from observations or experiments. Interpreting data is an important step in drawing conclusions.

You interpret data when you **study** daily weather tables and **conclude** that cities along the coast receive more rainfall than cities in the desert.

IDENTIFYING AND CONTROLLING VARIABLES

Identify anything that may change the results of an experiment. Change one variable to see how it affects what you are studying. Controlling variables is an important skill in designing investigations.

You can **control** the amount of light plant leaves receive. Covering some of the leaves on a plant with foil allows you to compare how plant leaves react to light.

HYPOTHESIZING

Make a statement that gives a possible explanation of how or why something happens. A hypothesis helps a scientist design an investigation. A hypothesis also helps a scientist identify what data to collect.

Saying that bean seeds germinate faster in warm areas than cold areas is a hypothesis. You can **test** this hypothesis by germinating bean seeds at room temperature and in the refrigerator.

DEFINING OPERATIONALLY

An operational definition tells what is observed and how it functions.

Saying the skull is a bone that surrounds the brain and is connected to the backbone is an operational definition.

DESIGNING INVESTIGATIONS

Plan investigations to gather data that will support or not support a hypothesis. The design of the investigation determines which variable will be changed, how it will be changed, and the conditions under which the investigation will be carried out.

You can **design an investigation** to determine how sunlight affects plants. Place one plant in the sunlight and an identical plant in a closet. This will allow you to control the variable of sunlight.

EXPERIMENTING

Carry out the investigation you designed to get information about relationships between objects, events, and things around you.

Experimenting pulls together all of the other process skills.

UNIT A

Life Science

Cells

Earth is more than 4.6 billion years old. The first life on Earth appeared about 3.5 billion years ago. Through millions of years, many different types of organisms developed. Today scientists estimate that there are more than 10 million kinds of organisms on Earth, but only 1.5 million of them have been identified.

Fossils have been found that tell us that many more types of organisms once lived on Earth and are now extinct, or no longer exist. In fact, more organisms have become extinct than the 10 million that are now living on Earth.

Although millions of different organisms have inhabited Earth, all have something in common. All organisms are made of cells.

The Big IDEA

All living things are made of cells.

CHAPTER SCIENCE INVESTIGATION

Learn how substances move into and out of a cell membrane. Find out how in your *Activity Journal.*

Looking at Cells

Find Out

- How microscopes were important to the beginning of cell study
- How cells can be alike and different
- How to identify some unicellular organisms

Vocabulary

compound microscope
cell
cell theory
unicellular organisms
multicellular organisms
flagellum
cilia
pseudopod

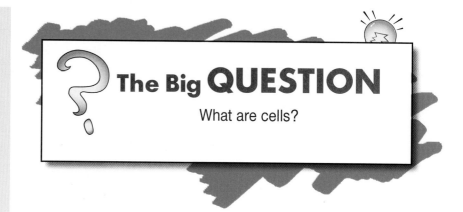

The Big QUESTION
What are cells?

*L*ook around you. What is the smallest living thing you can see? Can you think of other things that are even smaller? What about a flea or a seed? Even these tiny things have smaller parts that you can't see without help.

Early Microscopes and Cell Study

There is a whole miniature world that cannot be seen with the unaided eye. Before magnifying glasses and microscopes were used, no one imagined such a world existed. Without any knowledge of cells, some scientists believed that living things developed suddenly from dead and rotting material. When microscopes were invented, scientists began to see the world of cells and understand the importance of cells in all living things.

The very first microscopes were magnifying glasses. Many people have used magnifying glasses to observe things they could not otherwise see. Magnifying glasses are called simple microscopes because they use a lens to magnify the image of an object. It was not until the late sixteenth century that powerful microscopes using more than one lens were invented.

A Dutch maker of eyeglasses, Zacharias Janssen (yän′ sən), put two magnifying glass lenses in a tube and used it to view very small objects. Janssen's microscope made the objects look about 100 times larger than they appeared with the unaided eye. This type of microscope, which increases magnification by using more than one lens, is called a **compound microscope.** Janssen is credited with discovering the principle of the compound microscope in about 1590. This principle is still present in the modern compound microscopes that many scientists use today.

Microscopes can make objects or organisms look much larger than they actually are. How does this image of a black housefly compare to how the housefly would look without a microscope?

This microscope was used by Leeuwenhoek to study very small objects and organisms. With lenses that increased the magnification and with the use of light, this microscope allowed many details on the object or organism to be seen.

In the late 1600s, a Dutch linen merchant named Antonie van Leeuwenhoek (lā′ vən hŏŏk) made and used compound microscopes that were about twice as powerful as those made by Janssen. One of Leeuwenhoek's greatest contributions to the history of the microscope was his use of light to illuminate the object that he was viewing. By adding light, he could see not only the outline of the object, but also through it. This allowed him to see more details of an object than anyone before him had ever been able to see. When Leeuwenhoek used his compound light microscope to look at water from a nearby lake, he became the first person to see living things made up of only one cell moving in the water. Leeuwenhoek called these small organisms *animalcules.*

At about the same time that Leeuwenhoek was making his microscopic investigations, an English scientist, Robert Hooke, was also exploring the microscopic world. The microscope that Hooke used was not as powerful as Leeuwenhoek's, nor did it use light. However, in 1665, when Hooke looked at a sample of cork with his microscope, he noted that the cork appeared to be made of many boxes that had empty centers. Hooke called these boxes *cells*. Hooke made careful drawings and records of his cell observations. He published his findings, and the cell was introduced to many other scientists.

Since the seventeenth century, many different kinds of microscopes have been invented. Some of the microscopes are so powerful that they can look at objects much smaller than cells. We now know a great deal more about cells than the scientists of the seventeenth century did. Scientists have identified parts of cells, know how some parts function, and know how some cells are alike and different. Many of these findings have changed our understanding of how organisms, such as plants and animals, live and grow.

This instrument is a replica of the compound microscope used by Hooke.

This drawing is Hooke's record of the "cells" he saw when he looked at cork with his microscope.

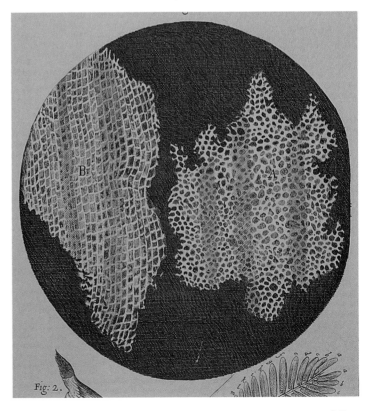

Fig: 2.

Cells Can Be Alike and Different

Many scientists have investigated cells and have increased our knowledge of what role they play in life. The **cell** is now understood as the smallest unit of living matter that can perform life functions. What most scientists consider to be generally true about cells has become the **cell theory.** The cell theory states the following:

1. All organisms are made up of one or more cells.
2. Cells are the basic units of structure and function in all living organisms.
3. All cells come from cells that already exist.

The cell theory did not result from the work of one person, but is based on the observations and discoveries of many scientists. The cell theory can help us understand some similarities that exist among living things. Once we know some characteristics that all cells share, the differences between cells can be more easily understood.

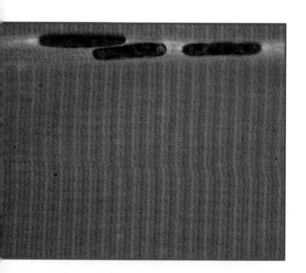

Cells are the smallest units of living matter that can perform life functions. Plant cells (right) perform some life functions, such as making food, that the animal cells (above) do not perform.

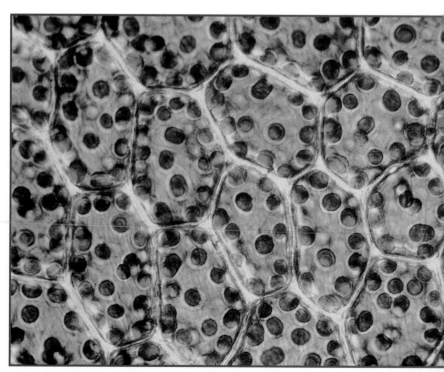

Cells can be different in many ways. Cells can be very different in size. Most cells are too small to be seen without a microscope, and the structures within them are even smaller. An average-sized cell is about ten micrometers in diameter. About 25 average-sized cells would fit on the period at the end of this sentence. Some cells, like a nerve cell in a giraffe, can be about a meter in length!

Cells can also have different shapes and colors. Some are spherical, like a ball. Others are shaped like cubes, with six sides, or have many sides. Some cells are flat and some are round. Many cells are colorless. Plants that make their own food have some cells that appear green. Cells can look very different from each other.

Some differences among cells are due to the function of each cell in an organism. Some organisms are made up of only one cell and are called **unicellular organisms.** These are the types of organisms that Leeuwenhoek saw when he used his light microscope to look at water. These organisms perform all of the processes necessary for life within one cell.

Organisms made up of more than one cell are called **multicellular organisms.** These organisms often have specialized cells that perform specific functions, such as muscle cells, nerve cells, and the cells that carry water and food in plants. Because of the different functions they perform, some cells of multicellular organisms can look very different from each other. Some organisms have billions of cells that work together to perform all of the processes necessary for life.

In Chapter 2, the way cells function in multicellular organisms will be looked at in greater detail. Now, let's take a closer look at how some unicellular organisms perform life processes.

Animals and plants, such as this hawk and cactus, are multicellular organisms, which are made up of many cells that perform specific functions.

Unicellular Organisms

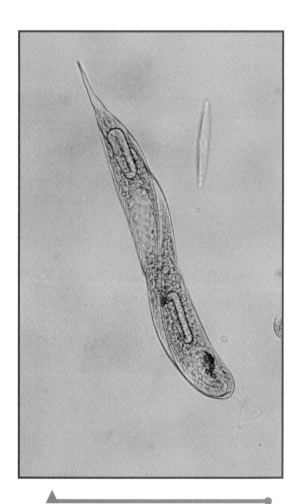

Euglena have flagella that can move them toward light and food.

Because unicellular organisms perform all of the processes necessary for life within one cell, they must also have a way to make or take in food. Some unicellular organisms make their own food, some move to find their food, and some do both. There are three basic structures that some unicellular organisms have to produce movement.

Some unicellular organisms use a flagellum to move. A **flagellum** (flə jel′ əm) is a long, whiplike structure that extends from a cell and moves the cell through water. An example of unicellular organisms that use flagella is euglena. These unicellular, green organisms are common in freshwater, such as ponds or lakes, but are not found in the ocean.

Euglena have a structure called a stigma, or eyespot, that contains material that is sensitive to light. The stigma allows the organism to sense the direction of a light source. When the stigma detects light, the flagellum moves the organism toward it. Euglena also have structures for food production and taking in food. The ability that euglena have to find light, make their own food, and also take in food helps them to survive.

A flagellum is the whiplike structure that is used by some unicellular organisms for movement.

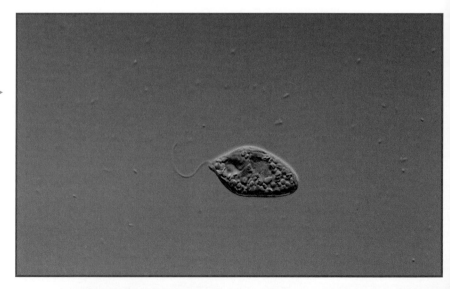

Other structures that some unicellular organisms use for movement are cilia. **Cilia** (sil′ ē ə) are short, hairlike parts on the surface of a cell. The cilia move back and forth very fast, causing the organism to move through water. Unicellular organisms with cilia are usually found in ponds and streams. One type of organism that has cilia is the paramecium.

The paramecium uses the cilia to move as well as take in food. The constant beating of cilia moves a paramecium through water. By controlling the movements of its cilia, a paramecium can stop suddenly, rotate like a spinning football, or go backward. Once food is located, cilia can sweep food particles toward a groove in the paramecium. In the groove, sacs are formed around the food particles and carried into the cell. The food is then broken down and used by the cell.

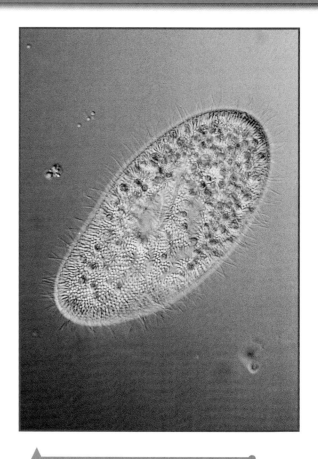

Cilia are small, hairlike extensions that move, causing the unicellular organism to move through water.

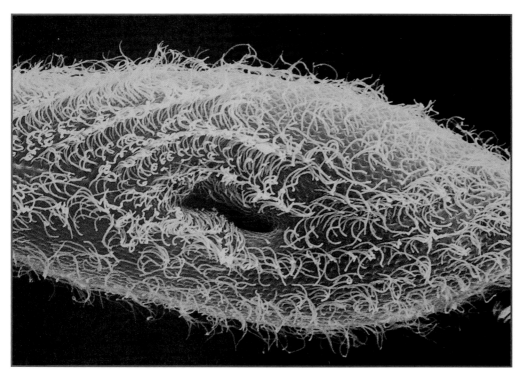

A paramecium uses its many cilia to move and sweep food toward the groove in the cell where food is broken down.

A **pseudopod** (so͞o′ də pod′) is an extension of the inside fluid of the cell that allows for the movement of some unicellular organisms. An amoeba (ə mē′ bə) is a unicellular organism that moves by using a pseudopod, or "false foot." The amoeba pulls or pushes itself over a surface by extending a pseudopod and then pulling the rest of the cell after it. Pseudopods are also used for feeding. An amoeba surrounds a particle of food or another organism with a pseudopod. The cell forms a sac around the food. This sac moves inside the cell, where it is broken down.

Amoebas have pseudopods to move and take in food. This amoeba is surrounding the food it is about to consume.

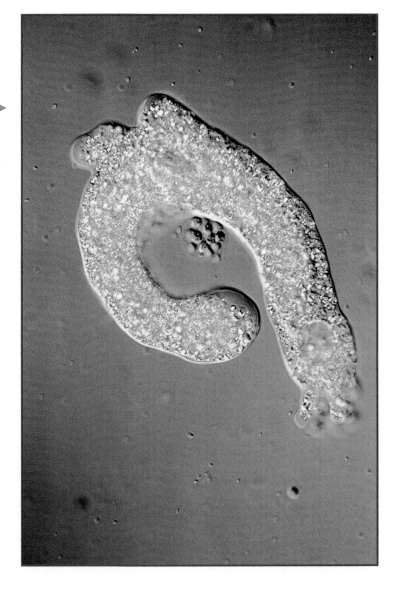

By having the ability to move, some unicellular organisms are able to find food, react to light, or take in food. For many unicellular organisms, the structures that allow movement are vital to their ability to survive and perform the processes necessary for life.

Living things can be found almost everywhere on Earth. Some of these living things have many cells, and some are made up of only one cell. Even though unicellular organisms and multicellular organisms can have many differences, both kinds of organisms perform all of the functions necessary for them to survive. Because of the microscope, which has been improved over many years, scientists have been able to learn a great deal about cells and about how cells function. Though cells are very small, they are very complex. Many things must happen inside a cell in order for it to live and grow. For us to understand how our bodies function or what makes up living things in our world, we first must understand the world of cells.

Living things can be found almost everywhere on Earth. This African elephant lives in very warm conditions and has many cells that allow it to live, grow, eat, and breathe.

CHECKPOINT

1. How were microscopes important to the beginning of cell study?
2. How can cells be alike and different?
3. Name two unicellular organisms and the structures that each uses to move.

 What are cells?

ACTIVITY

Investigating Pond Water Organisms

Find Out

Do this activity to see what kinds of organisms may be found in pond water.

Process Skills

Predicting
Observing
Communicating

WHAT YOU NEED

microscope

pond water

slide

dropper

coverslip

Activity Journal

WHAT TO DO

1. Place one drop of pond water on the middle of a slide and carefully cover it with a coverslip.

2. **Predict** what kind of organisms you might find in pond water.

3. Observe the slide through your microscope.

Safety! *Thoroughly wash hands after using pond water.*

4. Draw the organisms you see.

CONCLUSIONS

1. Compare your prediction with your observations.
2. How many cells made up the organisms you observed?
3. What parts did these organisms use for movement?

ASKING NEW QUESTIONS

1. Would you expect to see the same kinds of organisms in tap water as you did in the pond water? Why? What kinds of further information would be helpful to support your conclusion or to answer new questions that you have?
2. Based on the kind of microscope that you used, did you view cells more like Janssen, Leeuwenhoek, or Hooke did many years ago?

SCIENTIFIC METHODS SELF CHECK

✔ Did I **predict** what kinds of organisms I might find in pond water?

✔ Did I **observe** what was on the slide?

✔ Did I **record** my observations?

Cell Structure

Find Out

- What parts all cells have
- What organelles are and what they do
- How plant and animal cells can be alike and different

Vocabulary

cell membrane
cytoplasm
nucleus
eukaryotic cells
prokaryotic cells
organelles
vacuoles
mitochondria
cell wall
chloroplasts

The Big QUESTION

What parts make up cells, and what does each part do?

*A*s you have explored the world of cells, you have seen that cells can be different in many ways. They can have different sizes, shapes, and functions. Even though there are many differences among cells, cells can also have a lot in common. All cells have parts that allow them to live. Cells can have different parts, but there are some parts that all cells have.

Cell Parts Found in All Cells

In the last lesson, you learned that the cell is the smallest unit of living matter that can perform life functions. Cells have certain structures that allow them to perform their life processes. Because some cells live in environments that change, cells can meet great difficulties in trying to survive. A cell must be able to interact with its environment for its needs. All cells must bring in certain substances, keep out some substances, and perform their internal activities.

All cells have three basic parts. One part is the very thin covering that surrounds a cell, called the **cell membrane.** The membrane forms the boundary of the cell and allows certain substances to move into and out of the cell. The cell membrane allows needed materials to move into the cell and allows wastes to move out of the cell. Many different kinds of materials can pass through a cell membrane. Because the cell membrane is in direct contact with the cell's environment, it is a very important structure in the survival of the cell. The cell membrane is what separates the cell's contents from its environment.

Another part that all cells have is the gel-like substance inside the cell membrane, called **cytoplasm.** The cytoplasm contains a large amount of water, but it also contains chemicals and cell structures that carry out the life processes of the cell.

Cells have structures that allow them to perform their life processes.

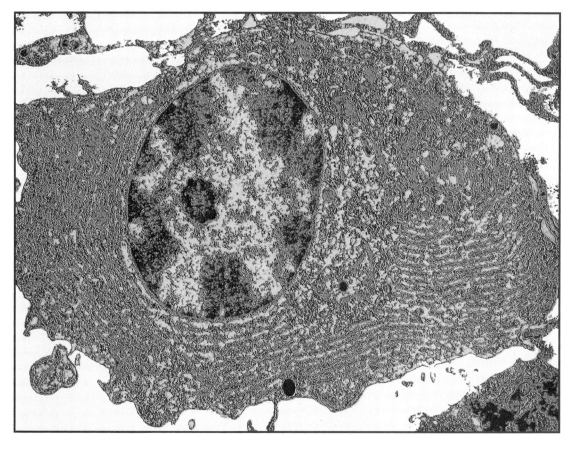

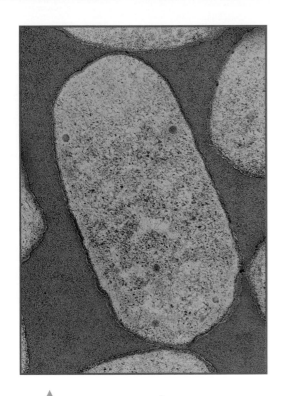

Prokaryotic cells do not have a nucleus.

The third structure that all cells have is a part that controls a cell's activities. This part acts as a kind of control center for a cell. Some cells have a control center called a nucleus. The **nucleus** is a structure that has a membrane around it and directs the activities of a cell. The nucleus also holds the cell's genetic material. This material is the information that tells the cell how to grow, change, and complete its life processes. Cells with a nucleus are called **eukaryotic cells** (yo͞o kâr′ ē o′ tik sels). The animal and plant cells that you will study in this lesson are eukaryotic cells.

Cells that do not have a nucleus are called **prokaryotic cells.** Even though prokaryotic cells do not have a nucleus, they do have genetic material that directs the activities of the cell. This material is clustered in part of the cell but does not have a membrane around it. A bacterium, a type of unicellular organism, is an example of a prokaryotic cell.

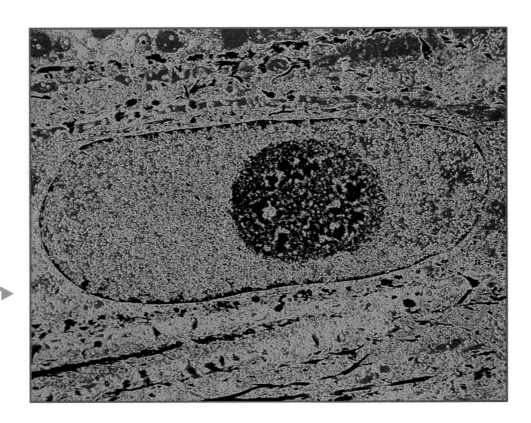

Eukaryotic cells have a nucleus.

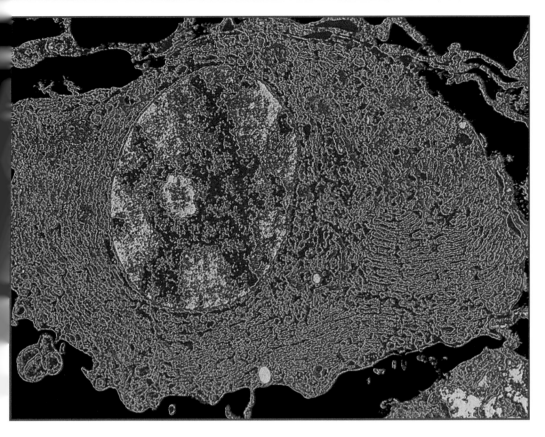

The nucleus is an organelle that contains the cell's genetic material and directs the cell's activities.

Organelles

A variety of structures can be found in eukaryotic cells. Many of the structures within the cytoplasm of a eukaryotic cell are called **organelles.** Each organelle has a specific job to do inside the cell. Organelles have a membrane that covers them.

In many cells, the largest organelle you can see is the nucleus of the cell. The nucleus is separated from the cytoplasm by a membrane. Materials can go into and out of the nucleus through very tiny openings in this membrane.

Other structures that can be found in some eukaryotic cells are vacuoles. **Vacuoles** are storage areas in cells. Vacuoles may store food, water, and other materials that a cell needs. They may also store a cell's wastes.

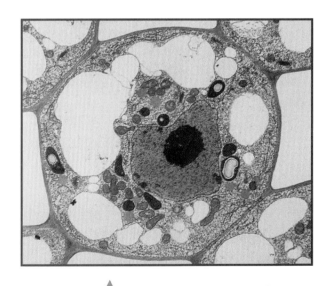

Vacuoles, which look like large, clear bubbles in this image, are storage areas in cells.

For a cell to function, it needs energy. **Mitochondria** are organelles in which energy is released from the cell's food. Mitochondria are like power plants for the cell. Cells need this energy for activities. Some cells, like the unicellular organisms you studied in Lesson 1, need this energy to move and find food or light. Some cells use more energy than others because they are more active. All cells need energy to perform their life processes. The mitochondria are the structures where this energy is released.

Mitochondria have an outer membrane, which faces the cytoplasm, and an inner membrane. The inner membrane has many deep folds in which energy is released from food.

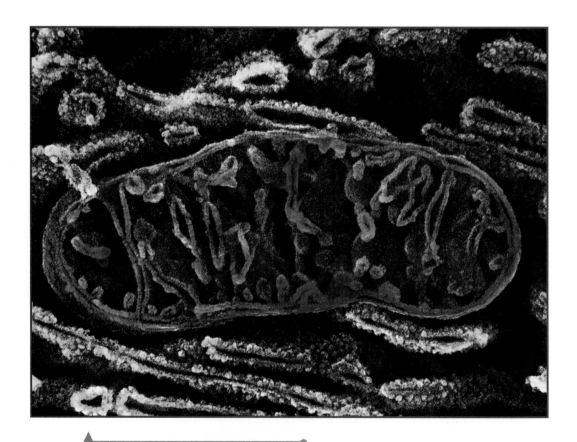

Mitochondria supply energy for cells to do their work. This image shows the deep folds of the inner membrane where energy is released from food in mitochondria.

The nucleus, vacuoles, and mitochondria are just a few examples of the kinds of organelles that can be found in the cytoplasm of cells. All organelles have specific roles they must perform to keep the cell alive and healthy. There are some organelles that move materials from one place to another inside a cell. Some package materials from inside the cell and move them outside. Others make chemicals that process wastes, worn-out cell parts, and materials that could be harmful to the cell. All of these parts must function properly for a cell to survive.

It is important to remember that there are many different kinds of cells. The organelles that you have been studying are only found in eukaryotic cells. Prokaryotic cells do not have organelles in the cytoplasm of their cells. In addition, not all eukaryotic cells have the same structures. Cells can have different needs and, consequently, different structures.

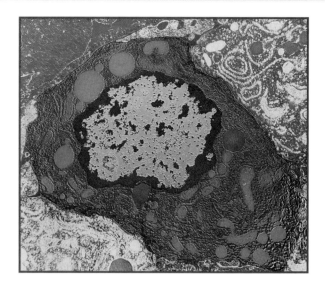

This animal cell has some different structures and functions than bacteria or plant cells.

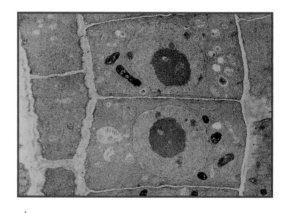

These plant cells are eukaryotic cells that help to support the plant and move materials from its roots to its leaves. The cells have structures that allow them to perform these functions.

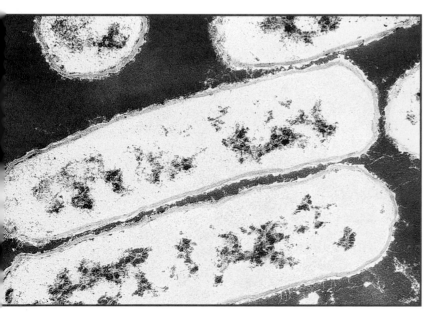

The bacteria in this image are prokaryotic cells that have some different needs and structures from those in plant and animal cells.

There are two basic types of eukaryotic cells—plant cells and animal cells. There are many structures that plants and animals have in common, but there are also some that are different. Look at the following diagrams of typical plant and animal cells. How are these cells alike? How are they different?

Animal Cell

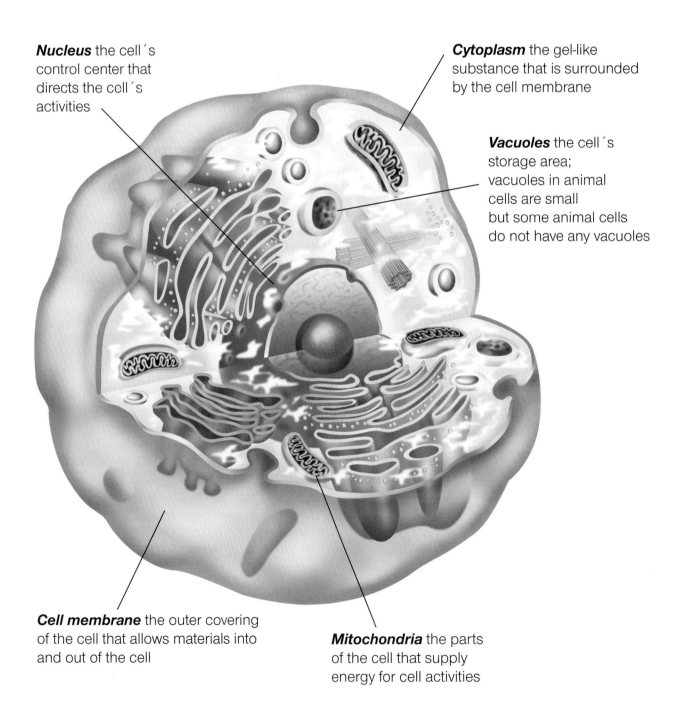

Nucleus the cell's control center that directs the cell's activities

Cytoplasm the gel-like substance that is surrounded by the cell membrane

Vacuoles the cell's storage area; vacuoles in animal cells are small but some animal cells do not have any vacuoles

Cell membrane the outer covering of the cell that allows materials into and out of the cell

Mitochondria the parts of the cell that supply energy for cell activities

Plant Cell

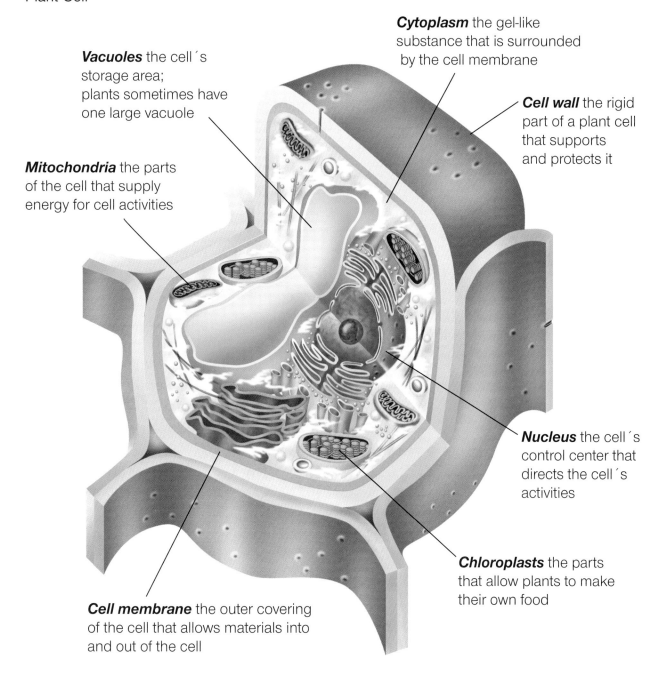

Vacuoles the cell´s
storage area;
plants sometimes have
one large vacuole

Cytoplasm the gel-like
substance that is surrounded
by the cell membrane

Cell wall the rigid
part of a plant cell
that supports
and protects it

Mitochondria the parts
of the cell that supply
energy for cell activities

Nucleus the cell´s
control center that
directs the cell´s
activities

Chloroplasts the parts
that allow plants to make
their own food

Cell membrane the outer covering
of the cell that allows materials into
and out of the cell

A23

Plant and Animal Cells

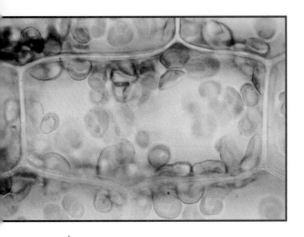

Cell walls protect, support, and give shape to some plant cells. The small, green, disk-shaped structures in these plant cells are chloroplasts.

By comparing the diagrams of the plant and animal cells, you could see that many of the structures appeared in both cells. There were also some structures that were not in both cells. What parts were not in both? Let's investigate what makes a typical plant cell different from an animal cell.

One structure that is not found in animal cells is a cell wall. The **cell wall** is a rigid structure outside the cell membrane that supports and protects the plant cell. The cell walls are made of tough fibers and other materials made by the cell. Like the walls of a building, cell walls shape and support plant cells. Cell walls provide support for a plant to stand and grow upright.

Unlike a building's walls, cell walls allow substances to move through them. Cell walls have tiny openings that allow water and other materials to pass through. Even the most solid-looking cell wall has microscopic spaces that allow substances into and out of the cell.

Do you remember Robert Hooke, the seventeenth-century scientist who identified cells in cork? Even though the cork cells were no longer alive, it was the remaining cell walls

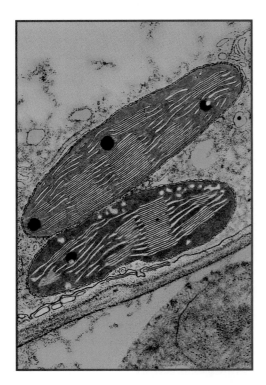

Chloroplasts have chlorophyll, a green pigment that allows plants to make their own food. This image shows two chloroplasts under very high magnification.

of cork that Hooke described as "cells." Cell walls can remain strong and rigid even when the contents of the cell are no longer there.

Other structures that can be found in some plant cells but not in animal cells are chloroplasts. **Chloroplasts** are small, oval- or disk-shaped structures that contain chlorophyll, a green pigment that allows plants to make their own food. It is the chlorophyll in plant cells that makes the plant look green. Most chloroplasts are found in the leaves of a plant, but chloroplasts also can be found in other plant parts.

Chloroplasts are organelles that can be found in the cytoplasm of some plant cells. Like mitochondria, chloroplasts have an outer and an inner membrane. The outer membrane faces the cytoplasm, and the inner membrane is organized into parts that look like stacks of pancakes. It is in these stacks that the plant cell traps energy from light to make its own food.

In each chloroplast, the inner membrane is organized into structures that can trap the energy from light.

CHECKPOINT

1. What parts do all cells have?
2. Name three organelles and describe what they do for a cell.
3. How are some plant cells different from animal cells?

 What parts make up cells, and what does each part do?

ACTIVITY

Comparing Plant and Animal Cells

Find Out

Do this activity to see how plant and animal cells compare.

Process Skills

Predicting
Observing
Communicating
Classifying

WHAT YOU NEED

microscope

slide labeled "A"

slide labeled "B"

Activity Journal

WHAT TO DO

1. Predict how the onion skin cells will be similar to and different from the cheek cells.

2. Observe the cells on both slides through your microscope.

3. Draw what you see in each cell. Label the cell parts.

CONCLUSIONS

1. Compare your prediction with your observations.
2. Did slide A contain plant or animal cells? Slide B?
3. How could you tell you were looking at plant cells?
4. How could you tell you were looking at animal cells?

ASKING NEW QUESTIONS

1. What are the functions of the cell parts that you labeled?
2. Based on your observations of the plant and animal cells, how might lettuce cells compare to cat cells?

SCIENTIFIC METHODS SELF CHECK

✔ Did I **predict** how the plant and animal cells would be alike and different?

✔ Did I **observe** how the plant and animal cells compared?

✔ Did I **classify** the cells and their parts?

LESSON 3

Cell Processes

Find Out

- Why cells need energy
- How materials can move into and out of a cell
- How cells get energy from food
- How some cells make food

Vocabulary

energy
diffusion
osmosis
active transport
respiration
photosynthesis

The Big QUESTION

What processes must cells perform to stay alive?

*F*rom the time you wake up in the morning until the time you go to sleep, you can notice ways that you interact with your environment. Your environment is everything that surrounds you. When you eat, drink, and breathe, you are meeting your needs with substances found in your environment. Cells also interact with their environment to meet their needs.

Cells Need Energy

When you looked at unicellular organisms through a microscope in the first activity of this chapter, you saw that some cells were very active and moved to find food or light. Through their movements, some cells were taking in light and materials found in the water droplet on the slide. Even as you watched them, the cells were using energy. They were also taking in materials that could provide them with more energy. All cells need energy to live and grow.

Energy is the ability to make things happen, to cause change, or to do work. You use energy when you clean your room. A cell also uses energy to make things happen, such as moving and organizing materials inside the cell.

One way in which cells interact with their environment is to find or make food for energy. All cells need energy to perform their life processes. Without energy, cells would not be able to live. If you did not have energy, you would not be able to eat, drink, or breathe. Every activity your body performs, even those that happen while you are asleep, requires energy.

It is important to know that the food a cell gets from its environment is different from the food you get from yours. Think of your favorite food. Can you hold this food in your hand? Compared to the food we eat, the food particles that cells need are very small. In fact, they are so small that you cannot even see them with your microscope.

All living things need energy to survive.

Movement of Materials in Cells

We know that the particles of food that cells use for energy are very small. In addition to food, cells also need other substances to perform their life processes. How do substances get through the cell membrane? The cell membrane has many tiny holes in it that allow some materials in and out of it, much like a fishing net. In a fishing net, the holes are big enough to let water and small organisms through but are small enough to catch larger fish. Similarly, the cell membrane allows water and some small substances to move into and out of the cell. Other substances, much like the large fish, are kept either inside or outside of the cell. Cell membranes allow some substances to pass through but not others.

Like a fishing net (left), the cell membrane allows some substances to pass through but not others. The cell membrane (right) has many tiny openings that allow substances to move into or out of the cell.

Like the materials dissolved in water in a cell or in its environment, the ink and water in the beaker are in constant motion. In time, the particles spread out evenly in the available space.

To understand the processes by which a cell moves materials inside and outside of a cell membrane, we first must look at the way a cell relates to its environment. Usually, cells are made up mostly of water. The environment in which a cell lives is also made up mostly of water. Many substances that a cell needs are dissolved in the water in the cell's environment as well as in the water inside the cell. The water and many of the materials dissolved in the water can move freely into and out of the cell. Even though you cannot see them, the materials dissolved in water are in constant motion. This natural motion results in the spreading out of particles. Particles have a tendency to spread out evenly in the space that is available to them.

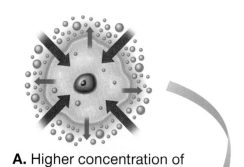

A. Higher concentration of particles outside the cell

B. Equal amount of particles on both sides of the cell membrane

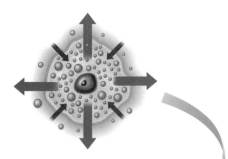

C. Higher concentration of particles inside the cell

D. Equal amount of particles on both sides of the cell membrane

Many of the materials that move into and out of cells do so because either the cell or its environment has a greater concentration of certain materials. This means there can be more dissolved particles inside or outside of the cell. When a cell has more dissolved particles inside its membrane, some of those particles will move out of the cell until the cell's environment has the same concentration of those particles as the cell does inside its membrane. If the cell's environment has more dissolved particles than the cell, some of those particles will move into the cell. **Diffusion** (dif yoo′ zhun) is the movement of particles from where they are more concentrated to where they are less concentrated. Particles in a solution can move through a cell membrane by diffusion. Many of the substances that cells need to perform their life processes, such as oxygen and carbon dioxide, can move into and out of cells by diffusion.

The diffusion of water through a membrane is called **osmosis.** If there is more water on one side of a cell membrane than the other, water will diffuse from high concentration to low concentration through a cell membrane. Water can enter a cell by osmosis. Diffusion of water into a cell causes pressure in the cell. This pressure pushes outward on the cell membrane and gives the cell shape.

Diffusion can occur through the cell membrane if the cell has a higher or lower concentration of a substance than its environment.

Water can also leave a cell by osmosis. If a cell is placed in a very concentrated saltwater solution, the concentration of water will be greater inside the cell than outside of it. Water will then move outside of the cell. The loss of water could cause the cell to shrink. If too much water moves out of a cell, the cell itself could die.

Cells also can move substances from lower to higher concentrations. This movement is the opposite of what happens in diffusion. **Active transport** is the movement of materials by living cells from areas of lower concentration to areas of higher concentration. Cells must use energy to carry out active transport. Cells must carry out active transport to keep many important life substances inside their cell membrane.

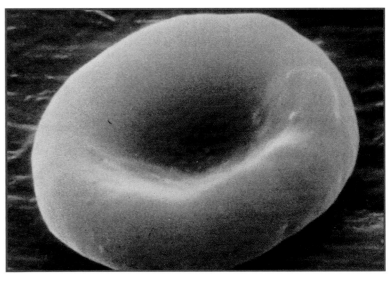

This normal red blood cell has equal amounts of water moving inside and outside of its cell membranes.

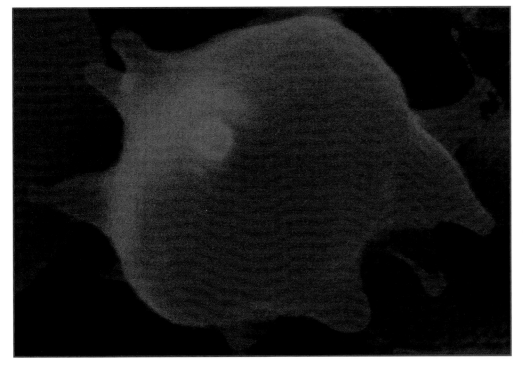

Because too much water has diffused into this red blood cell, it will burst due to the outward pressure exerted by the water on the cell membrane.

Cells Can Convert Energy

Once the cell takes in the food it needs for its life processes, the energy stored in food can be changed into energy that can be used by the cell. Neither you nor a cell can create energy. Energy can only be converted, or changed, from one form into another. Food has stored energy. This stored energy can be changed into energy to be used for work by cells.

The processes in a cell that release energy from food are very complex. As you know, the food particles that cells need are very small. When cells take in these particles and change them into a different substance, a chemical change occurs. A chemical change is a change that occurs when the chemical composition of a substance changes and a new substance is formed.

Cells get the energy they need to live and grow from a chemical change that takes place when the energy stored in food is converted to energy that the cells use to perform their life processes. **Respiration** is the process by which cells release energy from food. The food that a cell uses to get energy for work is called glucose. Glucose is a simple sugar. Most cells use oxygen to break down glucose. In respiration, oxygen and glucose are changed into two new substances— carbon dioxide and water. Energy is released in this process.

These in-line skaters get the energy they need from chemical changes that take place when food is used by their cells.

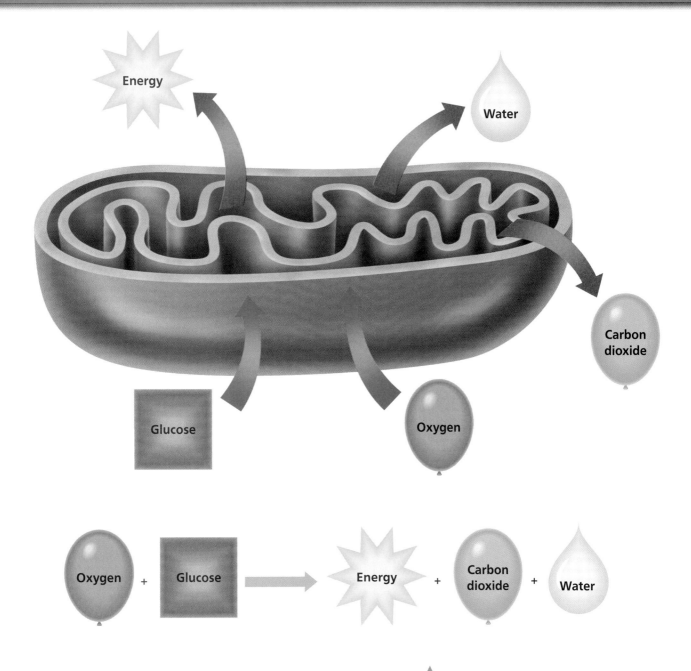

In mitochondria, oxygen breaks down glucose to produce energy, carbon dioxide, and water.

In eukaryotic cells, respiration takes place in mitochondria, the cells' "power plants." The number of mitochondria in a cell can vary. Cells with more mitochondria can release more energy than cells with fewer mitochondria. For example, a muscle cell may have more than 1000 mitochondria and can release more energy than the cells in fingernails, which have fewer mitochondria.

Some Cells Can Make Food

As you examined the way that cells can release energy from food to do work, you learned that some cells need to take in food and other cells make their own food. One important difference between animal cells and plant cells is that some of the cells of green plants trap energy to make food.

Photosynthesis is the process by which green plants use energy from light to produce food. In chloroplasts, chlorophyll traps the energy of light and stores it. Light energy, carbon dioxide, and water are needed for photosynthesis to occur. Carbon dioxide and water are combined to produce glucose. Light energy is changed into chemical energy, which is locked into the glucose that is produced.

What happens to the substances resulting from photosynthesis? Plant cells make use of the products of photosynthesis in many ways. Some of the oxygen is used by the plant cells for respiration and the rest of the oxygen is released. Sugar produced by plants is used right away for plant life processes such as growth, or it is stored in the plant. When you eat carrots or apples, you are eating the food stored by those plants.

The large leaves on this plant, which are almost a meter long, provide a large surface to receive sunlight for photosynthesis.

In photosynthesis, light energy is changed into chemical energy.

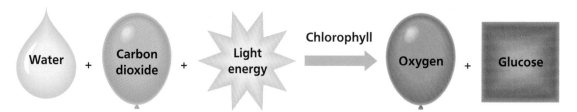

Water + Carbon dioxide + Light energy → Chlorophyll → Oxygen + Glucose

Comparing Photosynthesis and Respiration				
	Energy	Starting Products	End Products	In What Cells
Photosynthesis	stored	light energy, water, carbon dioxide	sugar, oxygen	cells with chlorophyll
Respiration	released	sugar, oxygen	water, carbon dioxide, energy	all cells

You might have noticed that the substances needed for photosynthesis to occur and the substances that result from photosynthesis seem familiar. These same substances are formed or used in respiration. Photosynthesis occurs only in cells that have chlorophyll. Respiration, however, occurs in all cells of all organisms. To see some of the ways that these two processes are alike and different, look at the chart above that compares photosynthesis and respiration.

CHECKPOINT

1. Why do cells need energy?
2. Name two processes that allow materials to move into and out of a cell.
3. What happens during respiration, and why is this process important to all cells?
4. How do some cells make their own food?

[?] What processes must cells perform to stay alive?

ACTIVITY
Investigating Osmosis

Find Out
Do this activity to see how osmosis occurs between a cell and its environment.

Process Skills
Observing
Communicating
Measuring
Predicting
Controlling Variables
Interpreting Data
Experimenting
Hypothesizing
Designing Investigations

WHAT YOU NEED

three slices of raw potato

three 250-mL beakers or glass jars

5 percent salt solution

10 percent salt solution

water

Activity Journal

WHAT TO DO

1. Label the beakers "1," "2," and "3."
2. Place a raw potato slice into each 250-mL beaker or jar.
3. Observe the texture and color of each of the potato slices and record your observations.
4. Measure 150 mL of the 10 percent salt solution and add it to beaker 1.
5. Measure 150 mL of 5 percent salt solution and add it to beaker 2.
6. Measure 150 mL of water and add it to beaker 3.

7. **Predict** what will happen in each of the beakers. Will osmosis take place between the potato slice and the salt solutions, the water, or all of them?

8. Allow the solutions to stand for 30 minutes.

9. Remove the potato slices and **observe** the texture and color of each slice.

10. **Record** your observations.

CONCLUSIONS

1. Compare your prediction with your observations.

2. Did osmosis occur between the cells in the potato slices and their environment in each beaker? How do you know?

3. Was there a higher concentration of water in the potato cells or in the salt solution in beaker 1? How do you know?

ASKING NEW QUESTIONS

1. Develop a testable question based on your observations in this activity.

2. Plan and conduct a simple investigation based on your question and write instructions that others can follow to carry out the procedure.

3. Prepare a report of your investigation that includes the tests conducted, data collected, or evidence examined, and the conclusions drawn.

SCIENTIFIC METHODS SELF CHECK

✔ Did I **predict** what would happen to the potato slices?

✔ Did I **observe** what happened to the potato slices?

✔ Did I **experiment** using different solutions?

CHAPTER 1

Review

Reviewing Vocabulary and Concepts

Write the letter of the answer that completes each sentence.

1. A ___ increases magnification by using more than one lens.
   - **a.** magnifying glass
   - **b.** vacuole
   - **c.** compound microscope
   - **d.** mitochondria

2. The smallest unit of living matter that can perform life functions is ___.
   - **a.** a chloroplast
   - **b.** a cell
   - **c.** an organelle
   - **d.** a nucleus

3. The gel-like substance inside a cell membrane is the ___.
   - **a.** nucleus
   - **b.** gelatin
   - **c.** cilia
   - **d.** cytoplasm

4. The ability to make things happen, to cause change, or to do work is ___.
   - **a.** energy
   - **b.** diffusion
   - **c.** active transport
   - **d.** movement

5. The process by which cells release energy is ___.
   - **a.** osmosis
   - **b.** respiration
   - **c.** photosynthesis
   - **d.** heat

Match the definition on the left with the correct term.

6. a long, whiplike structure used for movement by some unicellular organisms
   - **a.** mitochondria

7. very thin covering that surrounds a cell
   - **b.** cell membrane

8. cells with a nucleus
   - **c.** osmosis

9. the "powerhouses" of cells
   - **d.** flagellum

10. diffusion of water through a membrane
   - **e.** eukaryotic cells

Understanding What You Learned

1. Why was the invention of the microscope important to the study of cells?

2. How are unicellular and multicellular organisms different?

3. What cell structure allows movement into and out of cells?

4. Identify the three parts that can be found in all cells.

5. Name two parts found in some plant cells that are not found in animal cells.

Applying What You Learned

1. Describe how unicellular organisms use pseudopods.

2. How do cell walls help a plant live and grow?

3. Suppose a celery stalk became soft and limp after being in a salt solution for 20 minutes. Describe why the celery stalk became limp by explaining the osmosis that took place between the celery cells and their environment.

4. What substances do cells need to perform respiration, and what new substances are formed?

 5. Why are cell parts and processes important to the survival of living things?

For Your *Portfolio*

Think about all you have learned about cells. Draw a picture of a plant and an animal. Write about the similarities and differences between the plant and animal based on the cells that make up each organism.

CHAPTER 2

Structures of Life

Have you ever used a tool to make or fix something? If you needed to drive a nail into a wall, what tool might you use? What tool would you use if you wanted to cut a board in half? Tools like a hammer and saw have different parts that make them useful for one of these tasks but not the other. There is a definite relationship between the job these tools do and the size and shape of the parts they have.

The same is true of parts in multicellular organisms. There is a relationship between the shape and size of certain plant and animal cells and the jobs they do in an organism. In multicellular organisms, cells can work together to perform specific jobs or functions that the organism needs for life.

The Big IDEA

Living things have parts that work together to perform life processes.

SCIENCE INVESTIGATION

Learn how an individual plant organ is important to the survival of the organism. Find out how in your *Activity Journal.*

Tissues

Find Out

- How cells can work together
- What some animal tissues are and how they function in an organism
- What some plant tissues are and how they function in an organism

Vocabulary

tissues
epithelial
connective
muscle
nerve
vascular
dermal
ground

The Big QUESTION

What are tissues, and how do they function in plants and animals?

Have you ever watered a plant and wondered how the water got from the soil to the leaves? In the last chapter, you learned how individual cells take in water and food, but how do those cells work together in an organism? When you pull your hand away from something hot, brush your teeth, or eat a meal, the cells in your body are working together. Both plants and animals have cells that work together to protect the organism and perform the functions necessary for it to live and grow.

Cells Can Work Together

In the last chapter, you learned that some organisms are made up of only one cell and others are made up of many cells. Unicellular organisms perform all of their life processes in one cell. Multicellular organisms can have many different types of cells that work together to perform life processes.

Some plants and animals have billions of cells that must work together. In multicellular organisms, cells are specialized. That is, different cells have shapes and structures that allow them to perform specific functions. For example, animals may have nerve cells, muscle cells, and bone cells. Each type of cell has a different structure and function. Plants also have many kinds of cells with different structures and functions. Cells found in the leaf of a plant are quite different from those found in the root.

In both plants and animals, groups of similar cells that work together to perform a particular function are called **tissues.** In multicellular organisms, the cells in tissues can perform functions that an individual cell could not.

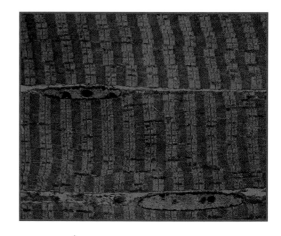

Muscle tissue allows animals to move.

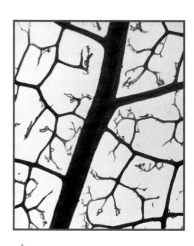

Vascular tissue allows plants to take in water and nutrients.

In multicellular organisms, cells work together to perform functions that an individual cell could not do by itself. The boy's muscle tissue allows him to hold the hose, and the plant's vascular tissue allows it to take in water and needed materials from the soil.

A45

Tissues in Animals

In both animals and plants, tissues perform important processes for an organism. Different tissues perform different functions to keep the organism alive. The kinds of cells that make up each tissue are designed to help the tissues carry out these functions.

In animals, there are four main kinds of tissue: epithelial, connective, muscle, and nerve. **Epithelial** (ep⁄ ə thē⁄ lē əl) tissue is made up of tightly packed cells that cover the bodies and make up the internal linings of some animals. The skin of animals is composed of epithelial tissue and can prevent harmful substances from invading the body. Epithelial tissue also makes up the inside lining of body openings such as the nose, mouth, throat, and stomach of animals. In the intestines, epithelial tissue absorbs nutrients. Epithelial tissue can protect an organism as well as help it to perform its life processes.

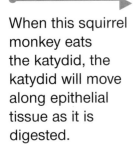
The lining of an animal's stomach is made up of epithelial tissue.

When this squirrel monkey eats the katydid, the katydid will move along epithelial tissue as it is digested.

A46

Connective tissue performs many functions in the body. One kind of connective tissue makes up the ligaments and tendons in an animal's body. These tissues hold muscles together and keep parts of the body in place. Fat, cartilage, and bone are also examples of connective tissue. Bones provide support and protection for some animals. Blood is also a kind of connective tissue found in animals. Blood transports food and oxygen to parts of an animal's body where they are needed. Blood also transports cells' wastes to areas where they can be eliminated from the body of the animal.

Muscle is another kind of tissue that can be found in animals. Muscle tissue is made up of cells that can contract, or get shorter, and relax. This allows the body and parts inside of an animal to move. There are different kinds of muscle tissues. Some muscle tissues can move an animal's bones, some can be found in its heart, and still others can be found in an animal's blood vessels, stomach, and intestines. The muscle types differ in where they are located, how their cells are joined, and how they are controlled.

The connective tissue in this white-handed gibbon is strong and elastic and performs many functions in its body.

Muscle tissue in the heart pumps blood through an animal's body.

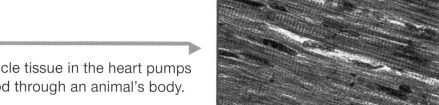

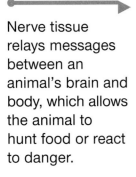

Nerve tissue relays messages between an animal's brain and body, which allows the animal to hunt food or react to danger.

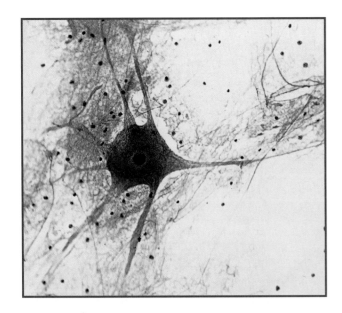

Nerve tissue relays information to and from an animal's brain.

Another type of tissue that some animals have is **nerve** tissue. Nerve tissue relays messages between the brain and the rest of the body. These messages allow the brain to keep all the parts of the body working together. Some nerve tissues receive messages from inside or outside an animal's body and send them to the brain. This type of nerve tissue tells the brain when it is time to get food and when the animal is in danger. Another type of nerve tissue carries messages from the brain to muscles. This tissue sends messages to muscles that cause them to move. Because of this type of tissue, an organism eats when it is hungry and runs away when there is danger.

Tissues in Plants

Some plants also have different kinds of tissues. Plants can be classified as either vascular or nonvascular. Vascular (vas′ kyə lər) plants have tubelike structures called vessels that move water and nutrients. Plants without vessels are called nonvascular plants. Nonvascular plants like mosses do not have stems, leaves, or roots, and their cells are not organized into tissues. Vascular plants, like trees and flowering plants, usually have roots, stems, and leaves with cells that are organized into tissues.

As the cells of vascular plants grow, they change and group together to form the different tissues of the plant. The three basic types of plant tissues found in vascular plants are dermal, vascular, and ground.

Vascular tissue is made up of vessels and is the tissue that moves substances throughout a plant. There are two types of vascular tissue: the xylem and the phloem. Xylem is a vascular tissue that carries water and minerals from the roots to the leaves of a plant. It is made up of dead cells with thick cell walls stacked end to end, like water pipes joined inside the wall of a house. The water and minerals taken in through the roots move up and through the cells to different areas of the plant. The phloem tissue is made up of living cells that move the sugars produced by photosynthesis from the leaves to the rest of the plant.

The vascular tissue in this giant sequoia move needed materials over the great distance between the tree's roots and leaves.

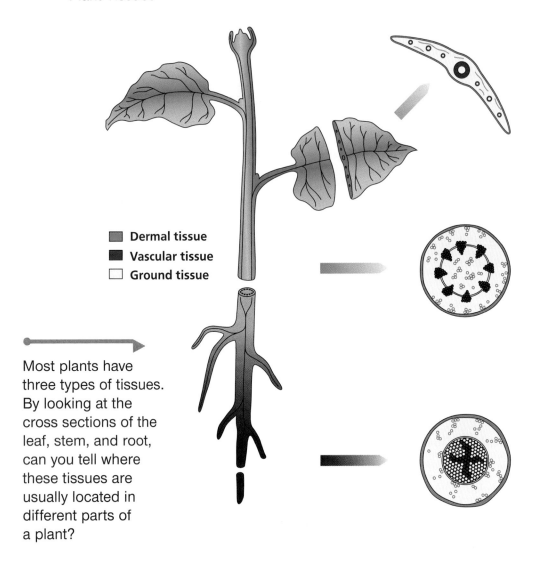

Dermal tissue
Vascular tissue
Ground tissue

Most plants have three types of tissues. By looking at the cross sections of the leaf, stem, and root, can you tell where these tissues are usually located in different parts of a plant?

Dermal tissue is sometimes called protective or surface tissue. This type of tissue forms the outermost tissue layer on leaves, roots, and stems. The dermal tissue on leaves can be covered with a waxy substance that prevents water loss from leaves. On stems, dermal tissue can sometimes be in the form of bark. Dermal cells can function to protect a plant. Some dermal cells also have chloroplasts and can perform photosynthesis, allowing the plant to make its own food.

All the remaining plant cells are part of the **ground** tissue, or fundamental tissue, in a plant. Some ground tissue cells perform photosynthesis and store sugars and nutrients. Others provide some support for plants.

There are many tissues that make up plants and animals. Tissues in plants and animals function when groups of cells work together to perform a job that one cell could not do by itself. Each type of tissue has many specialized cells, and these cells perform the processes that allow multicellular organisms to live and grow.

The cells in plants and animals work together to perform a job that one cell could not do by itself. How are cells working together in this organism?

CHECKPOINT

1. Name some ways in which cells can work together.
2. Give two examples of animal tissues and name some functions of each.
3. Give two examples of plant tissues and name some functions of each.

 What are tissues, and how do they function in plants and animals?

ACTIVITY

Investigating Plant Tissue

Find Out

Do this activity to see how the cells that make up a tissue can work together.

Process Skills

Predicting
Observing
Communicating
Interpreting Data

WHAT YOU NEED

plastic knife

water

dropper

food coloring

celery stalk with leaves

Activity Journal

600-mL beaker

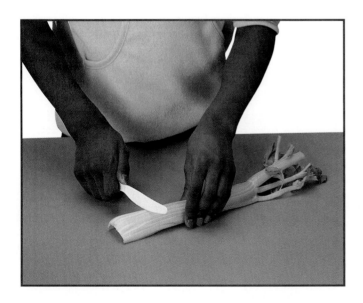

WHAT TO DO

1. Pour 100 mL of water into the beaker and put eight drops of food coloring in the water with the dropper.

 Safety! *Food coloring can stain.*

2. Cut off the end of the celery stalk that does not have leaves.

3. Place the celery stalk into the beaker so that its cut end is in the colored water.

4. **Predict** what will happen to the celery stalk in the colored water.

5. After one hour, **observe** the celery stalk and **record** your observations.

6. **Draw** an outline of the bottom of the celery stalk and show the parts that are stained. Now cut the celery stalk in half lengthwise. **Draw** what this cut edge looks like.

Conclusions

1. Compare your prediction with your observations.

2. What kind of tissue was stained by the food coloring?

3. How did the cells in this tissue work together?

Asking New Questions

1. How did you know what kind of tissue was stained by the colored water?

2. **Predict** what might happen if you left the celery stalk in the colored water for a day. Why might this happen?

SCIENTIFIC METHODS SELF CHECK

✔ Did I **predict** what would happen to the celery stalk in the colored water?

✔ Did I **observe** what happened to the celery stalk?

✔ Did I **interpret the data** I collected?

Organs

Find Out

- How tissues can work together
- What some animal organs are and how they function in an organism
- What some plant organs are and how they function in an organism

Vocabulary

organ
lungs
heart
intestine
roots
stems
leaves

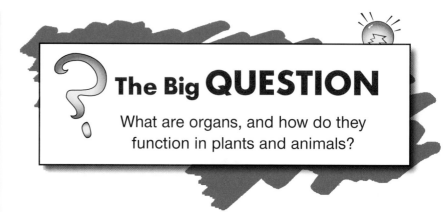

The Big QUESTION

What are organs, and how do they function in plants and animals?

Do you know what body part pumps blood in some animals? If you answered "the heart," you were right. Did you know that the heart is an organ? In the last lesson, you learned that specialized cells make up tissues that perform a specific task for an organism. Organs that are made up of tissues also perform certain jobs for an organism.

Tissues Can Work Together

In order to understand how a plant or animal performs its life functions, you must first understand how its parts are organized and how they work together. In the first chapter, you learned that cells are the smallest unit of a living thing that can perform life processes. Cells can be thought of as the most basic level of organization in a living thing, much like the letters in the alphabet. You know that multicellular organisms have specialized cells in tissues that work together to perform functions that an individual cell could not do by itself. In this way, tissues can be thought of as the words that are made up of letters. But what can words form? Organs can be thought of as the sentences that are made up of words.

Different types of tissues are often found working with other types of tissues in an organism. An **organ** is a structure made up of several different types of tissue that all work together to do a particular job.

Both plants and animals have organs that do a certain job for the organism. In multicellular organisms, organs perform functions that a single tissue could not do by itself. For example, your heart is an organ. Its job is to pump blood to all parts of the body. The heart is made up of connective tissue, muscle tissue, and nerve tissue. In order for this function to be performed successfully, all of the tissues that make up the heart must work together. Like the heart, all of the organs in plants and animals are made up of two or more kinds of tissue that must work together.

Like the heart, organs in living things are made up of two or more tissues that work together.

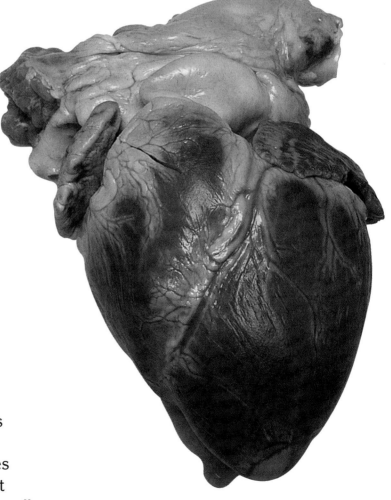

Animal Organs

An animal's lungs can have many tubes and air sacs that allow needed gases to be taken in and unneeded gases to be released.

Animals have many different organs that allow them to live and grow. Each organ is made up of a combination of tissues all working together to assist the organ in carrying out its particular function. In order to see how tissues work together in organs, we will look at three examples of animal organs and how they help the organism to survive.

One type of organ that is found in many animals is the **lungs.** The lungs are the breathing organs of mammals, birds, and reptiles. Most amphibians have lungs, too. The main job of the lungs is to exchange gases. As you learned in the last chapter, cells need oxygen for respiration. The lungs are the organs that bring the oxygen into the body. Lungs also eliminate carbon dioxide, the waste product of respiration.

Many animals have two lungs that are made up of different tissues that work together to exchange gases. Epithelial tissue lines the inside of the lungs and helps to keep harmful substances from invading the animal's body. The nerve tissue within the lungs carries messages from the brain that signal the lungs to bring oxygen to the body. A large sheet of muscle tissue found beneath the lungs helps the lungs take in and push out air.

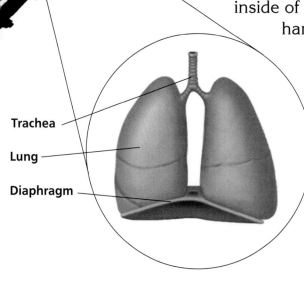

Trachea

Lung

Diaphragm

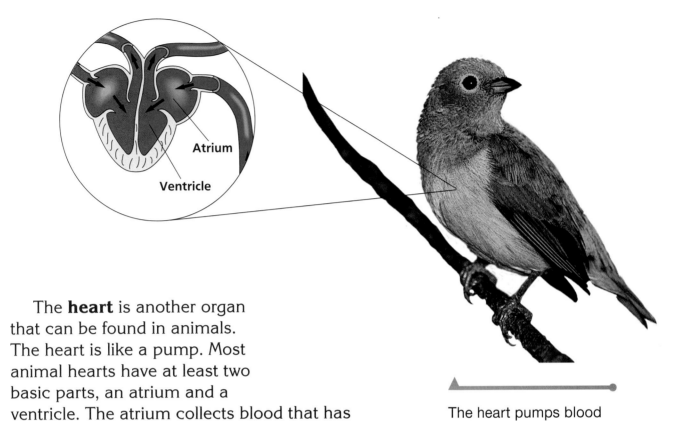

Atrium

Ventricle

The heart pumps blood throughout an animal's body.

The **heart** is another organ that can be found in animals. The heart is like a pump. Most animal hearts have at least two basic parts, an atrium and a ventricle. The atrium collects blood that has moved through the body and empties it inside a chamber called the ventricle. The ventricle is the part of the heart that pumps the blood into the animal's body. With each heartbeat, blood is pushed out of the heart and into the body of an animal. As the blood travels, it brings oxygen and food to cells in the animal's body. Blood also carries away the waste products that cells release and do not need.

As you know, the heart is made up of connective, nerve, and muscle tissues. The heart is made up of mostly muscle tissue. It is the muscle tissue that pushes the blood from the heart to the rest of the body. Nerve tissue in the heart relays messages from the brain to the heart muscles that tell the muscles when the body needs more blood. Connective tissue can be found throughout the heart. This tissue holds together some of the muscle tissues that make up the heart. Connective tissue also makes up the blood and blood vessels that run into and out of the heart.

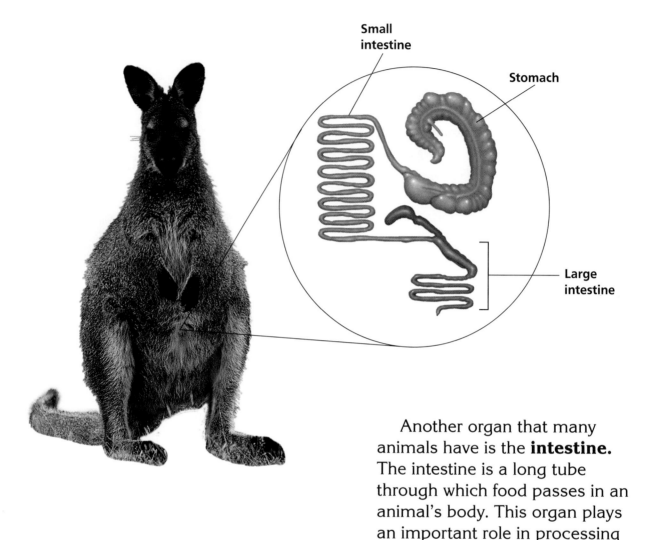

Small
intestine

Stomach

Large
intestine

The intestine is an organ
that helps to break down
food in an animal's body.

Another organ that many animals have is the **intestine.** The intestine is a long tube through which food passes in an animal's body. This organ plays an important role in processing the food an animal consumes. The intestine helps break down the food so that it can be used by the cells in the animal's body.

The intestine is made up of all four of the basic tissues that can be found in an animal's body. Epithelial tissue lines the inside of the small intestine. This tissue absorbs nutrients from food and carries them to the blood. The blood, a connective tissue, then carries the nutrients to all parts of the body. Muscle tissue in an animal's intestine helps move food through the body. The nerve tissue in the intestine alerts the brain that there is food to be processed. The brain sends a message back telling the muscle tissue and other tissues what jobs they need to do.

Plant Organs

Like animals, plants can have organs that are made up of two or more tissues that work together to perform a particular function. Plants have fewer organs than animals do. Roots, stems, and leaves are organs that can be found in some plants. Each of these organs is made up of vascular, dermal, and ground tissue. Although the organs are made up of similar tissues, each performs a distinct job that enables the plant to survive.

The **roots** perform many important functions for a plant. Most roots grow underground and anchor the plant in the soil. Roots also absorb the water and minerals that a plant needs to grow. In addition, many roots store food for the plant.

The tissues in a root work together to perform functions that the plant's other organs cannot do. The outer covering of the root is made up of dermal tissue. This tissue is made up of a single layer of cells that protect the tissue underneath. The ground tissue in a root consists of a thick layer of rounded cells just inside of the dermal tissue that store some of the plant's food and water. At the very center of the root is the vascular tissue. Here, the xylem carries the water and minerals taken in by the roots and moves them up to the stem and leaves. Phloem tissue moves food to the root cells so that they will have the energy they need to perform life functions.

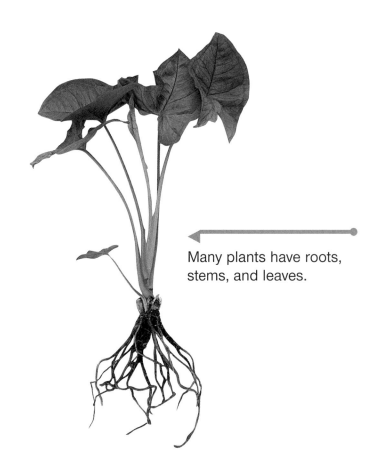

Many plants have roots, stems, and leaves.

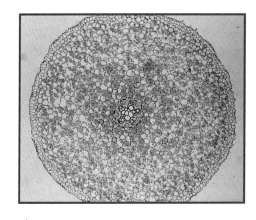

In this root cross section, vascular, dermal, and ground tissues work together to perform jobs necessary for the plant's survival.

A59

Stems are other organs found in plants that perform many functions for a plant. Stems support the leaves of plants. They help move the sugars made in the leaves to other parts of the plant that need food. Stems allow water to move upward from the roots to the leaves. Stems also carry minerals and sugars throughout the plant.

Like roots, stems are made up of vascular, dermal, and ground tissue. The dermal tissue surrounds the stem and protects the tissues that it encloses. The ground tissue makes up the majority of tissue found in stems and provides support and storage space for the plant. The vascular tissue in most stems is found in a ringlike pattern about halfway between the epidermis and the center of the plant. The position of the vascular tissue in stems allows water and minerals to move up the stem of a plant with support and protection on both sides of the tissue.

The stem of a tree is its trunk, which supports the tree and moves water, minerals, and sugars between the leaves and the roots.

In this stem cross section, the circular spaces are where water, minerals, and sugars move through vascular tissue. The ground tissue is found between the vascular tissue and the thin layer of dermal tissue that surrounds the stem.

Leaves are the organs that perform the majority of the photosynthesis in plants. The shape and structure of leaves can help a plant trap light and reduce water loss or can protect the plant. Leaves also exchange gases for a plant. Remember that plants need carbon dioxide to perform photosynthesis. In leaves, carbon dioxide can be taken in through tiny openings. Oxygen and water, released as a gas called water vapor, are released through a plant's leaves.

Leaves have tissues like those found in stems and roots. The dermal tissue is made up of a thin layer of block-shaped cells that cover the surface of a leaf. The vascular tissue in some leaves that looks like roads on a map are called veins. The veins help to support the leaves and contain the xylem and phloem tissue in the leaf.

By looking at some of the organs found in plants and animals, you might have noticed that the same kind of tissue can often perform different functions when found in different organs. Although the organs in plants and animals can be very different, all organs are made up of tissues that work together.

Wide leaves have a large surface that can trap light. The veins on this leaf contain xylem and phloem tissue and also help to support the leaf.

CHECKPOINT

1. Name some ways in which tissues can work together.
2. Name three animal organs and discuss the functions of each.
3. Name three plant organs and discuss the functions of each.

 What are organs, and how do they function in plants and animals?

A61

ACTIVITY

Investigating the Lungs

Find Out

Do this activity to see how an organ performs a particular function for an organism.

Process Skills

Measuring
Predicting
Observing
Communicating
Interpreting Data

WHAT YOU NEED

50 mL of bromothymol blue solution

drinking straw

250-mL beaker

safety goggles

graduated cylinder

balloon

tape

Activity Journal

WHAT TO DO

1. Tape the balloon to the end of the straw. The tape should hold the balloon onto the straw end and not let any air out when the balloon is inflated.

2. Put on safety goggles.

3. Measure 50 mL of bromothymol blue and pour it into the 250-mL beaker.

Safety! *Be careful not to swallow or inhale the bromothymol blue solution.*

4. When carbon dioxide is added to bromothymol blue, it turns green, then yellow. **Predict** what will happen when the air is released into the solution.

5. Blow into the straw to inflate the balloon. Pinch the straw so that the air is trapped in the balloon.

6. Put the straw into the beaker so that its end is under the surface of the liquid. Release the air from the balloon slowly.

7. **Observe** the color of the bromothymol blue solution and **record** your observations.

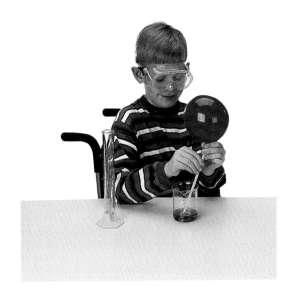

CONCLUSIONS

1. Compare your prediction with your observation.

2. Was carbon dioxide present in your breath? How do you know?

3. What particular function of your lungs was detected by this activity?

ASKING NEW QUESTIONS

1. What cellular process produces carbon dioxide as a waste product?

2. Would the gases released from the leaves of a plant change the color of bromothymol blue?

SCIENTIFIC METHODS SELF CHECK

✔ Did I **predict** what happened when I blew into the bromothymol blue solution?

✔ Did I **observe** what happened to the solution?

✔ Did I **record** my observations?

Organ Systems

Find Out

- How organs can work together
- What some animal organ systems are and how they function in an organism
- What a plant organ system is and how it functions in an organism

Vocabulary

organ system
circulatory system
skeletal system
nervous system
transport system

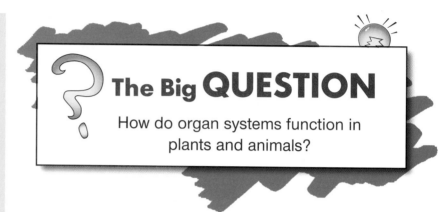

The Big QUESTION

How do organ systems function in plants and animals?

Have you ever played kickball with a friend? Did you realize that in order for you to run or kick the ball, many organs in your body need to work together? Your eyes see the ball, your brain sends messages to your body telling it when and how to move, and your muscles move according to messages sent by the brain. Organs in living things work together in many ways. Organs interact when you kick a ball, and they also interact to perform necessary functions that keep you alive and healthy.

Organs Can Work Together

In the last lesson, you looked at the way some parts are organized in living things. Cells are the basic units of organization in living things. Tissues are like words made up of letters, and organs are like sentences made up of words. The levels of organization in living things do not stop there.

The next level of organization in a multicellular organism is an organ system. An **organ system** is a group of organs that work together to perform a specific job. They could be thought of like a paragraph made up of sentences. The highest level of organization is an organism. An organism is made up of organ systems that work together, like paragraphs organized into a book. Each system plays an important role in keeping the organism alive and healthy.

In plants and animals, there are many organs that work together in systems to perform complex functions. Some organs in plants and animals produce chemicals that direct the growth of an organism. Others work to exchange gases between an organism and its environment. There are many functions that organ systems can perform. It is important to remember that although cells, tissues, and organs perform certain functions, the parts that make up an organism all work together. In multicellular organisms, any individual cell, tissue, organ, or organ system could not perform all of the functions necessary for the entire organism to live and grow. These parts rely on each other to perform their own specific functions.

The organs in living things must work together for an organism to survive. What organ systems in this Mediterranean chameleon are working together to catch the insect?

Animal Systems

Fish hearts have an atrium and a ventricle. Blood carrying carbon dioxide (blue) is pumped from the heart to the gills of a fish. The oxygen-rich blood (red) then moves through the body.

There are many systems that perform important life processes in animals. Although a certain type of system may be found in many animals, the parts that make it up can be quite different. The following pages will look at three systems that can be found in animals, discuss how the systems function, and show how these systems can be different in various kinds of animals.

One type of system that can be found in many animals is a circulatory system. A **circulatory system** is a system that moves nutrients and oxygen through an animal's body and removes waste products. Many circulatory systems are composed of a heart and a network of vessels that carry blood through the organism's body. The blood that leaves the heart is pumped to an area like lungs or gills where the blood can receive oxygen. The oxygen-rich blood is sent to the rest of the body, where it delivers nutrients and oxygen to cells and picks up wastes. The blood then returns to the heart.

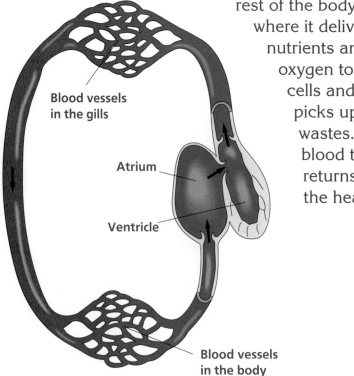

Blood vessels in the gills

Atrium

Ventricle

Blood vessels in the body

Multicellular organisms can have a circulatory system that is either open or closed. In an open circulatory system, blood does not stay within a network of vessels but moves freely through the animal. In a closed circulatory system, blood is pumped by the heart throughout the body in a network of connected blood vessels.

Animals like reptiles, amphibians, fish, and mammals have closed circulatory systems. Not all closed circulatory systems are the same. The heart and blood vessels can have differences in their structure that allow an animal to meet its needs in its particular environment.

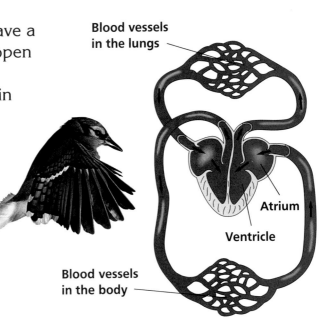

Blood vessels in the lungs

Atrium

Ventricle

Blood vessels in the body

Birds have four chambers in their hearts, two atria and two ventricles. One atrium and ventricle receive oxygen-rich blood (red) from the lungs and send it to the body. Blood carrying carbon dioxide and wastes (blue) enters the second atrium and ventricle, where it is pumped to the lungs.

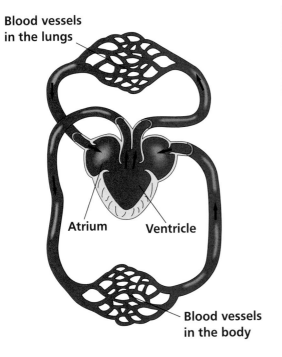

Blood vessels in the lungs

Atrium   Ventricle

Blood vessels in the body

Frog hearts have three chambers. The blood from two atria empties into one ventricle, where it is pumped in two different directions. The oxygen-rich blood (red) is pumped to the body, and the blood with carbon dioxide and wastes (blue) is pumped to the lungs.

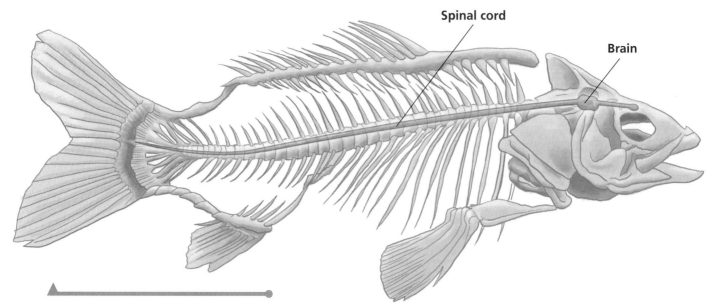

Spinal cord

Brain

In this fish, the skull protects the brain, and thick bones that stack together, called the spinal column, protect the spinal cord. Many of the internal organs of the fish are protected by the small, thin bones that run up and down along the fish's body. How does the structure of the fish's skeletal system help the fish to live and move?

The **skeletal system** is the system that provides shape and support in the body of some animals. In most animals, the skeletal system is made up mostly of bone. Some animals, like sharks, have skeletal systems that are mostly made of cartilage. Cartilage (kart′ əl əj) is a thick, tough, and flexible tissue that is harder than flesh but softer than bone. In addition to providing shape and support, the skeletal system protects the animal's organs. For example, some animals have a skull that protects the brain and ribs that protect the heart and lungs. The bones of the skeleton also contain many kinds of cells that play an important role in making and keeping an animal's blood healthy.

Like the circulatory system, a skeletal system can be found in some animals but can vary from organism to organism. The differences in size and structure of an animal's skeletal system can tell you something about its lifestyle and its needs.

The **nervous system** is the system that controls the activities of nearly all the other systems in the body of an animal. It enables the body to adjust to changes that occur within itself as well as to those that occur in its

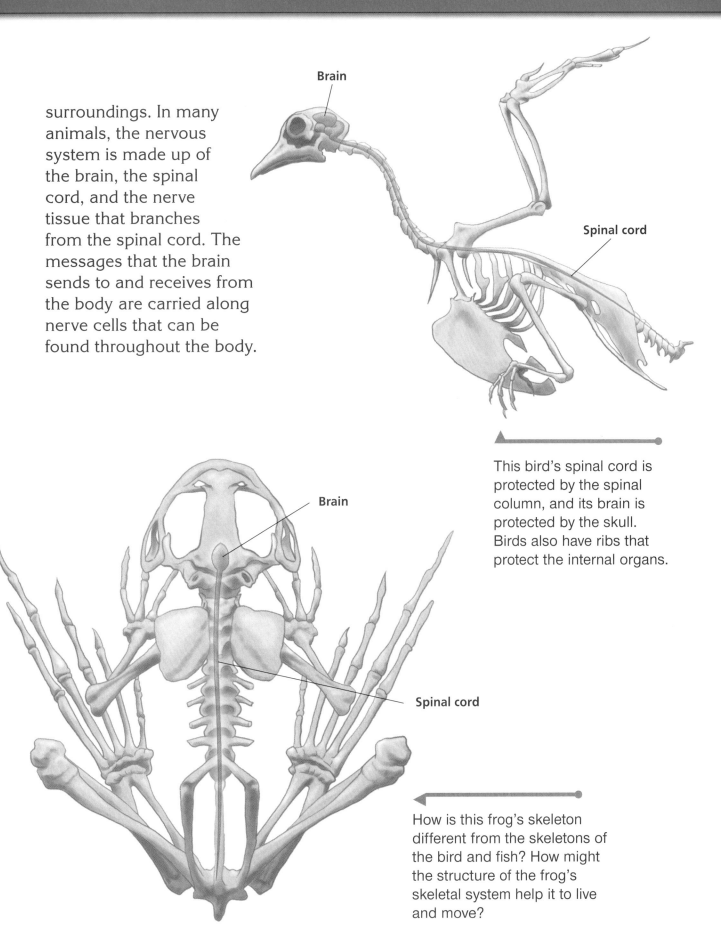

surroundings. In many animals, the nervous system is made up of the brain, the spinal cord, and the nerve tissue that branches from the spinal cord. The messages that the brain sends to and receives from the body are carried along nerve cells that can be found throughout the body.

Brain

Spinal cord

This bird's spinal cord is protected by the spinal column, and its brain is protected by the skull. Birds also have ribs that protect the internal organs.

Brain

Spinal cord

How is this frog's skeleton different from the skeletons of the bird and fish? How might the structure of the frog's skeletal system help it to live and move?

A69

Plant Systems

Unlike animals, plants do not have many distinct organ systems. In the previous lesson, you learned that animal organs could be made up of various tissues. You also learned that each organ in a plant is made up of dermal, ground, and vascular tissue. Even though plant organs are made of the same tissues, the tissues in each organ are arranged differently and perform different functions for the plant.

The transport system is made up of the leaves, stems, and roots. These organs must work together properly in order for the plant to survive.

Like the organ systems found in animals, the organ systems in plants work together to perform the life processes necessary for the organism to live and grow. The system by which the leaves, stems, and roots of a plant move water, nutrients, and minerals throughout the organism is called the **transport system.** A plant's transport system is made up of the leaves, the stems, and the roots. These three organs provide for the protection and survival of the plant. A plant needs the structures that allow it to make food; the structures that move and store water, nutrients, and minerals; and the structures that remove the plant's wastes. The transport system is made up of the organs that perform these important functions. If any of these jobs are not performed, the plant will not be able to survive. Although there are many differences in the organ systems found in plants and animals, all organ systems are made up of organs that work together to perform the life functions of an organism. By looking at the levels of organization in living things from cells to organ systems, you can see how complex organisms really are.

CHECKPOINT

1. How do some organs work together?

2. Name an organ system that can be found in animals, describe its function, and discuss ways in which the system could be different from animal to animal.

3. Describe a system that can be found in some plants and describe the organs that make it up.

 How do organ systems function in plants and animals?

ACTIVITY

Investigating Systems

Find Out

Do this activity to see how two animal systems can work together.

Process Skills

Observing
Communicating
Using Numbers
Predicting
Inferring
Interpreting Data

WHAT YOU NEED

a watch or clock
with a second hand

*Activity
Journal*

WHAT TO DO

1. Place two fingers on the side of your neck where your jaw and neck meet.

2. Push gently against your neck and move your fingers until you feel a strong beat. The beating you feel is from the blood being pushed through a large vessel called the *carotid artery* that runs along the sides of your neck.

3. Sit down and take a deep breath. In the sitting position, count the number of beats you feel for 20 seconds and **record** the number. **Multiply** this number by 3. This is your heart rate for one minute.

4. Also in the sitting position, place your hand in front of your mouth and nose. Count how many times you breathe out in 20 seconds and **record** this number.

5. **Predict** how your heart rate and breathing rate might change if you run in place.

6. Stand up and clear any objects that you might slip on off of the floor. Now run in place for two minutes.

7. Again, place your hand on your neck, count the number of beats you feel for 20 seconds, and **record** this number. Now count the number of times you breathe out in 20 seconds and **record**.

CONCLUSIONS

1. Compare your prediction with your observations.

2. What system did you observe when you felt your neck with your fingers? When you felt your breath?

3. What organ pumped the blood into the carotid artery that you felt in your neck?

4. Did you see a relationship between your heart rate and the number of times you exhaled?

ASKING NEW QUESTIONS

1. Based on what you know about the flow of blood in an animal, explain why a relationship might exist between your heart rate and the number of times you exhaled.

2. If your heart rate were measured while you were sleeping, how might it compare to the heart rates you recorded in this activity?

SCIENTIFIC METHODS SELF CHECK

✔ Did I **predict** how my heart rate would change?

✔ Did I **observe** how my heart rate changed?

✔ Did I **record** my observations?

Review

Reviewing Vocabulary and Concepts

Write the letter of the answer that completes each sentence.

1. ___ tissue is made up of tightly packed cells that cover the bodies and make up the internal linings of some animals.
   - **a.** Nail
   - **b.** Epithelial
   - **c.** Organ
   - **d.** Muscle

2. Tissue that is able to contract and then relax is ___.
   - **a.** rubber
   - **b.** bone
   - **c.** muscle
   - **d.** cartilage

3. The breathing organ(s) in mammals, birds, and reptiles is (are) the ___.
   - **a.** lungs
   - **b.** stomach
   - **c.** skin
   - **d.** hair

4. The ___ is a long tube through which food passes and is absorbed in an animal's body.
   - **a.** blood vessel
   - **b.** intestine
   - **c.** ligament
   - **d.** nerve

5. The organs in plants that release the most oxygen and water vapor into the air are the ___.
   - **a.** leaves
   - **b.** roots
   - **c.** stems
   - **d.** dermal tissue

Match the definition on the left with the correct term.

6. tissue that relays messages between the brain and the body
   - **a.** roots

7. the tissue in plants that moves water, nutrients, and other materials
   - **b.** vascular

8. the organ that pumps blood in most animals
   - **c.** nerve

9. the organs that anchor plants in the ground

d. circulatory system

10. the system that moves nutrients, oxygen, and other materials through an animal's body

e. the heart

Understanding What You Learned

1. How do cells work together in both plants and animals?

2. What does connective tissue do in an animal's body?

3. How does dermal tissue protect a plant?

4. How does oxygen move through an animal's body?

5. What system does a plant use to move water, nutrients, and minerals throughout the organism?

Applying What You Learned

1. Why is the heart made up of mostly muscle tissue?

2. Why are organ systems different in different animals?

3. What protective advantage does a snake, which has a skeletal system, have over an earthworm, which does not have a skeletal system?

4. How are plant organ systems different from animal organ systems?

 5. How do the systems in living things work together to perform life processes?

For Your *Portfolio*

Imagine that you are a frog for a day. Describe what you do and see during your day as a frog. As you describe your day, discuss what parts of your body allow you to do your daily activities and how your parts work together.

Populations and Ecosystems

Have you ever seen a spiderweb? The web that a spider makes is made up of many small, delicate strands. Some strands are attached to each other, and some are attached to surrounding objects that support the web. The web is strong enough to catch insects that the spider might eat, but it is also fragile.

Like the spider and its web, all living things interact with and depend on their environment. However, the relationship between organisms and their environment can become fragile and unbalanced. The ability of living things to meet their needs depends on their ability to successfully interact with their environment.

The Big IDEA

Organisms in an ecosystem interact with one another and their environment.

Learn how some organisms respond to a stimulus in their environment. Find out how in your *Activity Journal.*

A77

The Nature of Ecosystems

Find Out

- What an ecosystem is
- How physical factors affect organisms
- How niches and habitats relate in an ecosystem
- What population density is

Vocabulary

ecosystem
population
limiting factor
carrying capacity
community
habitat
niche
population density

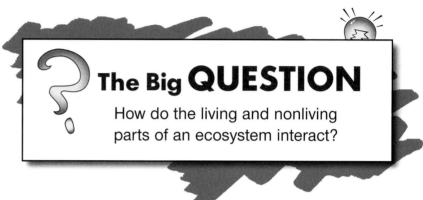

The Big QUESTION

How do the living and nonliving parts of an ecosystem interact?

All living things interact with their environment to meet their needs. How do you interact with your environment to meet your needs? Whenever you eat, speak to a friend, or ride in a car, you are affecting factors of your environment at the same time those factors of your environment are affecting you. There are many ways in which living things interact with their environment.

What Makes Up an Ecosystem

Surviving on Earth requires a complex set of interactions between an organism and its environment. The environment is made up of everything with which living things interact. The environment is made up of abiotic and biotic factors. Abiotic factors are nonliving things such as rainfall, oxygen, and minerals. Biotic factors include all the living organisms in an environment.

An **ecosystem** is all the living and nonliving things within a particular area and their relationship to each other. Ecosystems are always experiencing changes. Biotic factors change each day. Living organisms take in nutrients, grow, and reproduce. Some organisms are eaten for food. Others die and are decomposed by other organisms.

Abiotic factors in an ecosystem can also change. Abiotic factors such as forest fires or hurricanes can change an ecosystem very quickly. Other changes in the ecosystem happen over a long period of time. For example, the abiotic factors of an ecosystem change very slowly when rocks are broken down and form soil.

An ecosystem is all the living and nonliving things within a particular area and their relationship to each other.

Physical Factors and Organisms

Organisms interact with each other and with nonliving things in their ecosystem all the time. Water, light, temperature, and the availability of food affect the lives of organisms that live within an ecosystem. Some plants need cool, shady areas to live and some need bright, warm areas. Some animals live in hot ecosystems and some live in cold ecosystems. The abiotic factors help determine which and how many organisms can live in an ecosystem.

All ecosystems have a limit to the number of individuals they can physically hold. Although some plants and animals are well-suited to a particular ecosystem, there is a limit to the resources—such as food, water, and light—that plants and animals can share.

The abiotic and biotic factors that affect a pond ecosystem also affect what kind of populations will live there. Can you identify some populations in this pond ecosystem?

Ecosystems consist of populations. A **population** is all the organisms of the same species that live in an area. To describe the biotic factors of a pond, a scientist would identify the different species present and the approximate number of individuals of each species. For example, there might be populations of crayfish, ducks, and cattails.

The size of a population can change due to a number of factors. Suppose that near a pond you saw a raccoon catch and eat a crayfish. The population of crayfish would consequently decrease. If the cattails reproduced and more cattails grew, the population of cattails would increase.

Birth and death cause changes in the size of populations. So does migration—movement into or out of an area. If you returned to the pond in winter, you might find that the ducks were no longer there. The duck population decreased because the ducks flew to a warmer place.

Population size also can change because of the conditions in the ecosystem that affect the growth and reproduction of a population. When provided with perfect conditions for growth and reproduction, almost any organism will experience a rapid increase in its population. The number of individuals that could be produced in a population under perfect conditions is its biotic potential.

Because conditions are almost never perfect, populations do not reach their biotic potential. Limiting factors can prevent a population from reaching its biotic potential. A **limiting factor** is any condition that restricts the growth or survival of an organism or species. For example, a lack of resources that a population needs to survive—such as food, light, or water—is a limiting factor.

Overpopulation of wildebeests in Africa has resulted in overgrazing and an eventual decrease in the population.

What do you suppose happens to the size of a population if the changes due to birth and immigration are equal to changes due to death and emigration, or the movement out of an area? The answer is that the size of the population stays about the same, or stabilizes, at a level called carrying capacity. **Carrying capacity** is the largest population size in an area that the resources can support.

All the populations that live in an ecosystem make up a **community.** The community present in an area is mainly determined by the abiotic factors of the area. For example, a population of fish would be common in a pond due to its abiotic factors, such as water. Fish would not be able to live in a field because it lacks necessary abiotic factors that a fish population needs. Abiotic factors, such as the amount of available resources in an ecosystem, also affect the community that might live there.

Niches and Habitats in an Ecosystem

Each of the populations in a community has a place where it lives and meets its needs. A **habitat** is the place where a population lives. Populations can share the same habitat. For example, mice and grass might live in the same field habitat as a hawk. An ecosystem has many habitats within it, with many populations occupying each habitat. The ecosystem of a hawk might include a field, pond, stream, and clump of trees.

Each population has a particular role or function, much as you have a particular role in your household. The role or function of an organism in a community is its **niche.** Although many populations share a habitat, only one population can occupy a niche. The hawk's niche is eating small mammals in the field. The niche of a cattail is at the edge of a pond. Cattails can serve as a source of food for other organisms.

In this ecosystem, many different populations share the same habitat. Can you guess what niches these organisms have in this community?

Population Density

If you looked at a field or pond and counted the number of individuals that lived there, you would be calculating the population density of the area. **Population density** is the number of individuals per unit of living space in an ecosystem.

Population density can vary from place to place. Within a pond, the populations of some organisms might be greater in some areas than others. For example, there might be many cattails growing along one section of the pond while another section may not have any or only a few cattails.

All populations fall into one of three patterns of population density. The individual organisms are spread out evenly, unevenly, or into clumps. The most common pattern is clumping. Think about the lunchroom at your school. In what pattern is the population of students there usually distributed? Students are often clumped in the lunchroom by groups of friends.

Clumping happens when organisms form groups for protection, to help one another, or when resources such as food or water are concentrated in one spot. Some birds in flocks protect each other by giving warning cries when danger approaches. Kittens may huddle together when they sleep to keep warm. Wolves that clump in a pack hunt for food together and provide protection for each other.

These flamingoes clump together for protection.

Even spacing allows creosote bushes to get enough resources to survive.

Another pattern in which populations can be found is when they are spaced evenly. Creosote (krē′ ō sōt′) bush populations are evenly spaced. In the dry soil of the desert, creosote bushes need to be far away from each other to acquire all the resources they need to survive. The roots of the creosote bush produce chemicals that keep other creosote bushes from growing close enough to compete for water and nutrients.

The least common pattern of populations is uneven spacing. Trees and other plants in tropical rain forests come close to being unevenly spaced. Uneven spacing in populations can happen when organisms appear to be located randomly in an area due to abundant resources.

Ecosystems and the populations in them are changing all the time. Populations in ecosystems change constantly due to birth, death, or migration. Limiting factors affect the rate of change in a population. When an environment reaches its carrying capacity, a population stabilizes. Even though the size of populations might become steady, the organisms and the abiotic factors that make up ecosystems are still changing in many ways.

Trees and plants within some tropical rain forests grow in an uneven spacing pattern.

CHECKPOINT

1. What is an ecosystem?
2. How do the physical factors of an ecosystem affect where organisms live?
3. How are niches and habitats related in an ecosystem?
4. What is population density?

 How do the living and nonliving parts of an ecosystem interact?

ACTIVITY

Investigating a Population

Find Out

Do this activity to see what changes can affect a population.

Process Skills

Predicting
Using Numbers
Interpreting Data
Inferring

Year	Number of Mice per 1000 Square Meters
1989	97
1990	94
1991	91
1992	88
1993	79
1994	67
1995	52
1996	48
1997	30
1998	26
1999	17

WHAT YOU NEED

Activity
Journal

ruler

WHAT TO DO

1. Review the following information:

   In 1987, there were no houses in a large field. By 1999, there were 300 houses built upon the field. A biologist found a population of field mice living in this field. The biologist observed this population from 1989 to 1999.

2. **Predict** what you think happened to the mouse population between 1989 and 1999.

3. On a sheet of graph paper, draw a line across the bottom of the page. Mark this horizontal line with the years 1989 to 1999 and label it "Years Observed."

4. Now draw a vertical line along the left side of the page. Label it "Size of Mouse Population." Mark the vertical line with the numbers 0 to 100, with the zero on the spot where the horizontal and vertical lines meet.

5. Study the information in the table and plot the data for the field mouse population on the graph.

6. Connect the data points with a ruler to make a line graph. Continue the line to the right of the last point so you can estimate the size of the mouse population in the year 2000.

CONCLUSIONS

1. Was your prediction supported by the data? Why or why not?

2. Did the number of mice increase or decrease between 1989 and 1999?

3. Between which two years was there the greatest change in the population?

4. Infer what limiting factors affected the population size of the field mice.

ASKING NEW QUESTIONS

1. List two factors that could cause the mouse population to decrease.

2. List two factors that could cause the mouse population to increase.

SCIENTIFIC METHODS SELF CHECK

✔ Did I **predict** what happened to the field mice?

✔ Did I **interpret the data** on my graph?

Interaction in Ecosystems

Find Out

- How organisms in a community interact
- How resources are cycled through an ecosystem
- How energy flows through a community and an ecosystem

Vocabulary

predation
symbiosis
carbon cycle
nitrogen cycle
food chain
food web
energy pyramid

The Big QUESTION

What interactions take place in an ecosystem?

Every living thing needs energy to survive. Whenever you eat, energy is transferred from the food you eat into the energy you use or store in your body. In an ecosystem, energy is transferred from one organism to another when certain organisms eat others.

Organisms Interact in a Community

In the last lesson, you learned that a community is made up of all the populations that live together in an area. The niche of a hawk is to eat small mammals. **Predation** is when one organism hunts and eats another. In its relationship with field mice, the hawk is a predator. The field mice are prey that the hawk hunts and eats.

Other interactions also take place between organisms. Like predators, scavengers feed on other animals. Scavengers, however, feed on dead or dying animals or plants. Perhaps you've seen a vulture swoop down on a dead animal by the roadside. Scavengers are important in an ecosystem because they help get rid of dead and decaying material.

A decomposer is an organism that breaks down the remains of dead plants and animals. Decomposers also break down waste materials into simpler substances. Nitrogen, carbon, and other materials are returned to the soil as decomposers break down dead organisms. Living things need these materials to survive.

Organisms can also interact in other ways within a community. **Symbiosis** is a specific interaction between two species over a long time. *Symbiosis* means "living together." Organisms can have different kinds of symbiotic relationships. One kind is a relationship between two species in which both benefit. This kind of symbiotic relationship exists between a Seeing Eye dog and its owner. The Seeing Eye dog is fed and sheltered by the owner, and the owner is led and protected by the dog.

Another kind of symbiosis is a relationship between two species in which one benefits and the other is neither helped nor harmed. For example, some vines climb up the trunk of a tree where there is more sunlight. The vine benefits, but it neither harms nor helps the tree.

In some symbiotic relationships, one organism benefits while the other is harmed. Some fish, such as a lamprey, attach themselves to other fish and feed off their blood. The lamprey benefits, but the other fish is harmed.

Organisms can interact in many ways. In this relationship, the Seeing Eye dog helps its owner, and the owner provides food and shelter for the dog. This relationship is beneficial to both living things.

In this relationship, the small fish are benefiting by feeding off the shark's blood and body fluids. The small fish are benefiting from the relationship, while the shark is being harmed.

Cycles in Nature

In the last lesson, you learned that a population is made up of all the organisms of one species in the same area. You also learned that populations rely on biotic and abiotic factors such as food, water, and minerals to meet their needs. When many populations live in the same area and use similar resources, all the resources aren't used up because some resources in the environment are recycled through the ecosystem.

All parts of an ecosystem, living and nonliving, work together and continuously cycle water and other substances vital to life. This cycling provides organisms with an ongoing supply of materials for survival, growth, and reproduction in an ecosystem.

The **carbon cycle** is one of the continuous cycles that can be found in an ecosystem. In the carbon cycle, carbon is cycled through the ecosystem. This element is needed by and released from living things.

Two basic life processes, photosynthesis and respiration, are important to the carbon cycle. Green plants take in carbon dioxide from the air. You learned in the first chapter that during photosynthesis, green plants make their own food by using carbon dioxide, water, and sunlight. In the process, plants release oxygen into the air. Oxygen from the air is used by animals in respiration. Respiration uses oxygen to break down glucose and produces carbon dioxide and water as wastes. Carbon dioxide is released into the air and the cycle begins again. You are part of the carbon cycle when you exhale carbon dioxide into the atmosphere.

All organisms contain carbon. Waste products and the dead bodies of plants, animals, and simple organisms are broken down by bacteria called decomposers. The carbon in waste and decomposing bodies is released as carbon dioxide when they are broken down by decomposers. Look at the diagram below to see how carbon is cycled through an ecosystem.

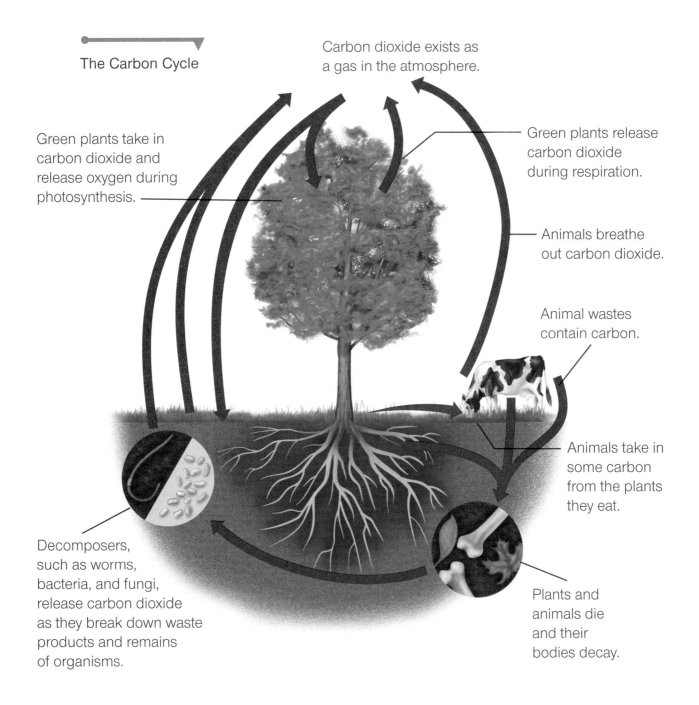

The Carbon Cycle

Carbon dioxide exists as a gas in the atmosphere.

Green plants take in carbon dioxide and release oxygen during photosynthesis.

Green plants release carbon dioxide during respiration.

Animals breathe out carbon dioxide.

Animal wastes contain carbon.

Animals take in some carbon from the plants they eat.

Decomposers, such as worms, bacteria, and fungi, release carbon dioxide as they break down waste products and remains of organisms.

Plants and animals die and their bodies decay.

The Nitrogen Cycle

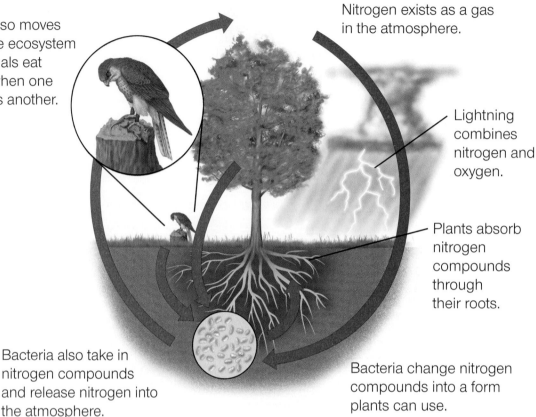

Nitrogen also moves through the ecosystem when animals eat plants or when one animal eats another.

Nitrogen exists as a gas in the atmosphere.

Lightning combines nitrogen and oxygen.

Plants absorb nitrogen compounds through their roots.

Bacteria also take in nitrogen compounds and release nitrogen into the atmosphere.

Bacteria change nitrogen compounds into a form plants can use.

Nitrogen is also essential to life. Genetic material and proteins, which are found in all organisms, are made with nitrogen. The **nitrogen cycle** is the continuous cycle by which nitrogen moves through the ecosystem. Nitrogen is found as a gas in the atmosphere, but most organisms cannot use it in this form. Instead, bacteria change the gas into a form that can be taken in and used by plants. Bacteria in the roots of bean and pea plants also change nitrogen into a form that can be used by other plants. Animals get nitrogen by eating plants or by eating other animals that have eaten plants. The nitrogen is returned to the soil when animals release waste products or when the animals die and decay. All parts of an ecosystem are involved in the cycling of carbon and nitrogen.

Energy Flows Through an Ecosystem

When one organism eats another, energy flows through an ecosystem. Energy is transferred through a community as organisms produce and consume food.

Plants use sunlight to make their own food. This food is stored as chemical energy.

Energy enters an ecosystem in the form of sunlight interacting with organisms and the physical environment. Green plants use energy from the sun to produce food in the process of photosynthesis. Because they make their own food, green plants are called producers. Organisms such as the hawk and the mouse, which do not make their own food but eat other organisms, are called consumers.

The hawk is called a carnivore because it eats only other animals. Frogs, snakes, and wolves are also carnivores. Animals that eat only plants are called herbivores. A dairy cow is an example of a herbivore. Omnivores are animals that eat both plants and animals. Humans are omnivores. So are bears and raccoons.

Energy flows from producers to consumers as populations eat and are eaten. A **food chain** is the transfer of energy as organisms feed on other organisms. In a food chain, green plants produce food for themselves by trapping the sun's energy. Animals eat plants, and these animals are eaten by other animals. In this way, energy from the sun moves through an ecosystem. Although energy is transferred from one organism to another in a food chain, only some of the energy that is trapped by plants is used by the animals that eat plants or by the animals that eat other animals.

A mouse eats plants. The mouse uses some of the plants' stored energy and stores the rest.

A hawk eats the mouse. The hawk's body uses some of the energy stored in the mouse's body.

The photos on this page show different producers and consumers in overlapping food chains. This network of interrelated food chains is called a **food web.** A food chain shows one population that eats or is eaten by another population. A food web shows how one population can be part of more than one food chain in a community.

Food webs show the interdependence of all the biotic factors in an ecosystem. The biotic factors in ecosystems affect each other in many ways. If an organism no longer fills its place in a food web, how will this affect the ecosystem? A change in the food web affects the entire ecosystem because it changes the way energy is transferred and the amount of energy available.

A food web is a model of the overlapping food chains in a community.

All the energy trapped by plants cannot be used by animals. An **energy pyramid** shows the amount of energy flowing from one organism to the next in a food chain. Producers such as grass change energy from sunlight into chemical energy through photosynthesis. Herbivores such as grasshoppers eat producers such as grass. Only some of the energy stored in grass will be used by a grasshopper. Similarly, when a bird eats a grasshopper, not all the energy that the grasshopper gained from the grass will be passed on to the bird. Consequently, a smaller amount of the chemical energy from grass will be made available to a hawk that eats the bird.

An energy pyramid is a model of the energy that is transferred from producers to consumers in an ecosystem.

CHECKPOINT

1. How can organisms in an ecosystem interact?
2. How can resources be cycled through an ecosystem?
3. How does energy flow through a community and an ecosystem?

 What interactions take place in an ecosystem?

ACTIVITY

Investigating What a Predator Eats

Find Out

Do this activity to see how owls interact with their environment.

Process Skills

Predicting
Observing
Classifying
Communicating
Inferring

WHAT YOU NEED

plastic gloves

petri dish

two forceps

paper towel

owl pellet

Activity Journal

WHAT TO DO

1. Based on what you know about a hawk's niche, **predict** what an owl might eat.

2. Place the owl pellet on the paper towel. Use the forceps to carefully separate the bones of the animals from the hair and fur.

   Safety! *Wear plastic gloves to perform this activity. Be careful with sharp objects.*

3. Remove the fur from the bones with the forceps and place the bones in the petri dish. Dispose of the fur as your teacher directs.

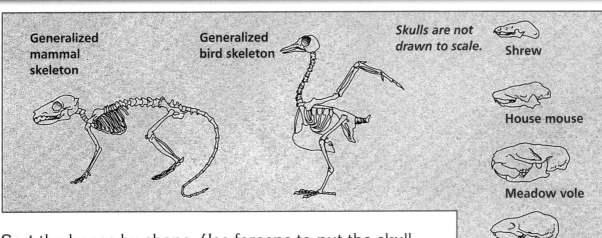

Generalized mammal skeleton

Generalized bird skeleton

Skulls are not drawn to scale.

Shrew

House mouse

Meadow vole

Deer mouse

Mole

Rodent

Rabbit

4. **Sort** the bones by shape. Use forceps to put the skull bones in one half of the petri dish.

5. **Match** the skulls that you found in the owl pellet with the skulls shown to the right.

6. **Record** the number of skulls of different animals.

7. On the chalkboard, make a class record of the kinds and numbers of animals found in the owl pellets.

8. Dispose of the bones as your teacher directs. Wash your hands thoroughly.

CONCLUSIONS

1. Compare your prediction with your observations.

2. What kinds of materials did you identify in the owl pellet?

3. Infer what the interactions and relationships were between the owl and the animals it ate.

ASKING NEW QUESTIONS

1. How are the owl and other predators important to Earth's ecosystem?

2. Infer what the owl's niche might be in its community.

SCIENTIFIC METHODS SELF CHECK

✔ Did I **predict** what I would find in the owl pellet?

✔ Did I **record** my observations?

✔ Did I **infer** what niche the owl might have in its community?

Behaviors and Adaptations

Find Out

- What some plant and animal behaviors are
- What adaptations are
- How some plants adapt to their ecosystem
- How some animals adapt to their ecosystem

Vocabulary

behavior
stimulus
response
tropism
innate behavior
learned behavior
adaptation

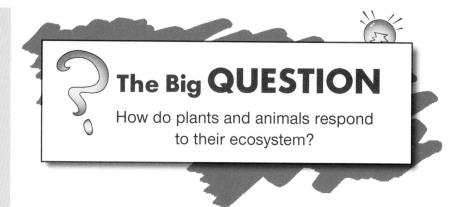

The Big QUESTION

How do plants and animals respond to their ecosystem?

In order to survive, living things must respond to their ecosystem. When you put on a winter coat or sit down in your seat when class begins, you are also responding to your ecosystem. How might plants and animals respond to their ecosystems?

Plant and Animal Behavior

All plants and animals respond to their ecosystems in ways that are unique to their species. Species of plants and animals have adaptations and behaviors that help them to survive. The adaptations and behaviors that plants and animals have are related to their needs and the demands of the ecosystems in which they live.

Behavior is an action or pattern of movements that may help plant and animal populations survive in an ecosystem. **Behavior** is the way an organism acts toward its ecosystem. A **stimulus** (stim′ yə ləs) is anything in the ecosystem that causes an organism to react. The action of an organism as the result of a stimulus is a **response.** Many different stimuli affect plants and animals. Some stimuli are outside of an organism's body, such as light and noise. Others come from within, such as thirst and hunger. All of these stimuli result in some response by the organism.

Gravity, the attraction between two objects, is a stimulus to which a plant responds. The response of plants to gravity is called geotropism. If a root is growing horizontally, because of gravity it will curve downward because the cells on the upper side of the root grow longer than the cells on the bottom side. As the upper cells become longer, the root curves and pushes down into the soil. How does this plant behavior help plants to survive?

Most plants spend their lives anchored in one place by their roots. But a plant can change its position slightly. The type of plant response that involves a change of position by growing toward or away from a stimulus is called **tropism.** Geotropism is just one example of tropism. Plants also respond to light (phototropism), water (hydrotropism), and touch (thigmotropism). All these tropisms are responses that help a plant survive by obtaining more sunlight, water, or dissolved nutrients from the soil.

A cobra reacts to danger by displaying its hood.

These birds migrate because of innate behaviors that they were born with and that they will pass on to their offspring.

Like plants, animals also respond to stimuli in their environments. Animals can have different kinds of behaviors—some they are born with and some they have learned. A behavior that an animal is born with and that is passed on from generation to generation is an **innate behavior.** Some innate behaviors are very complex. Migration is one such behavior that is thought to be largely innate. Other innate behaviors include hunting, nesting, feeding, and mating.

Another kind of behavior that animals have is **learned behavior,** or behavior that is taught. Learning involves choosing responses to a stimulus. This means that learned behavior can change as a result of experience and training. When you first started school, you might not have known what to do when you went into a classroom or how to find your way through your school. Now you have learned how to get to your classrooms and how to behave when class begins.

Both plants and animals behave in ways that help them to survive. Behavior in both plants and animals involves the organism and its ecosystem. An organism receives many stimuli from its ecosystem, and the better an organism is at responding to these stimuli, the more likely it will be to survive.

Adaptations

From the time a plant or animal begins to grow, there are many challenges that it must face to survive. If an organism has parts or behaviors that help it meet its needs, the organism is more likely to survive. An **adaptation** is a trait that helps an organism to survive in a particular ecosystem. The gills on fish, the lungs in animals, and the roots on plants are all examples of adaptations that help each organism survive in its ecosystem. The better adapted an organism is to its ecosystem, the more likely it is to complete its life cycle. The life cycle of a living thing is made up of all the changes that occur at the beginning of its life, during its growth period, during reproduction, and death.

In order to complete their life cycles, living things must obtain nutrients and energy, and they must reproduce. All organisms have many adaptations that help them complete these tasks. When food or space is limited, the organisms that survive are those that are best adapted to the conditions of their ecosystem.

Adaptations are traits that help an organism survive in a particular ecosystem. How do the adaptations of the green anoles (top) and Mexican horned lizard (bottom) help them to survive?

A101

Plant Adaptations

Plants have many adaptations that allow them to survive in various ecosystems. One way that plants have been able to respond to changes in an ecosystem is with reproductive adaptations.

Reproductive adaptations are traits that help an organism to reproduce in an ecosystem. Some plants are able to reproduce by producing seeds. This adaptation increases the chances that some of the plant's offspring will survive.

There are some plants, such as the lodgepole pine tree, that produce two kinds of seeds. Some of the lodgepole pine's seeds are released every year. These seeds will sprout if they land on fertile soil and if other conditions for growth are favorable. The second kind of seed is held in tightly closed cones. These cones will not release seeds unless they have been exposed to the heat of fire. This adaptation allows lodgepole pines to grow in areas of Yellowstone National Park where most trees were burned to the ground.

Cacti have structures to help them survive and reproduce in dry areas.

A lodgepole pinecone will not release seeds until it has been exposed to the heat of fire.

Some plants have another kind of adaptation that allows them to go without water for a long time. Many plants in the desert have adaptations for dealing with water shortages. Some desert plants have flowers that bloom when it rains. Some desert plants that produce flowers and seeds need more water than is available to them for most of the year. When water is available, many desert plants bloom immediately. The flowers produce seeds that can survive in dry conditions. The seeds begin to sprout the next time water is available.

Some deserts may not receive rain for several years in a row. In order to survive these harsh conditions, desert plants have a variety of adaptations for collecting, storing, and conserving water. A cactus is a common desert plant that has these kinds of adaptations. Cacti have a thick, waxy covering that reduces the amount of water they lose through their cell walls. Cacti also have long, shallow roots that stretch out beneath the surface of the soil to absorb rainwater quickly. Many cactus plants also have a thick center that swells to absorb and store water.

Thorns and irritating chemicals are also plant adaptations. Plants cannot run away from animals that might harm them, nor can they move away from other plants that crowd them. Some plants have developed structures such as thorns, and others, such as poison ivy, have developed irritating oils for protection and survival.

Some plants have developed protective structures such as thorns or poisonous oils that are irritating to skin.

Animal Adaptations

Some birds, such as blackbirds, have a long hind toe that helps them hold onto a perch.

Most aquatic birds, such as ducks, have webbed feet.

Birds of prey, such as hawks, have sharp talons to catch and hold their prey.

Like plants, animals have many adaptations that allow them to survive in different ecosystems. There are many kinds of adaptations. Adaptations include traits related to size, shape, color, and body functions involving the animal's body structure.

Examples of structural adaptations can be seen in birds. Two structural adaptations that most birds have are beaks and feet that help them survive in their ecosystem. Birds have many different kinds of beaks that make them better suited to their ecosystem. Birds, such as the hawk, that eat small mammals have large, thick beaks that allow them to tear apart small animals. Some birds eat insects that they pick out of bark. These birds have small, narrow beaks that can get into tiny places to get food. Bird feet are another example of an adaptation that involves the animal's body structure. Some birds have feet that help them perch, some have feet that help them swim, and others have feet to help them catch and hold their prey. What can you infer about each bird's lifestyle from the structure of its feet?

Some animals also have structural adaptations for breathing. Fish have gills that use oxygen from water for cellular respiration. Insects have small openings along the sides of their bodies through which oxygen enters. Most amphibians, such as frogs, have lungs but can also take in oxygen through their skin. Your lungs are also structural adaptations that help you survive in your ecosystem by allowing you to breathe.

The structural adaptations and behaviors that plants and animals have allow them to meet their needs in their ecosystem. Fish have adaptations that make it possible for them to live in water. Grasshoppers, wolves, and mice also have characteristics that make them suited for their ecosystems. Some plants have seeds that increase the chances of survival for their offspring. Other plants have structures that help them live in areas that do not get much rain. Some animals migrate during certain times of the year. Other animals learn better ways to find food sources or to interact with other animals.

These are just some behaviors and adaptations that can be seen in plants and animals that help them to survive in their ecosystems.

Underwater kelp grows toward the light. What kind of plant behavior is this?

Gills are one type of structural adaptation that help an animal survive in its environment.

CHECKPOINT

1. What are some plant and animal behaviors?
2. What are adaptations?
3. How do some plants adapt to their ecosystem?
4. How do some animals adapt to their ecosystem?

 How do plants and animals respond to their ecosystems?

ACTIVITY

Investigating Earthworm Behavior

Find Out

Do this activity to learn how an earthworm responds to stimuli.

Process Skills

Observing
Communicating
Inferring
Interpreting Data

WHAT YOU NEED

hand lens

paper towels

vinegar

bright light

water

live earthworms in slightly moist soil

cotton swab

600-mL beaker

shallow pan

Activity Journal

WHAT TO DO

1. Open the container of earthworms and immediately hold it under a bright light. **Observe** the behavior of the earthworms and **record** how the earthworms react.

2. With moistened hands, take an earthworm and place it in the palm of one hand. **Observe** and **record** how it responds.

   Safety! *Be sure your hands are moist when you handle the earthworms.*

3. Rub your hand along its body and notice its hairlike bristles.

4. After dipping the cotton swab in vinegar, place it on a wet paper towel in front of the worm. **Observe** and **record** how the worm reacts to the vinegar.

CONCLUSIONS

1. What were the different stimuli to which the earthworm responded?

2. What earthworm behavior did you observe?

3. If the earthworms were never before exposed to the stimuli used in this activity, was the earthworm's behavior learned or innate? Why?

ASKING NEW QUESTIONS

1. How might the earthworm's responses to light, touch, and vinegar help it to survive?

2. How else might you test an earthworm's responses to its ecosystem?

SCIENTIFIC METHODS SELF CHECK

✔ Did I **observe** how the earthworm reacted to each stimulus?

✔ Did I **record** my observations?

✔ Did I **interpret the data** I collected?

Review

Reviewing Vocabulary and Concepts

Write the letter of the answer that completes each sentence.

1. All the organisms of the same species that live in an area make up ___.
   a. a habitat
   b. an ecosystem
   c. an environment
   d. a population

2. The ___ is the maximum population size that the resources in an area can support.
   a. limiting factor
   b. carrying capacity
   c. adaptation
   d. community

3. The continuous cycle in which the exchange of oxygen and carbon dioxide is important is the ___.
   a. carbon cycle
   b. nitrogen cycle
   c. food web
   d. water cycle

4. A behavior that an animal is born with is called ___.
   a. conditioning
   b. tropism
   c. innate
   d. carrying capacity

5. ___ is a trait that helps an organism to survive in a particular ecosystem.
   a. Adaptation
   b. Stimulus
   c. Plant behavior
   d. Limiting factor

Match the definition on the left with the correct term.

6. all the living and nonliving things within a particular area

7. the role or function of an organism in a community

8. the number of individuals per unit of living space

9. the way an organism acts toward its ecosystem

10. anything in an ecosystem that causes an organism to react

a. population density

b. ecosystem

c. niche

d. stimulus

e. behavior

Understanding What You Learned

1. What are abiotic and biotic factors?

2. What do you call the role or function of an organism in a community?

3. What do all parts of an ecosystem cycle?

4. What do omnivores eat?

5. What factors could cause a plant to change its position?

Applying What You Learned

1. If half the people in your neighborhood suddenly moved away, what could restore the population?

2. A skunk spraying its scent when another animal approaches is an example of what?

3. How is the sun important to our ecosystem?

4. How are animals and other organisms useful and necessary to the ecosystem even after they die?

 5. How do organisms in an ecosystem interact with one another and their environment?

For Your Portfolio

Imagine an ecosystem in which you would like to live. Draw a picture showing the abiotic and biotic factors of that ecosystem. Describe what you would need to live there, and what adaptations and behaviors would help you and other organisms in that ecosystem to survive. The ecosystem and adaptations can be real or imaginary.

Unit Review

Concept Review

1. Explain the importance of cells.

2. What parts do living things have that work together to perform life processes?

3. What are some ways in which organisms interact with one another and their environment?

Problem Solving

1. How would plant and animal cells be affected if all of their mitochondria were removed?

2. Give an example of an organ that performs multiple functions in a plant organism. Give an example of an organ that performs multiple functions in an animal organism.

3. Suppose that a plant from an Arizona desert was transplanted to a Michigan forest, and a plant from a Michigan forest was transplanted to an Arizona desert. Would they do well?

Something to Do

Pick a type of animal or plant that you find interesting. Draw a picture of your animal or plant on posterboard. On the posterboard, draw or describe the organism's habitat. On a separate sheet of paper, describe how its organ systems and adaptations help the organism to survive.

UNIT B

Earth Science

CHAPTER

1

Earth's Atmosphere

When you look up on a clear day, what do you see? You're looking up through hundreds of kilometers of atmosphere. Humans and most other organisms depend on Earth's vast ocean of air for life. The air supports many living organisms. People can survive for weeks without food and for days without water. But without air, they can only live for a few minutes. Every day you breathe about 11,000 L of air!

If there were no atmosphere at all, Earth would not be able to support life as we know it. Earth's atmosphere contains the right amounts of certain chemicals at the right temperature for life to survive.

The Big IDEA

Air has properties, makes up Earth's atmosphere, and affects weather.

and Weather

CHAPTER SCIENCE INVESTIGATION

Geographic locations affect weather and air patterns. Find out how in your *Activity Journal.*

Properties of Air

Find Out

- What air is and why it is important
- How sound travels through air
- How temperature affects air pressure
- What instruments measure the properties of air

Vocabulary

air
air pressure
wind
barometer
anemometer
Beaufort scale

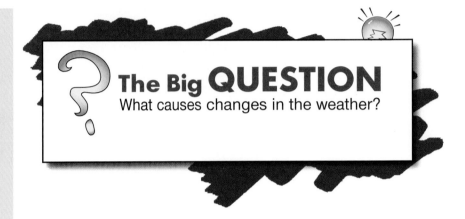

The Big QUESTION
What causes changes in the weather?

Have you ever heard the phrase, "It vanished into thin air"? This means that it's gone without a trace, right? There's nothing left, right? Although this phrase is often used, air is anything but "thin." A column of air in the atmosphere one centimeter square weighs 1.03 kg and that's not thin.

Even though we do not usually think about the properties of air, they affect many of the conditions on Earth's surface that allow life to exist. If your air supply is interrupted, even briefly, you are instantly aware of it. You might also notice air when it does something dramatic in the form of a tornado or storm. But let's take a really good "look" at air and its properties.

Air Has Properties and Supports Life

Air has many unique properties. Although you cannot see, smell, or taste air, it is all around you. Air is matter, takes up space, and has mass.

Because the air in the atmosphere is often referred to as an "ocean of air," it is easy to get the idea that air is made up of a single substance. Actually, air is a mixture of many gases.

The mass of air may not be as noticeable as that of liquids and solids. However, a simple demonstration can show that air has mass. If the mass of an opened plastic bottle is measured on a balance and then measured again after the air is squeezed out of it, the bottle will seem to have less mass the second time it is measured. The reason the bottle seems to have less mass is because the bottle contains less air the second time it is measured. So, even though you may not be able to see the properties of air, it has mass and takes up space.

This mixture of gases makes up Earth's atmosphere. Our atmosphere acts as an insulating blanket that keeps Earth from becoming too hot or too cold, which enables life as we know it to exist. It also acts as a shield against some harmful rays from the sun. Without the atmosphere, life as we know it would not exist on Earth.

You can demonstrate that air takes up space by blowing air into a balloon. The balloon expands as you blow it up. The difference between the mass of an empty balloon and an inflated balloon is the mass of the air.

Sound Travels Through Air

The properties of air are important to humans in many ways. Humans and other living things need air for life. Air also carries sound energy. That makes it very important in communicating many kinds of information.

Let's look at the way air carries sound. Because sound is made when something moves back and forth, or vibrates, sound can move through a substance like air or water. Sound is a form of energy. When a sound is made, energy is transferred to an object, or substance, that vibrates. Sound can travel in air because the sound energy vibrates the tiny particles, or molecules, that make up air. Each of these vibrating molecules bumps into other nearby molecules. Those molecules bump into yet other molecules. When you hear the teacher call out your name from the front of the classroom, you know the air between you and the teacher carried sound energy from your teacher's voice box to your ear.

The molecules that make up air can carry sound energy.

Every time you speak, you cause the air around you to move. When you speak, air causes your vocal chords to vibrate. These vibrations are then carried by your breath out of your mouth. The sound energy causing the vibrations spreads out through the air in all directions. These vibrations might be carried through the air next to someone else's eardrum. The vibrating air molecules cause his or her eardrum to vibrate. As the eardrum moves back and forth, that person hears sound. That person's eardrum repeats the vibrations and passes them on to the bones of the middle ear. Then, they are sent to a fluid in the inner ear. From there, nerve impulses send them to the person's brain, which interprets the sounds and understands what you have said.

When vibrating air molecules cause parts of the ear to vibrate, sound is heard and interpreted by the brain.

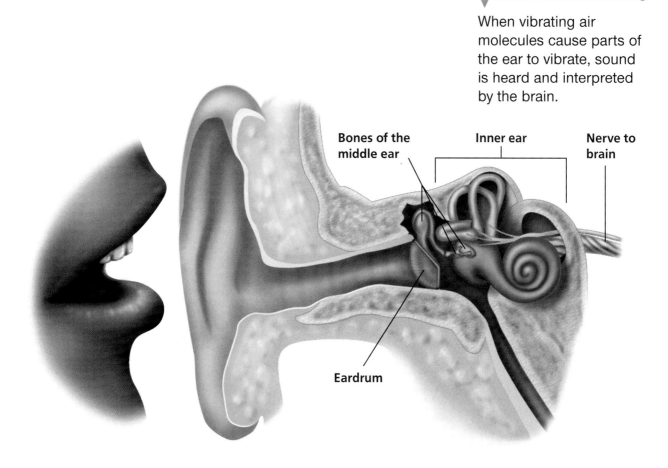

Bones of the middle ear

Inner ear

Nerve to brain

Eardrum

Temperature Affects Air Pressure

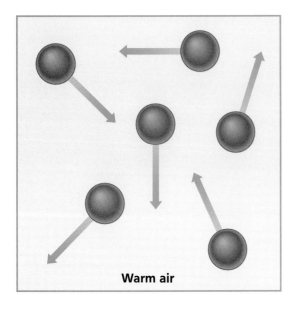

Warm air

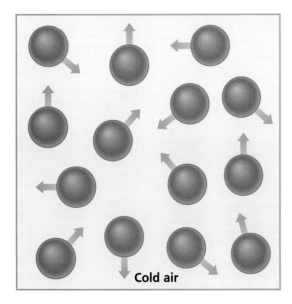

Cold air

Molecules of warm air move faster and farther apart than molecules of cold air.

You now know that when sound energy moves through air, the tiny molecules that make up air vibrate. Did you know that molecules of air are always moving? As air is warmed, its molecules move faster. When the molecules move faster, they also move farther apart, or expand. You can picture this if you think about people on a dance floor. If everyone stands still and close together, you can jam a huge crowd of people into the room. If everyone starts to dance slowly, they will need to move apart a little. The faster they dance, the more room they need and the farther apart they move.

Like the dancers, molecules of air take up more space when they are warmed. Cool air is more dense than warm air because it has more molecules in a given amount of space. Because it has more molecules in a given amount of space, a cubic meter of cold air has a greater mass than a cubic meter of warm air.

Because air has mass, it also exerts pressure. **Air pressure** is the force of air pushing against something. Just as air in a balloon exerts force against the sides of the balloon, air in Earth's atmosphere has pressure and pushes against Earth and the objects on it.

On Earth, the pressure that is exerted by air can be different from place to place. Differences in temperature can create differences in pressure. Because cold air is more dense than warm air, cold air exerts a greater amount of pressure on Earth's surface. Areas where more dense air is exerting a greater amount of force on Earth's surface are called high-pressure areas. Low-pressure areas are areas where less pressure is exerted by air that is less dense.

When there is a difference in air pressure, air is caused to move. When the air moves from one area of high to low pressure across Earth's surface, the moving air is called **wind.** The greater the difference in air pressure, the faster the wind. If the difference is slight, you may feel a gentle breeze. If the difference is great, the wind may blow at speeds that flatten buildings.

The surface of Earth also plays a part in the movement of the wind. Large bodies of water can have a significant effect on wind patterns. Land heats up more quickly than water during the sunny hours and loses its heat more quickly when the sun is no longer striking Earth's surface. Although it takes water longer to absorb heat, it also takes water longer to lose heat. As a result, warm air rises from the land during the sunny hours and from bodies of water during the time after sunset, when the land has lost much of its heat. Since warm air rises, there is an almost continual movement of air from land to water and back again as the colder air moves into the space emptied by rising warmer air.

Low-pressure areas contain rising warm air.

High-pressure areas contain sinking cold air.

The surface of Earth has areas of permanent high and low pressures. The air over the equator is very warm. It receives the most direct rays of the sun for much of the year. This hot, less dense air along the equator drifts upward and maintains an area of low air pressure. Meanwhile, the polar regions maintain high-pressure areas because the air in these regions becomes cold and sinks to Earth's surface. Warmer air then drifts into the area vacated by the sinking cold air. Look at the diagram on this page to see where other permanent high- and low-pressure areas are on Earth.

But air doesn't move just north and south or up and down. Every day, Earth makes a full 360° rotation on its axis. As Earth rotates from west to east, the northward or southward movement of air is bent in a westerly or easterly direction. Many wind patterns are the result of Earth's rotation.

Earth's Permanent High- and Low-pressure Areas

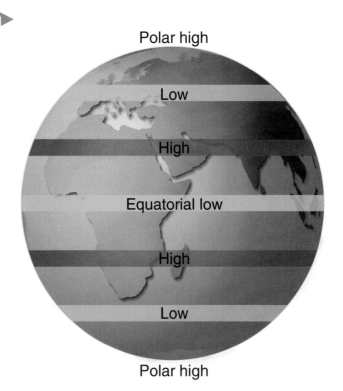

Polar high

Low

High

Equatorial low

High

Low

Polar high

Pressure systems and winds influence weather all over the world. The winds influence the direction in which weather systems move. Winds are also important because they help keep the temperature of Earth just right for life. If air moved only up and down, the equatorial regions of Earth would become too hot for most plant and animal life. In the polar regions, cold air would settle and areas would become exceedingly cold. Because air moves across Earth's surface, temperatures all over the world are more moderate and varied.

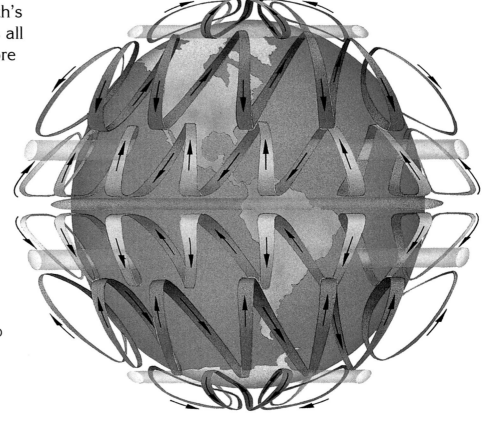

Because of Earth's rotation, winds move in a spiral pattern from high-pressure to low-pressure areas.

The trade winds are formed by air rushing from north and south toward the low-pressure area along the equator.

Prevailing westerlies move from southwest to northeast in the northern hemisphere and from northwest to southeast in the southern hemisphere.

In the polar regions, cold dense air flowing toward the equator causes winds called polar easterlies.

Cool air descending causes areas of high pressure.

Properties of Air Can Be Measured

Because of air's importance in our lives, humans develop and use instruments that measure the properties of air. They often use the data they collect from these instruments to forecast the weather. Today, there are very sophisticated instruments to measure air.

One instrument that can be used to measure air is a thermometer. A thermometer can tell us how hot or how cold the air is. When air becomes warmer, the liquid in a thermometer also becomes warmer. When the liquid is warmed, it expands, takes up more space, and moves upward in a narrow tube. What do you think happens when the air becomes cooler? On many thermometers, markings along the side of the tube indicate the temperature in Celsius or Fahrenheit degrees.

Other instruments can also be used to measure the properties of air. A **barometer** tells how much air pressure is being exerted on Earth's surface at a given spot. One common kind of barometer uses mercury, which responds quickly to changes in air pressure. At sea level, air exerts about 1.03 kg of pressure per square centimeter. This raises the mercury in a small tube to a height of 760 mm. If air pressure increases, the mercury is forced upward. When the air pressure drops, the mercury drops. A barometer is an instrument that could be used to show that Earth's atmosphere exerts a pressure that decreases with distance above Earth's surface and is the same in all directions.

The direction and speed of wind are other measurements of air that meteorologists use when forecasting weather. Wind speed is measured using an instrument with a rod and cone-shaped cups attached to spikes. This instrument is an **anemometer** (an ə mo′ mē tər). The wind spins the anemometer and the speed of its turning tells the speed of the wind.

A mercury barometer measures air pressure.

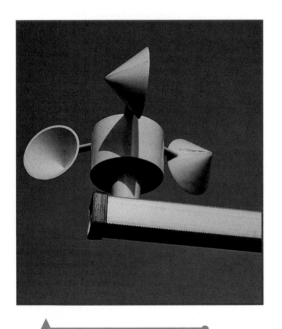

An anemometer measures the speed of wind.

	Type of Wind	km/h	Observations
0	Calm	< 1	Calm; smoke rises straight up
1	Light Air	1-5	Weather vanes don't move
2	Light breeze	6-11	Weather vanes move slightly
3	Gentle breeze	12-19	Leaves move; flags stretch out
4	Moderate breeze	20-28	Small branches sway
5	Fresh breeze	29-38	Trees sway; whitecaps on ponds
6	Strong breeze	39-49	Large branches sway
7	Moderate gale	50-61	Hard to walk into the wind
8	Fresh gale	62-74	Branches break off trees
9	Strong gale	75-88	Shingles blow off roofs
10	Whole gale	89-102	Trees are uprooted
11	Storm	103-117	Extensive damage
12	Hurricane	118 +	Violent destruction

Beaufort Wind Scale

Meteorologists sometimes use the **Beaufort scale** to label winds by speed and force. The scale was developed in the nineteenth century by Francis Beaufort. It uses numbers from 0 to 12 and names to identify the strength of winds. For example, a Force 3 wind, called a gentle breeze, blows 12–19 km/h.

Meteorologists can also use many other instruments to measure the properties of air. A hygrometer measures the amount of water vapor in the air. Weather balloons and weather satellites collect data on clouds and wind movements. By measuring the properties of air, we are better able to understand the weather and the atmosphere that allows for life on Earth.

CHECKPOINT

1. What is air and why is it important?
2. How does sound travel through air?
3. How does temperature affect air pressure?
4. What are some instruments that measure the properties of air?

 What are the properties of air?

ACTIVITY

Investigating Air Pressure

Find Out

Do this activity to learn how air moves from an area of high pressure to an area of low pressure.

Process Skills

Controlling Variables
Communicating
Predicting
Observing
Inferring

WHAT YOU NEED

small thread spool

two large balloons

Activity Journal

WHAT TO DO

1. Work with a partner. Blow up one balloon half way. Twist the neck and then stretch it over one end of a small spool. Keep the balloon twisted so the air doesn't escape.

2. Blow up the second balloon until it is nearly full. Twist the neck of the second balloon and stretch it over the free end of the spool.

3. Keep both balloons twisted so no air can escape. Draw a picture of the balloons and spool.

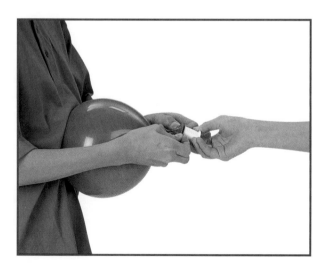

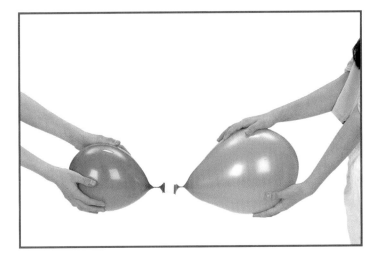

4. **Predict** what will happen if you hold the spool and let the balloons untwist. Construct a chart for recording your predictions and observations.

5. Untwist the balloons and **record** your observations on the chart.

CONCLUSIONS

1. What happened to the air in each balloon when they untwisted?

2. **Infer** how air pressure caused this to happen.

ASKING NEW QUESTIONS

1. **Infer** what would happen if you blew air into a balloon and then let go of it.

2. What does this tell you about the air pressure outside of the balloon?

SCIENTIFIC METHODS SELF CHECK

✔ Did I **predict** what would happen when the balloons untwisted?

✔ Did I **record** my observations?

✔ Did I **infer** how air pressure was related to my observations?

Earth's Atmosphere

Find Out

- What the atmosphere is
- What the chemical composition of the atmosphere is
- What layers make up Earth's atmosphere

Vocabulary

atmosphere
troposphere
stratosphere
ozone
mesosphere
ionosphere
thermosphere
exosphere

The Big QUESTION

What makes up Earth's atmosphere?

What do trees, air, and fish have in common? All of them are made up chiefly of the same four elements of matter—hydrogen, oxygen, carbon, and nitrogen. But how is air different from trees and fish? Air is a gas. In trees and fish, these elements usually exist in solids or liquids, two other states in which matter can exist.

The Atmosphere

The **atmosphere** is the layer of gases hundreds of kilometers thick that surrounds Earth. The gases that are in the atmosphere are a special kind of mixture called a solution. In a solution, tiny particles of a substance are evenly spread throughout another substance.

Scientists theorize that the atmosphere began to form when Earth itself was first forming. Gases escaped from Earth's interior through volcanoes and other openings in Earth's newly formed crust. By studying gases that volcanoes release today, scientists can speculate about what gases early volcanoes may have released. They theorize that Earth releases many of the same gases from its interior today as it did then. These gases include water vapor, carbon dioxide, nitrogen, ammonia, and methane. The newly formed atmosphere contained high concentrations of carbon dioxide and no oxygen. Life as we know it couldn't have survived in this early atmosphere.

Scientists speculate that gases released from Earth's interior made up Earth's early atmosphere. Today, the composition of the atmosphere allows Earth to support life.

The Composition of the Atmosphere

The atmosphere of Earth today contains many different kinds of gases and can support life. In the diagram on this page, you can see all of the gases that make up Earth's atmosphere. Nitrogen and oxygen are the two main gases in the atmosphere. Together, these gases make up about 99 percent of the volume of dry air. Argon, the third most common atmospheric gas, makes up less than 1 percent of the atmosphere. There are many other gases that can be found in the atmosphere as well, but only in trace, or very small, amounts. All of these trace gases make up less than 1 percent of the entire composition of the atmosphere.

Earth's atmosphere is not made up of only gases. Dust and ice are two common solids that are in the atmospheric solution. Dust gets

Gases in Earth's Atmosphere

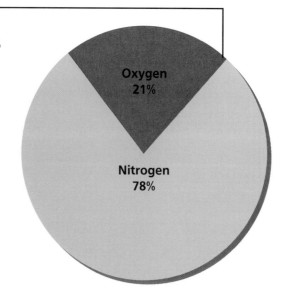

Argon 0.93%
Carbon dioxide 0.03%
Water vapor 0.0% to 4.0%
Traces of other gases

Oxygen 21%

Nitrogen 78%

carried into the air by wind, and ice forms in the air when water particles freeze. Water is the most common liquid in the atmosphere. Water is the only substance that exists as a solid, liquid, and gas in Earth's atmosphere.

Foreign substances, such as pollution or ash, are also in Earth's atmosphere. These foreign substances might be dangerous chemicals discharged by industries or by cars. Others might be released by volcanic eruptions or forest fires. They are suspended in the air and can be separated from air. This means that some of the substances that enter the air may be carried by air currents across great distances. For example, industrial pollution in the United States can be carried by air currents to Africa where the pollution can have a detrimental effect on the environment of the continent.

Forest fires release foreign substances into the air.

Water molecules in the air may attach themselves to foreign substances. If the clusters of water molecules on these particles become heavy enough, they will fall as rain. This can return the harmful substances to Earth's surface. Acid rain has already caused extensive environmental damage in industrialized countries. Vegetation has been harmed and metallic surfaces have been corroded. Many countries are increasingly concerned about this threat to our environment.

Layers of the Atmosphere

You now know the components that make up the atmosphere, but is there a difference between the air in the atmosphere closest to Earth and the air farthest away? How is the atmosphere structured? Earth's atmosphere has five main layers, each with its own unique characteristics.

The Layers of Earth's Atmosphere

Exosphere	480+ km	
Thermosphere	80–480 km	Ionosphere
Mesosphere	50–80 km	
Stratosphere	10–50 km	Ozone layer
Troposphere	0–10 km	

Picture the atmosphere as a multilayered blanket wrapped around Earth. Since air has mass, a gravitational attraction exists between Earth and each layer of this blanket based upon the distance between them. Earth's atmosphere exerts a pressure that decreases with distance above Earth's surface and is the same in all directions. The layer of the atmosphere closest to Earth's surface is called the **troposphere**. You live in the troposphere. The troposphere contains 75 percent of all Earth's gases, as well as dust, ice, and liquid water. This layer includes the air we breathe and is where weather occurs.

This layer of the atmosphere is the most dense, and is about 10 km thick. Water vapor and carbon dioxide in the troposphere absorb some of the sun's radiation and also capture some of the heat reflected from Earth's surface. This is what keeps the air around Earth warm enough to support life. But as the distance from Earth increases, the troposhere's temperature drops. At the top of the troposphere, the air temperature has dropped to about –60 °C.

Above the troposphere is the **stratosphere.** The stratosphere extends from about 10 to 50 km above Earth's surface. It is within the stratosphere that the ozone layer is found. **Ozone** is a gas that absorbs some of the harmful radiation from the sun. As a layer in the atmosphere, ozone filters much of the sun's ultraviolet (UV) rays, thus shielding Earth from the burning effect of the sun's rays.

In recent years, however, scientists have become increasingly aware of the possibility that the discharge of industrial and other chemicals into the air is harming the ozone layer. If the ozone layer is damaged or thinned, the ozone layer's capacity to absorb the sun's UV rays would be reduced and more UV rays would reach Earth's surface. This could change aspects of life on Earth as we know it.

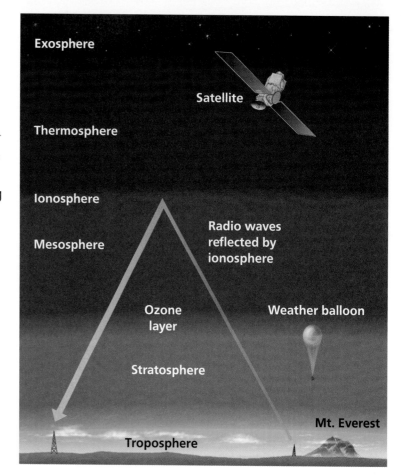

Some radio waves are sent across long distances by reflecting them off of the ionosphere.

Exosphere

Satellite

Thermosphere

Ionosphere

Radio waves reflected by ionosphere

Mesosphere

Ozone layer

Weather balloon

Stratosphere

Mt. Everest

Troposphere

Above the stratosphere are the mesosphere, thermosphere, and exosphere. The **mesosphere** is the layer of Earth's atmosphere that can be found above the stratosphere and extends between about 50 and 80 km above Earth's surface.

The top of the mesosphere has been useful for transmitting radio waves over long distances. Obstacles on Earth's surface block radio waves and make sending radio messages across long distances impossible. The solution to this problem has been to bounce radio waves off of a region at the bottom of the thermosphere called the **ionosphere.** This electrically conductive region reflects radio waves which allows them to be transmitted over much greater distances than radio waves sent across Earth's surface.

The **thermosphere** is the layer of Earth's atmosphere that is above the mesosphere. This layer is about 80 to 480 km above Earth. The air in this region is so thin that it contains only a relatively few, scattered air molecules. Since light is diffused or scattered by air molecules, the scarcity of air molecules in the thermosphere makes it appear dark. And because sound depends on matter, such as air, to travel, sound does not carry in the thermosphere. Although the temperature in the thermosphere is quite high—a couple of hundred degrees Celsius—there is so little air that molecules move around over large distances before colliding.

The **exosphere** is the uppermost part of Earth's atmosphere. Beyond the exosphere is outer space. This uppermost layer has no particular ending point. The air just becomes less and less dense until there is no air at all. There is essentially no air in outer space.

The layers of the atmosphere extend outward from Earth's surface. There are no clear dividing lines between the layers. Unlike the boundaries around states and countries, there are no exact boundaries that exist between one layer and the next. Each layer of the atmosphere blends into the layer above and below it.

CHECKPOINT

1. What is the atmosphere?
2. What is the chemical composition of the atmosphere?
3. What are the layers of the atmosphere?
?. What makes up Earth's atmosphere?

ACTIVITY

Oxygen in Air

Find Out

Do this activity to discover how much oxygen is in the air.

Process Skills

Measuring
Communicating
Predicting
Observing
Using Numbers
Interpreting Data

WHAT YOU NEED

measuring cup with mL gradations

test-tube stand

tongs

paper towels

steel wool

two pencils

test tube

test-tube stand and clamp

water

two rubber bands

beaker

white vinegar

Activity Journal

stopwatch

scissors

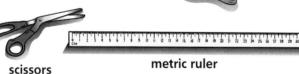
metric ruler

WHAT TO DO

1. Measure and record the length of the test tube in millimeters. Mix 30 mL white vinegar with 20 mL of water in the beaker.

2. Unroll a bale of steel wool and cut a strip 2 cm wide and 20 cm long. Soak it in the vinegar solution for one minute.

3. Using tongs, remove the steel wool from the vinegar solution, stretch it out, and dry it thoroughly.

4. Pour out the vinegar solution, rinse the beaker, and fill it about ⅔ full of water.

5. Using the pencils, push the steel wool into the test tube, keeping it as loose as possible.

6. Use rubber bands to attach the metric ruler to the test tube. Position the tube so that its open end is at the 0 mm mark on the ruler.

7. Turn over the test tube and insert it into the beaker so the opening of the tube is just below the surface of the water. Attach the tube to the stand with the clamp. Adjust the ruler's 0-mm mark to the water line.

8. Record the amount of air in your test tube.

9. Predict what percentage of air will be oxygen.

10. Observe and record the water level in the test tube every two minutes until the level stops changing.

CONCLUSIONS

1. About what percentage of the air in the test tube was oxygen? Use this formula to calculate the percentage.

$$\frac{\text{final water level (mm)}}{\text{tube length}} \times 100 = \% \text{ oxygen}$$

2. Compare your prediction with your observations.

ASKING NEW QUESTIONS

1. Why was it important to stretch the steel wool and pack it loosely before inserting it in the water?

2. Based on your observation, do you think that air is mostly oxygen?

SCIENTIFIC METHODS SELF CHECK

✔ Did I **predict** what the percentage of oxygen in the air would be?

✔ Did I **record** my observations?

✔ Did I **calculate** how much oxygen was in the test tube?

The Sun and Weather

Find Out

- How the sun warms Earth
- How landforms affect weather
- What the relationship is between climate and weather

Vocabulary

weather
radiation
lithosphere
convection current
hydrosphere
climate

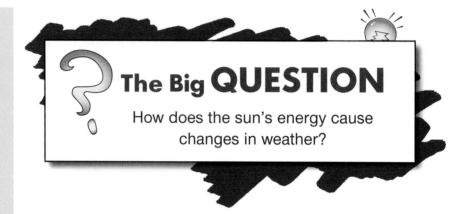

The Big QUESTION

How does the sun's energy cause changes in weather?

How many times in the last day or two have you heard people talk about the heat, the cold, or another day of gloomy fog? Probably a lot. In fact, one of the things strangers often discuss first upon meeting one another is what it is like outside—what will it be like tomorrow? There are many factors that are responsible for the weather you experience each day.

The Sun Warms Earth

Every day the sun rises and, depending on the time of year, we experience a bright, sunny morning, sleet, or maybe an overcast day. The sum of the outside conditions is our weather. **Weather** is the day-to-day conditions in the atmosphere.

What the weather is like is enormously important. You may know what it means to have a ball game canceled by rain or school called off because of snow. Weather can also affect crops and the price of food on our tables.

Although many factors affect weather conditions, the sun is the greatest influence on our weather. It puts many atmospheric forces into motion. Let's take a look at some of the reasons why the sun is so important to weather.

One reason why the sun is important to weather is because the sun warms the Earth. The sun is a ball of hot gases about 150 million km from Earth. That is far enough away so that Earth is not burned by the sun's incredible 6000 °C temperature. About 30 percent of the sun's rays that reach Earth is reflected back into space. Another 20 percent is absorbed by Earth's atmosphere. The remaining 50 percent supports the life and powers the vast system of weather on Earth.

Weather is the day-to-day conditions in the atmosphere.

The sun is the source of all energy in our atmosphere. The energy from the sun that reaches Earth is called radiant energy, or **radiation.** Radiation from the sun travels through space as well as through our atmosphere. You experience radiation when you warm your hands near a campfire. The sides of your hands facing the fire become warm even though you are not touching the fire. Similarly, Earth is not in direct contact with the sun, yet its radiation warms Earth. The sun warms the side of Earth that is in contact with the sun's rays, like the sides of your hands that face the fire.

Three different events take place when Earth receives radiant energy from the sun. Some of the energy will be reflected back into space, some is absorbed by the atmosphere, and some energy reaches the surface of Earth. The balance of these three events controls the characteristics of the atmosphere and the weather that Earth experiences.

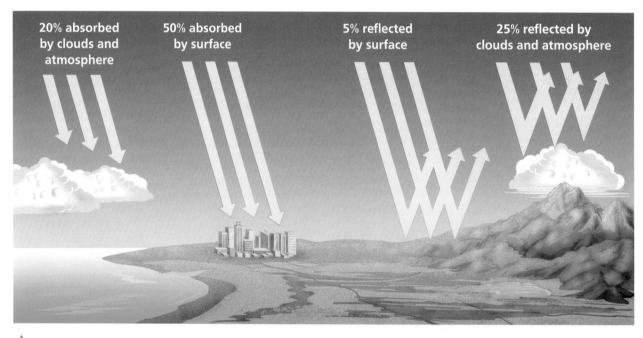

The radiant energy received by Earth from the sun can be reflected back into space, or absorbed by the atmosphere, as well as absorbed or reflected by Earth's surface.

The sun's rays have an enormous effect on Earth's atmosphere. The atmosphere is the layers of gases surrounding Earth. As the sun's energy hits Earth's **lithosphere,** the outermost layer of Earth's surface, it is absorbed and warms the air near the ground. Warm air is less dense than cold air. The warm air rises and as it does, cold air moves in to replace the warm air.

The circular movement of convection currents over land has a great effect on Earth's weather.

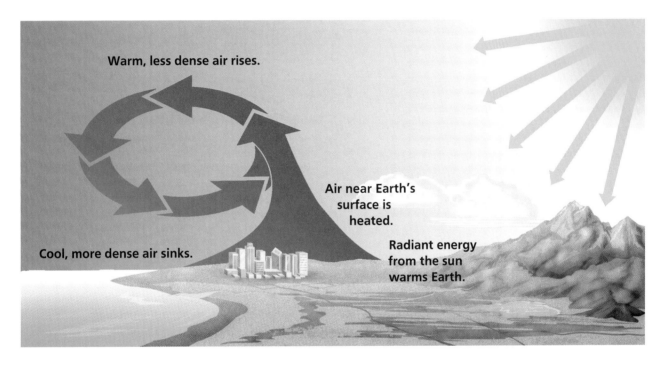

Warm, less dense air rises.

Cool, more dense air sinks.

Air near Earth's surface is heated.

Radiant energy from the sun warms Earth.

The movement of air caused by hot air rising and cold air moving in to replace it causes a convection current. A **convection current** is the movement of air caused when air is unevenly heated, so that part of it becomes less dense, rises and then cools, and other parts become more dense, and sink. Convection currents shape much of our weather.

Earth's Landforms Affect Weather

Earth's air current patterns and weather are also affected by features on Earth's surface. Large bodies of water, such as oceans and lakes, make up Earth's **hydrosphere.** They respond to the sun's energy differently than land. This uneven response of the lithosphere and hydrosphere to the sun's energy contributes to Earth's weather.

The uneven response of the lithosphere and hydrosphere to the sun's energy can cause air current patterns in coastal areas. Because a large body of water holds heat longer than land, a difference in the temperature of the air above water and land can cause convection currents.

Air movements occur when cool, dense air sinks and replaces rising warm air. During the day, land warms faster than water. When the warm, less-dense air over land rises, cooler air rushes over the ocean to the land causing a sea breeze. Because bodies of water hold heat longer than land, at night the air over the ocean is warmer than air over land. The cool, dense air over land sinks and replaces the warm, less-dense air that rises over water. The air that rushes over land to replace the warm, rising ocean air is called a land breeze.

The hydrosphere, which makes up almost three-fourths of Earth's surface, has a significant effect on weather. When the sun's rays strike the surface of a large body of water, some of the water turns into a gas called water vapor. When this moist air cools, the water in the air is released in the form of rain or snow. Therefore, large bodies of water affect the weather by supplying much of the water that later falls as precipitation.

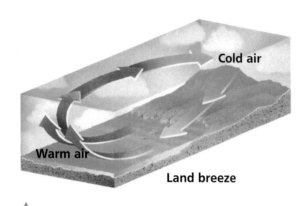

Air at night is warmer over the ocean. Cooler air from the land rushes over the ocean to replace the warm air in a land breeze.

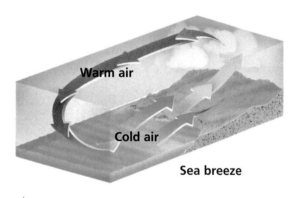

During the day, the air is warmer over the land. Cooler air rushes from over the ocean to the land in a sea breeze.

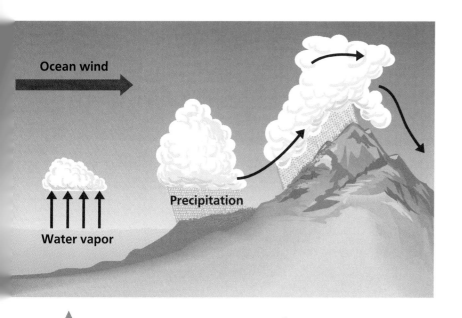

When moist air over an ocean moves over a mountain, one side of the mountain can receive much precipitation while the other side receives very little.

Heavy rains on one side of the Cascade range support a rain forest.

The features of the lithosphere can also affect weather. For example, a coastal mountain range can cause the weather on the ocean side of the mountain to be very different from the weather on the other side of the mountain. When the moist air over an ocean moves over a mountain, the air is cooled. Because the air is cooled as it moves up the side of the mountain, most of the moisture in the air is released as rain or snow on the ocean side of the range. After the moisture in the air is released, the air continuing to travel over the range is dry and the land on the far side of the range is arid.

This pattern of weather occurs in the northwestern United States over the Cascade Mountains. On the west side, or ocean side, heavy rains from ocean air support a rain forest. On the other side of the Cascade Mountains, the dry air and lack of rain cause desert conditions.

Lack of rain on the other side of the Cascade Mountains causes desert conditions.

Climate Is Related to Weather

Most places on Earth experience weather patterns that repeat over and over, year after year. The patterns of weather over many years are what we call **climate.** Weather may change from day to day, but the climate of an area is the average of all weather conditions over a long period of time.

Patterns of weather can be seen to repeat as seasons change. The amount of solar energy that is given off by the sun is about the same all year round. However, the amount of solar energy received on areas of Earth can change due to the changing position of Earth as it moves around the sun.

The angle of sunlight received at any place on Earth changes during the year because Earth is tilted 23½ degrees on its axis. In the temperate zones the angle at which the sun's radiant energy strikes Earth changes over the course of a year. As the angle of the sun changes, the seasons change and the hours of daylight increase or decrease. In the polar zones, the angle of Earth to the sun in summer can cause 24 hours of daylight. In winter, these zones are dark for 24 hours. These differences in the amount of solar energy received by Earth can cause weather patterns to change from season to season.

Solar energy spread out over a large area causes lower temperatures on Earth.

Solar energy spread out over a small area causes higher temperatures on Earth.

Solar energy

Polar zone

Temperate zone

Tropical zone

Temperate zone

Polar zone

Earth has three major climate zones. Do you see a relationship between the amounts of solar energy different parts of Earth receive and climate zones?

Beginning December 21 or 22, the southern hemisphere receives its largest amount of solar energy and has its longest day and shortest night.

Between June and September, days grow shorter in the northern hemisphere.

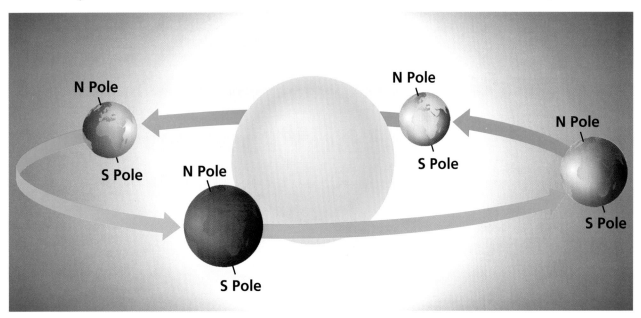

Between December and March, hours of daylight increase in the northern hemisphere until March 20 or 21.

On June 21, the northern hemisphere receives its largest amount of solar energy and has its longest day and shortest night.

You are now equipped to think about weather globally. You know that the sun and Earth's movement around the sun affect the weather and climates on Earth. You know that Earth is surrounded by the atmosphere. You also know that Earth's great landmass, or lithosphere, is continually interacting with its oceans, or hydrosphere, and influences Earth's weather.

Patterns of weather can be seen to repeat as seasons change, due to Earth's changing position as it moves around the sun.

CHECKPOINT

1. How does energy from the sun cause Earth's air to move?

2. How do landforms affect weather?

3. What is the relationship between climate and weather?

 How does the sun's energy cause changes in the weather?

ACTIVITY

Radiant Energy

Find Out

Do this activity to model how energy from the sun affects Earth.

Process Skills

Measuring
Controlling Variables
Hypothesizing
Communicating
Observing
Inferring
Interpreting Data
Constructing Models

WHAT YOU NEED

2-L bottle with cap

cotton balls

thermometer

watch or clock

funnel

sand

water

plastic cup

light source

Activity Journal

WHAT TO DO

1. Pour two cupfuls of sand through the funnel into the 2 L bottle. Slowly add water until the sand is soaked. Think of the bottle system as a model of planet Earth.

2. Place the thermometer into the bottle so that it is gently resting on the sand.

3. Wedge cotton balls in the bottleneck to keep the thermometer in place. Place the lid on the bottle.

4. Make a hypothesis by telling how the temperature will change in the bottle when it is in the shade and under a light source.

5. Create a chart for recording the data you collect.

6. Select the appropriate tool to **measure** and **record** the temperature in the bottle. Label it "Starting Temperature."

7. Set the bottle in the shade or a dark cool place for 30 minutes.

8. **Record** the temperature and the appearance of the bottle.

9. Set the bottle underneath a light source for 2 hours.

Safety! *Do not put the bottle too close to the lightbulb or you could cause a fire.*

10. Record the temperature and the appearance of the bottle.

CONCLUSIONS

1. Compare your hypothesis with your data.

2. Infer how the time that your model Earth spent under the light represented daytime.

3. Based on the data you collected, how does the sun's energy affect the temperature on Earth?

ASKING NEW QUESTIONS

1. What might have caused the moisture to build up on the inside of the bottle?

2. How was your model like and unlike the sun and Earth?

SCIENTIFIC METHODS SELF CHECK

✔ Did I **make a hypothesis** by telling what would happen to the bottle's temperature?

✔ Did I **observe** the temperature and the appearance of the bottle?

✔ Did I **construct a model** of Earth?

Weather Forecasting

Find Out

- How climate can help to predict weather
- How scientists predict weather
- What the causes and types of fronts are
- What causes some severe storms

Vocabulary

monsoons
cirrus
stratus
cumulus
cold front
warm front
tornado
hurricane

The Big QUESTION

How can weather be predicted?

Severe weather is coming! Some people who work outside can predict when the weather around them is going to change. What signals do these people read to make these predictions? How do scientists know when weather is going to become severe? Although weather is often difficult to predict, there are many indicators that people can use to determine when and how weather changes will occur.

Climate Can Help in Predicting Weather

You have learned that the greatest influence on weather is the energy from the sun. This energy causes air movements throughout Earth's atmosphere. In some parts of the world the weather is warm. In others it is cold. Some parts of the world have weather that is very different from the weather in other parts of the world.

Your climate may be warm in the summer and cold in the winter, or the temperature may be steady all year round. No matter what kind of climate your area has, your weather is always changing.

Precipitation and temperature are two major factors that determine the climate of a region. By observing and by recording the patterns of weather over a long period of time, the patterns found in a particular climate can be used to predict future weather events. For example, if a particular climate experiences heavy snows and very cold temperatures at the same time for many years, meteorologists can predict that similar weather patterns will occur in the future.

Warm climates can also have predictable weather. In warm and tropical areas, such as the Caribbean, the warm weather often leads to severe storms coming off the ocean. These storms often happen at particular times of the year. In a large part of the world, monsoons affect people's lives. **Monsoons** are seasonal winds that during the summer bring heavy rains. The farmers in these areas rely on these rains for water for their crops.

In some parts of the world, monsoons cause heavy rains.

Predicting the Weather

Humans have been studying and predicting the weather for a very long time. Meteorologists use many methods to help us know when the weather is going to be severe. Observation is a key factor in predicting weather. By using many different kinds of instruments, such as weather balloons, thermometers, and computers, to collect and analyze data, scientists predict what will happen in the atmosphere and on Earth's surface. Scientists watch temperature, air pressure, wind speed and direction, and humidity. They also watch the movements of air masses by using data relayed from satellites in space. By using instruments for observation, scientists look for recognizable patterns in the weather. This helps them know when and how weather might change.

Satellites can provide scientists with a great deal of information about the weather.

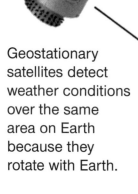

Geostationary satellites detect weather conditions over the same area on Earth because they rotate with Earth.

Because of Earth's rotation, polar-orbiting satellites cover different parts of Earth from one orbit to the next.

Cumulus clouds are puffy, billowing clouds associated with fair weather.

Clouds can also be used to predict weather. Both farmers and scientists in all parts of the world study clouds and know which ones usually bring certain kinds of weather. Different kinds of clouds can provide information about the kind of weather that may be coming.

Although there are many kinds of cloud formations, there are three basic types of clouds. **Cirrus** clouds are high and wispy, usually made up of ice crystals. Cirrus clouds are not associated with severe weather. **Stratus** clouds, which are layers of clouds, are usually associated with wind and rain or snow. **Cumulus** clouds are puffy, billowing clouds. These are usually associated with fair weather.

Every cloud is a collection of very small water droplets or ice crystals. When these droplets grow large enough, they fall to Earth in the form of rain, snow, sleet, or hail. The temperature of Earth and the temperature of the air determines which type of precipitation will occur.

Fronts and the Weather

If you have ever listened carefully to a weather forecast, you have probably heard a meteorologist refer to a "front." An incoming front always means that there will be a change in the existing weather pattern.

The word *front* is borrowed from the military. In military language, a front is the place where opposing armies clash. In meteorological language, a front occurs at the point where two large air masses collide. In a front, one of the air masses will "surrender" to the other one. When the collision happens, warm air will rise and clouds will form. These clouds are messengers of the kind of weather that is on its way.

One type of front that can affect weather is a cold front. A **cold front** occurs when a cold air mass moves into a region occupied by a warm air mass. When the colder air mass meets the warmer one, it slides under the warm air mass and forces it upward. The higher the warm air goes and the cooler it gets, the less able it is to hold the water vapor it contains. When this happens, meteorologists may predict heavy rains or snow. Because air masses in cold fronts move fast, the weather conditions they bring are often brief. Cold fronts often pass quickly and are followed by fair weather and clear skies.

Cold Front
In a cold front, dense, cold air moves into a region of warm air, forcing the warm air upward along the front.

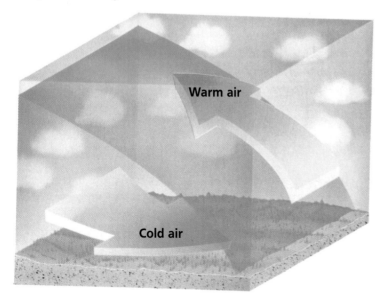

Warm air

Cold air

A **warm front** occurs when a mass of warm air catches up with a mass of cold air, probably because the cold air has settled or slowed. The warm air pushes the cold air out of the way and, at the same time, rises above the cold air. The warm air cools and clouds form as the air's water vapor cools. These clouds usually indicate that there will be prolonged precipitation and warmer weather.

Another type of front is formed when a cold front overtakes another cold or cool front, lifting the warmer air between them above Earth's surface. This type of front is called an occluded (ə klōōd′ əd) front.

Because each type of front causes disturbances in the atmosphere, weather conditions change as fronts occur. With any front, the amount of precipitation depends on how much water vapor is in the air. If the air contains a lot of moisture, the front produces heavy clouds and precipitation as the air cools. If the cooling air is dry, clouds may form but precipitation does not develop.

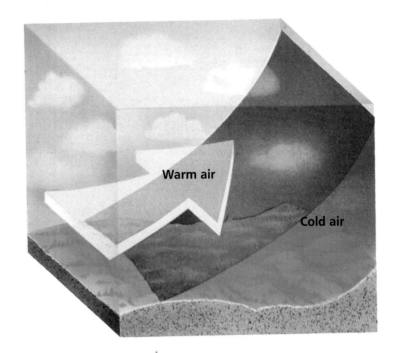

Warm Front
In a warm front, warm air advances and moves up the edge of the cold air mass.

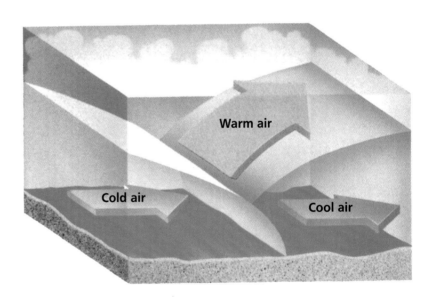

Occluded Front
In an occluded front, a cold front catches up with another cold or cool front. The warmer air between them is pushed up and away from the surface.

Causes of Severe Weather

The patterns that can be found in weather allow meteorologists to make reasonably accurate predictions. You might need to move your picnic indoors if the weather is bad, or you might have to cancel a baseball game if there is heavy rain. However, people can usually continue their normal activities through most kinds of weather.

But sometimes weather can become very dangerous and even deadly. Even though severe weather can often be predicted, there can be surprising, frightening, and destructive results when some types of severe weather strike. Severe weather often occurs when there is a great difference in temperature between two air masses that collide in a front.

One form of severe weather is a **tornado.** Perhaps you may have actually seen or experienced a tornado. If you have, you know how powerful and destructive it can be. Tornadoes occur over land.

Tornadoes occur when an updraft of air in a thundercloud is rotated by the winds near the top of the cloud. The speed of the rotation is increased by rising humid air. This air movement forms a column of whirling air that can appear as a funnel-shaped cloud. As the air around the center of the column of air continues to pick up speed, the funnel grows in length and begins to move downward from the bottom of the cloud. This funnel may even reach the ground. When this happens, a tornado warning is issued. If people are warned in time, they may be able to get out of the tornado's path. Anything in the path of a tornado may be destroyed by the force of its very strong air movements.

A **hurricane** is a severe storm that occurs over water. A hurricane occurs when strong winds begin to circle a low-pressure area over

Tornadoes occur when an updraft of air is rotated by the winds near the top of a cloud. If this funnel-shaped cloud reaches ground, it can be very destructive.

the sea. The wind speeds continue to increase and sometimes reach speeds of 360 km/h. The winds pick up moisture from the water, causing the storm to be accompanied by very heavy rains and wind. A hurricane can be huge, sometimes as large as 800 km across.

The center of the hurricane is called the "eye of the hurricane." The "eye" of the storm is free of clouds and has only light breezes instead of the gale force winds that accompany the hurricane. Because hurricanes rely on large bodies of water, they die out when they reach the land. However, before it dies out, a hurricane can cause extensive damage to everything in its path.

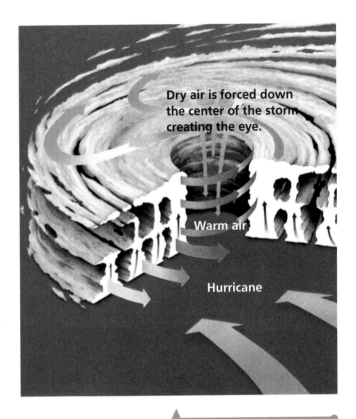

Dry air is forced down the center of the storm creating the eye.

Warm air

Hurricane

Warm, moist air rises rapidly, causing updrafts of air and an area of very low pressure. Surrounding air rushes into the low-pressure center, sometimes at terrific speeds, when a hurricane forms.

CHECKPOINT

1. How can climate help to predict weather?
2. How can scientists predict the weather?
3. What are fronts?
4. What causes some severe storms?

 How can weather be predicted?

ACTIVITY

Investigating Air Masses

Find Out

Do this activity to learn what happens when two air masses meet.

Process Skills

Controlling Variables
Communicating
Predicting
Observing
Measuring
Inferring
Hypothesizing
Designing Investigations
Experimenting

WHAT YOU NEED

250-mL beaker

food coloring

eyedropper

thermometer

water

tall, clear jar

Activity Journal

WHAT TO DO

1. Half-fill the jar with cold water and put it in the refrigerator or another cool place for one hour.

2. Fill the beaker with hot tap water and color it with the food coloring. **Record** the temperature of the water.

3. **Predict** what will happen when the warm water meets the cold water.

4. Gently pour the warm water carefully down the side of the tilted jar.

5. Observe the jar and **draw** a diagram of how the cold and warm water interact.

6. **Use** the thermometer to **measure** the temperature of the warm water. Put the thermometer deeper into the water to measure the temperature of the cold water. Wait ten minutes and again measure the temperature of the water and **record** your measurement.

CONCLUSIONS

1. Compare your prediction with your observations.

2. What happened to the temperature of the warmer water and cooler water when they were mixed?

3. Infer how the movement of the cold and hot water were like two air masses in a front.

ASKING NEW QUESTIONS

1. Develop a testable question. Plan and conduct a simple investigation based on this question and write instructions that others can follow to carry out the procedure.

2. Prepare a report of your investigation that includes the tests conducted, data collected, or evidence examined, and the conclusions drawn.

3. Identify the dependent and controlled variables in your investigation.

SCIENTIFIC METHODS SELF CHECK

✔ Did I **predict** how the hot and cold water would interact?

✔ Did I **observe** the interaction of the water?

✔ Did I **infer** how this interaction was like a weather front?

Review

Reviewing Vocabulary and Concepts

Write the letter of the answer that completes the sentence.

1. ___ is the force of air pushing against something.
   a. Ozone   **b.** Temperature
   c. Air pressure   **d.** Climate

2. The layer of gases closest to Earth's surface is the ___.
   a. biosphere   **b.** troposphere
   c. hydrosphere   **d.** exosphere

3. Wind and rain or snow are associated with ___ clouds.
   a. stratus   **b.** billowing
   c. cumulus   **d.** cirrus

4. The movement of air due to uneven heating and differences in densities is ___.
   a. a convection current **b.** sound
   c. ozone   **d.** atmosphere

5. A ___ is severe weather that occurs over water.
   a. tornado   **b.** blizzard
   c. ionosphere   **d.** hurricane

Match the definition on the left with the correct term.

6. matter that has mass and takes up space and is made up of a mixture of gases   **a.** monsoons

7. seasonal summer winds that bring heavy rain   **b.** ozone

8. measures the speed of wind   **c.** radiation

9. gas that absorbs much of the sun's ultraviolet (UV) rays   **d.** air

10. energy from the sun   **e.** anemometer

Understanding What You Learned

1. In order to predict weather, what conditions in the troposphere are scientists able to observe and measure?

2. What is the source of energy that causes most changes in air temperatures and weather?

3. Besides gases, what other things can be found in the atmosphere?

4. What three different events take place when Earth receives radiant energy from the sun?

5. Why does precipitation often occur when a cold front meets a warm front?

Applying What You Learned

1. Describe changes that might occur as a result of the sun heating Earth unequally over its surface.

2. Why do tornadoes usually occur over flat lands?

3. Why are meterologists often only able to predict weather a few days in advance?

4. If one city releases pollutants into the atmosphere, how can this be a global problem?

 5. How do the properties of the air that make up Earth's atmosphere affect weather?

For Your Portfolio

Use newspaper and tape to make a model of a tornado. On a separate piece of paper, describe what causes a tornado to form and how your model is like and unlike a real tornado. Display your model and paper in the classroom.

CHAPTER 2 *Water* on Earth

*W*ater, water everywhere, and not a drop to drink. Have you ever heard that expression? It comes from a poem in which an old sailor is stranded in the ocean. He is surrounded by water but dying of thirst because ocean water is too salty to drink.

About three fourths of Earth's surface is covered by water, and most of this water is salt water found in the oceans. Although humans cannot drink ocean water, there are many sources of freshwater on Earth. Water can be found in many places and in different states in the atmosphere and on Earth's surface. In fact, water is continuously cycled in what is known as the water cycle.

The Big IDEA

Water is a resource on Earth that is part of a system called the water cycle.

CHAPTER **SCIENCE** **INVESTIGATION**

Learn how the sun affects the water cycle. Find out how in your *Activity Journal.*

Sources of Water

Find Out

- What water is and why it is so important
- Where to find salt water and freshwater
- What can cause differences in water

Vocabulary

groundwater
water table
salt water
oceans
freshwater
glaciers
icebergs

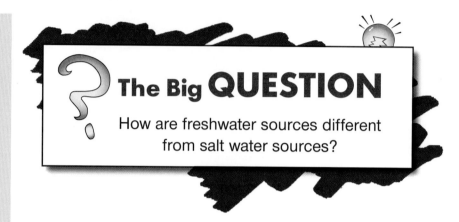

The Big QUESTION

How are freshwater sources different from salt water sources?

If you stood at the edge of the ocean and gazed out across it, you might think its waters stretched on forever. Our oceans are indeed huge. They cover almost three quarters of Earth's surface.

Although our oceans contain vast amounts of water, they provide humans with little drinking water. That water must come from other sources—lakes and rivers, rainwater, and water beneath Earth's surface.

Water and Its Importance

Because water is all around us—filling bathtubs and running from kitchen faucets—it is easy to take for granted. Only the air that you breathe is more immediately important to your survival than water. We need water to digest food, eliminate waste, and control our body temperature. You can live without food for nearly a month, but you would die in less than a week if you did not have water.

To learn about the different sources of water, it helps to know exactly what water is. In the 1780s, scientists discovered that water is a chemical compound containing two elements: hydrogen and oxygen.

Scientists also found that there were two hydrogen atoms for every one atom of oxygen. You have probably seen this written as H_2O. Scientists showed that one single drop of water contains billions of molecules of hydrogen and oxygen.

Water is the only substance in nature that occurs naturally in all three physical states: solid, liquid, and gas. If the temperature of water is below 0 °C, it is a solid and is called ice. Between 0 °C and 100 °C, water is a liquid. Above 100 °C water changes into a gas called water vapor.

Although there are many sources of water on Earth, rivers and lakes provide most of the drinking water we need.

Salt Water and Freshwater

Where does all the water that we drink, bathe in, and use for cooking come from?

There are many sources of water on Earth. Under Earth's surface there are large amounts of water called **groundwater.** Groundwater is stored in porous rock or large pockets between rocks. The highest level of groundwater is called the **water table.**

Water can also be found above ground. Ponds, lakes, rivers, and streams can be found in many places on Earth's surface. There are huge areas of ice and snow at the north and south poles. Water falls from the clouds in the form of rain, snow, hail, and sleet. And, of course, there are the oceans, with their vast amounts of water.

Groundwater is stored in porous rock or large pockets between rocks.

Sources of Salt Water

Ninety-seven percent of the water on Earth is **salt water.** Most of this salt water is found in Earth's **oceans,** the large bodies of water that cover most of Earth's surface. Salt water can also be found in many other bodies of water, such as the Great Salt Lake in Utah and the Dead Sea in Israel.

How did these bodies of water get their salt? Scientists aren't sure, but many believe it all began with the formation of Earth. As the molten rock that formed Earth cooled, it contained all the necessary materials to make minerals including oxygen and hydrogen.

The dense material, such as iron and nickel, within the molten rock sank, and less-dense material rose. Water vapor was released into the atmosphere as volcanoes erupted, releasing gases including hydrogen and oxygen, which combine as water vapor.

When the atmosphere cooled, the water vapor condensed and fell to the surface as rain. The water ran over Earth's surface, dissolving the salts and minerals in the rocks. Water carried these dissolved minerals with it as it moved. Finally, water flowed to low areas on Earth's surface and formed the oceans. All of the dissolved salts and minerals remained in the oceans, which caused the oceans to be salty.

About 75 percent of Earth's surface is covered with water, and most of that water is salt water found in the oceans. Due to the large amount of water covering its surface, Earth looks blue from outer space.

Scientists estimate that there are about 50 quadrillion metric tons of salt in the oceans of the world. The amount of dissolved salts in ocean water is referred to as salinity (sə lin′ ə tē). The greater the percentage of dissolved salts, the higher the salinity of ocean water. About 3.5 percent of the ocean is salt.

As mentioned above, some bodies of water are saltier than others. The Mediterranean Sea, for example, is relatively salty. It is in a hot, dry climate, and the hot air causes surface water to evaporate quickly. This leaves a high concentration of salt behind. Because the Mediterranean is almost entirely cut off from other bodies of water by land, little water flows in to reduce the concentration of salt in the water.

Ocean water is always in motion. This causes water masses with greater salt concentration to mix with those containing less salt. This keeps ocean salinity nearly constant over the globe.

In other areas, rain falls more rapidly than water can evaporate or large rivers dump freshwater into the oceans faster than water is being lost by evaporation. These areas, such as the Baltic Sea, have a lower-than-average salinity.

Icebergs are large masses of floating ice.

Freshwater Sources

Only about 3 percent of the water on Earth is **freshwater.** Freshwater is water that has a mineral content low enough to be consumed by people and land animals. Although the amount of freshwater on Earth is limited, its availability can be extended through recycling and decreased use.

Three quarters of the world's freshwater is frozen. Much of it is in **glaciers,** huge masses of ice that move across the land. The northern half of the North American continent was once nearly covered by glaciers. Water is also frozen in ice caps on Greenland and Antarctica, and in large masses of floating ice called **icebergs.**

Most of the freshwater now available to us falls to Earth as precipitation. Precipitation can take the form of rain, snow, sleet, or hail. It collects in lakes and rivers or soaks into Earth and becomes groundwater. This process will be discussed in greater detail in Lesson 2 of this chapter.

Differences in Water

Freshwater and salt water have many characteristics in common. Both contain salt and other minerals, but freshwater contains only a small fraction of salt.

The amount of rainfall in a region has a large impact on what is in the water. The amount of minerals in the land close by and the number of tiny organisms in the water are also important factors when determining whether a freshwater source can be used for drinking water.

Only about 3 percent of the water in the world is freshwater.

The Dead Sea contains so much salt that swimmers cannot sink.

If you found a spot far from people and pollution, you could drink the water from a freshwater source. But you could never drink water from the ocean, no matter how far from people or pollution you traveled.

The more salt dissolved in water, the more dense the water. The ability of water to exert an upward force on a body placed in it is called buoyancy. As water becomes saltier and more dense, this force increases. The Great Salt Lake in Utah is one of the saltiest bodies of water in the world. If you swam in it, you would float more easily than usual. The Dead Sea in the desert between Jordan and Israel contains so much salt that swimmers can't sink!

CHECKPOINT

1. What is water and why is it important?
2. Where can salt water and freshwater be found?
3. What can cause differences in water?

 How are freshwater sources different from salt water sources?

ACTIVITY
Comparing Buoyancy

Find Out
Do this activity to see how freshwater and salt water affect buoyancy.

Process Skills
Predicting
Communicating
Measuring
Controlling Variables
Interpreting Data
Experimenting

WHAT YOU NEED

3 L freshwater

3 L salt water

pencil with eraser

3 L cold salt water

3 L cold freshwater

3 L hot freshwater

3 L hot salt water

salt

metric ruler

spoon

thumbtack

waterproof felt-tip pen

tall, narrow jar

Activity Journal

paper towels

WHAT TO DO

1. **Predict** how hot and cold salt water and how hot and cold freshwater might affect the buoyancy of a pencil. **Record** your prediction.

2. Fill a jar with room temperature freshwater to within 1 cm of the top.

3. Push the thumbtack into the center of the eraser. Place the pencil, eraser down, into the water. Let the pencil float up naturally. Mark the pencil at the water line with the pen.

4. Remove the pencil and dry it with a paper towel. **Measure** its length above the water level in millimeters and record.

5. Repeat Steps 1–3 using both hot and cold salt water and hot and cold freshwater.

CONCLUSIONS

1. Compare your results with your prediction.

2. How does salinity affect the buoyancy of water?

3. How does the temperature of the water affect buoyancy?

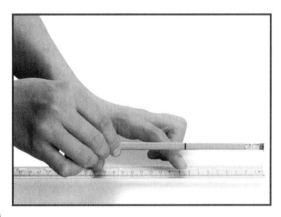

ASKING NEW QUESTIONS

1. Why is it easier to float in the ocean than in freshwater?

2. Could a boat carry a heavier load in freshwater or salt water? What kinds of further information would be helpful to support your conclusion or to answer new questions that you have?

SCIENTIFIC METHODS SELF CHECK

✔ Did I **predict** how the water would affect buoyancy?

✔ Did I **control the variables** in this activity?

✔ Did I **interpret the data** I collected?

The Water Cycle

Find Out

- What the water cycle is
- How water on Earth's surface moves into the atmosphere
- How water moves from the atmosphere to Earth's surface
- How the relative humidity of air is important to the water cycle

Vocabulary

water cycle
evaporation
humidity
condensation
precipitation
runoff
relative humidity
dew point

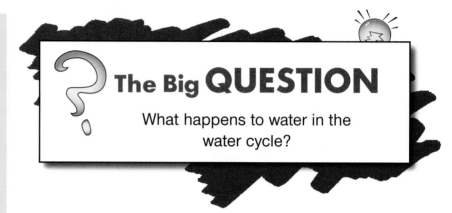

The Big QUESTION

What happens to water in the water cycle?

When you look at a drop of water, it seems calm and still. But if you come back a few hours later, chances are it will be gone. That's because all water is in constant motion. Water moves from Earth's surface into the atmosphere and back to Earth's surface over and over again in what we call the water cycle. This lesson will investigate the cycle and explore how the water cycle influences our weather.

The Cycle of Water on Earth

Water is the most abundant resource on Earth and one of the most important. All organisms depend on water for life. Water is constantly being cycled between living and nonliving parts of the ecosystems that make up Earth.

The **water cycle** is the continual movement of water from one place to another and from one state of matter to another. Let's look at what happens in the water cycle and then investigate these events with more detail in the pages that follow.

To examine the cycle we begin with water falling to the surface of Earth in the form of dew, rain, hail, or snow. Once water falls to the ground, it follows several routes. Some of the moisture seeps into the soil, and some collects in bodies of water like rivers, lakes, or oceans. Plants take in water and release it into the atmosphere. Heat from sunlight causes water held in soil or in bodies of water to become gas. The gas then cools and falls to Earth, beginning the cycle again.

In the water cycle, water changes states and moves from place to place.

Surface Water Moves into Earth's Atmosphere

Let's begin our close examination of the water cycle by looking at how water on Earth's surface moves into the atmosphere. You already know that water can be found in many places on Earth's surface. Water can be found in large quantities in lakes, rivers, and oceans. Water on Earth's surface can also be found in small amounts, such as the water in puddles and the water on your skin. Regardless of the quantity of water in a particular source, the water can change state and move into the air surrounding Earth.

The Water Cycle

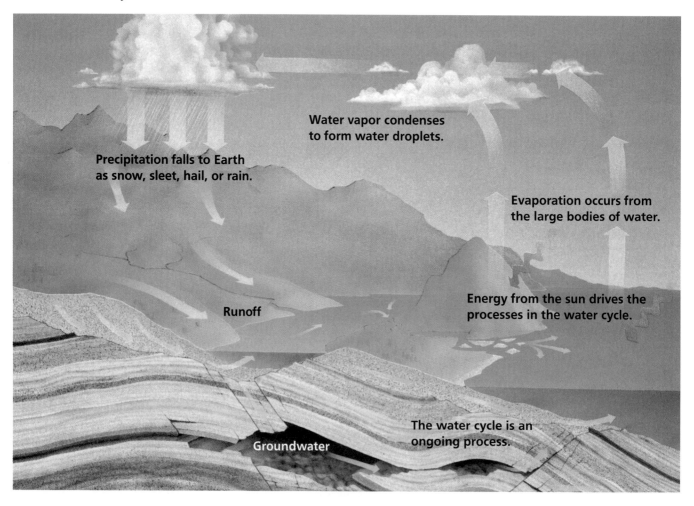

Water vapor condenses to form water droplets.

Precipitation falls to Earth as snow, sleet, hail, or rain.

Evaporation occurs from the large bodies of water.

Runoff

Energy from the sun drives the processes in the water cycle.

Groundwater

The water cycle is an ongoing process.

The sun is the driving force of the water cycle. When the sun's radiant energy, or radiation, strikes Earth's surface, it causes the surface to warm. This radiation can warm soil and rock as well as water. When water is warmed to a certain temperature, it changes from a liquid to a gas. When water exists as a gas, it is called water vapor. The process in which liquid water changes to water vapor is called **evaporation.**

When water evaporates, water vapor rises away from Earth's surface and mixes with the other gases that make up Earth's atmosphere. **Humidity** is a measure of the amount of water vapor in the air. You may have experienced a hot, sticky summer day when the air around you seemed almost heavy. The humidity on a day like this is probably very high. Evaporation occurs over large bodies of water as well as over land. Why might places like Miami, Florida, or Portland, Oregon, have more water vapor in the air than desert areas like Las Vegas, Nevada?

When evaporation occurs over the ocean, water vapor also rises into the atmosphere. Rising water vapor from the oceans contains no salt. What happens to the salt that makes ocean water undrinkable for humans? When ocean water evaporates, it leaves the salt behind. Have you ever been exercising on a hot day and, when you were done, felt as though you had a fine sand on your skin? When you exercise, your body releases sweat, which contains salts. When the water in your sweat evaporates from the surface of your skin, the salt is left behind. Similarly, salts are left behind in the ocean when ocean water evaporates and becomes water vapor.

Water Moves from the Air to Earth's Surface

Once in Earth's atmosphere, some of the water vapor in the atmosphere cools. When water vapor cools, it changes state again and forms tiny water droplets. This process of changing from a gas to a liquid is called **condensation** (kon′ dən sa′ shən). In clouds, the water vapor condenses on tiny particles that are always present in the atmosphere. These particles include dust, smoke, salt crystals, and soil. Fog occurs when water condenses close to the ground. When water vapor condenses on something cold on the ground, these water droplets are called dew. What time of day is dew likely to form? Why is this?

Fog occurs when air condenses as a cloud that rests close to the ground.

When water droplets condense, they can combine into larger drops and become massive enough to fall toward Earth's surface. This process is called **precipitation.** If the air temperature is relatively warm, precipitation will fall in the form of rain. If the air temperature is cold enough, the water droplets could freeze or partially freeze and fall in the form of snow, sleet, or hail.

The precipitation that falls over land drains into rivers and lakes or sinks into the ground. When the ground is saturated, or filled to its capacity, with water from heavy rains or rapidly melting snow, water becomes runoff. **Runoff** is water that flows across the surface of the ground. The water that does not flow across the surface seeps into the ground. Eventually this groundwater seeps into creeks and streams that flow into small rivers. Small rivers join large rivers flowing toward the oceans.

Only about 25 percent of the precipitation from clouds falls on land. The rest falls back into the oceans, maintaining the balance between evaporation and condensation, and preventing oceans from becoming even saltier.

Precipitation occurs when water vapor in the air condenses and falls toward Earth in the form of rain, snow, sleet, or hail.

Relative Humidity and the Water Cycle

To understand why water vapor condenses in the water cycle as air cools, it is important to understand relative humidity. **Relative humidity** is used to compare the amount of water vapor in the air to the amount of water it could hold at its present temperature. If a meteorologist states that the relative humidity is 25 percent, the air contains 25 percent, or one fourth, of the amount of water vapor it could hold at its present temperature. If the relative humidity is 100 percent, the air has all the water vapor it can hold at that temperature.

Humidity, or the amount of moisture in the air, should not be confused with relative humidity. On a hot summer day, the air might contain a lot of water vapor while its relative humidity may still be low. This is because warm air can hold more water vapor than the same volume of cold air. But if this same amount of air becomes cooler, its relative humidity will increase even though the amount of water vapor stays the same.

If the amount of water vapor remains the same, as air cools, its relative humidity increases. As air warms, its relative humidity decreases. Both the temperature and amount of water vapor affect daily weather changes. Without water vapor, there would be no precipitation.

Dew forms on objects when the temperature of air reaches the dew point. Dew can also freeze and become frost.

The amount of water vapor in the air depends partly on the amount of water available. Water evaporates into the air from bodies of water, and water vapor is given off from the leaves of plants in a process called transpiration. Thus, places near oceans, lakes, and forests usually have more water vapor in the air than places without bodies of water or vegetation.

The temperature affects the amount of water vapor in the air as well. As the air warms, it rises, carrying the water vapor with it. As the air rises higher into the atmosphere, it cools. As it cools, the relative humidity increases. When the air holds all the water vapor it can at that temperature, water condenses and the relative humidity is 100 percent. The temperature at which condensation occurs is called the **dew point.** The closer the air temperature is to the dew-point temperature, the higher the relative humidity is. Thus, the water cycle continues as water condenses and falls to Earth when the relative humidity increases and air reaches its dew point.

CHECKPOINT

1. What is the water cycle?
2. How does water on Earth's surface move into the atmosphere?
3. How does water move from the atmosphere to Earth's surface?
4. How is the relative humidity of air important to the water cycle?

 What happens to water in the water cycle?

ACTIVITY

Investigating Humidity and Precipitation

Find Out

Do this activity to see how humidity affects precipitation.

Process Skills

Measuring
Controlling Variables
Predicting
Observing
Communicating
Interpreting Data
Inferring

WHAT YOU NEED

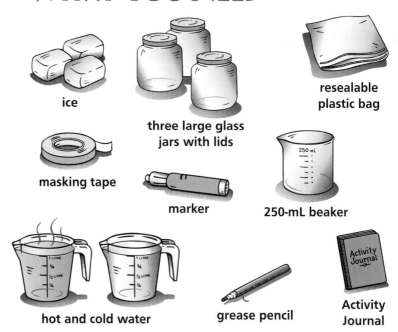

ice

three large glass jars with lids

resealable plastic bag

masking tape

marker

250-mL beaker

hot and cold water

grease pencil

Activity Journal

WHAT TO DO

1. With the marker and masking tape, label the jars "A," "B," and "C."

2. Measure 200 mL of cold water in the beaker, and pour into jar "A." With the grease pencil, draw a line at the water level.

3. Measure 200 mL of hot water and pour into each of the remaining jars, "B" and "C." Draw a line at the water level on each jar.

4. Place several ice cubes into the plastic bag and seal the bag. Put the bag on top of jar "C."

5. **Predict** which jar will be most humid and which will have the most precipitation in ten minutes.

6. **Observe** the jars for ten minutes, again mark the water level on each jar, and **record** your observations.

CONCLUSIONS

1. How could you tell which jar was most humid? Least humid?

2. Which jar had the most precipitation? Why?

ASKING NEW QUESTIONS

1. If you poured 200 mL of hot water into a small jar and large jar, in which jar would the relative humidity be higher? Why?

2. How is condensation different from precipitation?

SCIENTIFIC METHODS SELF CHECK

✔ Did I **predict** which jar would be most humid and which would have the most precipitation?

✔ Did I **interpret the data** I collected?

✔ Did I **infer** which jar was most humid?

Oceanography

Find Out

- How the ocean has been and is currently explored
- What features can be found on the ocean floor
- What ocean currents and ocean waves are

Vocabulary

oceanography
sonar
continental shelf
abyssal plain
mid-ocean ridges
ocean trenches
rift zones
ocean current
ocean waves

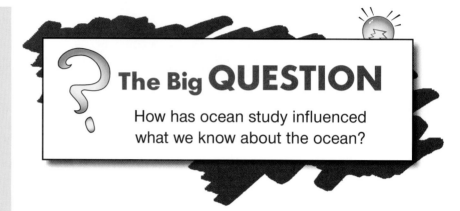

The Big QUESTION

How has ocean study influenced what we know about the ocean?

When early ocean explorers set sail, their maps held large blanks because areas were unknown and not yet explored. There's still much we don't know about our vast oceans, but we are learning more every day. Let's examine how we study oceans, what features can be found beneath the water, and how ocean water moves.

Ocean Exploration

Early explorers faced many limitations when attempting to find out about what exists in the vast oceans. They did not have access to the technology that allows scientists to probe the depths of the sea with advanced equipment and computer-driven instruments and cameras. Step by step, new ideas and inventions expanded the range of human explorations of the oceans.

Many early explorers, such as Christopher Columbus and Ferdinand Magellan, used the ocean to travel great distances in search of wealth and new lands. These explorers were more interested in the lands they found than in the oceans themselves. Many of these early explorers believed the ocean was bottomless and extended to the end of the world.

Matthew Fontaine Maury conducted the first intensive study of the ocean in 1839. He published the first map of the ocean floor and a book about the sea. His work marked the beginning of **oceanography,** the study of the seas and oceans.

In 1872, the British ship HMS *Challenger* set sail to explore the deep sea. The ship had an on-board laboratory that the scientists used to study the ocean floor and ocean life.

Challenger's voyage lasted three-and-a-half years and the ship traveled 111,000 km. Its scientists brought back a remarkable wealth of information, including 4717 species of organisms never seen before. The scientists had also succeeded in taking the deepest water-depth measurement that had been recorded at that time. The *Challenger* mission established the practice of scientific observation and experimentation that many oceanographers use today.

The scientists aboard HMS *Challenger* studied the ocean floor and ocean life. The voyage established scientific practices that are used by oceanographers today.

The oceanographers of our time have advanced technology available to them for studying the ocean. Like the scientists on the *Challenger* voyage, oceanographers today are interested in the depth of the ocean and what features can be found on the ocean floor.

Features of the Ocean Floor

Did you know that less than one fourth of 1 percent of the ocean floor has ever been seen by human eyes? How do we know what features are on the ocean floor? As they have investigated features on the floor of the ocean, oceanographers have been able to "see" with sound.

You learned in the first lesson that sound travels through air, but did you know that sound travels through water, too? Sound waves can be sent through water to help oceanographers find out about the depth of water and the features on the ocean floor.

Continental shelf

Continental slope

Abyssal plain

Continental shelf
The continental shelf is the gently sloping underwater plain that extends from the shoreline out into the ocean.

Continental slope
The continental slope is the outer edge of the continental shelf. It drops sharply toward the seafloor, like a steeply slanted wall.

Abyssal plain
The abyssal plain is the flat bottom of the ocean. It is covered with a layer of mud, sand, and the remains of organisms that have drifted down from above for millions of years.

Sonar is an instrument that uses sound waves to locate objects underwater. Sonar equipment carried on a ship sends out into the water a pulse of sound, which then bounces off an object and returns to the ship. If we know how fast the sound travels and how long it takes to return to the ship, we can calculate how far away the object is. This technique, which allows oceanographers to measure depth, is called echo sounding. Echo sounding has provided oceanographers with information about the location and size of many of the features of the ocean floor.

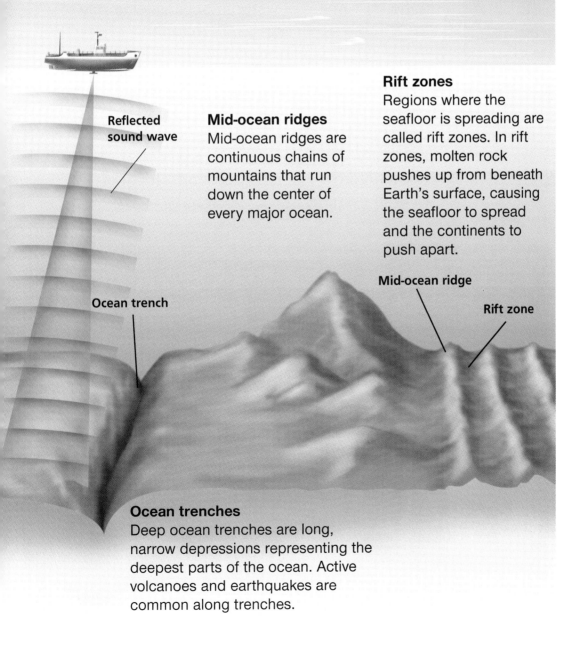

Reflected sound wave

Mid-ocean ridges
Mid-ocean ridges are continuous chains of mountains that run down the center of every major ocean.

Rift zones
Regions where the seafloor is spreading are called rift zones. In rift zones, molten rock pushes up from beneath Earth's surface, causing the seafloor to spread and the continents to push apart.

Mid-ocean ridge

Rift zone

Ocean trench

Ocean trenches
Deep ocean trenches are long, narrow depressions representing the deepest parts of the ocean. Active volcanoes and earthquakes are common along trenches.

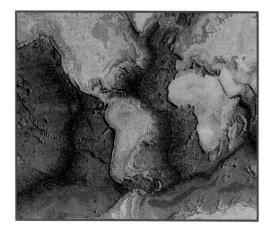

Bathymetric maps show the major features of the world's ocean floor.

In spite of the fact that we cannot adequately see the ocean floor at great depths, there are excellent maps of the ocean floor showing the location of a wide variety of features. Maps showing the depth of area on the ocean floor are called bathymetric (bath′ ə met′ rik) maps. Sonar readings from different areas of the ocean floor can give a picture of the ocean floor. The bathymetric map on this page shows the major features of the world's ocean floor.

In addition to the features on the ocean floor, many oceanographers are also interested in the movement of water in oceans. One way that today's oceanographers map the movement of ocean waters is through the use of satellites. Sonar is often used to map the ocean floor and satellites are often used to map ocean currents. The satellite image on this page shows the ocean currents as twisting paths of bright colors. The image also shows how landforms can affect the movement of water in currents.

Satellite maps help oceanographers understand the movement of water over Earth's surface. Can you see the eastern coast of the United States in this photograph? How does the coastline affect the ocean currents?

Ocean Currents and Waves

An **ocean current** is a sustained, or long-lasting, movement of ocean water. An ocean current travels in a horizontal direction through the ocean, like a river, moving water caught up in its flow. Some currents travel across the surface of the ocean, and some flow at great depths near the ocean floor. Other currents flow in the area between the surface and the bottom of the ocean.

The currents that occur on the surface of the ocean are most often powered by wind. The wind blows across the surface of the ocean and pushes on the water. The force exerted by the wind sets the water in motion.

Currents move water horizontally from one place to another in the ocean.

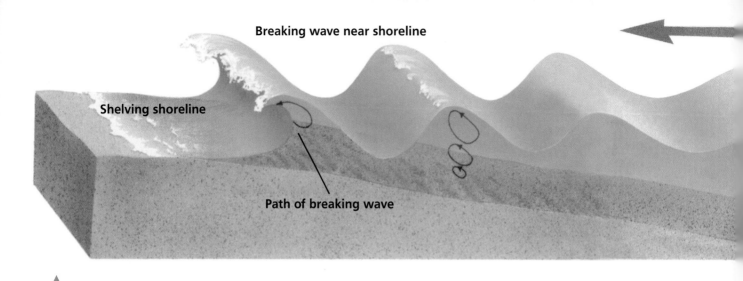

Breaking wave near shoreline

Shelving shoreline

Path of breaking wave

Water waves transfer energy, but not matter, as they move from deep to shallow water.

The deep-water currents are caused by differences in the density of water. You know that circular movements of air due to differences in density are called convection currents. Convection currents also occur in water. Warm water is less dense and will rise to the surface. Cold water is more dense and will sink in the direction of the ocean floor. When the cold, dense water sinks, it pushes ahead water that is warmer and less dense. This interaction between less-dense and more-dense water causes large-scale movements of water.

Ocean waves do not move water or other substances from one place to another. **Ocean waves** are caused by the passage of energy through water. Waves bob up and down but do not move far. Think of the way you move in an inner tube when a wave passes by. You bob up and down, but stay in the same place. But if you were in a current, you and your inner tube would be swept downstream.

Wind causes most ocean waves. You know that you can make ripples in a pan of water by blowing on the surface. Winds blow on the ocean's surface with great force and over a longer period of time. The longer and harder the winds blow, the bigger the waves become.

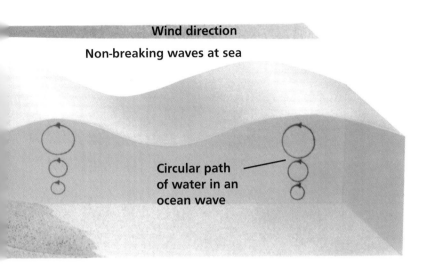

Wind direction

Non-breaking waves at sea

Circular path of water in an ocean wave

Waves can travel hundreds of kilometers. As waves move, they transfer energy, but not matter.

Ocean waves slow down as they move from deep water into shallow water. As they slow down, the crests rise higher and get closer together. This causes crests to become steeper until they fall over. We say that waves "break" near the shore. This is called surf.

Waves and currents both affect the movement of water within an ocean. The technologies that oceanographers use have helped them to understand the features and movements of oceans. There is still much that we do not know about the ocean, but ocean exploration continues to give us a greater understanding of the ocean and the interactions that take place within its waters.

CHECKPOINT

1. Describe some ways in which the ocean has been studied or explored.

2. What features can be found on the ocean floor?

3. What are ocean currents and ocean waves?

 How has ocean study influenced what we know about the ocean?

ACTIVITY

Sonar Mapping

Find Out

Do this activity to find out how sonar echoes are used to map the ocean floor.

Process Skills

Constructing Models
Measuring
Communicating
Interpreting Data

WHAT YOU NEED

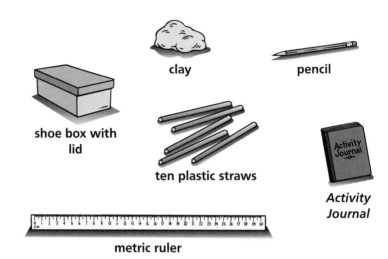

clay

pencil

shoe box with lid

ten plastic straws

Activity Journal

metric ruler

WHAT TO DO

1. Make a **model** of the ocean floor by molding the features of the ocean floor out of clay along the inside edge of the shoe box.

2. Mark a straight line down the opposite side of the box. Use your pencil to poke ten evenly-spaced holes in the lid along the line. Number the holes 1–10. Place the lid on the box.

3. Exchange your box with that of another group. Gently insert a plastic straw into the first hole and mark the straw at the top of the box. Remove the straw. In centimeters, **measure** and **record** the length of the straw between the mark and the end that touched the "ocean floor."

4. Use a new straw for each hole and repeat Step 3 for holes 2–10.

5. Use the data to make a graph showing depth in centimeters of each hole location.

CONCLUSIONS

1. How does your graph compare with the actual model?

2. The straw represents the sonar echo in this model. How is the straw like and unlike sonar?

ASKING NEW QUESTIONS

1. Which areas of the model you tested would you compare to actual ocean floor features?

2. Would it be possible to create a three-dimensional map of the shoe-box seafloor using the data from this activity?

SCIENTIFIC METHODS SELF CHECK

✔ Did I **construct a model** of the ocean floor?

✔ Did I **measure** the depth accurately?

✔ Did I **record** and **graph** my data?

Review

Reviewing Vocabulary and Concepts

Write the letter of the answer that completes each sentence.

1. The highest level of groundwater is called the ___.
   a. waterfall
   b. tidal pool
   c. puddle zone
   d. water table

2. The amount of dissolved salts in the ocean is referred to as its ___.
   a. movement
   b. salinity
   c. density
   d. buoyancy

3. ___ is a measure of the amount of water vapor in the air.
   a. Temperature
   b. Dew
   c. Humidity
   d. A cloud

4. The temperature at which condensation occurs is called ___.
   a. the freezing point
   b. the melting point
   c. fog
   d. the dew point

5. Sonar is an instrument that uses ___ to locate objects underwater.
   a. sound waves
   b. light
   c. radiation
   d. sight

Match the definition on the left with the correct term.

6. makes up 97 percent of the water on Earth's surface   a. salt water

7. sustained movement of water between the atmosphere and Earth's surface   b. evaporation

8. process where a liquid changes to water vapor   c. oceanography

9. water that flows across Earth's surface   d. water cycle

10. the study of seas and oceans   e. runoff

Understanding What You Learned

1. What is water and why is it important?

2. Where is most of the world's freshwater? Salt water?

3. Describe the water cycle.

4. What is the difference between condensation and precipitation?

5. Describe the main features of the ocean floor.

Applying What You Learned

1. What would happen to the salinity of a large area of salt water, such as the Gulf of Mexico, if rainfall was much higher than usual over a period of years?

2. Why does the salinity of the ocean stay about the same?

3. What is the difference between fog and dew?

4. How did the measurements and specimens collected by the scientists on HMS *Challenger* help them learn more about the ocean?

 5. How does water cycle between Earth's surface and air?

For Your Portfolio

Draw an illustration of the water cycle on posterboard showing freshwater and salt water sources. Label the steps of the cycle and use arrows in your illustration to show the movement of water. Show where water changes states. Display your illustration in your classroom.

Earth's Changing

The surface of Earth is constantly changing. Some changes, such as the eruption of a fiery volcano, are rapid and dramatic. Earthquakes happen quickly and can change the landscape in a matter of minutes. We can observe such changes and their effects as they happen. Other changes to Earth's surface occur very slowly over thousands, even millions, of years. For example, the forces of rain, gravity, and the river have been at work for millions of years gouging out the spectacular Grand Canyon. Some changes occurring within the surface of Earth have resulted in the formation of coal, oil, and natural gas. We can't actually observe these changes as they occur, but we can see their effects.

The Big IDEA

Change on Earth's surface can be rapid or slow and can affect Earth's natural resources.

Surface

CHAPTER SCIENCE INVESTIGATION

Learn how a glacier can affect Earth's surface. Find out how in your *Activity Journal.*

Earth's Surface and Rapid Change

Find Out

- What layers make up Earth
- How volcanoes can change Earth's surface
- How earthquakes can change Earth's surface
- What changes occur on the ocean floor

Vocabulary

magma
vent
lava
caldera
mass wasting
faults
rift valley

The Big QUESTION

What causes Earth's surface to change quickly?

Few sites are as awesome as an erupting volcano. Just as amazing are the spectacular, rapid effects a volcano can have on the landscape. Before it exploded in 1980, Mount Saint Helens in Washington was 2950 m high. After its eruption, the mountain was about 400 m shorter. The force literally blew the top off the mountain!

Earth's Layers

Much of what we know about how Earth changes comes from our knowledge of Earth's structure. Understanding Earth's makeup can provide information that can help to answer many of the questions that you may have about volcanoes, earthquakes, and other forces that can affect Earth's surface.

Earth consists of three main layers: the crust, the mantle, and the core. The crust is the top layer. It consists of many different kinds of rock and pockets of liquid rock called **magma.** Where do you think Earth's crust is thickest? Thinnest? Earth's crust is thickest beneath the continents—the major land areas. Beneath the continents the crust averages about 40 km in thickness. Under the oceans the crust averages only about 8 km in thickness. Magma within the crust is under tremendous pressure. This pressure causes the magma to flow upward toward the surface.

Earth's second layer, the mantle, is made of extremely hot molten rock that can flow. The mantle is about 2900 km thick. Temperatures vary from 870 °C near the top of the mantle to 3700 °C at its base.

The core is the center-most layer of Earth and is made up of metal. The inner core is a dense solid ball of iron and nickel at the center of Earth. The outer core is made up of molten metals. The closer to Earth's center, the higher the temperature and pressure become.

Earth consists of many layers: a rocky crust surrounding the mantle and a core of solid iron and nickel.

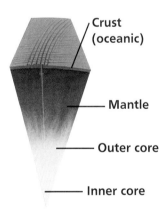

Crust (oceanic)

Mantle

Outer core

Inner core

Earth's Layers

Volcanoes Can Change Earth's Surface

Pressure within the crust is so great that it can force magma to flow through vents in the crust. A **vent** is an opening or a crack that reaches Earth's surface. At these openings, the magma erupts, or breaks through the surface. The hot molten rock that erupts may build a volcano on that spot or flow out on the ground as **lava.**

Volcanic eruptions can be loud explosions or quiet outpourings of lava. Eruptions can also vary greatly in intensity and duration.

One particularly violent volcanic eruption occurred in Oregon more than 6000 years ago. The eruption of Mount Mazama caused the top 1524 m of the volcano to collapse, leaving a huge **caldera** (kal der′ a), or bowl-shaped depression. As lava was cooled by the air, it sealed the opening of the volcano. Over time, the sealed crater filled with water from melted snow and rain. Today, we call this body of water Crater Lake.

Although much less powerful than the eruption of Mount Mazama, the eruption at Mount Saint Helens significantly changed the area's landscape. Before the eruption, the mountain had a steep, conical peak capped by snow and small glaciers. The explosion caused the peak to collapse and the side of the mountain to blow away.

Crater Lake, the deepest lake in the United States, was formed when lava sealed the vent of the volcano after Mount Mazama violently erupted.

The collapse of Mount Saint Helens illustrates how quickly land can change. According to scientists, the movement of debris reached speeds as high as 250 km/h. Much of the debris ended up almost 21 km away, leaving a deposit of debris about 150 m deep and more than 1 km wide.

Volcanic eruptions often affect a wide area of the surrounding land. During the Mount Saint Helens eruption, ash was carried by winds for hundreds of kilometers. Forests were devastated and about 10 million trees were destroyed. In addition, mass wasting also affected the landscape. **Mass wasting** is the movement of rock, snow, mud, or soil down a slope. Floodwaters created by melting snow mixed with ash caused mudflows. In a mudflow, sediment and soil are mixed with water, forming a thick, pasty substance. Gravity then causes this mass to slide downhill. These mudflows caused considerable damage in river valleys beyond the mountain.

Another example of rapid change caused by volcanic activity can be seen in the eruption in Parícutin, Mexico. Unlike the eruption at Mount Saint Helens, no mountain existed at Parícutin— just farmlands, trees, and a nearby town.

One day, residents noticed steam and a low rumbling sound coming from a crevice in a farmer's field. Soon cinders and ash began blowing out of the crevice. Over a period of nine years, the vent spouted cinders, ash, and lava— sometimes at the rate of a million tons a day! When the eruption finally stopped, a 369-m volcano stood where there had once been a village and farmers' fields.

The top photograph shows Mount Saint Helens before the volcanic eruption. The bottom photograph shows Mount Saint Helens after the eruption.

Earthquakes Can Change Earth's Surface

Like the volcanoes at Mount Saint Helens and Parícutin, earthquakes can change Earth's surface quickly and dramatically. Also like volcanoes, earthquakes are the result of pressures built up within Earth's crust.

During an earthquake, pressure in the crust causes cracks and movements along weak sections of Earth's surface. These weak, broken areas are known as **faults.** The energy released at a fault travels outward from the fault in waves. These waves cause the crust to tremble and quake, often causing it to buckle.

In any given year about 50,000 earthquakes occur around the world. Out of those, only about 100 are significant enough to cause damage.

Pressure in Earth's crust causes cracks and movement along weak sections of Earth's surface known as faults.

Within the past 200 years, several large quakes have hit the United States. The eight largest earthquakes in the United States occurred in Alaska. While most people think of California when they think of earthquakes, only three of the largest U.S. earthquakes have been in California. In 1811 and 1812, New Madrid, Missouri, was at the center of extremely powerful earthquakes. Three of the eight largest earthquakes in the contiguous United States occurred in this area between 1811 and 1812. The New Madrid quake in December 1812 caused the ground to sink up to 3 m over a very large area. Gravity caused nearby rivers to pour into the newly created low areas which changed the course of the Mississippi River!

The largest earthquake in the U.S., and the second largest of the twentieth century, struck Alaska in 1964, causing major rising and sinking of land over a 120,000 sq. km area. Coastal areas were particularly hard-hit from seismic sea waves that formed as a result of the earthquake. Huge waves crashed against the Pacific Coast as far south as California, causing serious erosion and property damage.

During an earthquake, the energy released at a fault can cause areas of the crust to buckle. This coastal road in Costa Rica was damaged from the buckling effect of an earthquake.

Changes on the Ocean Floor

Contrary to what some people might think, the ocean floor is not a flat, featureless bed of sand. Like Earth's land surface, the ocean floor has a variety of landforms. Mountains, plains, valleys, canyons, and many other features occur on the ocean floor.

Many features beneath the ocean are more impressive than those found on land. Did you know, for example, that Earth's longest mountain range lies beneath the sea? This mountain range is a mid-ocean ridge. It is four times longer than the combined lengths of the Rockies, Andes, and Himalayas!

The tallest mountain in the world is Mauna Kea, an inactive volcano that forms part of the island of Hawaii, rising 9087 m above the seafloor.

In the middle of the Pacific Ocean are some of the world's tallest mountains. The tallest is Mauna Kea, an inactive volcano that rises above the surface to form part of the island of Hawaii. This mountain stands 4207 m above sea level. This is an impressive height for a mountain, yet most of its height is beneath the surface of the ocean. If you measured Mauna Kea from its base on the sea floor, its height would be 9087 m. By comparison, the tallest mountain on land—Mount Everest—is a little more than 8839 m.

Another feature that exists both on land and on the ocean floor is rift valleys. A **rift valley,** which is caused by the pulling apart of Earth's crust, is a long, narrow depression with steep walls.

Volcanoes, earthquakes, and mass wasting cause rapid changes not only on land but also on the ocean floor. In fact, scientists estimate that 90 percent of all volcanic activity on Earth occurs on the ocean floor. Much of it occurs along the mid-ocean ridge. Earthquakes are also common along this ridge. Each of these forces helps change the look of the ocean floor. As on land, some of these changes occur rapidly, whereas others take many years to unfold.

CHECKPOINT

1. What are the three layers of Earth?
2. How can volcanic eruptions change Earth's surface?
3. How can earthquakes change Earth's surface?
4. What kinds of changes can occur on the ocean floor?

   What causes Earth's surface to change quickly?

ACTIVITY

Modeling A Volcano

Find Out

Do this activity to learn how volcanic calderas form.

Process Skills

Predicting
Observing
Communicating
Constructing Models
Defining Operationally

WHAT YOU NEED

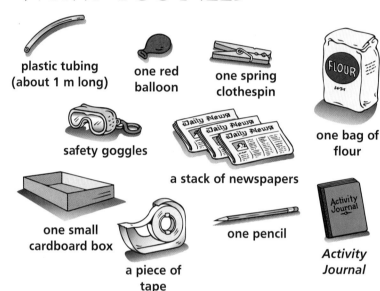

plastic tubing (about 1 m long)

one red balloon

one spring clothespin

one bag of flour

safety goggles

a stack of newspapers

one small cardboard box

a piece of tape

one pencil

Activity Journal

WHAT TO DO

1. Line the bottom of the box with a layer of newspaper. With the pencil, poke a hole through the center of the newspapers and the box.

   Safety! *Press downward when piercing the papers and box with the pencil, never upward.*

2. Pass the plastic tubing through the hole in the center of the newspapers and box. The tubing should stick out of the top of the newspapers by 5 cm or so. The other end of the tubing—the longer end—should be pulled out from beneath the box.

3. Tape the balloon to the short end of the tubing above the newspapers.

4. Blow through the long end of the tubing to inflate the balloon. Clamp the long end of the tube with the clothespin.

5. Bury the balloon under a cone of flour. Shape the flour so that it looks like a mountain.

6. Predict what will happen when the balloon deflates.

7. Remove the clothespin from the clamp and observe what happens when the balloon deflates.

8. Record what you observed.

CONCLUSIONS

1. What happened to the flour when you released the air from the balloon?

2. Explain how the activity showed the forces that create calderas in volcanoes.

ASKING NEW QUESTIONS

1. Based on the result of the activity, define a caldera.

2. What might have happened to the mound of flour if pressure had been increased to the point that the balloon burst?

SCIENTIFIC METHODS SELF CHECK

✔ Did I **predict** what would happen when the balloon deflated?

✔ Did I **observe** what happened to the flour?

✔ Did I make an **operational definition** of a caldera?

Change Over Time

LESSON 2

Find Out

- How mountains form and change
- How glaciers change the shape of the land
- How the ocean can change over time

Vocabulary

folding
faulting
dome
breakwater
seawalls
jetties

The Big QUESTION

What causes Earth's surface to change over time?

Landforms above and beneath the sea do not always change quickly or dramatically. Sometimes the changes are more gradual, often taking thousands or even millions of years.

How Mountains Form and Change

Scientists have evidence that Earth is more than 4 billion years old. During that long period, many changes have taken place due to forces that continually act on Earth's crust. Some of these forces build up landforms, creating new mountains, islands, and other features. Other forces work to erode these landforms. Let's take a look at the processes of mountain building and erosion to see how these forces operate on Earth's crust.

Four basic processes form mountains. These processes are folding, faulting, doming, and volcanic eruptions. Each of the processes occurs because of pressures exerted within Earth's crust.

In the **folding** process, Earth's crust responds to pressures by literally folding. If you laid a sheet of paper on your desk and pushed two opposite sides of the paper together, the paper would buckle or fold. In the United States, the Rocky Mountains and Appalachian Mountains were formed by folding.

The Sierra Nevada of California and the Teton Mountains in Wyoming were formed by faulting. **Faulting** occurs when huge cracks form in Earth's crust. Pressure forces sections of Earth's crust either to slip down or to be thrust upward along these cracks.

Occasionally, mountains form when pressure within the crust causes the surface to warp upward. Mountains formed in this way are called **dome** mountains. The Black Hills in South Dakota are dome mountains that were formed as ancient volcanic rocks were lifted and the sediments covering them were eroded.

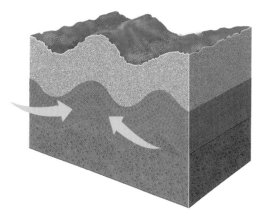

Folding

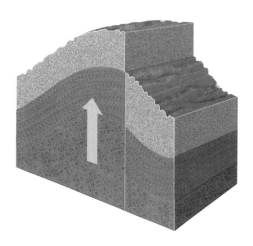

Faulting

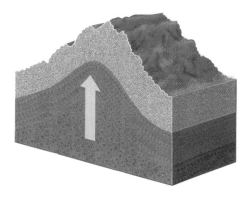

Dome

Even as mountains are forming, the process of erosion begins. Comparing the Rockies and the Appalachians illustrates the effects of erosion. Both these mountain chains were formed by the same process of folding, and yet the two chains look very different. The Rockies are high, jagged, and pointed. They are made of folded igneous, sedimentary, and metamorphic rocks. The Appalachians are low, smooth, and rounded, and made of only sedimentary rocks.

The Appalachian Mountains were formed by folding, but are much older than the Rockies. Erosion has worn away many of the mountains' jagged peaks.

Why don't they look the same? Erosion caused by rainwash, mass wasting, and running water has been working much longer on one of the mountain chains than on the other. Can you guess which one? The Appalachians are much older than the Rockies. They began forming about 460 million years ago. Erosion has carved many of the weak rocks away.

Compared to the Appalachians, the Rockies are mere youngsters. They started forming about 80 million years ago. In fact, some scientists believe that the Rockies are still in their formative years. This is evidenced by occasional earthquakes in the area. But erosion continues to work on these mountains, day by day, year by year. In a few hundred million years, they could look much like the Appalachians do today. Weathering, rainwash, and mass wasting will round their peaks, washing sediments to other places. And the Appalachians? Erosion may eventually wear them down to the point where they are no longer considered mountains.

The forces of erosion affect other landforms, too. Beaches, for example, are diminishing in many parts of the world, including the United States. According to scientific research, 70 percent of the world's sandy beaches are slowly being washed into the sea.

Some of the loss is due to natural erosion. The wind and ocean currents gradually change beach shapes and structures by moving sand from one location to another. Sand is sometimes blown into dunes and deposited inland. Sometimes currents transport the sand many kilometers away.

The Rockies were also formed by folding, but are younger than the Appalachian Mountains. The peaks of the Rockies are high and jagged.

The gradual warming of Earth's climate may also be contributing to the erosion of beaches. As the climate warms up, polar glaciers melt. This causes the sea levels around the world to rise and the beaches to be eroded. The warming of the climate is being caused by a complicated mix of environmental factors that affect Earth's surface and atmosphere.

People build breakwaters, seawalls, and jetties to prevent the natural course of change along shorelines. A **breakwater** is like an artificial sandbar, but it is made of concrete or rock. **Seawalls** are walls built just behind the shoreline to help keep the ocean away from the shore. **Jetties** are barriers that are usually built in pairs. They extend on both sides of the mouth of a river into the ocean. Sometimes these developments are costly and ineffective. Some have interfered with natural processes and have created additional problems.

This breakwater is designed to weaken the effects of ocean waves.

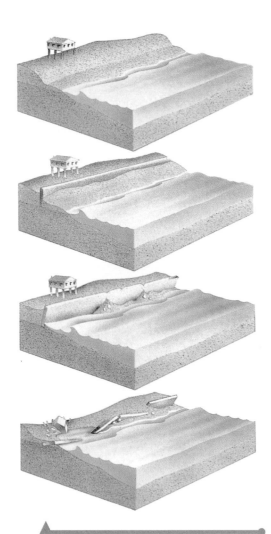

Seawalls are often eroded by the natural force of ocean waves, causing shoreline property to be destroyed.

Jetties are designed to keep drifting sand from blocking the river mouth.

Glaciers

You have seen how rainwater, mass wasting, and running water slowly shape and mold mountains, and how ocean waves, currents, and wind can change beaches. Glaciers can also slowly shape the land.

The most recent ice age began between 2 and 3 million years ago. As recently as 20,000 years ago, huge ice caps covered much of the northern half of North America and northern Europe. Huge rivers of ice called valley glaciers also have moved slowly out of mountain ranges. As these glaciers moved over the land, they gouged deep valleys into the landscape.

About 12,000 years ago, the climate on Earth began to warm up. As the weather warmed, the glaciers melted, revealing valleys, lakes, and waterfalls where none had existed before. The Great Lakes were formed when huge depressions gouged by the ice filled with water.

Today, ice caps and valley glaciers cover about 10 percent of Earth's surface. Just as they did during the Ice Age, they are still shaping valleys and creating other landforms.

Huge rivers of ice called valley glaciers can shape valleys and other landforms.

These rocks were gouged from the action of a moving glacier.

Ocean Changes

As you discovered in the previous chapter, the ocean floor contains some of the most spectacular landforms on Earth. Like the features on land, the ocean landforms are undergoing continual change. Some of these changes take many years.

If you were to drain all of the water from the ocean, what would you find? On the outer edges—the areas that skirt the continents—you would find continental shelves along much of the shoreline. The continental shelf is a plain that gently slopes away from the present shoreline. Water depth on the shelf averages 200 m. About 8 percent of the ocean's total area is made up of continental shelves, but along some active continent margins there are no shelves.

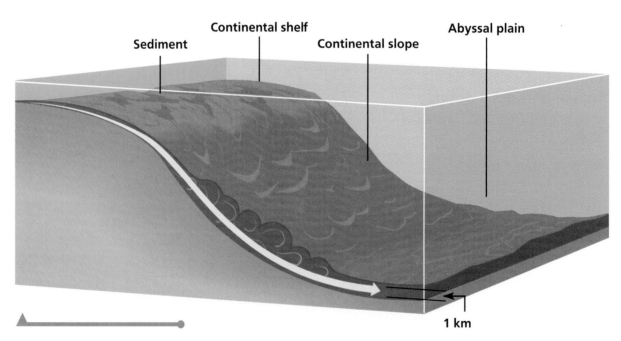

The sediment on the continental shelf is constantly changing due to the deposition of materials from rivers, currents, and erosion.

The sediment on the continental shelf is always changing. Rivers empty materials onto the shelf, and currents deposit materials from along the shore. Erosion of the coastal areas also adds material to the shelf.

Beyond the shelves at the bottom of the continental slope is the abyssal plain, or the ocean bottom. The abyssal plain ranges in depth from 4000 to 6000 m. It is covered with a layer of sediment about 1 km deep. The sediment is thought to be the accumulation of millions of years' worth of assorted materials from the land, including sand, mud, and the remains of organisms.

Scientists have only begun to understand some of the many mysteries of the ocean floor. As scientists are discovering, the oceans store a vast treasure of natural resources, including deposits of petroleum and natural gas. You will read about some of these resources in the next lesson.

CHECKPOINT

1. What processes can form and change mountains?

2. How do glaciers change the landscape?

3. How can the ocean floor change over time?

 What causes Earth's surface to change over time?

ACTIVITY

Investigating Mountain Formation

Find Out

Do this activity to learn how Earth's crust can respond to pressures.

Process Skills

Observing
Communicating
Predicting
Inferring
Constructing Models

WHAT YOU NEED

four colors of clay

waxed paper

two sturdy wooden rulers

Activity Journal

WHAT TO DO

1. With each color of clay, form four thin squares of equal size (about 8–10 cm on each side).

2. Stack the four different colored squares on top of one another and pinch them together along two opposing sides.

3. Place the clay on a sheet of waxed paper.

4. Observe the layers of clay and draw the layers of the clay.

5. **Predict** what will happen to the layers of clay as you push on the clay from two sides with equal force.

6. Gently place one ruler flat against each of the pinched sides of the clay and slowly move the two rulers together.

7. **Observe** what happens to the clay and **draw** the layers of clay.

CONCLUSIONS

1. What happened to the clay as you moved the rulers toward each other?

2. Of the four mountain-forming processes that you studied, which type of mountain-forming process did the movement of the clay most resemble? Why?

ASKING NEW QUESTIONS

1. **Infer** and **draw** how the clay would look if faulting had occurred.

2. Compare your pressed clay with the photograph of real mountains above. What evidence would you look for to find out if specific mountains were formed by the method modeled in this activity?

SCIENTIFIC METHODS SELF CHECK

✔ Did I **predict** what would happen to the clay?

✔ Did I **observe** what happened to the clay?

✔ Did I **draw** the layers of clay?

Earth's Changes and Natural Resources

Find Out

- How mineral deposits form and are mined
- How fossil fuels are formed and used
- How we can protect our environment

Vocabulary

ores
fossil fuels
coal
peat
lignite
bituminous coal
anthracite
petroleum
natural gas

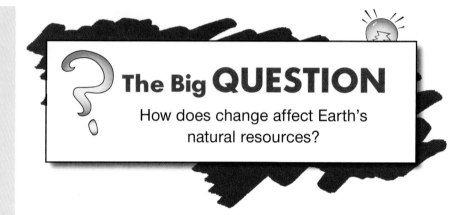

The Big QUESTION

How does change affect Earth's natural resources?

Some events that occur on Earth's surface can change the way the landscape looks in a matter of minutes, some events change the landscape very slowly, and others take place within Earth's surface. For example, many different processes work together over a long period of time to transform one kind of rock into another, for mineral deposits to form, and for coal, oil, and natural gas to form within Earth's surface. In this lesson, we will look at some of these slow changes that can occur within Earth's crust.

Mineral Deposits and Mining

Minerals are just about everywhere. They make up the vast majority of the material found on Earth. Besides air, water, and organic matter, almost everything else on Earth is a mineral.

Wherever you find rocks you'll find minerals. Rocks are made up of combinations of minerals. For example, granite is composed of the minerals feldspar, quartz, mica, and amphibole.

Different processes work together over long periods of time to transform one kind of rock into another. Granite is an igneous rock formed from magma. Over many years, wind, water, and ice break down granite. Water can dissolve feldspar, one of the main minerals in granite. After a time, only grains of the mineral quartz are left. Other processes cement these quartz grains together to form sandstone, a type of sedimentary rock. Heat and pressure can change the sandstone into quartzite, a type of metamorphic rock.

Water on or within Earth, such as groundwater, can transport minerals from place to place and then deposit them at various locations. These mineral deposits can be found in large or small quantities. Rocks and minerals that are found in quantities large enough to make them worth mining are called **ores.**

Fragments of gold are sometimes in certain sand and gravel deposits near riverbeds. One of the oldest methods of mining gold is known as placer mining. It works by separating the dense gold fragments from other grains that aren't as dense. Miners fill a pan with water and place handfuls of dirt and sand into the pan. The pan is then swirled, and the dense materials settle in the center of the pan. Today, minerals are usually mined with large machines that can locate and remove great quantities of minerals relatively quickly from within Earth's surface.

Different processes work together over long periods of time to transform one kind of rock into another.

Granite

Quartz

Sandstone

Fossil Fuel Formation and Use

Inorganic resources, or resources from nonliving materials such as minerals, are not the only natural resources valuable to people. **Fossil fuels**, which are substances formed from organisms that lived on Earth millions of years ago, are important to people because of their energy value. Coal, oil, and natural gas are fossil fuels.

When organisms die, such as decomposed plants that grew in a swamp, their remains become buried under loose Earth materials called sediment. As the organisms decay and become compressed by masses of overlying sediment, all the water is squeezed from them. Over millions of years, pressure and heat can turn the organic material into coal or oil.

Coal is a sedimentary rock. It is also an organic substance made mostly of carbon and hydrogen. Most organisms have these two elements. When they die and their decomposed remains are subjected to heat and pressure by overlying sediment, carbon and hydrogen remain.

Much of the coal mined today was formed from the great forests that grew in subtropical swamps during the Carboniferous period between 285 and 360 million years ago.

Coal forms in swampy areas when plants decay. It takes between 1 and 2 m of plant matter to make a bed of coal 0.3 m thick.

Coal forms in a series of steps during which it gradually loses its moisture content and hardens. In the first stage, peat is formed. **Peat** is a mixture of water and plant materials that will eventually form coal if the conditions are right. Peat is forming today in swamps along the Atlantic and Gulf coasts of the United States. Coal will form in these areas if the swamps eventually become buried by layers of sediment, and peat is compressed and hardened.

Stages of Coal Formation

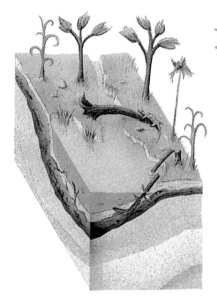  

Peat consists of rotting plant matter found in bogs and swamps. It is about 75 to 90 percent water and is burned as fuel in many parts of the world.

Lignite consists of soft brown coal that has lost much of its moisture.

Bituminous coal is a soft, black coal that has lost all of its moisture and most other impurities. Coal that is formed due to intense pressure and heat is the metamorphic rock **anthracite**, which is the last stage of coal.

In the second stage of coal development, lignite is formed. **Lignite** is a soft, dark brown coal often having a woody texture. Lignite has much less moisture than peat.

Although peat and lignite are both used as fuels, they are not as valuable as coal that reaches the third stage—bituminous coal. **Bituminous coal,** also called soft coal, has been compressed for a very long time. The intense pressure squeezes all of its moisture out, and thus it burns very easily and efficiently. It has its drawbacks, however. Bituminous coal produces many pollutants when it is burned. As a result, many countries have passed laws that put limits on how much of it can be burned.

The fourth stage in coal formation produces **anthracite,** or hard coal. Anthracite is the result of extreme pressures and heat applied by Earth's crust. Anthracite is almost pure carbon and burns more cleanly than bituminous coals. Anthracite is more valued because it does not produce as much pollution when it is burned.

Bituminous coal produces many pollutants when it is burned. Many countries have passed laws limiting the amount of pollutants that can be released into the air from the burning of fossil fuels.

Petroleum, also called oil, and **natural gas** are fossil fuels that result from Earth processes that compact sediment on top of decaying marine organisms that lived millions of years ago. After existing for many years beneath the sediment, heat and chemical reactions turned the organic matter into liquid—in the case of petroleum—or into gases, in the case of natural gas.

Because it is liquid, petroleum can move through porous rocks such as sandstone and limestone. In places where large quantities of oil became trapped, oil reservoirs were formed. Natural gas, which is often formed along with petroleum, is not as dense as petroleum. Thus, it is usually found above the surface of oil reservoirs.

Today, petroleum is the most widely used fossil fuel. Gasoline, a product of petroleum, is the most common form of fuel for automobiles. Natural gas, on the other hand, is the preferred fuel for heating homes in the United States because it burns very cleanly. Coal, meanwhile, is the preferred fuel for power plants because it is inexpensive.

Petroleum is located in reservoirs that are trapped in porous rock.

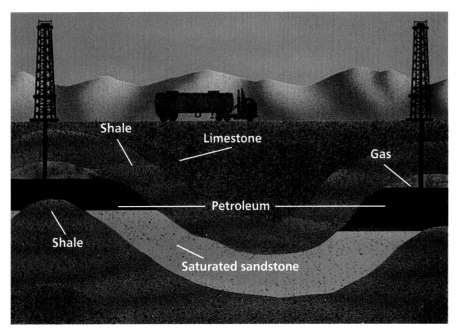

Shale

Limestone

Gas

Petroleum

Shale

Saturated sandstone

Protecting Our Environment

People use minerals and fossil fuels every day. Our world—which is growing in population all the time—has developed a tremendous need for the energy produced by fossil fuels. But the use of these sources of energy and the methods we use to get them out of the ground often harm the environment.

The mining of coal, for example, sometimes pollutes groundwater supplies if not done properly. Such techniques as strip mining can also damage the landscape. In strip mining, cuts are made side by side, and trenches are dug to reach the coal. Then, mechanical shovels are used to dig out the coal. As each new trench is excavated, the materials that are dug out are dumped into an old trench.

Environmentalists have long been opposed to strip mining because of the damaging effects it has on land and on the wildlife. Laws in the United States now require waste rock to be replaced and then covered with topsoil. The land that was once stripped of its mineral resources may now be ready to grow crops, forests, or grass.

Although most countries now have laws that reduce or eliminate much of the pollution caused by the burning of fossil fuels, problems still exist in many areas. In fast-growing cities in some of the world's developing nations, governments are not always able to protect the environment as well as they should. There will always be environmental costs and benefits associated with development.

A crane removes coal from a strip mine in Oklahoma

The burning of fossil fuels has also contributed to many pollution and health-related problems around the world. For example, the ash and sulfur compounds released into the air when coal is burned can cause illnesses, and in large amounts can pose significant threats to the environment.

Some natural resources are plentiful. For example, the world has reserves of iron ore that should last for many years. Other resources, such as petroleum, will not last as long, because all of our known petroleum will likely be used up in 45 years. How do we replace these dwindling resources?

One solution is to develop alternative resources to meet our energy needs. Another is to explore the resources of the ocean. The ocean floor possesses great quantities of petroleum, as well as an array of other natural resources. So far, however, these resources are too deep to efficiently mine.

Another solution is to conserve the resources we have by using them wisely. For example, people can recycle many of the materials that are often thrown away as trash. Recycling not only reduces the demand on our natural resources, it can save energy and reduce pollution.

CHECKPOINT

1. How can minerals be deposited and mined?
2. Name three fossil fuels and describe their formation process.
3. What are two environmental effects associated with our use of fossil fuels?

 How does change affect Earth's natural resources?

ACTIVITY

Investigating the Mining of Minerals

Find Out

Do this activity to learn the costs and benefits associated with mining.

Process Skills

Observing
Communicating
Predicting
Using Numbers
Interpreting Data

WHAT YOU NEED

one sandwich (two slices of raisin bread with layers of peanut butter and sliced bananas in between)

one round toothpick

one plastic knife

one clear plastic straw

one sheet of paper toweling

Activity Journal

Selling Price	
1 Gold deposit	$100,000
1 Molybdenite deposit	$350,000
Mining Cost	
Mineral rights	$10,000
Surface deposit removal	$15,000
Core sample	$10,000
Whole layer removal	$100,000
Restoration Costs	
Restoration of whole layer	$20,000
Filling area of gold deposit	$70,000
Filling area of molybdenite deposit	$70,000
Unrestored Area	$100,000

WHAT TO DO

1. Imagine you are trying to locate materials beneath Earth's surface. Your team has a beginning budget of $500,000. Look over the lists of associated costs.

2. Your "mineral lease area," the sandwich, is land, the raisins are deposits of gold ore, and the banana slices are larger deposits of molybdenite. You must purchase mineral rights to begin.

3. Before you mine each layer, **observe** and **draw** the area. You will need your drawings to restore the site.

4. Use a toothpick to mine the area's "surface deposits."

5. Hidden ore deposits may be located by examining "drill cores," which can be made by pushing the plastic straw through the mineral area. **Predict** what the drill core from the straw will look like.

6. Draw your core sample and decide if you will mine a deposit. Remember your budget is limited and you must restore the area to its original condition.

7. **Record** how many surface deposits and how many total deposits you found.

CONCLUSIONS

1. **Calculate** the percentage of total deposits represented by those found at the surface. How does this compare to the percentage of "deep" deposits?

2. Describe the financial condition of your "mining company."

ASKING NEW QUESTIONS

1. Tell how you decided how many core samples to purchase and how you decided the location of each sample.

2. Explain why it is more expensive to mine deeply hidden deposits than those located at the surface.

SCIENTIFIC METHODS SELF CHECK

✔ Did I **predict** what the core sample would look like?

✔ Did I **observe** the core sample and surface sample?

✔ Did I **interpret the data** I collected?

Review

Reviewing Vocabulary and Concepts

Write the letter of the answer that completes each sentence.

1. A crack leading up to a weak spot in Earth's crust may become a ___.
   - **a.** river
   - **b.** glacier
   - **c.** vent
   - **d.** ore

2. Avalanches, mud slides, and landslides are all forms of ___.
   - **a.** mass wasting
   - **b.** natural resources
   - **c.** snow formation
   - **d.** new material

3. ___ valleys, or long, narrow depressions with steep walls, are found both on land and in the ocean.
   - **a.** Caldera
   - **b.** Rift
   - **c.** Coal
   - **d.** Seawall

4. A ___ is an artificial sandbar used to reduce the impact of water on land.
   - **a.** breakwater
   - **c.** fault
   - **b.** wave
   - **d.** dune

5. ___ are substances formed from organisms that lived on Earth millions of years ago.
   - **a.** Artificial fuels
   - **b.** Minerals
   - **c.** Rocks
   - **d.** Fossil fuels

Match each definition on the left with the correct term.

6. hot, melted rock that erupts from a volcano — **a.** faulting

7. a bowl-shaped depression created by a volcanic eruption — **b.** coal

8. when huge cracks form in Earth's crust due to pressure inside Earth's surface — **c.** lava

9. walls built just behind the shoreline to lessen the impact of ocean waves — **d.** caldera

10. sedimentary rock made up of carbon and hydrogen — **e.** seawalls

Understanding What You Learned

1. Name two events that can cause Earth's surface to change quickly.

2. Describe what causes earthquakes to occur, and how they affect Earth's surface.

3. What types of forces cause changes on the ocean floor?

4. Name two ways that mountains form.

5. How can mineral deposits be mined, and what are some costs and benefits of mining?

Applying What You Learned

1. Name three ways the eruption of Mount Saint Helens affected the surface of Earth.

2. How does erosion affect Earth's surface?

3. If you wanted to explore the deepest part of the ocean's floor, describe what you would need for the exploration.

4. What are some environmental risks associated with the use of fossil fuels?

 5. Describe the changes that can occur on or in Earth's surface, including those that are rapid and those that are slow.

For Your Portfolio

Write a story describing how your town would be affected if an earthquake, volcano, mudslide, or other Earth-changing event occurred. You might describe the event, how long it took to happen, and how you and your friends responded.

Stars and the Solar

For thousands of years, people have gazed at the night sky and wondered about the stars and planets. A Greek astronomer named Ptolemy who lived nearly two thousand years ago believed Earth was the center of the universe and all the other heavenly bodies revolved around Earth. For thousands of years, this is what most people believed.

Today we know that the sun is the center of the solar system and that Earth and other planets revolve around the sun. In this chapter, you will learn how planets and stars are different. You'll also discover what stars are and why they shine.

The Big IDEA

Planets and stars have diverse compositions.

System

CHAPTER **SCIENCE** INVESTIGATION

Surface conditions of the moon and Earth are different. Find out how in your *Activity Journal.*

Earth, Moon, and Gravity

Find Out

- How gravity affects the movement of Earth and the moon
- How gravity affects the tides
- How gravity affects the atmosphere and the ability to support life

Vocabulary

gravity
weight
spring tides
neap tides
craters
friction

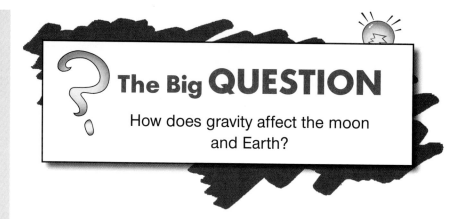

The Big QUESTION

How does gravity affect the moon and Earth?

Did you know that the moon and Earth are in constant motion? The moon moves around Earth at the same time that Earth moves around the sun. Why does this happen? What keeps the moon and Earth from colliding? In this lesson, you will see how gravity and other forces can affect the surface conditions of the moon and Earth as well as their movement through space.

Gravity Affects Movement

There are many differences between the moon and Earth. The size, surface, and composition of the moon and Earth are quite different. However, Earth and the moon also have some similarities. For example, both are affected by gravity and other forces, and both rotate and revolve. Let's find out more about these movements and forces that affect Earth and its satellite, the moon.

One factor that accounts for the differences in movement between the moon and Earth is gravity. **Gravity** is the attraction between two objects based upon the mass of each object and the distance between them. The larger the mass of an object, the greater its gravitational force on another object will be. **Weight** measures the gravitational force exerted on one object by another. The gravitational force of Earth on your body mass equals your weight on Earth. Earth's gravitational force is about six times greater than the moon's gravitational force because its mass is six times as great as the moon's. Consequently, you would weigh one sixth as much on the moon.

Gravitational forces are also important to the way the moon and Earth move through space. Gravity affects the way one object in space moves around another. When one object in space moves around another in a circular path, it is said to revolve.

Because the moon has less mass than Earth, the moon exerts less gravitational force on Earth than the gravitational force that Earth exerts on the moon. Because Earth's gravitational force is greater, the moon revolves around Earth.

Gravitational attraction allows the moon to orbit Earth and Earth to orbit the sun.

→ Orbits
↔ Gravitational Attraction

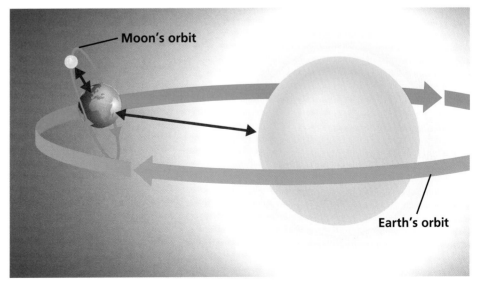

Moon's orbit

Earth's orbit

B119

Similarly, Earth is smaller and has less mass than the sun. Earth revolves around the sun because the sun has a greater mass and gravitational force than Earth. But if the moon is smaller than the sun, why doesn't the moon revolve around the sun like Earth does?

The moon does not revolve directly around the sun because the gravitational attraction between objects is based upon the mass of each object and the distance between them. Because Earth is closer to the moon, its mass exerts a greater gravitational force on the moon than the sun's mass does. The sun has a greater mass but is farther away.

Gravity Affects the Tides

The difference in water levels between high tides and low tides is due to the gravitational attraction of the moon and sun on Earth's oceans.

The gravitational force of Earth affects the moon, but the gravitational force of the moon also affects Earth. As the moon revolves around Earth, the gravitational attraction of the moon causes Earth to "stretch out" along the line toward the moon. The moon's gravity causes ocean water to bulge, or stretch away from Earth's surface, on the side facing the moon and the side opposite of the moon. The effect is much stronger in the ocean water than in the solid crust, so the water bulges are higher than those found in the crust. Although Earth's crust is not affected as much as the oceans, the solid part of Earth moves several centimeters due to the gravitational attraction of the moon.

The areas of the ocean that bulge due to the moon's gravitational attraction are called high tides. The areas of the ocean between the bulges experience low tides. Low tides occur in the places where the water is drained to flow into the two high-tide bulges. Smaller bodies of water, such as lakes, do not have tides because the whole body of water is raised all at one time, along with the land beneath it.

The sun also affects the tides, but because the sun is so much farther away from Earth, its effect on the tides is not as great as the moon's. During a new moon or a full moon, the sun, moon, and Earth are in a straight line. When they are aligned, the gravitational attraction of the sun reinforces the gravitational attraction of the moon. This compounded gravitational attraction of the sun and moon causes the highest tides, called **spring tides.** At the quarter moons, the sun and moon are at right angles. The gravitational attraction of the sun works in opposition to the gravitational attraction of the moon. Consequently, the tides are at their lowest point. These tides are called **neap tides.**

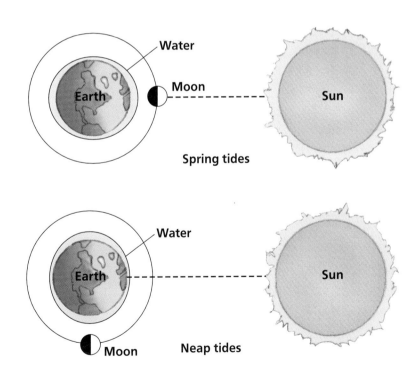

Water

Moon

Earth

Sun

Spring tides

Spring tides occur when the sun, moon, and Earth are in a straight line. Neap tides occur when the sun, moon, and Earth are at right angles.

Water

Earth

Sun

Moon   Neap tides

Gravity, Atmosphere, and Life

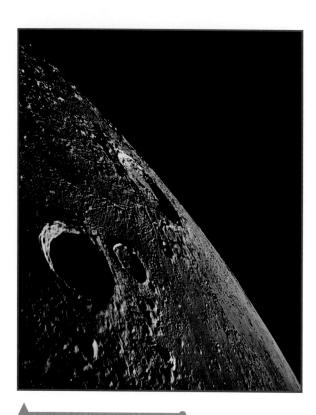

The surface of the moon is covered with craters, caused by space objects hitting the surface.

In addition to the movement of the moon and Earth, gravity also affects the atmosphere. You know that you are affected by gravity because you are held to Earth's surface and have weight. Did you know that the gases in the atmosphere are also affected by Earth's gravitational force? You learned that air is matter, takes up space, and has mass. Air is attracted to Earth's surface due to Earth's gravitational force on the mass of air.

The atmosphere that surrounds Earth enables Earth to support life. One way that the atmosphere affects Earth's ability to support life is by allowing the temperatures on Earth's surface to be mild enough to support life as we know it.

Earth's atmosphere also contains chemicals that support life and life processes. The atmosphere is made up of 78 percent nitrogen and 21 percent oxygen. The elements in the atmosphere are necessary for all of Earth's life-forms.

The presence of an atmosphere also accounts for some of the differences in appearance between the surfaces of the moon and Earth. Earth's surface is made of land and water. Land makes up about one fourth of Earth's surface, and has mountains, plains, rain forests, and deserts. The remaining three fourths of Earth's surface is covered with oceans. This is why Earth is sometimes called the "Blue Planet."

How does this compare with the surface of the moon? Unlike Earth, the moon has no large bodies of water. The moon also lacks the plant and animal life that is found on Earth. Like Earth, the moon has mountains as well as plains that stretch for miles. The surface of the moon is also covered with large depressions in the ground called **craters.**

Virtually all of the moon's craters were formed billions of years ago when objects moving through space hit the moon.

Earth also has a few visible craters, but most have been destroyed or buried by erosion. A few are hidden underneath the oceans.

Earth has just a few visible craters. This crater in Arizona is over a kilometer in diameter.

Scientists believe that Earth's atmosphere also provides a blanket of protection for the planet. Some space objects fly through space randomly. Other objects, like comets, travel in long orbits. If either Earth or the moon is in the path of an oncoming object, there will be a collision. Because of Earth's atmosphere, most of these objects burn up before hitting Earth's surface.

When objects moving through space enter Earth's atmosphere, the friction between the object and the air molecules results in an immense amount of heat being given off. **Friction** is the force that opposes motion, causing heat to be given off when two surfaces rub together. The intense heat resulting from friction causes most objects falling rapidly through Earth's atmosphere to burn up before they reach Earth's surface. If you have ever seen a meteor or "shooting star," you have seen objects burning up in Earth's

Earth and the Moon		
Feature	**Earth**	**Moon**
Size (distance across)	12,756 km	3476 km
Day length	12 hours	about 15 days
Night length	12 hours	about 15 days
Day temperature (highest recorded temperature)	+58 °C	+127 °C
Night temperature (lowest recorded temperature)	about −90 °C	−173 °C
Does it have air?	Yes	No
Does it have water?	Yes	No
Does it have soil?	Yes	No
Can living things survive there?	Yes	No
Does it have craters?	Some	Thousands
Does it have gravity?	Yes	Yes

atmosphere. Space shuttles are covered with as many as 24,000 heat-resistant tiles that protect the shuttle from the immense heat caused by friction during reentry into the atmosphere.

By studying the moon, we can predict what would happen on Earth if Earth lost its atmosphere. Without an atmosphere, more meteorites would likely hit Earth's surface. Temperatures on Earth would reach widely variant extremes. With no atmosphere to reflect and absorb the sun's energy, temperatures during a lunar day can climb to 127 °C. During a lunar night, temperatures can drop to −173 °C. Without an atmosphere, there would be no water, nitrogen, or oxygen on Earth.

Without an atmosphere, Earth would not have the life that makes it unique.

Space shuttles are covered with heat-resistant tiles. The surface of the tiles cools so quickly that you could touch the tiles seconds after they were white-hot, and you would not be burned.

CHECKPOINT

1. How does gravity affect the movement of Earth and the moon?

2. How does gravity affect the tides?

3. How does gravity affect the atmosphere and the ability to support life?

 How does gravity affect the moon and Earth?

ACTIVITY

Investigating Moon Craters

Find Out

Do this activity to see how craters are formed.

Process Skills

Predicting
Communicating
Observing
Measuring
Controlling Variables
Interpreting Data
Inferring

WHAT YOU NEED

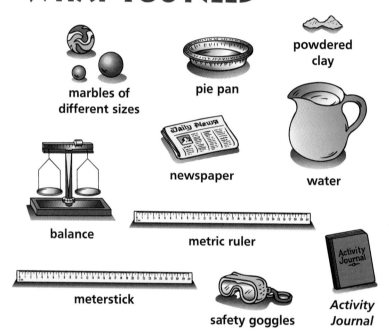

marbles of different sizes

pie pan

powdered clay

balance

newspaper

water

metric ruler

meterstick

safety goggles

Activity Journal

WHAT TO DO

1. Cover a square meter area with newspaper. Place the pie pan in the center of the area.

2. Put on safety goggles. Mix the clay and the water until a thick paste forms.

3. Pour the clay mixture into the pie pan. Smooth the surface of the clay mixture.

4. **Predict** which marble will make the biggest crater and why.

5. Select a marble and use the balance to find its mass. Drop the marble into the clay. **Record** the height from which you dropped the marble. **Observe** and **draw** the surface of the clay.

6. Repeat Step 3 with the other marbles. Drop the marbles from the same height. **Record** the mass and height and **draw** what you observe.

7. Using the metric ruler, **measure** the width and depth of each crater. **Record** your measurements.

CONCLUSIONS

1. What effect, if any, did the mass of the marbles have on the surface of the clay?

2. **Infer** what force caused the marbles to fall into the clay.

3. How were the marbles like objects moving through space and striking a planet?

ASKING NEW QUESTIONS

1. What might have happened to the clay "craters" if the marbles were dropped from a greater height?

2. How did the craters in this model compare to actual craters?

SCIENTIFIC METHODS SELF CHECK

✔ Did I **predict** which size marble would make bigger craters?

✔ Did I **measure** the craters?

✔ Did I **infer** what force caused the marble to fall?

The Solar System

Find Out

- What the solar system is
- What the inner planets are
- What the outer planets are
- What some other objects in the solar system are

Vocabulary

solar system
terrestrial planets
Jovian
asteroids
comet
meteoroids

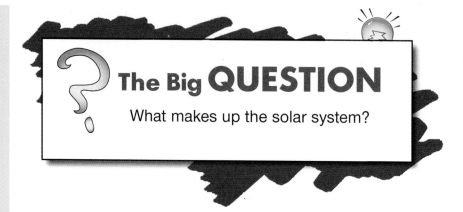

The Big QUESTION

What makes up the solar system?

Have you ever built a model? In the last lesson you put together a model of the moon's surface. Models are miniature representations that show the form, shape, size, and other characteristics of a real object. Scientists often use mathematical models of some physical process to show what might have happened in the past or to predict what might happen in the future.

What The Solar System Is

No one was around to watch when or how the objects that make up the solar system were formed. In order to answer many of the questions that scientists have about what makes up outer space, they use mathematical models to investigate what might have happened or how objects relate to one another.

Scientists now know that Earth is one of nine planets and many smaller objects that circle, or orbit, the sun. These nine planets, the sun, and other smaller objects like asteroids and comets make up the **solar system.**

The solar system includes a vast territory extending billions of kilometers in all directions from the sun. If all matter in the solar system, except for the sun, were combined, it would make up less than 1 percent of the sun's total mass. The sun contains 99.8 percent of the mass of the whole solar system. Because of its tremendous mass, the sun is the central object around which other objects of the solar system revolve.

The nine planets that make up the solar system are different from each other in many ways. Each planet's size, characteristics, and composition make it unique. Each planet also takes a different amount of time to orbit the sun.

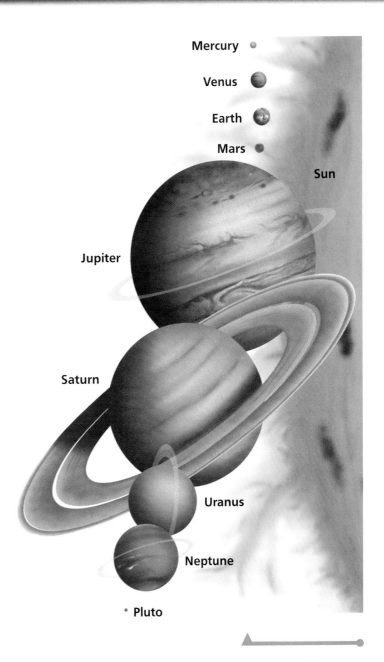

The Solar System

There are also some similarities among the planets. The four planets that are closest to the sun are made mostly of rock. These planets are called the inner, or terrestrial, planets. The five planets that are farthest away from the sun are called the outer planets. The outer planets, except Pluto, are mostly made up of gases.

The Inner Planets

The four inner planets are Mercury, Venus, Earth, and Mars. These inner planets are known as **terrestrial planets** because they are solid and are made mostly of rock, like Earth. The inner planets follow elliptical orbits around the sun. An elliptical orbit is more oval-shaped than circular.

Mercury

Mercury is the closest planet to the sun. It is less than half the size of Earth. Mercury has a rocky surface dotted with craters and looks a lot like our moon.

Unlike our moon, Mercury has an atmosphere. But the atmosphere is too thin to protect the planet from temperature extremes. On the day side of Mercury, the side facing the sun, temperatures can get as high as 425 °C. On the night side of Mercury the side facing away from the sun, temperatures can drop as low as −173 °C.

Venus

Venus, the second planet from the sun, is just slightly smaller than Earth. Like the other inner planets, Venus has an elliptical orbit but it rotates in the opposite direction from Earth and the other inner planets.

Venus receives almost twice as much sunlight as Earth does because it is closer to the sun. Most of this sunlight is reflected away from the planet by its thick cloud cover. Only 2 percent of the sun's energy reaches the planet's surface. However, heat is trapped by Venus's thick atmosphere, which is 90 times heavier than Earth's. Temperatures on the surface can reach 482 °C.

One day on Mercury equals 59 Earth days and one year is 88 Earth days long.

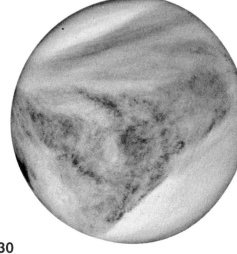

A day on Venus lasts 243 Earth days. A year lasts 225 days.

Earth

The third planet from the sun is Earth. Earth is the only planet we know of that has life. As we learned in Lesson 1, Earth's atmosphere enables plants and animals to live on the planet. Scientists have not found evidence of life on any other planet in our solar system. Earth's average temperature is 22 °C and Earth has one moon.

Mars

The fourth planet away from the sun is Mars. The soil on Mars is similar to what we know as rust. Dust storms are commonplace on Mars, and the dust is what gives Mars its reddish color.

By observing the changes in Mars's polar caps, we know the planet has seasons. During the warmest summer, temperatures on Mars climbed to about 20 °C. During the winter, temperatures can go as low as −124 °C.

Mars's atmosphere is mostly carbon dioxide gas and it is as thin as Earth's atmosphere at an altitude of 40 km. Small amounts of ozone and argon can also be found in the atmosphere. There are clouds and fog on Mars. Water vapor condenses during the night and evaporates during the day.

Mars has two satellites, or moons, Deimos and Phobos. Both of these moons are pockmarked with craters.

Most of Earth is covered with water. It is the only planet we know of that has life.

A Martian day lasts 39 minutes longer than an Earth day. A Martian year is almost two Earth years long.

The Outer Planets

The five outer planets are Jupiter, Saturn, Uranus, Neptune, and Pluto. Jupiter, Saturn, Uranus, and Neptune are known as the **Jovian,** or gas-giant, planets. Even though these planets are much larger than the terrestrial inner planets, they are less dense. The four gas-giant planets have deep hydrogen-helium atmospheres wrapped around hot cores of molten rock.

The fifth outer planet, Pluto, is the smallest planet in the solar system. Pluto seems to be made of ice and rock, and is smaller than Earth's moon.

Jupiter

Jupiter is the largest planet in the solar system. It has over ten times the diameter of Earth. Because of its great size, Jupiter has a tremendous gravitational force. Its gravity keeps 16 moons in orbit around the planet. In addition to the moons, a thin ring of dust surrounds Jupiter.

Jupiter is the first of the gaseous planets. Instead of being made of rock, Jupiter is made almost entirely of hydrogen, helium, and other gases. You could not walk on the surface of Jupiter because it has no firm land surface.

At the planet's core, temperatures reach 30,500 °C. This heat rises through the layers of hydrogen and causes violent storms and lightning on the planet's surface.

A day on Jupiter equals about ten Earth hours. But this giant planet takes almost 12 Earth years to complete one revolution around the sun.

Jupiter has a permanent storm raging on its surface. The storm, which appears in photographs as a gigantic red spot, is three times as wide as Earth.

Saturn

Saturn is the second largest planet in our solar system. Like Jupiter, Saturn has a powerful gravitational force. Eighteen moons are held in orbit by the planet's gravity. A large, wide system of rings, made of ice and rock, also surrounds the planet.

Saturn's atmosphere is made mostly of hydrogen gas. The density of Saturn is so low that it could float on one of Earth's oceans! A rain of ammonia constantly falls through Saturn's hydrogen atmosphere. The temperature on Saturn at cloud level is $-180\ °C$.

A day on Saturn is only 10 hours and 40 minutes on Earth. But it takes Saturn almost 30 Earth years to complete one revolution around the sun.

Uranus

If you look through a powerful telescope, Uranus, the third largest planet, looks bluish-green. The color is caused by the presence of the gas methane in the planet's hydrogen-helium atmosphere. The temperature at cloud level is about $-200\ °C$.

One planetary day on Uranus lasts for about 17 Earth hours. However, the planet takes about 84 Earth years to orbit the sun.

Uranus is different from the other planets in two ways. First, its rotational axis is tilted, or inclined, 98 degrees from its orbit. This means that Uranus is almost lying sideways from Earth's perspective. Second, Uranus's rotation is retrograde. This means that Uranus rotates opposite in direction from all the other Jovian planets.

Eleven dark rings made of rock and ice, together with 15 moons, orbit the planet Uranus.

Neptune

In 1989, the space probe Voyager 2 passed by Neptune. Data sent back to Earth from the space probe show that at least eight moons orbit Neptune. Four thin rings of rock, dust, and ice also circle the planet.

Neptune, which is almost four times as large as Earth, has a core of molten rock and metal. Violent storms rage over the surface of the planet. The planet is very cold, with temperatures on the surface falling to −214 °C.

A planetary day on Neptune equals 16 Earth hours. A planetary year for Neptune equals 165 Earth years.

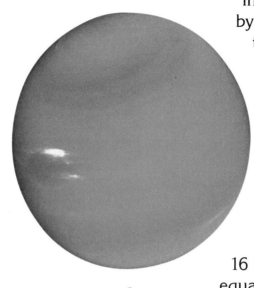

Neptune is almost four times as large as Earth. A day on Neptune is 16 Earth hours.

Pluto

Pluto, which is less than half the size of our moon, is the smallest and coldest of all the planets.

Pluto has a thin nitrogen atmosphere that condenses as snow and frost when the planet is farthest from the sun.

Pluto rotates very slowly. A day on this distant planet lasts almost six and one-half Earth days. It takes Pluto 248 Earth years to orbit the sun. Pluto has one moon, named Charon.

Pluto has the most eccentric orbit of any planet. Between 1979 and 1999 Pluto was inside Neptune's orbit. When this happened, Neptune was the farthest planet from the sun.

Pluto is a small cold planet and has one moon.

Other Objects in Space

The planets and their moons are not the only objects in our solar system. **Asteroids** (as′ te roidz) are rocky fragments made of materials similar to those of the inner planets. Asteroids can range in size from tiny dust particles to over 1000 km in diameter. Most asteroids' orbits can be found in the main asteroid belt between Mars and Jupiter.

Comets and meteors also travel through our solar system. A **comet** is a mass of dust, ice, frozen gas, and rock particles. As a comet approaches the sun, solar energy evaporates the ices in the comet, causing a halo, or coma, to appear around the comet. The closer a comet is to the sun, the brighter it will look. A comet's tail, made of gas and dust, points away from the sun.

Meteoroids are small fragments of material that are falling through space. Most meteoroids are tiny particles, a gram in size. As they enter Earth's atmosphere, the friction of entry burns up the particles. Meteoroids that enter Earth's atmosphere are called meteors. Sometimes, the piece of debris is large and solid enough to actually hit Earth's surface. A meteor that strikes Earth is called a meteorite. Meteor Crater in Arizona was caused by a large meteorite.

In this image of Halley's comet, its coma and tail can be seen.

CHECKPOINT

1. What is the solar system?
2. What are the inner planets?
3. What are the outer planets?
4. What are some other objects in the solar system?

 What makes up the solar system?

ACTIVITY

Modeling Planets

Find Out

Do this activity to learn how to make a model of our solar system.

Process Skills

Communicating
Using Numbers
Measuring
Classifying
Interpreting Data
Constructing Models

WHAT YOU NEED

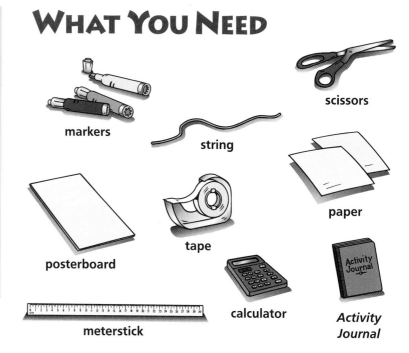

markers

string

scissors

paper

posterboard

tape

calculator

Activity Journal

meterstick

WHAT TO DO

1. Use the chart in the Almanac on page R9 to find the diameter of each planet. Record the diameters.

2. Multiply each of these numbers by .01 and record the numbers. These will be the scaled-down diameters of the planets in millimeters.

3. Divide the class into nine groups, and each group will work on one planet.

4. Using the meterstick, carefully measure and draw a straight line showing the scaled-down diameter of the planet on the posterboard.

Cut out your scaled-down planet by cutting around the diameter in a circular shape.

5. For the larger planets, **divide** the scaled-down diameter of your planet by 2. **Measure** a length of string this many millimeters long. Tape one end of the string to the center of the posterboard and trace the other end of the string while you move it in a circular motion to draw the outline of the planet to scale. Cut out the planet and remove the tape and string.

6. Color each planet the appropriate colors. Use the chart in the Almanac as a reference.

7. On a separate piece of paper, write your planet's name, its distance from the sun, and whether it's a terrestrial or Jovian planet, and describe the planet including its composition, surface features, atmosphere, or other unique characteristics.

CONCLUSIONS

1. How are the posterboard planets like the planets in our solar system? How are they different?

2. In this lesson, the planets were classified as terrestrial or Jovian. On the basis of the characteristics of the planets, name two other ways the planets could be classified.

ASKING NEW QUESTIONS

1. Based on their diameters, how many Earths would fit in Jupiter?

2. How many Plutos would fit in Earth?

SCIENTIFIC METHODS SELF CHECK

✔ Did I **calculate** the diameter for each planet?

✔ Did I **record** my calculations?

✔ Did I **classify** the planets?

Stars

Find Out

- What features stars have
- What affects a star's brightness
- How telescopes help us learn about stars

Vocabulary

photosphere
corona
absolute magnitude
apparent magnitude
red giant
white dwarf
red dwarf
refracting telescope
reflecting telescope

The Big QUESTION

What are stars and what affects how humans can see them?

Stars have fascinated people for thousands of years. From Earth, stars seem to twinkle. They seem to disappear in the day, only to return again each night. The rotation and revolution of Earth affects the way stars appear from Earth's surface. The atmosphere also limits our ability to see stars. Stars have many fascinating characteristics that can be seen only with a telescope.

Features of a Star

What is the sun? What makes it a star? What do we know about the sun?

We know that the sun gives off energy, which is converted to light and heat. We also know that the sun is a huge ball of extremely hot gas. But what else is there to know about the sun?

Scientists have been able to identify many features of stars. Let's begin by examining the surface of a star.

The **photosphere** is a star's surface. The photosphere emits the visible radiation, or light, that we see.

The chromosphere is the layer of gases above the photosphere. The chromosphere is less dense than the photosphere, but hotter.

The **corona** is the star's outermost layer. This thin transparent layer is made of super hot gases. Our sun's corona is visible only during a total eclipse, when the moon blocks the light from the photosphere.

When we draw pictures of the sun, we often draw rays coming from its surface. The sun doesn't have rays, but it does have loops of hot gases, called prominences, that stand above the photosphere.

Sunspots are relatively cooler, dark areas that appear on the sun's photosphere. Sunspots can quickly increase in size, last for a day or for several months, then disappear.

Solar flares are sudden bursts of radiation that often occur near clusters of sunspots. Solar flares are so powerful that they can excite gases in Earth's atmosphere. This produces lights known as the aurora borealis in the northern hemisphere and the aurora australis in the southern hemisphere.

Loops of hot gases, called prominences, stand above the photosphere.

What Affects Star Brightness

When you look up at the sky on a clear night, you might be able to see more than a thousand stars. If you look closely, some stars appear to shine more brightly than others.

When you refer to the brightness of a star, you can refer to either its absolute magnitude or its apparent magnitude. The **absolute magnitude** of a star is a measure of the amount of light it actually gives off. **Apparent magnitude** is the brightness of a star as viewed from Earth. A star that's actually rather dim can appear quite bright in the sky if it is close to Earth. A very bright star can appear dim if it is far away.

Imagine that you are standing outside on a clear, starry night. One star looks brighter than the others. But that large, bright star may actually be smaller or cooler than a star that looks faint and small. How is this possible? The star that looks so large and bright may be millions and millions of kilometers closer to Earth than the small, faint star.

Pretend that your friend is holding a huge, powerful flashlight. Another friend is holding just a regular flashlight. If your friend with the strong flashlight stands three blocks away, and your friend with the regular flashlight is standing right in front of you, which flashlight would seem brighter? The smaller flashlight would look brighter, even though the other flashlight is actually more powerful.

Because the sun is much closer to Earth than any other star, it appears much larger and brighter than other stars. One of those tiny stars in the night sky might actually be a thousand times larger than our sun but looks small because it is very far away.

Temperature, in addition to the amount of light a star gives off, affects a star's brightness. Stars have different surface temperatures. This difference in temperature can depend on the age of the star and its mass. Some stars, like our sun, are yellow stars. Other stars can be white, blue, or red. A star's color can tell us the star's temperature and its size.

If our sun were a small red star, it might be only as bright as a full moon. The sky would look dark, and Earth, even in summer, would be a frozen, lifeless planet.

Rank	Color	Average Surface Temperature °C
coolest	red	3500
average	yellow	5800
hot	white	10,000
hottest	blue	11,000–25,000

Stars can be different colors because of differences in temperatures.

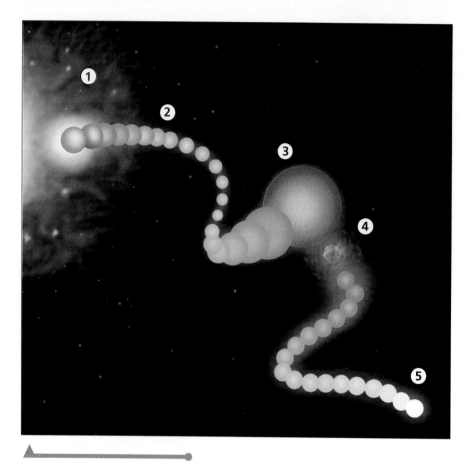

Stars form in all sizes. A star is born from a cloud of dust and hydrogen gas, mixed with helium and many other elements. If the cloud is large, the star that forms will be big, bright, and very hot. It will lead a short life and will shine blue-white. As the star's life comes to an end, it will probably explode as a supernova, a star that experiences a sudden outburst of energy.

If the star that forms is smaller, about like the sun, it will shine yellow-white and live for some 10 billion years. As it nears the end of its life, it will swell to become a **red giant** with a cool, greatly expanded surface. Then it will cast off its outer layers of gas. Its final state will be a small, hot star called a **white dwarf**, which is essentially the leftover core of a bygone star.

The smallest stars never get very big or shine brightly. Because they are small, they stay relatively cool and shine "only" red hot. Astronomers call this type of star a **red dwarf**. Red dwarfs live extremely long lives. A red dwarf that was born long before the sun will still look almost the same ages from now, well after the sun has run through its entire life.

Life Cycle of a Star

1. Gases and dust particles exert a gravitational force on each other and begin to move closer together.

2. When this mass of dust and gas becomes hot enough, a star begins to form and a huge amount of energy is released that radiates into space.

3. When this beginning star runs out of fuel, it expands and becomes a giant.

4. While the core of the giant collapses, the outer portions of the giant are blown away. When the giant collapses, a white dwarf is formed.

5. Eventually, the white dwarf uses up its fuel and becomes either a cold, dead star or implodes and becomes a supernova (supernova not shown).

The Telescope

Astronomers use telescopes to observe stars and planets. A telescope is an instrument that magnifies distant objects. The telescope makes it possible to study and photograph many objects in space that were formerly unknown.

In 1609, Galileo built his first simple telescope. Using his invention, Galileo was able to see four of Jupiter's moons, as well as craters and mountains on our moon. He also detected the rings of Saturn, but wasn't certain what they were.

The simplest telescope is a **refracting telescope.** At one end of the tube is a convex lens. The lens may be small or large in diameter. This lens is called the objective lens and its job is to gather light. At the other end of the tube is a small lens called an eyepiece. Its job is to magnify the image formed by the objective lens.

Light rays coming from an object strike the objective lens and are bent, or refracted, until the rays come to a single point called the focal point. This is similar to the way eyeglasses bend, or refract, light going into the eye. The eyepiece allows an astronomer to see the image in precise detail.

In a refracting telescope, a large objective lens gathers light from a star or planet. The light travels to a small eyepiece, or ocular. The eyepiece magnifies the image, which appears upside down.

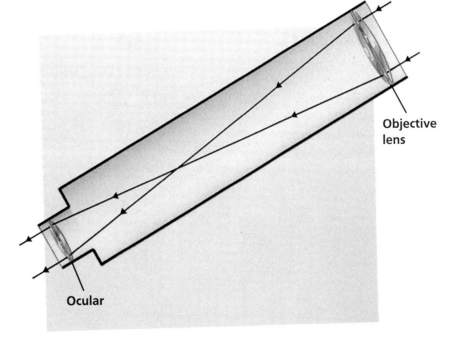

Objective lens

Ocular

Another type of telescope is a **reflecting telescope.** Instead of using a glass lens as the objective, a reflecting telescope uses a mirror as the objective. Reflecting telescopes can be built much larger than refracting telescopes and, thus, have a much greater light-gathering ability. Most astronomy today is done with large reflectors.

The Hale Telescope at California's Palomar Observatory has a 508 cm diameter reflecting mirror. The telescope at Kitt Peak National Observatory is used to photograph and study the sun, solar flares, and sunspots.

Astronomical observatories are often located in desert regions, where the sky is usually clear, or high on mountaintops, above the clouds.

The best location for a telescope is in space. In space, the telescope's image is not distorted due to the atmosphere. There is no interference from clouds, airplanes, weather, or lights.

A reflecting telescope uses two smooth mirrors to magnify distant objects. The biggest reflecting telescopes are larger than the biggest refracting telescopes and gather more light.

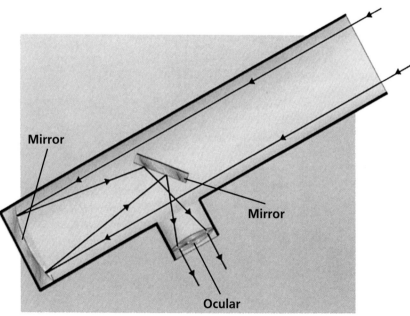

Mirror

Mirror

Ocular

In 1990, the Hubble Space Telescope was launched into space. The Hubble telescope is in orbit around Earth but is focused on objects in deep space. The Hubble telescope allows astronomers to see objects in space ten times more clearly than any telescope on Earth.

The Kitt Peak National Observatory sits on a mountaintop where images will be less distorted by clouds or other atmospheric conditions.

CHECKPOINT

1. What are some features stars have?
2. What affects how bright a star appears?
3. How do telescopes help us learn about stars?

 What are stars and what affects how humans can see them?

ACTIVITY
Investigating Brightness

Find Out
Do this activity to learn how distance affects brightness.

Process Skills
Measuring
Observing
Communicating
Predicting
Controlling Variables
Interpreting Data

WHAT YOU NEED

meterstick

two regular
flashlights of the
same size

Activity
Journal

WHAT TO DO

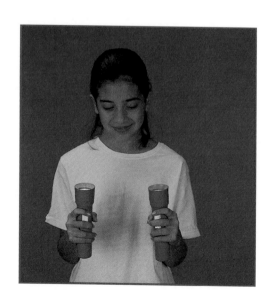

1. In a large, dark room, have a partner turn on both flashlights and stand about 5 m away from you. Observe the brightness of each light and record your observations.

   Safety! *Before turning off lights, make certain the walk areas are free of obstructions.*

2. Predict which light will seem brighter if one partner moves closer to you and one moves farther away.

3. Again, in a large, dark room, have one partner hold one flashlight about 3 m away from you. Have another partner hold the other flashlight about 20 m away. Compare the brightness of the two flashlights.

4. **Record** your observations.

CONCLUSIONS

1. Compare your prediction with your observation.

2. Was the absolute magnitude of the two flashlights different? Why?

3. Was the apparent magnitude of the two flashlights different? Why?

ASKING NEW QUESTIONS

1. How were the flashlights like stars you see from Earth?

2. What did this activity tell you about the way distance affects brightness?

SCIENTIFIC METHODS SELF CHECK

✔ Did I **predict** which flashlight would seem brighter?

✔ Did I **observe** the brightness of both flashlights?

✔ Did I **record** my observations?

Review

Reviewing Vocabulary and Concepts

Write the letter of the answer that completes each sentence.

1. The effect of gravity on you is your ___.
   - **a.** scale
   - **b.** weight
   - **c.** rotation
   - **d.** force

2. All the planets and other objects orbiting the sun make up our ___.
   - **a.** Milky Way
   - **b.** galaxy
   - **c.** planetary year
   - **d.** solar system

3. A tiny fragment of material that enters Earth's atmosphere and burns up is called ___.
   - **a.** a moon
   - **b.** an asteroid
   - **c.** a meteoroid
   - **d.** a particle

4. While we call a star's surface its photosphere, its outermost layer is its ___.
   - **a.** equator
   - **b.** corona
   - **c.** asteroid belt
   - **d.** planetary year

5. The amount of light a star actually gives off is its absolute magnitude, but what we see is a star's ___.
   - **a.** corona
   - **b.** atmosphere
   - **c.** sunspots
   - **d.** apparent magnitude

Match each definition on the left with the correct term.

6. the surface of a star, which emits the visible light that we see
   - **a.** terrestrial

7. the depressed areas visible on the moon and some other planets
   - **b.** reflecting telescope

8. inner planets having solid cores
   - **c.** photosphere

9. gaseous planets in our solar system
   - **d.** craters

10. an instrument that uses lenses to view the sky
   - **e.** Jovian

Understanding What You Learned

1. Why would you weigh less on the moon than you do on Earth?

2. Why is the atmosphere important for life on Earth?

3. How are the inner planets different from the outer planets?

4. Which star appears brightest to people on Earth?

5. Why do telescopes work better in space?

Applying What You Learned

1. Describe how objects in space are able to stay in orbit.

2. Why is the sun the center of our solar system?

3. Why do the planets take different amounts of time to orbit the sun?

4. List the factors that might affect a star's brightness if you were looking at the night sky from Earth's surface with a reflecting telescope.

 5. How are the compositions of the planets in our solar system and stars different?

For Your Portfolio

Choose three objects in space. Make a model of each using different colored clay or any other material that would be appropriate. For example, blue cellophane could be water on a clay Earth. Try to make the three objects relative in size to each other.

Unit Review

Concept Review

1. How do the properties of the air that makes up Earth's atmosphere affect weather?

2. How does water cycle between Earth's surface and air?

3. What forces can change the surface of Earth?

4. How are planets and stars different?

Problem Solving

1. Think about some of the problems of global warming due to the loss of ozone in Earth's atmosphere. Suggest some solutions for how these problems can be solved.

2. Because water is an important resource, we need to use it carefully, and recycle and conserve it. Think about ways that you can help conserve water in your school and home.

3. How might the landscape of your town change if a large earthquake or volcanic eruption occurred in your town? Describe what might occur in your town and describe which changes would be fast or slow.

4. How could you tell if one star was hotter than another?

Something to Do

Imagine that you are a meteorologist for a local television station. Pick a type of severe weather and imagine that it is heading in the direction of your town. The severe weather could be a tornado, snowstorm, monsoon, or any type of weather that might be out of the ordinary for your town. Tell your television audience what causes this type of severe weather, what atmospheric conditions are associated with this weather, and what they should do for safety. Create some type of visual aid or sound effects to go along with your broadcast.

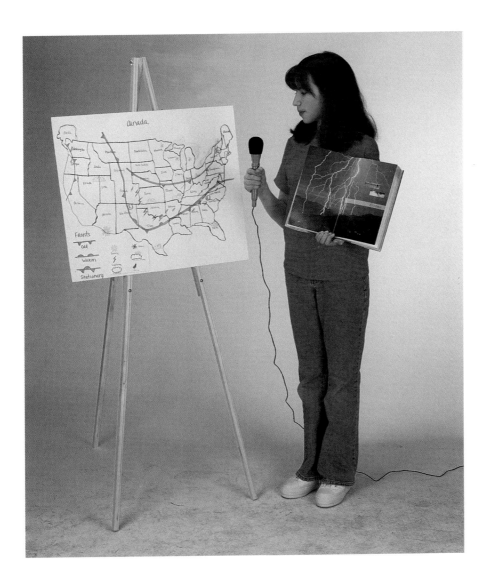

UNIT C

Physical Science

Properties of

Earth and everything on it is made up of matter. Not all matter is the same. We describe the differences in matter by discussing its properties.

Some properties provide information about the form of a material. For example, describing a material as a liquid describes the form of the material. Some properties provide information about a material's chemical composition and how it is used. For example, because wood burns, it would not be a good material to use for a chimney.

People identify and classify properties of matter in many ways. The way that some substances chemically change and the way that some change form are both properties of matter that help us understand the world and the interactions in it.

The Big IDEA

Matter can be identified by its physical and chemical properties.

Matter

CHAPTER SCIENCE INVESTIGATION

Different materials mixed with water can form different kinds of mixtures. Find out how in your *Activity Journal.*

C3

Physical and Chemical Properties

Find Out

- What physical properties of matter are
- What three states of matter are
- What a chemical property of matter is

Vocabulary

physical property
mass
volume
density
melting point
boiling point
chemical property

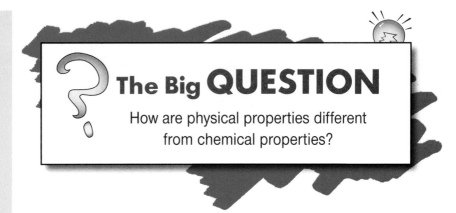

The Big QUESTION

How are physical properties different from chemical properties?

Take a look around the room. What do you see? All of the objects you see are made up of matter. In fact, every object in the universe, such as stars, planets, rocks, water, air, and all living things, is made of matter.

Physical Properties

Matter is anything that takes up space and has mass. We use the properties of matter to describe and classify the materials around us. In this part of the lesson you will discover some different physical properties of matter. A **physical property** is a characteristic of matter that can be observed without changing the chemical composition of the substance. By learning about a material's physical properties, we can learn about the world and discover how best to use Earth's resources.

Some physical properties of matter can be discovered through careful measurement. One physical property that scientists often use to describe matter is mass. **Mass** is the quantity of matter in a material. Sometimes people confuse an object's weight with its mass. Weight is a measure of the gravitational attraction between two objects. On the moon, for example, an object's weight would be different than the weight of the object on Earth. This is because the moon's attraction, or gravitational force, on the object is different from Earth's gravitational force. Scientists measure the gravitational force exerted on an object in newtons, the unit used for measuring weight. If you have a mass of 60 kg on Earth, your weight is about 600 newtons. You would have the same mass of 60 kg on the moon, but you would weigh only about 100 newtons. That's because the amount of matter that makes up your body does not change from place to place, but the moon's gravitational force is much weaker than Earth's.

Volume and density are two other physical properties that describe a substance through measurement. **Volume** is the amount of space something takes up. **Density** is the mass of an object divided by its volume.

An easy way to understand density is to imagine identical 2-L containers. One container is filled with popped popcorn and the other is filled with cement. Because the two materials fill identical containers, they have the same volume. But the 2 L of cement has more mass than the same volume of popcorn, and therefore, the cement-filled container has a greater density than the popcorn-filled container.

This "weightless" chamber at the United States Space Camp in Huntsville, Alabama, simulates the moon's gravitational pull, which is one sixth of Earth's.

Some properties of matter can be determined by using your senses. For example, some physical properties of matter can be determined by touch. The texture of a material, whether it is rough, grainy, or smooth, is one kind of physical property that can help us to know how to use a material. Have you ever felt sandpaper? Sandpaper is grainy and abrasive. This physical property lets us use sandpaper to file and smoothen materials such as wood. Some stones are very hard and abrasive. This physical property has allowed humans to use them for sharpening tools for centuries.

Some physical properties of matter can be detected by the sense of sight. Light can pass through some substances but not others. The ability of a substance to let light pass through it is one of the physical properties that allows us to make informed decisions about building materials. Glass, for example, is one substance that is valued for its ability to allow light to pass through it. Glass is important for allowing

Because glass allows light to pass through it, glass is used in homes and automobiles.

Because some materials are rough and abrasive, they are used for sharpening tools.

light into our homes and automobiles. Glass is also used in hand lenses, microscopes, and telescopes. By allowing light to pass, glass in these tools enables us to see very small things as well as things that are very far away.

The density of a material also helps us to determine how it can be used. Most metals are relatively strong and may be used to build things. Both aluminum and steel could be used to build, for example, camping equipment. Since the equipment must be a certain thickness to resist bending, a steel tube can be thinner and have a smaller volume than one made with aluminum, because the steel is stronger. Even with the added thickness, the thicker aluminum piece will have a smaller mass than the thinner steel piece because of the difference in their densities. Since the aluminum pieces have a smaller mass, they weigh less and are therefore easier to carry. However, when it is strength that is most important, such as for a building or bridge, stronger metals will be used even though they weigh more.

Hardness is also a physical property that allows us to make decisions about which materials would be best to use for certain functions. For minerals, hardness is tested by scratching one mineral against another. The harder of the two minerals will scratch the softer mineral. Diamonds are the hardest minerals and talc is one of the softest. This property of diamond allows it to be useful as a cutting tool in factories and a durable gemstone in rings, whereas talc is sometimes used in skin-softening powders.

Because of iron's density, it is used to build deep-sea vessels that must withstand extreme pressures deep within the ocean.

States of Matter

The state of a sample of matter is another physical property of matter that helps us to understand and use materials. Depending on its temperature, a sample of matter may exist as a solid, a liquid, or a gas. These conditions are called states of matter. States of matter are physical properties, because the chemical composition of the original substance does not change when the substance changes from one state to another.

States of Matter

In a solid, particles are arranged closely together. Solids have a definite shape and volume.

When the temperature of a solid rises to or above its melting point, it becomes a liquid. Liquid has a definite volume but takes on the shape of its container.

When the temperature of a liquid rises to or above its boiling point, it becomes a gas. A gas does not have a definite shape or volume and takes on the shape of its container.

Think about what happens when water changes states. When water is a solid, it is called ice and has a definite shape and volume. Regardless of the container into which ice is placed, its shape remains the same. When ice melts, it becomes a liquid. Liquid water has a definite volume but takes on the shape of the container in which it is placed. When water changes from a liquid to a gas, it becomes water vapor. Water vapor, like all gases, has no definite shape or volume. A gas takes on the shape and volume of whatever container it is in.

The temperature and pressure of a sample of matter determine whether it is a solid, liquid, or gas. Ice turns into liquid water when the temperature rises to or above its **melting point,** the point at which a substance changes from a solid to a liquid state. Liquid water becomes a vapor if the temperature rises to or above its **boiling point,** which is the point at which a liquid becomes a gas.

Melting point and boiling point are both physical properties of matter. Most types of matter have their own specific temperatures and pressures at which they melt and boil. When you think of water, you probably think of the liquid because that is the state it is in at room temperature. A piece of gold, on the other hand, is a solid at room temperature. You would have to heat it to a much higher temperature to make it become a liquid or gas. You can say that if the temperature of a material is above its melting point, the material is a liquid. If the temperature is above the material's boiling point, it is a gas.

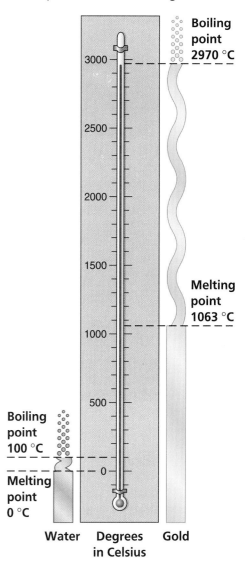

No two substances have exactly the same set of physical properties. Compare the melting point and the boiling point of water and gold.

Boiling point 2970 °C

Melting point 1063 °C

Boiling point 100 °C

Melting point 0 °C

Water   Degrees   Gold
         in Celsius

Chemical Properties

A **chemical property** describes the way a substance reacts with other substances. If you have ever left your bike out in the rain, you might know that iron interacts with the oxygen in water to form iron oxide, better known as rust. Because the chemicals iron and oxygen need one another for the action to take place, we say they react.

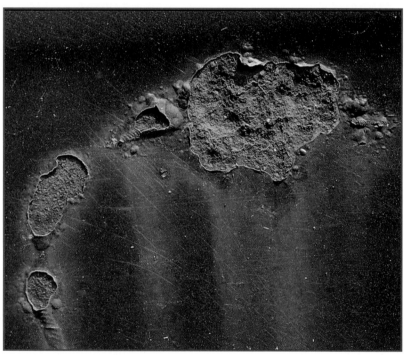

Rust develops because of the chemical properties of iron and oxygen. Iron reacts with the oxygen in water to form rust, which is why cars and bikes sometimes become rusty when exposed to rain.

Houses, cars, and ships are painted to protect their surfaces from rotting or rusting. Because paint does not have the same chemical properties as wood or metal, paint is often used to protect surfaces that are exposed to the environment. Marble is calcium carbonate, which reacts with acids. Acid rain corrodes statues and monuments in many parts of the world due to the chemical properties of marble.

The fact that a material does not react with another material is also a chemical property. A brick will not burn, so we say it is nonflammable. We know that gasoline burns, so we say that it is flammable. Being nonflammable is a chemical property just as being flammable is a chemical property.

Chemical properties of materials determine whether or not, and how, one material will react with another material. Some substances can undergo a chemical change when they contact oxygen and water vapor in the air. One such substance is sodium. Sodium must be stored in oil, because if it comes into contact with water, it will react violently, sometimes even explosively.

Expensive materials are destroyed every year because of chemical changes that occur in these materials. For example, steel structures such as bridges sometimes collapse as the metal they are made of rusts and weakens. Iron water pipes, automobiles, and many other items will also corrode as the metal in these objects rusts.

Chemical properties of materials enable us to use matter for countless commercial applications every day. Bleach, for example, is used as a product to whiten clothes. Bleach is also combined with many other substances in cleaning supplies. In addition, bleach is a vital ingredient in the making of paper.

CHECKPOINT

1. What are three examples of physical properties?
2. What are three states of matter?
3. What is a chemical property of matter?
 How are physical properties different from chemical properties?

ACTIVITY

Investigating Physical Properties

Find Out

Do this activity to learn how physical properties can be used to classify matter.

Process Skills

Measuring
Observing
Communicating
Using Numbers
Interpreting Data
Classifying

WHAT YOU NEED

beaker

4 percent solution of polyvinyl alcohol in water (PVA)

4 percent solution of powdered borax

graduated cylinder

balance

dropper

stir rod or craft stick

goggles

apron

food coloring

Activity Journal

WHAT TO DO

1. On the balance, measure and record the mass of the beaker.

2. Measure 30 mL of PVA solution into the beaker and add two drops of food coloring. Observe and record the physical properties of the material.

3. Using the dropper, add about 3 mL of borax solution to the beaker and measure and record the mass of the beaker and material. Record the volume of the material.

4. Stir the liquid vigorously for two minutes, then transfer the material into your hands.

5. **Observe** and **record** the physical properties of the substance.

6. Form the material into a ball and put it back into the beaker. **Record** whether or not it takes the shape of the container.

7. Again, **measure** and **record** the mass of the beaker and the material on the balance. **Record** the volume of the material.

8. Wash your hands thoroughly.

9. **Calculate** the density of the starting material and the ending material. From both the mass of the starting material and the mass of the ending material, subtract the mass of the beaker. Use this number as the mass when calculating density. Remember: density = mass ÷ volume.

CONCLUSIONS

1. Was the starting material most like a liquid, a solid, or a gas? The ending material?

2. Compare the physical properties of the ending material with the physical properties of the starting material.

ASKING NEW QUESTIONS

1. What other materials have you seen that have properties similar to the ending material?

2. What properties would the ending material have for it to be classified as a solid or a gas?

SCIENTIFIC METHODS SELF CHECK

✔ Did I **observe** the solution and new material?

✔ Did I **record** my observations?

✔ Did I **classify** the new material based on its physical properties?

Changes in Matter

Find Out

- What a physical change is
- What a chemical change is
- What can happen in a chemical reaction

Vocabulary

physical change
chemical change
chemical reaction
reactants
products
acids
bases
indicators

The Big QUESTION

How can matter change?

*W*hat are some changes that you see in the world around you? You might see a tree grow leaves in the spring and lose its leaves in the fall. You might see a worn-out place in clothes that were once brand new. You might also see changes that have taken place within you. There are many changes that take place in the world. Changes in matter can be classified as physical or chemical changes.

Physical Changes

Some changes that you may see around you take place in the shape and size of a substance. Think about making a picture by cutting out different colors of construction paper and gluing them on a posterboard. When you cut or tear the paper, you are changing the shape and size of the piece of paper. How did the glue change? The shape of glue changes as it moves from the bottle onto the posterboard.

When we talk about the changes that take place in matter, changes that alter the size, shape, or form of a substance are classified differently than changes that take place in a substance's chemical makeup.

A **physical change** takes place when a substance keeps the same chemical properties but changes form. You learned about states of matter in the last lesson. When water changes from ice to water or from water to water vapor, a physical change occurs. The water has changed form but still has the same chemical properties.

Change in the state of matter is one way that a material may change form. A change in the shape of matter is another way the form of a material may change. For example, the shape of a piece of paper changes when you cut it to make a picture. A change in shape involves only altering the appearance of the material. The chemical properties of the paper do not change.

Material also changes form when the amount of a substance changes. Imagine that you woke up one morning and had a block of lead the size of a car sitting outside of your home. You might describe the block as huge, heavy, and immovable. However, if this large block was cut down into a block of lead the size of a marble, you might describe it as small, dense, and movable. Even though the quantity of the lead caused you to describe its physical properties differently, the substance in both blocks is the same. The chemical properties of the lead did not change because the quantity of the lead was changed.

Clay undergoes a physical change when its shape is changed.

Chemical Changes

You now know that changes are classified as physical changes when only the form of matter changes and the chemical properties remain the same. There are also other kinds of changes. What happens to cause the chemical properties of a substance to change?

A **chemical change** happens when two or more substances react and new substances are formed. When a chemical change occurs, small particles of matter are actually rearranged and a new substance is formed. This new substance can be taken apart only by another chemical change or many chemical changes. For example, when you burn a piece of wood, the chemical properties of the wood change. The particles that made up the wood are rearranged and combine with substances in the atmosphere in the burning process. The burning process forms ash and a combination of gases, which are released in the form of smoke.

Sometimes it can be confusing to recognize the differences between physical and chemical changes. In general, chemical changes result in a new substance with different chemical properties. Physical changes involve only a change in form or amount. In addition, all chemical changes either release some form of energy or need energy for the chemical change to occur.

When wood is burned, the chemical properties of the wood change and new substances, ash and smoke, form.

Chemical changes can provide us with useful products. One example of a material formed by a chemical change is rubber. If you came to school today in a car, on a bus, on your bike, or even walked in your tennis shoes, you used rubber in moving from one place to another. More than 100 years ago, Charles Goodyear discovered a chemical reaction that improved rubber by making it less sticky, less smelly, and more springy. This made rubber a better material for use in tires, shoes, and thousands of other materials.

Rubber is a substance that comes from the sap of certain trees. When it is first harvested, it is called India rubber. This raw rubber becomes brittle when it is cold and sticky when it is hot. While Goodyear was experimenting with it, he accidentally spilled a mixture of rubber and sulfur onto a hot stove. He was surprised that the mixture didn't melt. The rubber had reacted chemically with the sulfur. It was a chemical reaction that needed a high temperature to make it happen. The new rubber material was tough and resistant to heat and cold.

Like rubber, many useful materials are formed as a result of chemical changes. By understanding the chemical properties of substances, scientists and engineers can predict and investigate how certain substances will react with others. The chemical changes that result from such reactions can provide us with different kinds of materials that can be used in buildings, homes, tools, foods, and many other items that humans use in their lives.

India rubber is the sap harvested from certain trees.

The rubber Goodyear developed was tough and resistant to heat and cold, making it a good material to use for tires.

Chemical Reactions

Chemical changes are involved in nearly everything that occurs in your life. Chemical changes take place in your brain and are necessary for you to think. You can see evidence of chemical changes everyday in the form of rust and in the food you eat. A **chemical reaction** is the activity that occurs during a chemical change. In a chemical reaction, substances are chemically changed and one or more new substances are formed. The substances that undergo change are called **reactants.** Substances that are formed during a chemical reaction are called the **products.**

When charcoal burns, carbon in the charcoal reacts with oxygen in the air to form carbon dioxide.

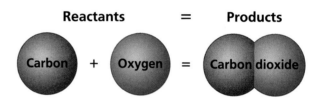

Reactants = Products

Carbon + Oxygen = Carbon dioxide

When a chemical reaction takes place, energy can be given off or absorbed. Think about how charcoal burns during a cookout. Carbon in the charcoal combines with oxygen in the air to form carbon dioxide. During the chemical reaction, energy is given off in the form of light and heat. In chemical reactions, energy is transferred from one form to another but is not lost.

Even though there are countless varieties of substances that can react with one another, there are four basic types of chemical reactions that occur when a chemical change takes place.

The first type of chemical reaction is when two substances join together to form a new substance. This type of reaction takes place when sodium and chlorine join together to make salt.

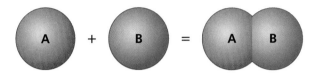

The second type of chemical reaction occurs when one substance is broken down into two new substances. This takes place when salt is broken down into sodium and chlorine.

Another basic type of chemical reaction is one that occurs when two substances are joined and one particle switches places with another.

The last type of basic chemical reaction is one in which two substances are formed and the particles that make up both switch places.

There are many very common chemical reactions and some of them you already know. You know that the cells of all plants and animals use oxygen to burn sugar for energy to perform their life processes during respiration.

Respiration

Oxygen + Sugar = Energy + Carbon dioxide + Water

Another common chemical reaction that you already know is photosynthesis. The chemical reaction that takes place during photosynthesis allows green plants to make their own food.

Photosynthesis

Carbon dioxide + Water + Sunlight = Oxygen + Sugar

Another common type of chemical reaction in nature is one that occurs between acids and bases. **Acids** are substances that react with metals and contain hydrogen. **Bases** are substances that contain hydroxide and can neutralize an acid. When an acid mixes with a base of equal concentration, a chemical reaction takes place that produces salt and water. This process is called neutralization. Can you tell which reaction pattern neutralization follows?

Neutralization

Acid + Base = Water + Salt

Acids can be strong or weak. Acids that aren't very strong are found naturally in many of the foods we eat. These weak acids can be found in substances like lemons, vinegar, and soft drinks. Some acids are made by humans for industrial uses and can be very dangerous. Strong acids, such as sulfuric and nitric acids, eat away at tough materials like wood or metal.

Bases also can be weak or strong. Some hand soaps are weak bases. Like the acids, strong bases can eat away at other materials.

Acids and bases are measured on a scale called a pH scale. The scale goes from 0, the strongest acid, to 14, the strongest base. Pure water would be in the middle with a pH of 7.

Chemicals that are used to test for acids and bases are called **indicators.** An easy way to test for an acid or a base is to use litmus paper. This is a type of treated paper that turns red if it comes into contact with an acid or blue if it contacts a base. The brighter the red or blue the litmus paper becomes, the stronger the acid or base. In addition to litmus paper, there are also other chemicals that can be used as indicators of acids and bases. The activity that follows will show you another way to see if a substance is an acid or a base.

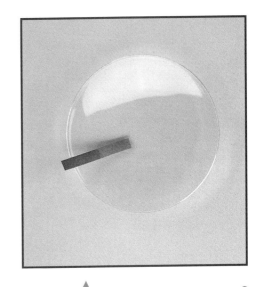

When litmus paper comes into contact with an acid, it turns red.

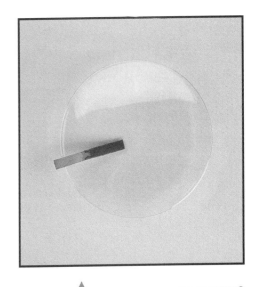

When litmus paper comes into contact with a base, it turns blue.

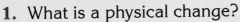

CHECKPOINT

1. What is a physical change?
2. What is a chemical change?
3. Describe what can happen in a chemical reaction.

   How can matter change?

ACTIVITY

Investigating pH

Find Out

Do this activity to learn how to use cabbage juice as an indicator to test the pH of different substances.

Process Skills

Measuring
Predicting
Controlling Variables
Observing
Communicating
Classifying
Interpreting Data
Inferring

WHAT YOU NEED

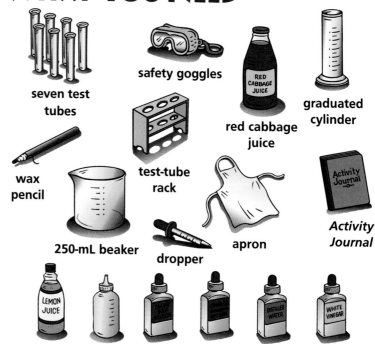

seven test tubes

safety goggles

red cabbage juice

graduated cylinder

wax pencil

test-tube rack

250-mL beaker

dropper

apron

Activity Journal

lemon juice, powdered dishwashing-detergent solution, baking soda solution, colorless carbonated soft drink, distilled water, vinegar

Color of Cabbage Juice	Relative pH
bright red	strong acid
red	medium acid
reddish purple	weak acid
purple	neutral
blue green	weak base
green	medium base
yellow	strong base

WHAT TO DO

1. Mark each test tube with the name of a substance.

    *Wear an apron and goggles.*

2. Measure and pour 10 mL of cabbage juice into each test tube.

3. Refer to the relative pH table. For each test solution, **predict** whether it will be an acid or a base.

C22

4. Add five drops of each test solution to each test tube. Be sure to add the test solution to match the name on the test tube. For example, add five drops of water to the test tube labeled *water.*

Safety! *Be careful with the solutions. If you spill any liquids on your clothes or skin, rinse the area immediately. Tell your teacher if any liquid is spilled.*

5. Observe any changes in color of the cabbage juice. Record your observations in your chart.

CONCLUSIONS

1. Which solutions did you classify as acids? Which did you classify as bases?

2. What happened when you added distilled water to the cabbage juice? Why?

3. How did your predictions compare with your results?

ASKING NEW QUESTIONS

1. What remained the same in each test tube?

2. What caused the results to be different in each test tube?

SCIENTIFIC METHODS SELF CHECK

✔ Did I **predict** whether the liquid would be an acid or a base?

✔ Did I **observe** the changes in the test solutions?

✔ Did I **record** my observations?

✔ Did I **classify** the different substances?

C23

Mixtures

Find Out

- What a mixture is
- What a homogeneous mixture is
- What a heterogeneous mixture is
- What a colloid is

Vocabulary

mixture
homogeneous mixtures
soluble
insoluble
alloys
heterogeneous mixture
suspension
colloid

The Big QUESTION

How do different kinds of mixtures compare?

There are many different kinds of mixtures. Scientists classify mixtures by the way that different materials interact when they are mixed together and by the properties of the mixture. Sometimes when two materials are mixed, one material seems to disappear because it dissolves. In some mixtures, such as salt mixed with water, the materials might be difficult to separate. Some mixtures, such as the fruit in a fruit salad, can be separated easily. In this lesson, we will look at a variety of mixtures and how they are classified.

Mixtures

There are combinations of matter all around you. Fruit salads, ink, salt water, and pizza are all combinations of matter. Each of these combinations is a mixture.

A **mixture** is formed when two or more substances are physically combined, or simply mixed together. Mixtures can be made up of many different types of substances. The materials used in mixtures retain their own properties, and the amount of each material can vary. Because there's no chemical change involved, mixtures can be physically separated.

Mixtures are everywhere around us. In fact, mixtures are the most common forms of matter. Oceans are a mixture of various salts in solution, including sodium chloride, and water. So are many fabrics. You're probably wearing a fabric mixture right now. Brass is a mixture of the metals copper and zinc. You might have a brass doorknob in your home. Can you think of any other mixtures? What about a cup of coffee with cream and sugar in it? Cream is a mixture containing calcium, fat compounds, water, and other substances. Coffee with sugar and cream in it is also a mixture.

Fruit salad is an example of a mixture in which the materials that make up the salad do not chemically change and can be easily separated.

Homogeneous Mixtures

Mixtures can be divided into two groups—homogeneous (hō mō jē′ nē əs) mixtures and heterogeneous (het ə rō jē′ nē əs) mixtures.

Homogeneous mixtures are composed of ingredients that are evenly spread throughout the mixture. In a homogeneous mixture, the particles stay mixed. However, they can be separated by physical methods, such as filtering, using a magnet, or evaporation.

Homogeneous mixtures are also called solutions. Solutions can form when one material dissolves in another. The material being dissolved is a solute. The material in which the solute dissolves is called the solvent. When a substance can be dissolved in a given substance, it is said to be **soluble.** When a substance cannot be dissolved in a given substance, it is said to be **insoluble.** For example, sugar can dissolve in water. The solute is sugar and the solvent is water. Sugar

When sand is added to water, a mixture is formed of sand and water. Because sand does not dissolve in water, sand is said to be insoluble in water. This mixture is not homogeneous because the sand is not spread evenly throughout the mixture.

is said to be soluble in water. In contrast, sand is said to be insoluble in water.

How does the sugar dissolve in the water? Remember that unlike liquids or gases, solids have a definite shape. The small particles, or molecules, that make up solids are arranged in patterns. The solid is held together by forces between the molecules. However, the molecules of liquids move about freely. When sugar mixes with water, its molecules attract the molecules of water. The water molecules surround the sugar molecules and separate them from each other. This makes the sugar seem to disappear. The sugar is still there, it is just separated by the water into single molecules so small they cannot be easily seen.

Water is the most common solvent in solutions, but it will not dissolve all substances. Oils, fats and many other chemicals are insoluble, or cannot be dissolved, in water.

When sugar dissolves in water, the sugar molecules are separated by the water into single molecules too small to easily see. This makes the sugar seem to disappear.

Not all homogeneous mixtures exist as liquids. Mixtures can be found in all states of matter. Air is a solution made up of gases. Tap water consists of pure water, dissolved minerals, and gases from the air. Fruit juices, coffee, and tea contain a number of different solids dissolved in water. The material that your dentist uses to make fillings for your teeth may be a mixture of metals called an alloy.

Alloys are homogeneous mixtures of two or more pure metals. They are made by heating the metals until they become a liquid and then mixing them together. The metals in alloys remain mixed after they are cooled.

Steel is an alloy in which different metals are mixed together and are spread evenly throughout the mixture.

Can you think why metals are mixed to form alloys? Most metals in their pure forms are too weak for some purposes. By mixing two or more metals, the strength of the metal can increase. There are also other reasons to mix metals. For example, stainless steel is an alloy of iron and other metals. Iron is a strong metal but by itself rusts easily. The alloy, however, resists rusting because of the other metals that were added.

Heterogeneous Mixtures

Can you think of methods that could be used to separate the different materials in a mixture? Not all mixtures can be separated in the same way. How could you separate a mixture of rocks and sugar? A solution of sugar and water? The sugar could be separated from the rocks by sifting the mixture through a screen. The sugar could be separated from the water through evaporation. If you placed a cup of sugar water on a hot sidewalk on a sunny day, the water would likely evaporate, leaving behind the dry sugar at the end of the day. Not all mixtures can be physically separated with the same method.

In a **heterogeneous mixture,** components are spread unevenly throughout the mixture and sometimes can be seen and separated easily. Soil, a pizza, a drawer full of loose socks, and concrete are examples of heterogeneous mixtures.

One type of heterogeneous mixture is called a **suspension.** A suspension is what results when something is mixed in a liquid or gas and it doesn't dissolve. In a suspension, the mixed materials will eventually separate if left undisturbed. You can stir or shake a suspension but the components always separate. Italian salad dressing is a suspension of spices in a mixture of liquid that will separate into layers of spices, vinegar, and oil. Dust in the air is also a type of suspension, as is muddy water.

Pizza is a heterogeneous mixture made up of materials that are spread unevenly throughout the mixture.

Italian salad dressing is a suspension of spices, oil, and vinegar that will separate into layers if left undisturbed.

Colloids

You might have noticed that the materials in mixtures can be many different sizes. In solutions, the particles are very small. In fact, the size of a particle in a solution is about one-millionth of a micrometer in diameter. In a suspension, however, the particles can be very large. The size of the particles in a suspension can be more than a thousand times larger than those in a solution.

Spray paint is an example of a colloid called an aerosol, in which a liquid (paint) is dispersed in a gas (air).

If the size of the particles in a mixture is between a solution and a suspension, the mixture is a colloid. A **colloid** is a heterogeneous mixture that has particles which, like a solution, stay evenly distributed throughout the mixture.

Many substances in everyday life are colloids. Ketchup is a colloid mostly made up of pureed tomatoes. You eat a colloid for dessert every time you have gelatin.

Colloids come in many combinations. A liquid in a liquid, such as homogenized milk, is called an emulsion. The particles of cream in milk are so small that they do not settle out of the mixture. Liquids or solids dispersed in gases, like spray paint, are called aerosols, and a gas dispersed in a liquid or solid, such as whipped cream, is called a foam.

Because the size of the particles in a colloid are smaller than those in a suspension and larger than those in a solution, a colloid has some properties of both a solution and a suspension. Both a suspension and a colloid have particles that do not settle out of the mixture when left undisturbed. If a beam of light is directed through a solution, the light goes straight through it. If a beam of light is directed through a colloid or a suspension, the light is scattered. Look at the chart below to see how the properties of a colloid compare to a solution and a suspension.

Properties of Solutions, Colloids, and Suspensions			
Description	Solutions	Colloids	Suspensions
Particles settle out	No	No	Yes
Can be separated using filter paper	No	No	Yes
Scatters light	No	Yes	Yes
Size of particles	0.1–1 nm*	1–1000 nm*	Larger than 1000 nm*

*One nanometer (nm) equals one billionth of a meter.

CHECKPOINT

1. What is a mixture?
2. What is a homogeneous mixture?
3. What is a heterogeneous mixture?
4. What is a colloid?

 How do different kinds of mixtures compare?

ACTIVITY
Separating Mixtures

Find Out
Do this activity to see how some mixtures can be separated by physical methods into their different components.

Process Skills
Measuring
Predicting
Observing
Communicating
Inferring
Interpreting Data

WHAT YOU NEED

scissors

pencil

paper towels

grease pencil

washable color markers

water

tall, wide-mouthed jar

tape

filter paper

metric ruler

Activity Journal

WHAT TO DO

1. Measure and cut five strips of filter paper 2 cm wide and 21 cm long. Draw a pencil line 2 cm from the bottom of the strips.

2. On each piece of filter paper put a different-colored marker dot on the center of the pencil line.

3. Measure 1 cm up from the bottom of a wide-mouthed jar and mark it with the grease pencil. Pour water into the jar until the water level meets the mark.

4. **Predict** what you think will happen to the dots of ink on the filter paper when the filter paper is put in water.

5. Fasten the filter paper strips to the inside of the jar with tape, with the dots toward the bottom so that the dots are just above the water level. Let the water rise up the paper until it's roughly 1 cm from the top of the strip.

6. Remove the paper strips from the jar and lay them on a paper towel to dry. **Observe** the filter paper and **record** your observations.

CONCLUSIONS

1. What happened as the water moved up the paper through the ink dots?

2. Describe the differences you observed in the different colors of ink. Was the change physical or chemical?

3. Is ink a mixture? Why?

ASKING NEW QUESTIONS

1. If a student from another class showed you filter paper results from several unknown materials, could you identify a sample of black ink?

2. Would all washable inks produce the same results? Why or why not? What kinds of further information would be helpful to support your conclusion or to answer new questions that you have?

SCIENTIFIC METHODS SELF CHECK

✔ Did I **predict** what would happen?

✔ Did I **observe** what happened to the ink on the filter paper?

✔ Did I **record** my observations?

Review

Reviewing Vocabulary and Concepts

Write the letter of the answer that completes each sentence.

1. ___ is the quantity of matter in a material.
   a. Mass   b. Volume
   c. Density   d. Reactivity

2. ___ is a physical property of matter that describes how much space something takes up.
   a. Freezing point   b. Boiling point
   c. Volume   d. Weight

3. A ___ takes place when a substance changes form but keeps the same chemical properties.
   a. chemical change   b. physical change
   c. loss of energy   d. neutralization

4. Homogeneous mixtures made up of two or more pure metals are ___.
   a. solutes   b. alloys
   c. suspensions   d. acids

5. A heterogeneous mixture that has particles which, like a solution, stay evenly distributed is ___.
   a. base   b. suspension
   c. reactant   d. colloid

Match the definition on the left with the correct term.

6. the substances that undergo change in a chemical reaction   a. reactants

7. the new substances formed in a chemical reaction   b. homogeneous mixtures

8. substances with a pH of 1–6   c. acids

9. substances with a pH of 8–14   d. products

10. solutions containing particles that stay evenly mixed in another substance   e. bases

Understanding What You Learned

1. Describe the difference between melting point and boiling point.

2. Give an example of a physical change and a chemical change.

3. Describe a neutralization reaction. Is it a physical or chemical change?

4. How is litmus paper used to determine whether a substance is an acid or a base?

5. What is the difference between a colloid and a solution?

Applying What You Learned

1. The wax in a candle first melts and then burns. What kinds of properties are melting and burning?

2. Which of the following has greater density—a bucket of sand or a box of cereal?

3. In what states does a substance take the shape of its container?

4. Give an example of a homogeneous mixture and a heterogeneous mixture.

 5. How can matter be identified by its physical and chemical properties?

For Your *Portfolio*

Design a baking recipe. Use cookbooks to design a recipe that requires a chemical change. List the steps for making the recipe. Describe any chemical or physical changes that occur.

The Structure

Have you ever watched a mason building a brick wall? On top of a concrete foundation, the mason spreads a layer of mortar, then a row of bricks. When the mason starts the second row, the bricks are set in an alternating pattern so that the wall will be strong enough to stand. This process is continued until a solid wall that is comprised of many smaller parts is put together in an orderly pattern.

Similar to walls made of small bricks, matter is made of atoms and combinations of atoms held together in varied arrangements. Most things look like solid objects, but they are actually made of many tiny particles too small for the eye to see.

The Big IDEA

All matter is made up of atoms and their combinations.

# of Matter

CHAPTER SCIENCE INVESTIGATION

Learn what makes up different elements and where those elements might be found. Find out how in your *Activity Journal.*

Atoms and Elements

Find Out

- What an atom is and how models of atoms have changed over time
- What elements are
- How elements are identified

Vocabulary

atoms
electrons
nucleus
proton
neutron
electron cloud model
element
chemical symbol

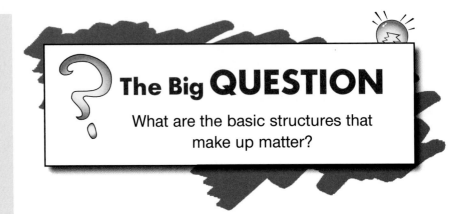

The Big QUESTION

What are the basic structures that make up matter?

Have you ever dusted in your home? You might have had a hard time seeing the dust because the particles of dust are very small. Even though you couldn't see the dust in the air, you know that the air must have carried it onto the different surfaces in your home. Dust particles are very small, but do you know matter has parts that are even smaller?

Atoms and Atomic Models

In the first chapter of this book, you learned that living things are made up of cells. Even though most cells are very small and most cannot be seen with the unaided eye, we know they exist. Scientists now know that even smaller particles of matter exist, although they too cannot be seen with the unaided eye. These tiny particles that are the basic units of matter are called **atoms.**

Discovering that atoms exist has been like putting together a jigsaw puzzle. Over the course of many years, different scientists have contributed information that has improved our understanding of what an atom looks like and how it is structured.

About 400 B.C., a Greek philosopher named Democritus (də ma′ kri təs) developed the idea that a piece of matter could be divided into smaller and smaller pieces until it reached the smallest possible piece. This piece could no longer be divided. The word Democritus used for the smallest piece of matter is *atomos,* which means "uncuttable." Centuries later, scientists confirmed Democritus's idea.

One scientist who contributed to our understanding of the atom is the English chemist John Dalton. In 1803, Dalton proposed a new atomic theory stating that matter is made up of single building blocks called atoms. He believed that all the atoms of a substance were identical and differed from the atoms of other substances. Dalton's ideas were groundbreaking for the study of the atom, but much remained to be learned. Dalton did not know that there were even smaller particles that make up matter!

Dalton Model

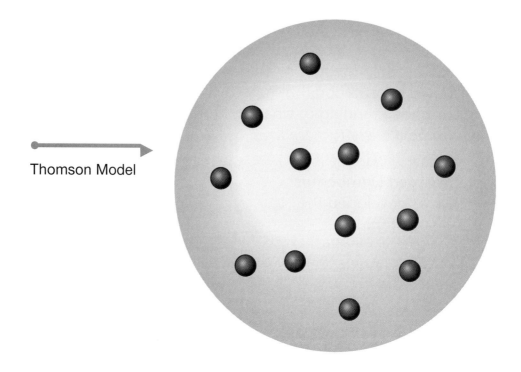

Thomson Model

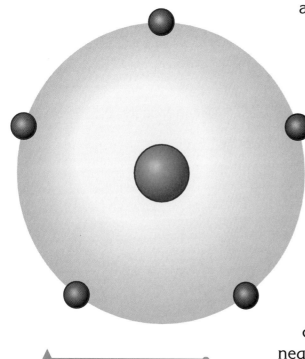

Rutherford Model

In the next 100 years, scientists experimented and learned that the atom was not the smallest particle making up matter. In the late 1800s, the British scientist J.J. Thomson discovered that atoms contain particles that have a negative electric charge. These negatively-charged particles are called **electrons.**

Scientists discovered that electrons were the same regardless of the atom they were in.

At about the same time, Ernest Rutherford, another British scientist, learned that atoms had a tiny but very dense center with a positive charge called a **nucleus** (nōo′ clē əs). He suggested that the atom was made up of a tiny nucleus with electrons traveling in empty space around it. The positive charge of the nucleus balances the negative charge of the electrons, and, thus, the overall charge of the atom is neutral.

In 1913, Niels Bohr formed a new model of an atom, called the planetary model. Bohr

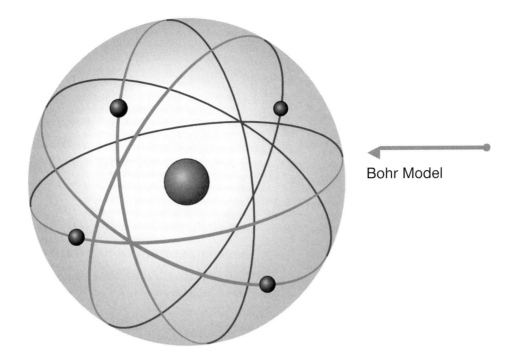

Bohr Model

suggested that electrons move around the nucleus in a pattern that resembles planets moving around the sun in the solar system. Each electron moves in a specific energy level.

Other scientists discovered that the nucleus was made up of two different particles, the **proton** (prō′ ton) and the **neutron** (n$\overline{oo}$′ tron). The proton has a positive electrical charge, whereas the neutron has no charge, or is neutral. The proton and the neutron make up the nucleus of an atom. They have about the same mass, and together they account for most of the mass of an atom. Electrons have very little mass.

Later, scientists found that an atom is composed of a nucleus made of protons and neutrons surrounded by electrons in a series of "shells." The electron shell model shows a predictable location and movement of electrons by placing certain electrons in different energy levels, or "shells," around an atom's nucleus.

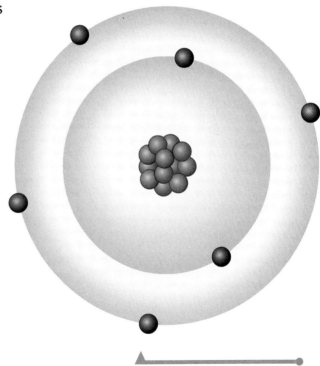

Electron Shell Model

Elements

You now know of some similarities that exist in the structure of atoms. They have a central nucleus with positive and neutral parts called protons and neutrons. Atoms also have negatively-charged electrons that surround the nucleus. Most scientists today use an atomic model that is structured somewhat differently from those you just studied.

Today, scientists use a model called the **electron cloud model.** In this model, electrons are not shown within shells that have specific orbits around the nucleus. Instead, this model shows electrons in an area, or "cloud," around the nucleus where an electron's charge will be found. Unlike the electron shell model, the exact location and movement of the electrons in this model are not shown.

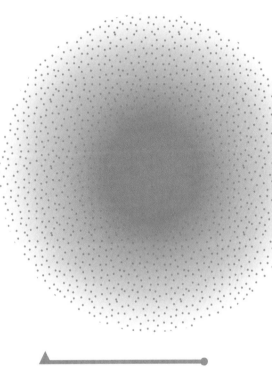

Electron Cloud Model

Scientists have learned that an atom's physical and chemical properties are determined by the number and arrangement of electrons that surround the atom's nucleus. Even though atoms can have similar parts and are believed to have a similar basic structure, each particular kind of atom is different from all others due to the number of protons in its unique nucleus.

You can tell that there are different kinds of substances by looking at the different types of matter around you. Many of the materials that make up the clothes you wear, the chairs you sit on, or the cars that take you from place to place are made up of many different kinds of substances. Scientists consider some substances to be pure substances. Let's take a look at what we mean by a pure substance.

When scientists talk about a pure substance, they are referring to a material that has the same structure all the way through. Aluminum is a metal that has certain physical and chemical properties. Suppose you had a 5 kg block of aluminum. If you took samples from many different parts of the block and studied each one, you would find that all of the samples had the exact same structure. Aluminum is an example of a pure substance.

Pure substances are exactly the same all the way through because they are made up of the same kinds of atoms. An **element** is an atom or a substance that is made up of only one kind of atom. Aluminum is one of the many elements that scientists have discovered. If you cut a piece of aluminum into smaller and smaller pieces until you got to an aluminum atom, you would not find a piece of this metal that differs from the larger piece. This is true because the atoms that make up aluminum are the same.

If you cut a block of aluminum into smaller and smaller pieces until you got to an aluminum atom, you would not find a piece that differs from the larger piece. This is true because aluminum is an element and is made up of only one kind of atom.

There are over 100 elements that make up our universe, and each of these elements is unique and unlike any other element. Like fingerprints, no two elements or types of atom are exactly alike.

Identifying Elements

One way that scientists identify elements is by using a chemical name. Each element has its own chemical name. Gold, iron, aluminum, and calcium are examples of some chemical names of elements. Each element also has a shortened, or abbreviated, form of its name.

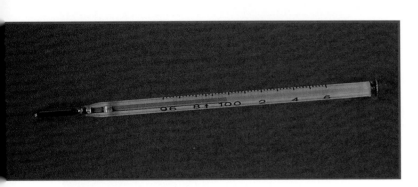

When you write down a doctor's name, you might use the abbreviation Dr. instead of spelling out the word *doctor*. Like an abbreviation, each element has its own symbol that represents its chemical name. The symbol that represents an element's name is called a **chemical symbol.** Chemical symbols are either one, two, or three letters.

The element mercury is a metal that exists as a liquid at room temperature. Its chemical symbol is Hg.

Some elements have symbols that are easy to remember. Oxygen's chemical symbol is O. Hydrogen's is H and helium's is He. These symbols use the first one or two letters of the element's chemical name.

Other chemical symbols are harder to remember, and sometimes a clear connection between the symbol and the chemical name of the element cannot be easily seen. For example, why is the symbol for gold Au? With further investigation, you would learn

The element gold, Au, is also a metal but it exists as a solid at room temperature.

that the chemical symbol was taken from the Latin word for gold, *aurum.* Knowing this, the chemical symbol Au makes more sense.

There are many sources for the chemical names and symbols of elements. Some elements were named after people and places. Who or what do you think the elements californium and einsteinium were named after?

You know that atoms are units of matter. You also know that everything in our world is made up of matter. This means that everything in the world is made up of atoms. You can easily see that not everything around you is made up of the same kind of substance.

The atoms in elements can combine to form many different kinds of substances. Imagine elements as letters in an alphabet. Each letter is different from other letters but can be combined to form many words that have very different meanings. Similarly, atoms can combine with other atoms to form many different substances. The combinations of the atoms that make up our world provide the variety of matter that we see around us every day.

Some elements exist as a gas at room temperature, such as chlorine, Cl_2.

CHECKPOINT

1. What is an atom and how have models of atoms changed over time?

2. What are elements?

3. How are elements identified?

 What are the basic structures that make up matter?

ACTIVITY
Investigating Matter

Find Out

Do this activity to describe matter that you cannot see.

Process Skills

Observing
Communicating
Measuring
Inferring
Interpreting Data

WHAT YOU NEED

magnet

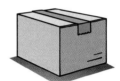

sealed container provided by your teacher

Activity Journal

ruler

WHAT TO DO

1. Observe the shape of the container you are given and record your observations.

2. Select any appropriate tools to make measurements of the container that you think might help you describe its contents and record your measurements.

3. Tilt the box. Shake it gently. Hold the magnet next to the box and run it over the surface. Record your observations.

4. Infer what is inside the box based on the data you collected.

5. Draw a picture of what you think is inside the box and explain why you think this, based on your data.

CONCLUSIONS

1. What information did you use to infer what was in the box?

2. Did any articles in the box roll or slide about? Did anything inside the box respond to the magnet?

3. How did your prediction compare to those of the other members in your group? How can you explain any differences?

ASKING NEW QUESTIONS

1. How do you think that this activity might resemble the way scientists investigate atoms?

2. Do you think the theory that all matter is made up of atoms will ever be changed? Why or why not?

SCIENTIFIC METHODS SELF CHECK

✔ Did I **observe** characteristics of the container?

✔ Did I **make measurements** of the container?

✔ Did I **interpret the data** I collected and **infer** what was in the container?

Molecules and Compounds

Find Out

- What molecules are
- What compounds are
- How compounds are structured
- How scientists can understand the activity of atoms when individual atoms are not seen

Vocabulary

molecule
compound

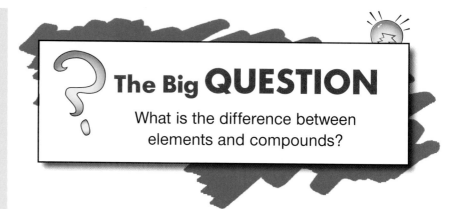

The Big QUESTION

What is the difference between elements and compounds?

Look around you. How many different kinds of things can you see? You know that all of the matter that you see around you is made up of atoms. Does everything around you look the same? If the objects and living things around you are different from one another, then the atoms that make them up must also be different, or found in different combinations.

Molecules

Many different types of atoms can be found in our world. All matter, including any living thing, is made up of atoms. Atoms can combine in many different ways to form all of the different living and nonliving things that make up our world.

Scientists know of over 100 different kinds of elements. The atoms that make up each of these different kinds of elements can combine to form a multitude of different substances. You could think of the atoms in each element as a unique building block. How many different structures could you make out of over 100 different kinds of blocks?

One way that atoms combine is with other like atoms. For example, oxygen in the air you breathe is made up of two oxygen atoms (O_2) joined together. When two or more atoms join together, a **molecule** is formed.

A molecule can form when like or unlike atoms join together. When two oxygen atoms join, a molecule forms consisting of two like atoms. An oxygen tank that you might find in a hospital is filled with billions upon billions of oxygen molecules. Even though the atoms in the oxygen molecules pair up, oxygen molecules do not cling to other oxygen molecules in the tank. Each molecule has a definite composition. The molecules move around randomly within the tank.

Nitrogen and oxygen in Earth's atmosphere exist as gases. The gas nitrogen is made up of molecules consisting of two joined nitrogen atoms. Two oxygen atoms join to form the molecules in the gas oxygen.

Compounds

Another way that atoms form molecules is when atoms combine with unlike atoms. When different kinds of atoms combine, a compound is formed. A **compound** is a substance made up of two or more elements chemically combined. In other words, when unlike atoms join, they form molecules that are compounds. By examining compounds, you can discover that the atoms in compounds are organized in a variety of patterns and arrangements.

Let's take a look at a compound that you use every day—water. Although water appears to be made up of only one kind of substance, it is actually made up of two different elements. The water molecule is made up of atoms of hydrogen and oxygen. Because it has two different kinds of atoms that combine, water is a compound.

In water, one atom of oxygen combines with two atoms of hydrogen (H_2O). Suppose you could cut a drop of water in half again and again until you had a particle so small that if you took any part of it away, the remaining substance would no longer be water. That tiny particle would be a molecule of water.

Water is a compound made up of molecules consisting of one oxygen and two hydrogen atoms.

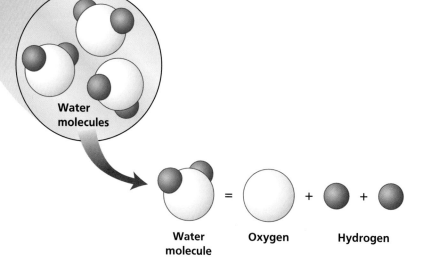

Water molecules

Water molecule = Oxygen + Hydrogen

Salt is also a compound. If you investigated salt, you would find that salt is made of more than one substance. Salt is made of two different elements present in equal amounts. Salt forms when one sodium atom combines with one chlorine atom (NaCl).

Look at the photos of the elements sodium and chlorine. Both sodium and chlorine are highly reactive elements. For example, if sodium is exposed to the oxygen in the air, it can explode. Chlorine is a yellow-green gas that also is very reactive. However, when these two elements combine in the compound salt, the individual properties of the compound are different from the properties of either of the individual elements. Salt does not react violently when exposed to air, nor does it have the properties of the yellow-green gas, chlorine. Whenever two elements combine in a compound, the properties of the compound are different from the individual properties of the atoms that make up the compound.

Sodium is a highly reactive element that must be stored in oil to keep it from reacting to the oxygen in air.

Salt is made up of sodium and chlorine atoms. The individual properties of sodium and chlorine change when they combine in the compound salt.

Chlorine is an element that exists as a highly-reactive yellow-green gas at room temperature.

Structure of Compounds

In the last lesson, you learned that elements are pure substances that have the same structure all the way through. Compounds are also pure substances that have orderly arrangements. For example, if you pour some salt into your hand, you might notice that it is a dry solid. If you were to look at one single grain of salt, you would see that it looked like a cube. If you were able to look at salt through a very powerful microscope, you would find that the salt cube has an organized composition. From the handful of salt, to the tiny particles that make up the grain, the deeper you explore the salt the more orderly it becomes.

Molecules are the smallest units of compounds in the same way that atoms are the smallest units of elements. Both are types of matter that have a definite composition.

What exactly do we mean by a definite composition? Elements and compounds both have an exact ratio of atoms that makes them

Copper
6.646 g Cu

Sulfur
3.354 g S

66.46 g Cu

33.54 g S

up regardless of where the element or compound is found. Let's look at a sample of copper and sulfur. In both copper and sulfur, the atoms are arranged in an orderly fashion. The number per unit volume and position of the copper atoms are the same throughout the sample.

When copper and sulfur combine they can form copper sulfide. In copper sulfide, one atom of copper joins with one atom of sulfur. If you investigated copper sulfide, you would find that the copper and sulfur atoms are also arranged in an orderly fashion. The ratio of copper atoms to sulfur atoms is the same throughout the sample.

Look at the copper and the sulfur in these photographs. You may wonder why it appears that more sulfur than copper was used if copper sulfide has a one-to-one ratio of each atom. Even though it appears that more sulfur is used, more grams of copper were used because copper atoms have a greater mass than sulfur atoms. Even though copper and sulfur have different masses, their atoms still join in the same ratio.

Copper Sulfide

10.000 g CuS

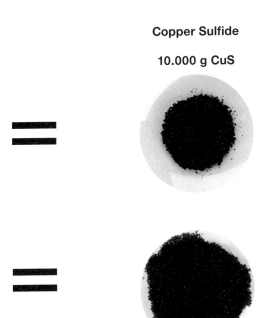

Copper sulfide (CuS) is made when copper atoms join with sulfur atoms. Each molecule of copper sulfide has one copper atom and one sulfur atom in an orderly arrangement.

100.00 g CuS

Understanding the Activity of Atoms

Because atoms are very tiny particles, even millions and billions of atoms take up a very small amount of space. For this reason, we usually look at substances that are made of many atoms. From the way that the substance acts on a large scale, scientists can understand what is happening on a smaller scale. In other words, we cannot see how individual atoms interact with other atoms, but we can infer how individual atoms are interacting by seeing how large quantities of atoms react to others.

It is important to remember that when we talk about the activity of individual atoms, we do not actually observe each atom in a substance. Rather, we are observing the combined activities of millions or billions of atoms.

Although we cannot see the individual atoms responding to other atoms, scientists have developed instruments that can create images of atoms and molecules that show they have a definite composition. This image of a silicon molecule shows its orderly arrangement.

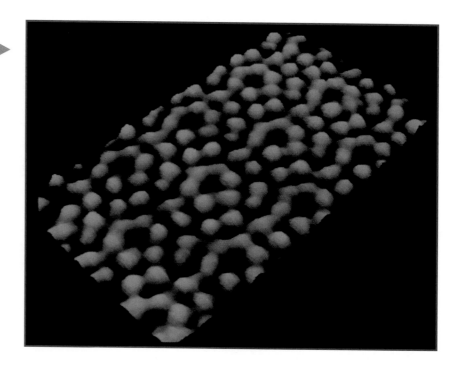

You have learned a lot about atoms and how they combine. Before moving on to the next lesson, let's take a look at some of the things that you have learned about atoms.

All of the matter in the world is made up of atoms. Each atom has smaller parts that define how it reacts with other atoms. Every element is made up of like atoms that are different from atoms of all other elements. Atoms can combine with either like or unlike atoms and form molecules. When atoms combine with unlike atoms, compounds are formed. Each particular type of compound is made up of atoms that are in an exact ratio. When a compound forms, the compound has different properties from the elements that make it up. By learning about atoms, you are not just studying particles too small for you to see. You are learning about how the world is structured and why the matter around you interacts the way it does.

Salt is a compound made up of sodium and chlorine that join in a one-to-one ratio in each molecule of salt. In just one grain of salt, millions of atoms are joined in an orderly fashion, resulting in a cube-shaped grain of salt.

CHECKPOINT

1. What are molecules?
2. What are compounds?
3. How are compounds structured?
4. How can scientists understand the activity of atoms when individual atoms are not seen?

 What is the difference between elements and compounds?

ACTIVITY

Making a Model of a Molecule

Find Out

Do this activity to learn how compounds are formed.

Process Skills

Constructing Models
Observing
Communicating
Inferring

WHAT YOU NEED

four different colors of modeling clay

plastic knife

Activity Journal

WHAT TO DO

1. Water is a compound formed when two atoms of hydrogen combine with one atom of oxygen. Salt is a compound formed when one atom of sodium joins with one atom of chlorine. Place four different colors of modeling clay on your desk. Choose one color of clay for each kind of atom in salt and water.

2. Use your plastic knife to cut off slices of the different colored clays to make atoms of chlorine, sodium, hydrogen, and oxygen. Roll each piece of clay into a small ball. Make two small atoms of hydrogen, one larger atom of oxygen, one large atom of sodium, and one large atom of chlorine.

3. Make the water molecule first. Press each of the hydrogen atoms onto the oxygen atom to make a water molecule.

4. Next make a salt molecule by joining the chlorine and sodium atoms.

5. Observe how the water molecule and salt molecule differ from one another. Record your observations.

CONCLUSIONS

1. Infer how your models of a water molecule and a salt molecule are different from a real salt molecule and water molecule.

2. Infer how your models are like the actual molecules.

ASKING NEW QUESTIONS

1. What structures of the hydrogen, oxygen, sodium, and chlorine atoms were not shown in your model?

2. Do you think that any two elements could combine to form a compound? Why?

SCIENTIFIC METHODS SELF CHECK

✔ Did I **construct models** of water and salt molecules?

✔ Did I **observe** differences between the two kinds of molecules?

✔ Did I **infer** how my models compared to real molecules?

The Periodic Table

Find Out

- How elements have been classified
- How the periodic table is structured
- What metals, nonmetals, and metalloids are

Vocabulary

periodic table
atomic number
mass number
families
periods
metals
nonmetals
metalloids

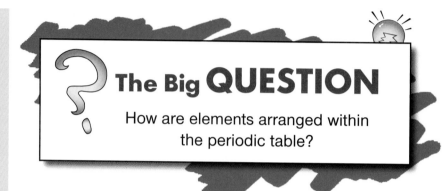

The Big QUESTION

How are elements arranged within the periodic table?

Have you ever used a calendar to organize your time? On a calendar, days of the week are arranged in a predictable order. Monday always follows Sunday, Tuesday always follows Monday, and so on. Did you know this repetition of days was periodic? On a calendar, the days of the week are periodic because they repeat themselves every seven days. What do a calendar and the periodic table have in common? Both a calendar and the periodic table of elements show a repeating pattern. The periodic table shows a repeating pattern in elements, and a calendar shows a repeating pattern of days.

Classifying Matter

About 100 years ago, scientists developed a table of the elements called the **periodic table.** The periodic table helps to organize elements based upon their characteristics and properties. The periodic table is one of a scientist's most useful tools. Let's look at how elements have been organized and how the periodic table is used to classify and show similarities and differences among the elements.

Many centuries ago, the Greeks invented a system of classifying matter. They believed that the universe consisted of four basic elements— earth, fire, wind, and water. For a long time, many people believed that these four substances made up everything in the world.

Later, people began to classify different substances, such as gold and silver, as elements. People known as alchemists believed that they could change one element into another. They tried to make elements such as iron into very valuable ones such as gold. Although the alchemists were not successful, they identified many important properties of elements.

In the early nineteenth century, scientists figured out that the atoms in each element have a different mass. For example, an atom of oxygen has a mass about 16 times greater than that of a hydrogen atom.

In 1869 the Russian chemist Dmitry Mendeleyev arranged the elements in order according to the atomic mass of each element in a table. By arranging elements with similar properties underneath one another, in order of their atomic masses, the periodic nature of the table was established. When organized in terms of increasing atomic mass, there were some gaps between elements where properties were similar. Mendeleyev believed that new elements would be discovered to fill those gaps. From the patterns he saw in the table, he was able to predict the properties that the unknown elements would have!

This photo shows a Mendeleyev periodic table reproduced on an outside wall of a technical school in St. Petersburg, Russia.

Structure of the Periodic Table

Although Mendeleyev's arrangement of elements in the periodic table was successful, the structure of the periodic table needed some changes. When Mendeleyev organized elements by their properties, the atomic mass of some elements did not fit. If the elements were arranged strictly according to their atomic masses, then the properties did not all match.

Later, scientists developed a way to measure the atomic number of elements. An element's **atomic number** is the number of protons in the nucleus of its atom. The atomic number is also the same as the number of electrons that can be found in an atom of an element. In 1913, a young English scientist named Henry Moseley arranged the elements on the periodic table according to their atomic numbers instead of their atomic masses. This solved the problem that Mendeleyev had when organizing the table by increasing mass, while grouping elements with similar properties.

Today, the periodic table also shows the atomic mass of each element, which is the average mass number of each element as it occurs in nature. The **mass number** of a particular element is the number of protons and neutrons in the nucleus of an atom.

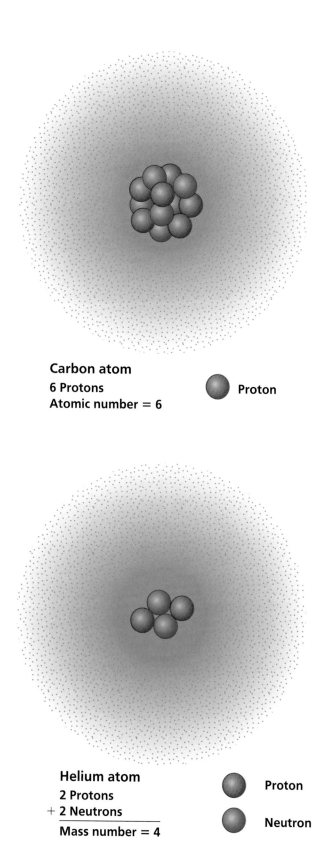

Carbon atom
6 Protons
Atomic number = 6

● Proton

Helium atom
2 Protons
+ 2 Neutrons
_____
Mass number = 4

● Proton

● Neutron

In the periodic table, elements are arranged in vertical columns. These columns are called groups, or **families.** On some periodic tables, these groups are numbered 1 through 18. Some groups contain elements with similar properties. For example, group 18 is made up of very stable gases. The elements in this group are found in nature as single atoms that do not normally form compounds.

Earlier, you learned that, like a calendar, the periodic table is arranged in order to show a repeating pattern. In a calendar, the repeating pattern is the number and order of days in a week. What is this repeating pattern in the periodic table?

The repeating pattern of the periodic table can be seen by looking across the table, as well as by looking up and down at the elements in a group. The horizontal rows of the periodic table are called **periods.** The periods are numbered 1 through 7, with some elements from sections 6 and 7 shown beneath the main body of the table.

Each element across a period is in a different group. How an element reacts with other elements can sometimes be determined from its group. If you moved across period 4, you would find that each element reacts differently compared to other elements. If you then moved across period 5 in the same direction, you would find a similar pattern of reactivity in the elements as in period 4. In the periodic table, the chemical properties of elements show a periodic pattern of reactivity.

Helium, He, is in group 18 and is a very stable gas. Helium is often used in balloons because it has less mass and is less dense than most of the gases that make up air. This is why helium balloons will rise through air.

Periodic Table of the Elements

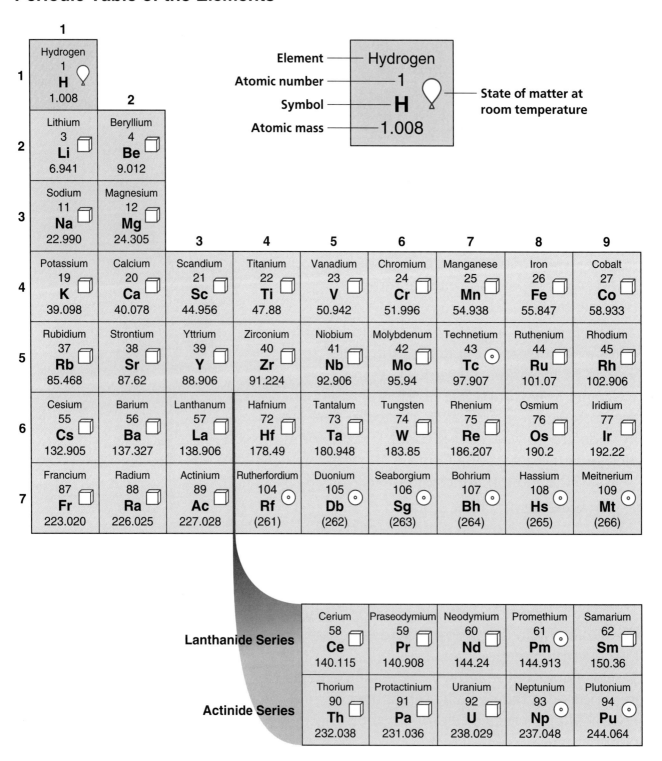

	1								
1	Hydrogen 1 **H** 1.008								
2	Lithium 3 **Li** 6.941	Beryllium 4 **Be** 9.012							
3	Sodium 11 **Na** 22.990	Magnesium 12 **Mg** 24.305							
			3	4	5	6	7	8	9
4	Potassium 19 **K** 39.098	Calcium 20 **Ca** 40.078	Scandium 21 **Sc** 44.956	Titanium 22 **Ti** 47.88	Vanadium 23 **V** 50.942	Chromium 24 **Cr** 51.996	Manganese 25 **Mn** 54.938	Iron 26 **Fe** 55.847	Cobalt 27 **Co** 58.933
5	Rubidium 37 **Rb** 85.468	Strontium 38 **Sr** 87.62	Yttrium 39 **Y** 88.906	Zirconium 40 **Zr** 91.224	Niobium 41 **Nb** 92.906	Molybdenum 42 **Mo** 95.94	Technetium 43 **Tc** 97.907	Ruthenium 44 **Ru** 101.07	Rhodium 45 **Rh** 102.906
6	Cesium 55 **Cs** 132.905	Barium 56 **Ba** 137.327	Lanthanum 57 **La** 138.906	Hafnium 72 **Hf** 178.49	Tantalum 73 **Ta** 180.948	Tungsten 74 **W** 183.85	Rhenium 75 **Re** 186.207	Osmium 76 **Os** 190.2	Iridium 77 **Ir** 192.22
7	Francium 87 **Fr** 223.020	Radium 88 **Ra** 226.025	Actinium 89 **Ac** 227.028	Rutherfordium 104 **Rf** (261)	Duonium 105 **Db** (262)	Seaborgium 106 **Sg** (263)	Bohrium 107 **Bh** (264)	Hassium 108 **Hs** (265)	Meitnerium 109 **Mt** (266)

Element ——— Hydrogen
Atomic number ——— 1
Symbol ——— **H**
Atomic mass ——— 1.008
State of matter at room temperature

Lanthanide Series

Cerium 58 **Ce** 140.115	Praseodymium 59 **Pr** 140.908	Neodymium 60 **Nd** 144.24	Promethium 61 **Pm** 144.913	Samarium 62 **Sm** 150.36

Actinide Series

Thorium 90 **Th** 232.038	Protactinium 91 **Pa** 231.036	Uranium 92 **U** 238.029	Neptunium 93 **Np** 237.048	Plutonium 94 **Pu** 244.064

Legend:
- Gas
- Liquid
- Solid
- Synthetic elements
- Metal
- Metalloid
- Nonmetal

18

Helium 2 He 4.003

13 14 15 16 17

Boron 5 B 10.811	Carbon 6 C 12.011	Nitrogen 7 N 14.007	Oxygen 8 O 15.999	Fluorine 9 F 18.998	Neon 10 Ne 20.180
Aluminum 13 Al 26.982	Silicon 14 Si 28.086	Phosphorus 15 P 30.974	Sulfur 16 S 32.066	Chlorine 17 Cl 35.453	Argon 18 Ar 39.948

10 11 12

Nickel 28 Ni 58.693	Copper 29 Cu 63.546	Zinc 30 Zn 65.39	Gallium 31 Ga 69.723	Germanium 32 Ge 72.61	Arsenic 33 As 74.922	Selenium 34 Se 78.96	Bromine 35 Br 79.904	Krypton 36 Kr 83.80
Palladium 46 Pd 106.42	Silver 47 Ag 107.868	Cadmium 48 Cd 112.411	Indium 49 In 114.82	Tin 50 Sn 118.710	Antimony 51 Sb 121.757	Tellurium 52 Te 127.60	Iodine 53 I 126.904	Xenon 54 Xe 131.290
Platinum 78 Pt 195.08	Gold 79 Au 196.967	Mercury 80 Hg 200.59	Thallium 81 Tl 204.383	Lead 82 Pb 207.2	Bismuth 83 Bi 208.980	Polonium 84 Po 208.982	Astatine 85 At 209.987	Radon 86 Rn 222.018
(unnamed) 110 Uun	(unnamed) 111 Uuu	(unnamed) 112 Uub						

Europium 63 Eu 151.965	Gadolinium 64 Gd 157.25	Terbium 65 Tb 158.925	Dysprosium 66 Dy 162.50	Holmium 67 Ho 164.930	Erbium 68 Er 167.26	Thulium 69 Tm 168.934	Ytterbium 70 Yb 173.04	Lutetium 71 Lu 174.967
Americium 95 Am 243.061	Curium 96 Cm 247.070	Berkelium 97 Bk 247.070	Californium 98 Cf 251.080	Einsteinium 99 Es 252.083	Fermium 100 Fm 257.095	Mendelevium 101 Md 258.099	Nobelium 102 No 259.101	Lawrencium 103 Lr 260.105

Metals and Nonmetals

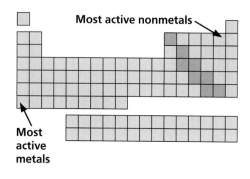

Most active nonmetals

Most active metals

The most active metals are in the lower left corner of the periodic table. The most active nonmetals are in the upper right corner, not including the gases in group 18.

As you looked at the periodic table, you probably noticed that many of the elements were colored differently from others. The difference in color represents the difference in the way scientists classify these elements.

Notice the stair-step line that separates the elements of different colors. The elements to the left of this line, shown as blue on this periodic table, are metals. Iron, nickel, and copper are examples of metals. Most **metals** have the common properties of existing as solids at room temperature, being shiny, and being good conductors of heat and electricity. The metals at the bottom left of the periodic table are the most reactive of the metals.

The elements to the right of the stair-step line, shown as pink on this periodic table, are classified as **nonmetals.** Most nonmetals at room temperature are gases, but some are hard, brittle solids. Most nonmetals do not conduct electricity or heat well. Oxygen, nitrogen, and helium are examples of nonmetals. The most reactive nonmetals are at the top right of the periodic table, excluding the elements in group 18.

Property	Metal	Nonmetal
Physical state	Solids (except mercury)	Solid, liquid, or gas (bromine is the only liquid)
Appearance	Shiny	Mainly non-shiny (iodine is one of the exceptions)
Conductivity	Good	Poor (except graphite)
Melting point	Generally high	Generally low
Boiling point	Generally high	Generally low

The elements that are located on the boundary of the stair-step line are called **metalloids** (me′ təl oidz′). Metalloids have some properties of both metals and nonmetals. The element boron is considered a metalloid along with silicon, germanium, arsenic, antimony, tellurium, polonium, and astatine.

There are many ways in which the periodic table organizes and classifies the elements that make up our world. There are now 112 known elements. When Mendeleyev created the periodic table, he knew of only 62 elements and predicted four more would be discovered. Even though we know much more about the world of atoms today than Mendeleyev did over a century ago, elements are still being discovered and more is being learned about the structure of matter.

CHECKPOINT

1. How have elements been classified?
2. How is the periodic table structured?
3. What are metals, nonmetals, and metalloids?

 How are elements arranged within the periodic table?

ACTIVITY

Investigating Metals and Nonmetals

Find Out

Do this activity to learn how metals and nonmetals can be different.

Process Skills

Observing
Communicating
Predicting
Experimenting
Inferring
Interpreting Data

WHAT YOU NEED

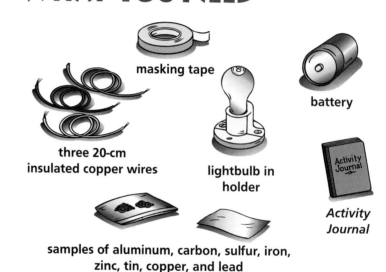

masking tape

battery

three 20-cm
insulated copper wires

lightbulb in
holder

Activity
Journal

Activity
Journal

samples of aluminum, carbon, sulfur, iron,
zinc, tin, copper, and lead

WHAT TO DO

1. Observe the physical properties of each element and record the appearance and texture of each.

2. Make a circuit tester by attaching the ends of two copper wires to the metal part of the lightbulb holder. Tape one of the wires from the bulb holder to one end of the battery. Tape the third wire to the other end of the battery. Bring the two unattached ends of the wires together to make sure the circuit tester works.

3. **Predict** which elements will conduct electricity.

4. Touch the two unattached wires to each sample. If the bulb lights, the element is conducting electricity.

5. **Record** the results when each sample is tested.

CONCLUSIONS

1. Which samples conducted electricity?

2. By looking at the periodic table, which of the elements that you tested are metals and which are nonmetals?

3. Based on the data you collected, what characteristics do most metals have and most nonmetals have?

ASKING NEW QUESTIONS

1. Which elements you tested are in the same family? Period?

2. What are some other properties of metals and nonmetals?

SCIENTIFIC METHODS SELF CHECK

✔ Did I **observe** the properties of the elements?

✔ Did I **predict** which elements would conduct electricity?

✔ Did I **interpret the data** I collected?

Review

Reviewing Vocabulary and Concepts

Write the letter of the answer that completes each sentence.

1. A ___ is a structure in an atom that has a neutral charge.
   - **a.** colloid
   - **b.** electron
   - **c.** neutron
   - **d.** proton

2. Today, to show the structure of atoms, scientists use the ___.
   - **a.** electron cloud model
   - **b.** planetary model
   - **c.** nucleus model
   - **d.** uniform structure model

3. A shortened form that represents the name of an element is the element's ___.
   - **a.** chemical name
   - **b.** mass number
   - **c.** chemical symbol
   - **d.** atomic number

4. When two or more unlike atoms join, they form ___.
   - **a.** a compound
   - **b.** an element
   - **c.** a mixture
   - **d.** a larger atom

5. Substances that have some of the properties of metals and some of the properties of nonmetals are called ___.
   - **a.** conductors
   - **b.** metalloids
   - **c.** families
   - **d.** periods

Match the definition on the left with the correct term.

6. negatively-charged particles

7. positively-charged particles

8. a chart that currently organizes elements by their atomic numbers and chemical properties

9. the number of protons and electrons in an atom

10. shiny solids that usually conduct electricity

- **a.** protons
- **b.** periodic table
- **c.** atomic number
- **d.** metals
- **e.** electrons

Understanding What You Learned

1. How was the Rutherford model of the atom different than the models that came before it?

2. What parts can be found in an atom?

3. How are elements different from compounds?

4. What does it mean to say that a compound has a definite composition?

5. Dmitry Mendeleyev developed an early version of the periodic table. How does the periodic table we use today differ from Mendeleyev's table?

Applying What You Learned

1. Why does an atom have a neutral electrical charge?

2. What would happen to the charge of an atom if the atom somehow acquired an extra electron?

3. What is one advantage of being able to form compounds?

4. If you came across an unknown solid substance, how could you determine if it was a metal or a nonmetal?

 5. What makes up all matter?

For Your *Portfolio*

Choose an element from the periodic table and make a drawing of what an atom of the element might look like. Use different colors for the different particles in the atom. Then describe how your drawing compares to the atomic models you studied.

CHAPTER 3

Forms and Uses of

Every day, people around the world use energy. How did you use energy today? People use energy in different ways. Energy stored in your body allows you to get out of bed in the morning. Energy used in the motor of a school bus moves students to school and back home again. Energy is also used to cook food, watch TV, and light your home.

You can see how people use energy, but what exactly is energy? How does energy enable buses to move or allow you to cook food? In this chapter, we will explore the answers to these questions by investigating the forms and uses of energy.

The Big IDEA

Energy can be found in many forms, has many sources, and is used in a variety of ways.

Energy

CHAPTER SCIENCE INVESTIGATION

Learn how you and your community depend on energy sources. Find out how in your *Activity Journal.*

Forms of Energy

Find Out

- How energy is defined
- What some different forms of energy are
- How energy can be transferred

Vocabulary

radiant energy
thermal energy
energy transfer
heat
chemical energy

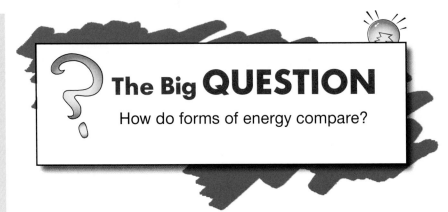

The Big QUESTION

How do forms of energy compare?

Energy is in the world around you as well as in your body. The activities you do during the day, the sports you play, even the thinking you do requires energy. Energy allows you to cook food and listen to music. Energy is a word that you may have used many times. But what exactly is energy?

How Energy Is Defined

Energy is defined as the ability to do work. Work is done when a force causes something to move over a distance. Energy is needed to exert the force needed to do work. You could also say that energy is the ability to cause changes in matter. In other words, the energy of an object can cause changes to the object or its surroundings. Is energy needed by the bicyclist on the opposite page? How is energy being used?

You may not be able to see energy, but you can see what it does. Energy is defined by what it does, not by what it is. For example, when you turn a switch on your radio and music plays, you know that energy is present. The results of work done by energy let us know that energy is present.

An object can have energy because of its motion or its position. Look at the bicyclist. Work is being done because both the cyclist and the bicycle are moved by the force that is exerted on the pedals. The cyclist and the bicycle both have kinetic energy as the bicycle

Energy is the ability to do work. Do both the cyclist and the bike have energy? If so, how is work being done by the cyclist on the bike?

is pedaled and steered. Kinetic energy is the energy of matter in motion. The blades of a moving fan have kinetic energy, as does a person who is bicycling.

The amount of kinetic energy in an object depends on two factors: the mass of the object and how fast the object is moving. The cyclist and the bicycle have kinetic energy because they are both moving. Force is exerted on the pedals, which move as a result; this means that work is being done by the cyclist. Can you tell whether the cyclist or bicycle has more kinetic energy? Because the cyclist has more mass than the bicycle, the cyclist has more kinetic energy even though both are going the same speed.

Objects that are not in motion may also have energy. A bobsled positioned at the top of the hill has energy even though it is not in motion. At the top of the hill, the bobsled has the potential to do work, but because it is not in motion, the bobsled does not have kinetic energy.

Remember that energy is the ability to do work. A bobsled at the top of the hill has the ability to do more work than a bobsled at the bottom of the hill. This is because the bobsled at the top can move down the hill. Since the bobsled could exert a force and do work due to its position at the top of the hill, the bobsled has greater potential energy than a bobsled positioned at the bottom of the hill. The stored energy, or energy an object has because of its position, is called potential energy.

Potential energy can change to kinetic energy when a force causes a change in an object's position. If the bobsled at the top of the hill begins to move downhill, some of its potential energy changes to kinetic energy.

Kinetic energy can also be changed to potential energy. The bobsled must be pushed up the hill in order for it to race down the hill. When the bobsled is being pushed up the hill, the bobsled has kinetic energy because it is in motion. The kinetic energy then changes to potential energy as it moves up the hill.

It is important to remember that at times an object's energy can be all kinetic or all potential. At other times, an object can have a combination of kinetic and potential energy. For example, when the bobsled has slid halfway down the hill, it has both kinetic and potential energy. It has kinetic energy because it is in motion and potential energy because of its position on the hill.

When a bobsled has slid halfway down the hill, it has both kinetic and potential energy.

Radiant energy and mechanical energy are two forms of energy. In what ways are mechanical energy and radiant energy shown in this photograph?

Different Forms of Energy

Energy can exist in different forms. When you think of an activity that takes a lot of energy, you might think of waterskiing. In waterskiing a lot of energy is used to move the boat and the skier across the water. Did you know that the boat and the skier have mechanical energy? Mechanical energy is the total kinetic and potential energy of an object. A moving bicycle, bobsled, boat, and water–skier all have mechanical energy.

They all have the ability to do work. An engine supplies the energy for a boat to move in the water. The force of the boat's propeller on the water does work, moving both the boat and the skier from one place to another in the water.

Radiant energy is a form of energy that travels in waves. Solar energy is radiant energy from the sun. Solar energy warms objects by causing the particles in objects to move more rapidly. The faster the particles move, the higher the temperature of the objects. How might radiant energy affect the water and the water–skier in the photograph?

Solar energy travels through space and is important to Earth. Plants would not grow without radiant energy from the sun. Solar energy also warms the air and surface of Earth, which allows the planet's temperature to stay mild enough for living things to survive.

Light is radiant energy that your eyes can detect. Like all radiant energy, light can travel through empty space. It can also travel through some kinds of matter. Light travels through air and through some solids and liquids.

In the previous chapter, you learned that all matter is made up of tiny particles called atoms. The atoms that make up matter are constantly moving randomly. They have kinetic energy. The energy of the random movement of atoms in matter is called **thermal energy.**

You may remember that an element is a substance made of only one type of atom. An atom has a nucleus containing protons and neutrons. Protons have a positive charge and neutrons have no electrical charge. The nucleus is surrounded by negatively–charged electrons.

Atoms are in constant motion. The amount of kinetic energy in an object is related to how rapidly the particles are moving. All atoms in an object have kinetic energy. However, they do not all have the same amount of kinetic energy. Temperature is a measure of the average amount of kinetic energy of all the particles in an object. The atoms of an object with a high temperature have more kinetic energy than the atoms of the same object with a lower temperature.

The atoms that make up matter are constantly moving and have kinetic energy. The atoms of an object with a high temperature have more kinetic energy than the atoms of the same object with a lower temperature.

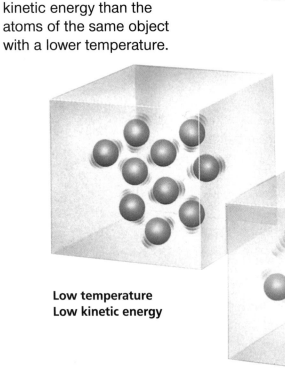

Low temperature
Low kinetic energy

Medium temperature
Medium kinetic energy

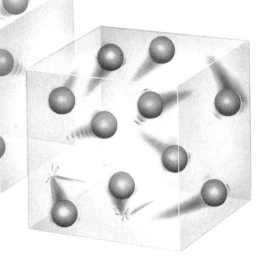

High temperature
High kinetic energy

Energy Can Be Transferred

You can tell that an object has thermal energy when you sense that the object is hot. When an object is hot, some of that object's thermal energy flows from the object to your hand. Any flow of energy from one place to another is called **energy transfer.**

Thermal energy that is being transferred between objects at different temperatures is known as **heat.** Heat flows from an object of higher temperature to an object of lower temperature.

Suppose you have a bowl of hot soup. When you first pick up your spoon to eat the soup, the spoon is cool. After leaving the spoon in the bowl for some time, you might find that the spoon is warmer. Thermal energy has transferred from the soup to the spoon.

Two objects at the same temperature may not have the same amount of thermal energy. Think about a large pot of hot soup. Suppose you take some soup out of the pot and put it in your bowl. The pot and the bowl both contain liquid that is the same temperature. The pot, however, has more thermal energy than the bowl because it contains more hot soup. Similarly, a lit match may have the same temperature as parts of a forest fire, but the forest fire has more thermal energy.

A forest fire has a large amount of thermal energy. The thermal energy transferred from this blaze to the air can be felt kilometers from the site of the fire.

Another form of energy is chemical energy. **Chemical energy** is energy stored in matter when atoms join together. It can be released when the matter undergoes a chemical change. When chemical energy is stored, it is called chemical potential energy.

Chemical energy may be converted to other forms of energy and is often released as thermal, radiant, or electric energy. Wood and other fuels contain chemical energy. Soup in a bowl also contains chemical energy. When fuels are burned, whether to warm your home or provide energy for your body, chemical energy is converted and heat is released. When energy is released in your body during cellular respiration, thermal energy is also being given off. The transfer of this thermal energy to your body as heat keeps your body at about 37 degrees Celsius. When fuels are burned in factories, a tremendous amount of heat is produced. Whenever heat is released, thermal energy is being transferred.

Green plants convert light energy to chemical energy during photosynthesis. When an animal, such as this sloth, eats the plant, the chemical energy from the plant is transferred to the animal. This is another way that energy transfer occurs.

When energy is passed between objects, energy can be converted and can be transferred. When a fuel is burned, some of the chemical energy in the fuel is converted to thermal energy. This thermal energy heats the air surrounding the fire. Thermal energy is then transferred from the fuel to the air.

Energy can be transferred in many ways. Sound is a form of mechanical energy that moves through solids, liquids, and gases. You learned that sonar transfers sound energy to water in ocean exploration. Light travels through space and other kinds of matter. Energy transfer also can occur when thermal energy is transferred to air around a forest fire.

Energy is transferred from one object to another in many ways, but it is always important to remember that energy is never lost or gained when it is transferred or converted. If you light a candle and let it burn itself out, you may think that the candle's stored energy disappears into thin air. However, the same amount of chemical energy stored in the candle wax is given off as light and thermal energy when the candle burns.

Energy transfer affects our lives in many important ways. In the next two lessons, we will explore some of the ways in which the transfer of energy has an impact on our lives.

CHECKPOINT

1. How is energy defined by what it does?
2. What are some different forms of energy?
3. How can energy be transferred?
 How do forms of energy compare?

ACTIVITY

Investigating Kinetic and Potential Energy

Find Out

Do this activity to learn how an object can change the energy it has.

Process Skills

Measuring
Communicating
Predicting
Hypothesizing
Controlling Variables
Experimenting
Interpreting Data
Designing Investigations

WHAT YOU NEED

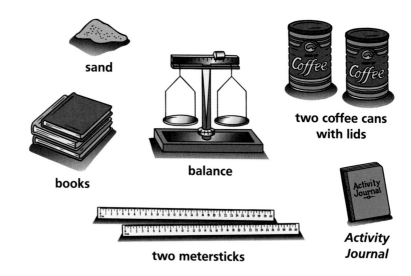

sand

books

balance

two coffee cans with lids

two metersticks

Activity Journal

Activity Journal

WHAT TO DO

1. Fill one coffee can with sand. Carefully place a lid on the can with sand and one on the empty can.

   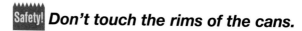 **Safety! *Don't touch the rims of the cans.***

2. Select the appropriate tool to measure the mass of each can. Record the mass.

3. Make a ramp with two metersticks and one book. The metersticks should be a few cm apart but even with each other. Line up the cm mark on the two metersticks to check that they are even.

4. **Predict** which coffee can will roll the farthest and why.

5. Roll each coffee can down the meterstick ramp. Have your partner mark where each can stops. Select the appropriate tool to **measure** the distance that each can traveled. **Record** the distance.

6. **Make a hypothesis** telling what will make the coffee cans roll farther and why. Use the materials to change your setup according to your hypothesis. **Record** your hypothesis and the data you collect.

CONCLUSIONS

1. Which can had more potential energy at the top of the ramp? Why?

2. What type of energy did the can have at the bottom of the ramp?

3. Describe how the height of the ramp and the mass of the cans affected the amount of kinetic and potential energy of the cans.

ASKING NEW QUESTIONS

1. What variables did you adjust according to your hypothesis?

2. What variables in the activity remained the same, or were constant?

SCIENTIFIC METHODS SELF CHECK

✔ Did I **observe, measure,** and **record** how far the coffee cans traveled?

✔ Did I **make a hypothesis** telling what would make the coffee cans roll farther and why?

✔ Did I **interpret the data** I collected?

LESSON 2

Electricity and Energy Use

Find Out

- How some machines use thermal energy to do work
- How fossil fuels are used for electricity
- How efficiency relates to electricity
- What nuclear energy is and how it can be used

Vocabulary

electrical energy
nonrenewable energy
efficiency
electric current
nuclear energy

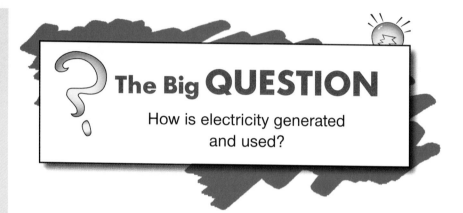

The Big QUESTION

How is electricity generated and used?

How does a car use the energy in gasoline to move you from place to place? Where does the energy come from that lights and heats your home? In the last lesson, you learned about many forms of energy. Now let's look at yet another form of energy, electrical energy.

Machines and Thermal Energy

It took a long time for humans to learn about energy, energy transfer, and how to use energy in a predictable way. Our ancestors looked for ways to use energy to help them travel quickly over far distances or do work with less effort. Through the ages, it took the efforts of many different people to develop methods of using energy in machines to make work easier for humans.

Energy is used to operate many of the machines you see each day. In a car, gasoline burns rapidly inside the cylinders of the engine. The up-and-down motion of pistons in the cylinders causes the forward motion of the car. The chemical potential energy in the gasoline changes to the mechanical energy of pistons in the car.

Before gasoline was used for powering cars, engines, such as those found in the first cars and locomotive trains, were driven by steam. They burned wood or coal that heated water to make steam. The steam made pistons move in cylinders. The energy of the moving pistons drove the machinery.

Internal View of Steam Engine

Steam pushes the piston back and forth and turns the wheel.

In early steam engines, steam was piped into one side of a cylinder. As the steam expanded, it pushed a piston. The steam then cooled and was piped out as more hot steam was let into the other side of the cylinder, pushing the piston back again.

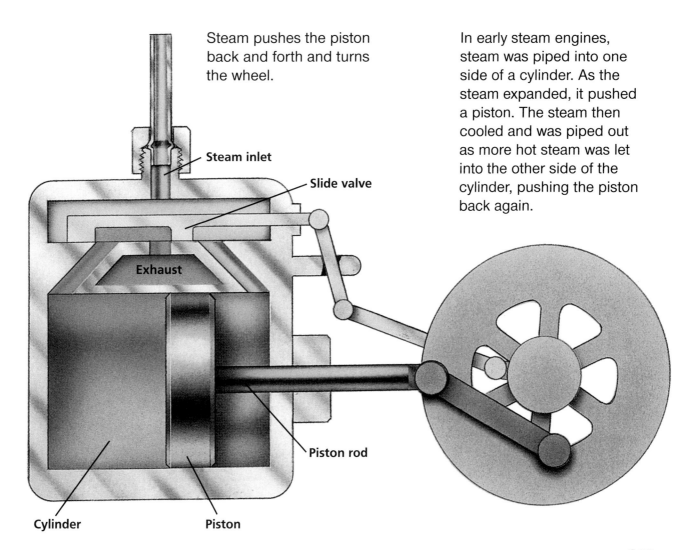

Steam inlet

Slide valve

Exhaust

Piston rod

Cylinder

Piston

Fossil Fuels and Electrical Energy

During the 1800s, steam engines changed the way people did work. Factories sprang up where coal, wood, and water were plentiful. These factories used the energy from coal or wood to do weaving, metalworking, and other work on a large scale.

Steam still helps us today. Many modern generating plants burn coal and oil to make steam. The kinetic energy of rapidly expanding steam is turned into something useful—electricity. **Electrical energy,** or electricity, is the form of energy caused by the presence or movement of electrons which exert an electric force.

Coal Burning Power Plant

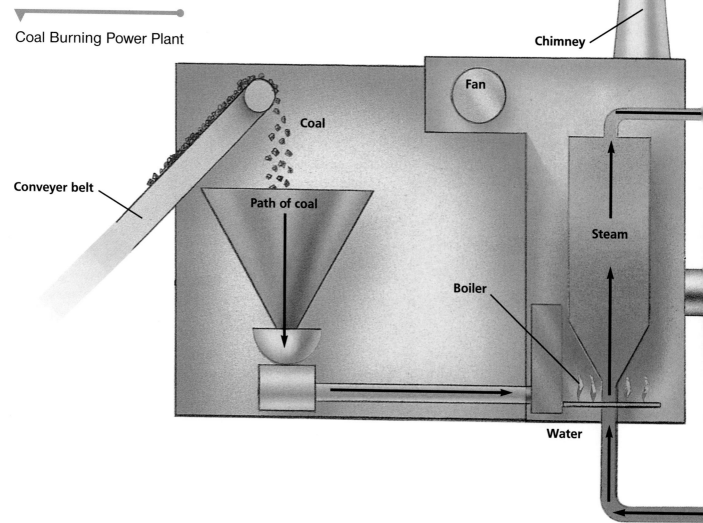

Chimney

Fan

Coal

Conveyer belt

Path of coal

Steam

Boiler

Water

When fossil fuels are burned, the chemical energy in some of the fuels is converted to thermal energy. The thermal energy transfers to water, producing steam. Thermal energy in steam is converted to mechanical energy when steam spins turbines. When the mechanical energy of the turbines spins generators, electricity is produced.

Coal, oil, and natural gas used to produce electricity are called fossil fuels because they formed from the remains of plants and animals that lived on Earth millions of years ago. While they were alive, plants and animals stored chemical potential energy.

Fossil fuels are a nonrenewable energy source. **Nonrenewable energy** sources are those that cannot be replaced by natural means in less than 30 years. It took millions of years to make a supply of these fuels, and it will take millions of years for another supply to form. Fossil fuels are found only in areas that used to be seas or swamps millions of years ago.

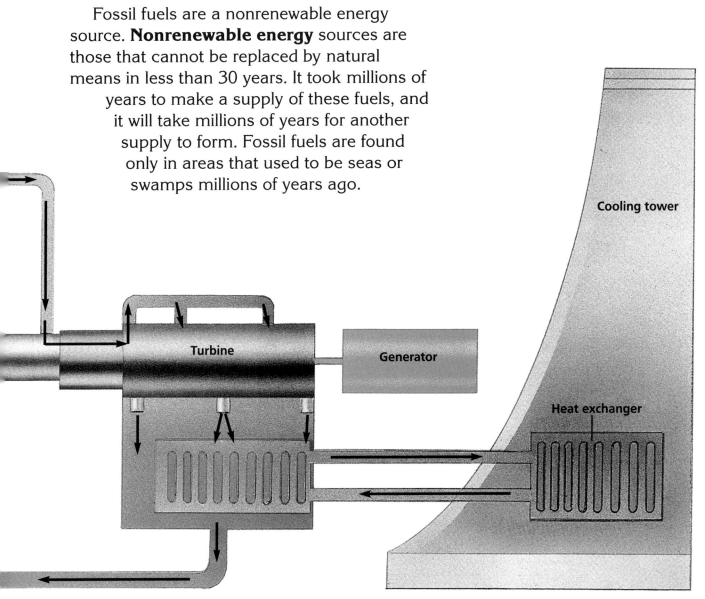

Cooling tower

Turbine

Generator

Heat exchanger

Electricity and Efficiency

Many different kinds of energy are converted and transferred to make the electricity that we use every day. Chemical potential energy from coal, oil, and natural gas is often converted to kinetic energy to make electricity.

When one form of energy is converted, usually only part of the energy is converted into the desired form. For example, when coal is burned, some of the chemical energy is given off as radiant energy, or light. The coal power plant uses the coal's energy to produce steam, and doesn't use the light that is given off in the burning process. **Efficiency** is the proportion, usually given as the percentage, of the energy that is converted into another usable form.

Steam Turbine and Generator

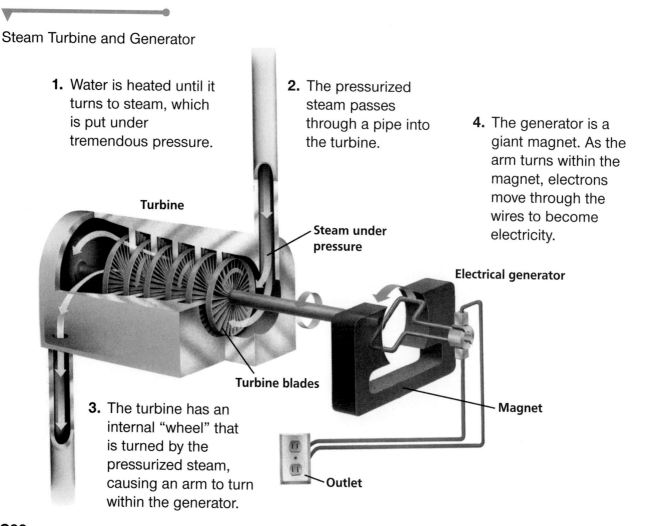

1. Water is heated until it turns to steam, which is put under tremendous pressure.

2. The pressurized steam passes through a pipe into the turbine.

4. The generator is a giant magnet. As the arm turns within the magnet, electrons move through the wires to become electricity.

Turbine

Steam under pressure

Electrical generator

Turbine blades

3. The turbine has an internal "wheel" that is turned by the pressurized steam, causing an arm to turn within the generator.

Magnet

Outlet

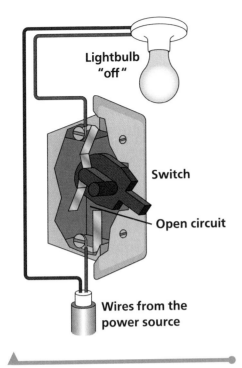

Lightbulb
"off"

Switch

Open circuit

Wires from the
power source

The switch prevents the electrons from
flowing through the circuit.

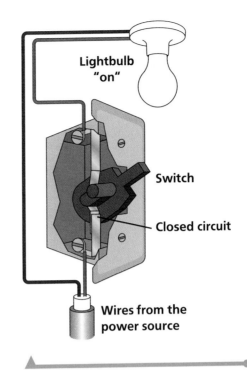

Lightbulb
"on"

Switch

Closed circuit

Wires from the
power source

The switch allows the flow of electrons
through the closed circuit.

Most oil burning power plants are about 30 to
40 percent efficient, which means only 30 to 40
percent of the energy in the oil is converted into
electricity.

Thermal energy is given off as heat
whenever energy is converted. For example,
95 percent of the electrical energy in an
incandescent lightbulb is converted to thermal
energy and given off as heat. Only five percent
of the electrical energy is converted into light.
Therefore, the lightbulb is only five percent
efficient.

In addition, much energy is lost as heat
when electricity flows along the wires used to
transport it. The movement of electrons along a
path or circuit is called **electric current.** You
can find many circuits, or paths, that electricity
moves through in your home. A switch inside
your home can send an electric current
through a circuit to a light, through a lightbulb,
and then back to the switch.

Nuclear Energy

Because so much of our electricity comes from coal and oil, finding new energy sources is as important as finding ways to use less coal and oil. Fuels such as coal, oil, and natural gas are not the only sources of energy for generating electricity. Nuclear energy can also be used to generate electricity.

The potential energy stored in the nucleus, or center, of atoms, is called **nuclear** (nu′ klē ər) **energy.** When atoms are split, some of the stored energy in the nuclei of the atoms is converted into thermal energy. The thermal energy is used to produce steam, which can be used to produce electricity.

Nuclear power plants are also used to produce electricity.

When the nucleus of an atom is split, energy is released.

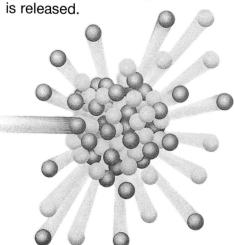

The energy released from splitting an atom is mostly in the form of thermal energy. Thermal energy is used to boil water and produce steam to produce electricity.

It does not cost much to run nuclear generating plants, but building them is very expensive. The waste from nuclear power plants can be dangerous for hundreds or thousands of years. Because the waste is dangerous, it must be stored safely. The safety of operating nuclear power plants is always a concern. A 1986 accident at a nuclear power plant in Chernobyl (chər no′ bel) in the former U.S.S.R. took many lives. The results continue to endanger a great many other lives.

Every source of energy has its costs and benefits. Both nuclear energy and fossil fuels produce waste when they are used. The more we use them, the more we pollute. It is important to balance the benefits of energy with the problems of pollution and waste.

We get much of our electrical energy from burning fossil fuels and splitting atoms. We use this electrical energy in many ways. However, we seem to need more and more energy as we find new ways to use it. The costs and benefits of different energy sources must be studied to make wise choices for the future.

CHECKPOINT

1. How do some machines use thermal energy to do work?

2. How are fossil fuels used for electricity?

3. How does efficiency relate to electricity?

4. What is nuclear energy and how can it be used?

 How is electricity generated and used?

ACTIVITY

Investigating Steam and Work

Find Out

Do this activity to learn how steam can be used to do work.

Process Skills

Measuring
Predicting
Communicating
Observing
Inferring
Defining Operationally

WHAT YOU NEED

beaker

rubber stopper with two holes in it

metal pinwheel

hot plate

water

250-mL Erlenmeyer flask

Activity Journal

small pan

WHAT TO DO

1. With the beaker, measure 200 mL of hot water into the Erlenmeyer flask. Tightly close the flask using the rubber stopper.

2. Place the pinwheel in one hole of the stopper.

3. Predict what will happen to the pinwheel when the flask is placed on the hot plate. Record your prediction.

4. Have your teacher put the flask on the hot plate in a small pan of water. When the water in the flask begins to boil, **observe** what happens to the pinwheel and **record** your observations.

CONCLUSIONS

1. Compare your prediction with your observations.
2. **Infer** what caused the pinwheel to move.
3. Describe how energy was converted in this activity.

ASKING NEW QUESTIONS

1. Would this activity have been different if cold water had been used? Why?
2. How is the simple engine you made like or unlike the steam engines you studied in this lesson?
3. Based on this activity, how would you **define** a simple engine?

SCIENTIFIC METHODS SELF CHECK

✔ Did I **predict** what would happen to the pinwheel?

✔ Did I **observe** how the expanding gas exerts force?

✔ Did I construct an **operational definition** of a simple engine?

Alternative Energy

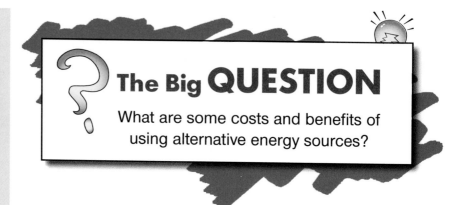

The Big QUESTION

What are some costs and benefits of using alternative energy sources?

When fossil fuel sources become too difficult or costly to find, what will be our alternative sources of energy? Today we are finding that very old sources of energy are being used in new ways to assist us in our search for sources of energy.

Alternative Resources

How do you think people used light and kept warm before they discovered coal and oil? How did they get from one place to another? How did they run machines? As fossil fuel sources are used up, people are rediscovering early energy sources and finding new uses for them. These energy sources will also play an important role in providing energy for your future.

When you studied weather and ocean waves, you learned that wind can move air and water. Wind can produce a force that moves air and water over a distance, which means that wind has energy and that it transfers energy. Did you know that wind can be used as an energy source?

There are different kinds of energy sources. Wind, the energy inside Earth, and solar energy are considered to be inexhaustible sources of energy. **Inexhaustible resources** cannot be used up and are constantly being used and recycled. **Renewable** energy sources are sources of energy that can be replaced by natural means in less than 30 years. Renewable energy sources include moving water and once-living matter. Just as there are advantages and disadvantages to using nonrenewable resources, such as fossil fuel, there can be both costs and benefits from using alternative energy sources, too.

This windmill in Alkmaar, Holland, uses the energy from wind to do work.

Wind Energy

Do you remember how convection currents caused movement in air when you studied high- and low-pressure systems? Winds and weather develop from the convection currents caused by the uneven heating and cooling of Earth's atmosphere.

Wind is caused by solar energy that unevenly heats Earth's surface and atmosphere. When the sun heats Earth's surface, air near the ground is heated. Convection currents occur when warm air rises and colder air moves in below. This movement causes wind.

Humans have used the energy of wind to do work for hundreds of years. Wind has been used to grind grain and sail ships. Some people in the world were using wind machines more than 1300 years ago to grind grain. Some windmills are still used to grind grain and pump water.

To make the best use of wind, turbines must be built in areas where wind blows most of the time at 12 km or more per hour. Because the wind doesn't occur all the time, storing energy to use during less

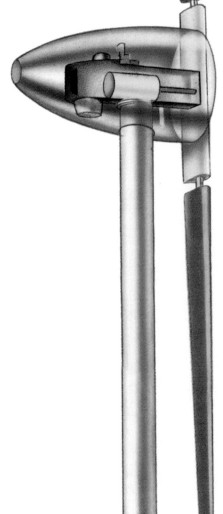

Modern wind turbines are windmills used to produce electricity. They may measure up to 100 meters across and are computer-programmed to use energy from the wind.

The turning of the turbines is used to generate electricity. The electricity is either stored in batteries or sent out for people to use right away.

windy times can be a problem. More than 90 percent of the land in the United States suitable for using wind energy is concentrated in the western states from Texas to Montana.

However, wind energy can be a source of energy in many other places as well. A large wind-generator farm located near Palm Springs, California, produces about one percent of the state's electricity. Wind is a very economical energy source for that part of California. To get that kind of electrical energy from fossil fuels, you would have to burn almost three million barrels of oil.

Wind energy produces almost no pollution. Some argue, however, that large wind-generator farms detract from the beauty of the landscape. Wind-generator farms are expensive to build, but the price of wind energy is becoming competitive with coal, oil, and natural gas.

This large wind-generator farm located near Palm Springs, California, produces about one percent of the state's electricity.

Solar Energy

The sun is the primary source of almost all of Earth's energy. The sun's energy creates virtually no pollution on Earth. Each day, the amount of energy the United States receives from the sun is equivalent to the energy from 22 million barrels of oil. To capture all that radiant energy, the entire country would have to be covered with solar collectors, which is not practical.

Solar energy is most often used to heat water or homes. The most common solar collectors are rooftop water heaters and windows that face the sun.

Solar energy can also be converted and used as electricity. **Solar cells** convert solar energy directly into electrical energy. When sunlight strikes the cell, electrons separate between two layers of semiconducting material and can flow through an external circuit. Solar-powered calculators use small solar cells to do this. However, calculators use only a small amount of electricity.

This solar power facility in the Mojave Desert is the world's largest.

This solar-energy power station in San Bernardino, California, harnesses solar energy by using mirrors to focus sunlight on a central receiver. This is used to produce steam which can then generate electricity.

In order to produce enough electricity for larger appliances or houses to use, large panels containing hundreds or thousands of solar cells are needed. Converting large amounts of solar energy directly to electricity is often expensive.

At one station in California's desert, a million mirrors are using the sun's energy to generate electricity. The solar energy is converted to thermal energy and used to boil water. The steam from the water turns turbines to generate electricity.

When sunlight is most intense, air conditioners work their hardest. Solar energy can provide extra electricity during the hottest part of the day when it is needed most. However, it is expensive to buy and build solar-energy-powered generators. Once the equipment is bought, collecting and using the energy do not cost much. In the end, solar energy can cost less than other sources.

Hydroelectric Energy

Waterwheels have been used to capture the kinetic energy of falling or flowing water since 100 B.C. Waterwheels are simple machines that are turned by flowing water. Today, the energy of moving water is often used to generate electricity. Water is considered to be a renewable resource because freshwater is a limited resource and needs to be conserved, recycled, and used wisely. Electricity generated by falling or flowing water is called **hydroelectric** (hi′ drō e lek′ trik) energy.

Hydroelectric plants at dams do not produce much pollution. However, dams do change the land around them. When they are built, a lake is formed and the people and animals living there must move. All the trees under the lake die and the environment of the area changes.

Hydroelectric Plant

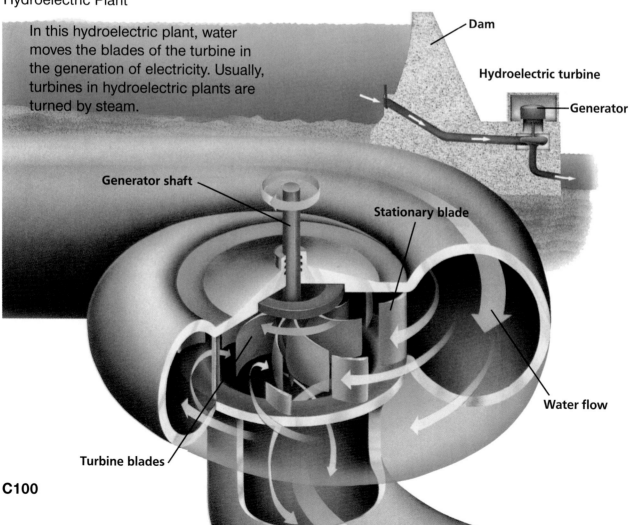

In this hydroelectric plant, water moves the blades of the turbine in the generation of electricity. Usually, turbines in hydroelectric plants are turned by steam.

Dam

Hydroelectric turbine

Generator

Generator shaft

Stationary blade

Water flow

Turbine blades

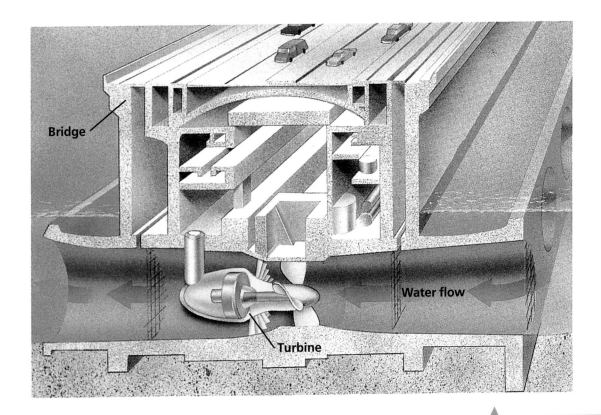

Bridge

Water flow

Turbine

The ocean's tides can generate electric energy in much the same way that hydroelectric energy is produced from running water. The rising tidewater flows through turbines to generate electricity. When the water level falls, the water flows out through the turbines.

Tide generators work best where there is a big difference in water level between high and low tides. This limits the number of places turbines can be built to use this energy. Most places that would be good sites for tide-energy generators are far from population centers. They would require long wires to be installed to transport electricity over long distances.

Tidal generators produce little pollution. However, they change the flow of water in the environment where they are constructed. Many plants and animals living in the harbors and river mouths can be affected by tide-energy generator stations.

Not many tidal energy stations are in operation because of their high cost. A large, working, tidal energy station was completed in France in 1967. The turbines shown in the illustration are below the bridge across the bay.

Geothermal Energy and Biomass

Because science has helped us learn more about Earth, we now have a more complete explanation of geysers and hot springs. Water under Earth's surface is heated as it passes over very hot rock. When steam pressure builds up, the steam and hot water escape through Earth's crust. The steam can be used to heat buildings and generate electricity. Energy from within Earth is called **geothermal** (jē ō thur′ mel) **energy.**

There are not many places where geothermal energy is easy to use for generating electricity. In areas where geothermal energy is available for electrical generation, such as Iceland and New Zealand, it is a relatively inexpensive and pollution-free energy source.

Scientists and engineers are trying to use geothermal energy for electricity where they need it by drilling wells five to six km deep and pumping water deep into Earth's crust to be heated. They plan to use the heat they extract from the crust to boil water, turn turbines, and generate electricity.

Castle Geyser in Yellowstone National Park is caused by water moving over very hot rock within Earth's surface. When the steam pressure builds up, steam and hot water escape through Earth's surface.

Another source of energy is energy from biomass. **Biomass** (bī′ ō mas′) is any matter that is or was living. Remember how fossil fuels were formed from dead plants and animals? Biomass can be thought of as the early stage of coal. You can burn biomass or products of biomass to get thermal energy. More than 50 percent by weight of landfill waste is paper, cardboard, and yard wastes. These can all be burned for thermal energy. Solid wastes of animals and humans is another waste product that can be dried and burned.

In some areas, products from biomass are burned. Brazil is trying to use alcohol burned from biomass to run cars to reduce pollution and the country's dependence on expensive, imported fossil fuels. Heat and a gas called methane are produced when biomass decomposes. This heat and gas can also be used for generating electricity.

Burning biomass can produce less of some kinds of pollution than burning fossil fuels. However, you must burn much more biomass than coal to generate the same amount of electricity. This makes biomass more expensive to use because so much more has to be transported and used to yield the same amount of power.

This biomass-fired power generating station in San Bernadino, California, generates electricity by burning wood residues from forest clearance and agricultural waste.

Energy Where You Live

Fossil fuels have been used for hundreds of years to provide light and heat for homes. Other sources have been used for much longer. Having other energy sources available to do work is very important to how you live. Many of the sources you have learned about depend on climate and location.

Hong Kong, Bombay, Boston, Chicago, San Diego, and London all have at least one thing in common. They are cities built near oceans, lakes, or rivers. In the past, water provided inexpensive transportation and a source of energy for producing food and building materials. Inland cities such as Dallas, Texas, are more likely to have developed near major roads or railroad lines.

Sources of energy are important for making and using the things people need to live and work, and for transportation. In the past, towns were built near forests or easy-to-get coal.

What sources of energy have been used in your area? What sources are being used today? The energy of moving water may have been used for transportation or manufacturing products. Your town or city may have started near a source of water, wood, or biomass. Solar energy for crops also may have been important to your town or city.

Trash-burning power plant in Bridgeport, Connecticut

Dam and power station in Chile

Where we get the energy to do day-to-day work will depend on decisions we make in the future. There are benefits and costs to any choice made concerning energy use. Some of the factors that have to be weighed when making energy choices include present and future costs in time and money, the safety of a given energy source, the location where energy is needed, and the resulting impact on the surrounding environment.

Nesjavellir Geothermal Powerstation, Southwest Iceland

CHECKPOINT

1. What are some alternative resources?
2. How can wind be used as a source of energy?
3. How can energy from the sun be used for energy?
4. How can water be used as a source of energy?
5. How can geothermal energy and biomass be used as energy sources?
6. What factors might influence the energy source used in your area?

 What are some costs and benefits of using different sources of alternative energy?

ACTIVITY

Comparing Energy Sources

Find Out

Do this activity to learn how solar energy compares to a traditional heat source.

Process Skills

Predicting
Measuring
Communicating
Observing
Inferring
Hypothesizing
Designing Investigations
Experimenting
Controlling Variables

WHAT YOU NEED

masking tape

two straws

pushpin

scissors

two 250-mL beakers

clear plastic wrap

20-cm-length rubber hose

thermometer

clay

water

funnel

newspaper

hot plate

cardboard shoe box

black plastic

Activity Journal

WHAT TO DO

Straw or tube
End plugged with clay
Holes punched with push pin
Clear plastic
Outlet tube
Box
Black plastic
Crumpled newspaper or insulation

1. Select the appropriate tools to make a solar energy collector. Line the shoe box with crumpled newspaper and cover with black plastic.

2. Plug one end of a straw with clay. With the pushpin, punch 12 holes in one side of the straw.

3. Attach the rubber hose on the straw's open end. Tape the straw in place at the top of the box. Attach the other end of the hose to the end of the funnel. Cover the box with clear plastic.

4. Cut the other straw to make a drainage pipe. Make a hole at the base of the box and insert the straw into it. Seal the area around the straw with clay and masking tape.

5. Predict whether the solar collector or a burner would heat water more quickly.

6. Place a beaker under the drainpipe. Measure and record the starting temperature of 250 mL of water. Pour the water into the funnel.

7. Record the time it takes for the water to drain into the beaker. Record its temperature. Repeat this process three times using the same water.

8. Measure 250 mL of water into a beaker. Observe the teacher heat the water over the hot plate.

9. Record the time at which the temperature of the water equals that heated by the solar collector.

CONCLUSIONS

1. Compare your prediction with your observations.

2. Infer what caused the temperature of the water to increase in the solar collector.

3. Infer what caused the temperature of the water to increase on the hot plate.

ASKING NEW QUESTIONS

1. Develop a testable question. Plan and conduct a simple investigation and write instructions that others can follow.

2. Prepare a report of your investigation.

3. Identify a single independent variable and explain what will be learned by collecting data on this variable.

SCIENTIFIC METHODS SELF CHECK

✔ Did I **predict** whether the hot plate or solar collector would heat water more quickly?

✔ Did I **observe** the temperature of water?

✔ Did I **record** my observations?

CHAPTER 3

Review

Reviewing Vocabulary and Concepts

Write the letter of the answer that completes each sentence.

1. ___ is the ability to do work and to cause changes in matter.
   - **a.** Energy
   - **b.** Biomass
   - **c.** Efficiency
   - **d.** Chemical energy

2. The energy of the random movement of atoms in matter is ___.
   - **a.** thermal energy
   - **b.** solar energy
   - **c.** potential energy
   - **d.** chemical energy

3. Fossil fuels are a ___ energy source.
   - **a.** renewable
   - **b.** nonrenewable
   - **c.** geothermal
   - **d.** hydroelectric

4. ___ is the percentage of the energy that is converted into another usable form.
   - **a.** Biomass
   - **b.** Energy transfer
   - **c.** Efficiency
   - **d.** Nonrenewable energy

5. Electricity generated by falling or flowing water is ___.
   - **a.** solar energy
   - **b.** biomass energy
   - **c.** hydroelectric energy
   - **d.** geothermal energy

Match the definition on the left with the correct term.

6. the energy an object has because of its position

7. a flow of energy from one place to another

8. the movement of electrons along a path or circuit

9. the potential energy stored in the nucleus, or center, of atoms

10. objects that convert sunlight directly into electrical energy

- **a.** energy transfer
- **b.** nuclear energy
- **c.** electric current
- **d.** solar cells
- **e.** potential energy

Understanding What You Learned

1. What two factors determine the amount of kinetic energy an object has?

2. How can solar energy warm objects?

3. What type of energy is found in fossil fuels and how can this energy be used for work?

4. What are some renewable energy sources?

5. What is one disadvantage of wind as a source of energy?

Applying What You Learned

1. How can an object at rest have energy?

2. Why don't all objects with the same temperature have the same thermal energy?

3. What is meant when it is stated that a lightbulb has only five percent efficiency?

4. What are the pros and cons of burning biomass to get thermal energy?

 5. Name three forms, sources, and uses of energy.

For Your **Portfolio**

Write a one-page advertisement promoting an alternative energy source of your choice. The advertisement should tell the other students of the costs and benefits of this energy source. Present your advertisement to the class. Props, visual aids, music, or other media can be used in your promotional advertisement.

Unit Review

Concept Review

1. What are some physical and chemical properties that can be used to identify matter?

2. What makes up all matter?

3. What are some forms, sources, and uses of energy?

Problem Solving

1. Suppose you found a piece of metal and did not know what kind of metal it was. How might you identify the metal?

2. If all matter is made up of similar basic structures, how can there be so many different kinds of substances?

3. When you help make dinner at home, what types of energy have gone into the making of the meal?

Something to Do

Design a plan to conserve energy in your community. You could contact your local gas and electric companies for brochures that list ways to save energy. The Internet and library might also have useful information. Make a brochure or flyer containing the tips you've gathered. Present the information in your brochure or flyer to your class and distribute the brochures or flyers in your community.

UNIT D

Health Science

CHAPTER 1

BODY SYSTEMS

Some cities have highways on which people drive their cars or trucks. Each of the cars and trucks moves people around the city. Some people may be on their way to work or to school. Some people may be picking up or delivering goods to stores or warehouses. Others may be collecting garbage around the city. Did you know that your body has a kind of "highway system" of its own? Your body has systems that pick up and deliver oxygen and nutrients as well as take away wastes. Like the many roads and highways that connect to each other in a city, the systems in your body are connected and have parts that work together to perform life processes.

The Big IDEA

Systems in the human body work together to perform functions necessary for life.

CHAPTER SCIENCE INVESTIGATION

Learn how systems in your body are interrelated. Find out how in your *Activity Journal.*

The Cardiovascular System

Find Out

- How the circulatory system moves blood through your body
- How the respiratory system moves air into and out of your body
- How gases are exchanged in your body

Vocabulary

valves
arteries
veins
capillaries
trachea
epiglottis
bronchi
alveoli

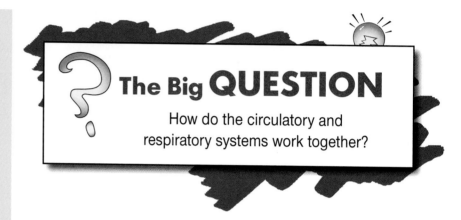

The Big QUESTION

How do the circulatory and respiratory systems work together?

Like the highways that carry people and vehicles, you have special vessels that carry blood through your body. Each of the blood cells, like cars, moves certain substances from one place to another. Like the city that has many kinds of roadways, such as highways, streets, and alleys, your body has many different sizes of vessels that allow blood and other substances to move throughout your body.

The Circulatory System

Your body is made up of billions of cells. Each cell must be supplied with certain substances in order to survive. Your body has a pickup and delivery system that supplies these substances to your cells. This system is called the circulatory system.

Do you remember studying the different kinds of circulatory systems that animals can have? Like the bird you studied in the life science unit, you have a closed circulatory system. In a closed circulatory system, blood moves through a network of vessels to and from your heart. The vessels in a closed system are directly connected to each other.

The circulatory system in your body is made up of blood, blood vessels, and the heart. Blood delivers materials that your cells need, such as oxygen, water, and food. Blood also picks up cell wastes, such as carbon dioxide. Blood travels along a series of tubes called blood vessels. Your heart acts as a pump that moves blood through the blood vessels in your body.

The circulatory system is made up of the heart, blood vessels, and blood. Some blood vessels are large and some, like the capillary below, are very small.

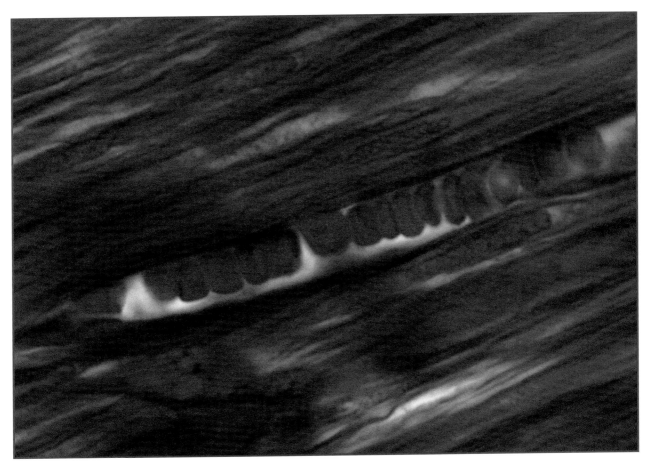

The heart is the central organ of the circulatory system. It is responsible for delivering blood to your body's cells. The diagram below shows the parts that make up the heart and how those parts function together to circulate blood.

The oxygen-poor blood (blue arrows) from the body enters the right atrium of the heart. When the atrium fills with blood, the muscle tissues in the atrium contract and blood is forced through a valve and into the right ventricle.

The left atrium collects the oxygen-rich blood (red arrows) that returns to the heart from the lungs. This blood is forced into the left ventricle when the muscle tissue in the atrium contracts.

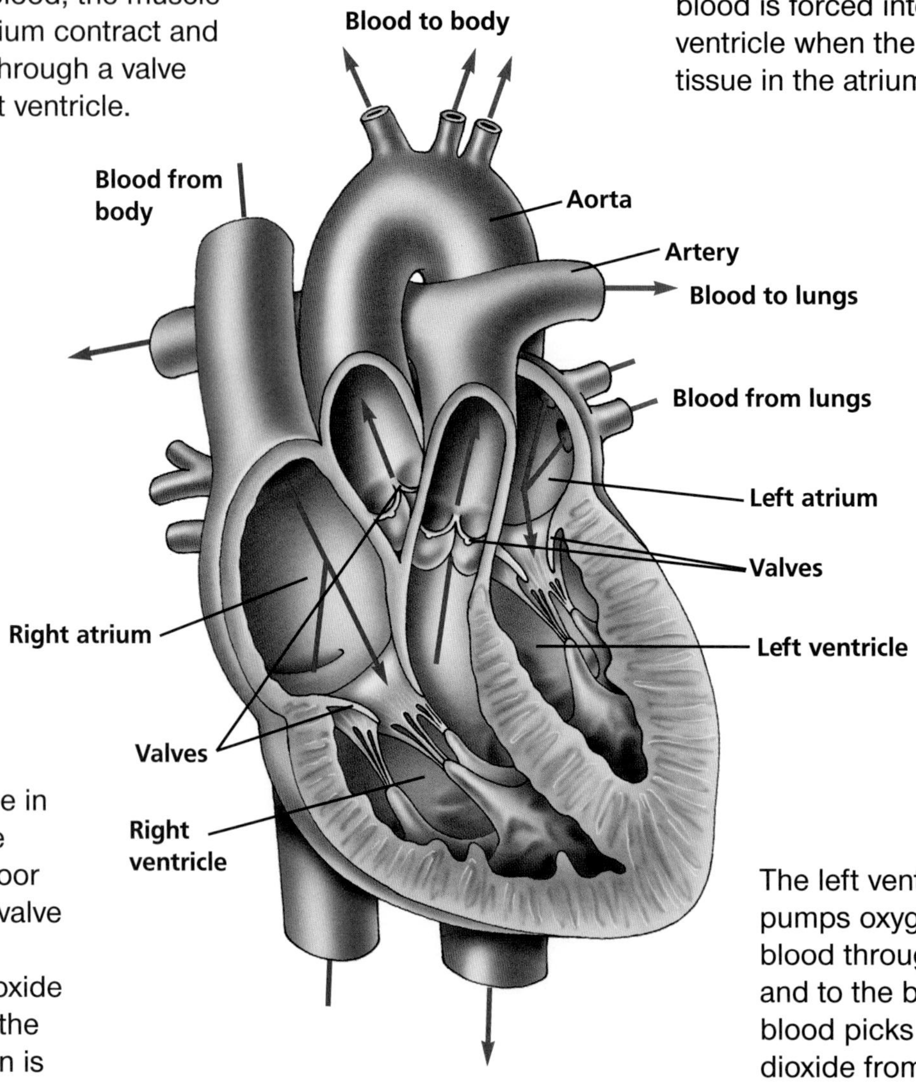

Blood to body

Blood from body

Aorta

Artery

Blood to lungs

Blood from lungs

Left atrium

Valves

Right atrium

Left ventricle

Valves

Right ventricle

The muscle tissue in the right ventricle pumps oxygen-poor blood through a valve and to the lungs, where carbon dioxide is released from the blood and oxygen is picked up.

The left ventricle pumps oxygen-rich blood through a valve and to the body. This blood picks up carbon dioxide from body cells and delivers oxygen.

The four valves in the heart allow blood to move in one direction through the heart.

The heart has two separate sides, each with a holding chamber called an atrium and a pump called a ventricle. The right atrium and ventricle receive blood coming back to the heart from the body. This blood is low in oxygen but high in carbon dioxide. This blood is sent from the heart to the lungs where the blood can unload the carbon dioxide and pick up a fresh supply of oxygen. From the lungs, the oxygen-rich blood returns to the heart. The left atrium and ventricle collect and then send the oxygen-rich blood to the body.

The heart also has parts called **valves,** which are the flaps that keep blood flowing in one direction through the heart. Each ventricle has two valves. One valve allows blood into the ventricle but keeps it from flowing back into the atrium. Another valve allows blood out of the ventricle but keeps it from flowing back into the ventricle.

During a single heartbeat, both atria contract at the same time, then relax. Then both ventricles contract at the same time and then relax. After the atria release their blood into the ventricles, the valves slam shut. When the ventricles release their blood into the blood vessels, the other set of valves slams shut. The sound of each set of valves closing can be heard as the "lub-dub" rhythm of your heart.

When ventricles contract and force the blood into the body or lungs, blood exerts pressure against the walls of the blood vessels. The pressure blood exerts against the inner walls of blood vessels is called blood pressure. When the left ventricle contracts, it forces blood under the highest pressure into your aorta, the largest blood vessel in your body. The blood vessels that carry blood away from your heart swell and then contract, and have a greater blood pressure than the blood vessels that carry blood returning to the heart.

This bottle is like the heart's ventricle filled with blood. When the bottle is not squeezed, the fluid is not pushed out.

When the bottle is squeezed, like the muscle tissues contracting in the ventricles, the fluid is forced out of the container.

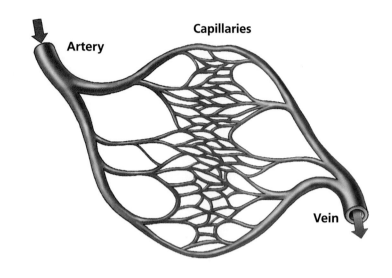

Artery

Capillaries

Vein

Arteries carry blood away from the heart. In the diagram, the artery is carrying oxygen-rich blood to the cells of the body. The vein is carrying the blood back to the heart. Based on what you know about the movement of blood into and out of the heart, did this artery come out of the right or left ventricle? Will this vein return to the heart's right or left atrium?

Like a city that has many kilometers of roadways, you have many blood vessels in your body. Did you know that you have about 96,000 km of blood vessels in your body? If they were placed end-to-end, they would go around Earth about two and one-half times. There are three different types of blood vessels in your body: arteries, veins, and capillaries.

Imagine that you had a field trip in the "heart," or downtown, of a city. Suppose you were traveling in a school bus on the highway pictured at the beginning of this chapter. If the school bus was going to drop you off at home, it would have to get off the highway and travel on a street or road. Once you got to your neighborhood, you might get out of the school bus and walk on a sidewalk to your home. Which type of roadway allows the greatest number of people to travel the quickest: the highway, the street, or the sidewalk?

Like the highways around the downtown of a city, your biggest blood vessels are those that go into or come out of the heart. **Arteries** are the blood vessels that carry blood away from the heart. **Veins** are the blood vessels that carry blood back toward the heart. Arteries and veins branching off the heart carry the greatest volume of blood at one time, like the highways that can carry the greatest number of travelers.

As the blood vessels move into tissues, they get smaller and smaller until they are so small that only one blood cell can move through at a time, like a narrow sidewalk. **Capillaries** are the smallest type of blood vessel, with walls that are only one cell thick. Like a sidewalk that can bring you close to your home, capillaries bring blood close to every body cell. All of the body's pickups and deliveries occur in the capillaries.

In the capillaries, blood performs many important jobs for your body. Blood is a connective body tissue that moves through blood vessels and delivers oxygen, food, and other materials to cells. Blood also picks up the wastes, such as carbon dioxide, that cells do not need. Blood also helps fight diseases that attack your body's cells.

There are three main types of cells that can be found in your blood: red blood cells, white blood cells, and platelets. Red blood cells carry oxygen to the body tissues. White blood cells destroy harmful microorganisms, remove dead cells, and make substances that help prevent disease. Platelets help your blood to clot if a blood vessel is broken. These blood cells work together to protect your body and keep your body's cells supplied with the materials they need to live, grow, and stay healthy.

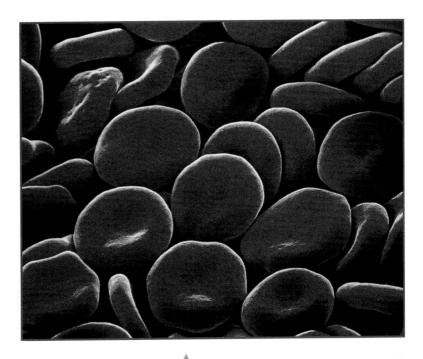

Red blood cells in the blood pick up many of the substances that cells need taken away and deliver substances that cells need to live and grow.

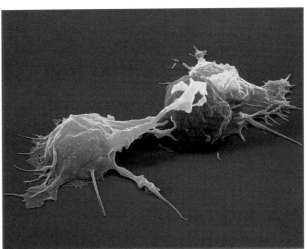

White blood cells can remove dead cells and destroy harmful microorganisms.

The Respiratory System

You now know how your circulatory system works to provide the body's cells with oxygen and take away carbon dioxide. But how do these gases get into and out of your body? The respiratory system is the system that is responsible for breathing. Breathing brings oxygen into your body and removes carbon dioxide.

When you breathe in, or inhale, air flows into your nose or mouth. The nose is lined with small hairs and a mucous membrane that trap dust and other particles in air, and keep them from reaching the lungs. In your nasal chamber, air is also warmed and moistened.

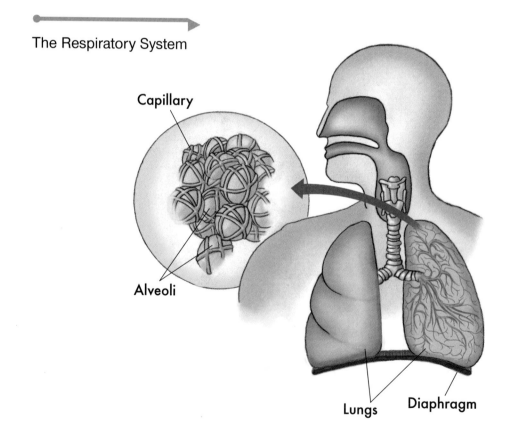

The Respiratory System

Capillary

Alveoli

Lungs   Diaphragm

From your nose or mouth, air travels through a windpipe called the trachea (trā′ kē ə). The **trachea** is a tube about 15 cm long that carries air to two shorter tubes that lead to your lungs.

Your trachea's entrance is covered by a small flap that closes over the windpipe when you swallow. The flap is called the epiglottis (ep ə glôt′ əs). The **epiglottis** is a respiratory organ that stops food from passing into the windpipe when you swallow. This flap keeps you from choking.

From the trachea, air moves through the bronchi and into the lungs. **Bronchi** (bron′ kī) are the two short tubes that carry air from the trachea to the lungs. Your lungs are the major organs of your respiratory system. Lungs are large, soft organs in which oxygen and carbon dioxide are exchanged. Air is brought into and out of the lungs by the action of your diaphragm. The diaphragm is a flat, powerful muscle that is found beneath your lungs.

The movement of your diaphragm causes air to move into and out of your lungs. When you inhale, your diaphragm moves downward, making more space in your lungs. Your ribs move up and outward, filling your lungs with air. When you exhale, your diaphragm moves upward and your ribs sink back down, forcing the air back out of your lungs.

When you inhale, air enters each lung through the bronchi. Each bronchus branches into thousands of smaller and smaller tubes. Each tiny tube leads to a very small air sac. **Alveoli** (al vē′ ə lī′) are the tiny air sacs that are found in the lungs. There are about 300 million alveoli in each lung. Each alveolus is surrounded by capillaries. The small area where the alveoli and the capillaries meet is the site where gases are exchanged between the respiratory system and the circulatory system.

The Exchange of Gases

The blood that moves through your body must bring oxygen from the lungs to the cells of the body. The blood entering the capillaries around the alveoli is low in oxygen. As you breathe in, air with oxygen fills each alveolus. Oxygen passes out of the air sacs and into the blood of the capillaries by diffusion. Red blood cells then carry oxygen to all the cells in the body. Oxygen diffuses out of the red blood cells and enters body cells.

Carbon dioxide is formed by all body cells as a waste during cellular respiration and must be eliminated from cells by blood. The carbon dioxide that is produced in respiration moves by diffusion from the cells of the body into the red blood cells. Blood that becomes loaded with carbon dioxide will be carried back to the lungs. When the blood arrives in the lungs, carbon dioxide diffuses out of the blood in capillaries and into the alveoli. Once there, it leaves your body and is released into the environment when you exhale.

It takes just one-tenth of a second for the oxygen to pass through the cell membrane of an alveolus and into the blood and for the carbon dioxide to pass through and into the air that you exhale.

Oxygen

Alveolus

Blood entering capillaries of lungs

Carbon dioxide

Blood leaving capillaries of lungs

This exchange of gases between the cells in your body and the cells in your lungs is how the circulatory and respiratory systems work together in your body. The cardiovascular system is another name for the circulatory system that is made up of the heart, blood, and blood vessels, which work to exchange gases in your body's cells.

The amount of oxygen that your body needs can change depending on how active you are. If you increase your level of activity, both your cardiovascular system and your respiratory system must work harder. To get the extra oxygen the body needs, the heart pumps faster. Blood circulates faster so that all parts of the body get the extra oxygen. The body's cells will be making more carbon dioxide, so the lungs must work harder to get rid of the waste. The lungs also take in extra oxygen. Many parts of the body all work together to supply your body's cells with the oxygen they need as well as remove the carbon dioxide waste so that your body functions properly and remains healthy.

CHECKPOINT

1. Describe the flow of blood through your circulatory system.

2. Describe the flow of air through your respiratory system.

3. How are oxygen and carbon dioxide exchanged in the body?

 How do the circulatory and respiratory systems work together?

ACTIVITY

Investigating Blood Pressure

Find Out

Do this activity to model how the blood pressure in arteries and veins compares.

Process Skills

Predicting
Observing
Measuring
Communicating
Using Numbers
Inferring
Interpreting Data
Constructing Models

WHAT YOU NEED

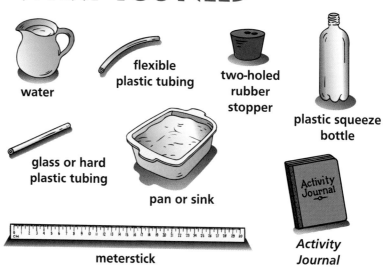

water

flexible plastic tubing

two-holed rubber stopper

plastic squeeze bottle

glass or hard plastic tubing

pan or sink

Activity Journal

Activity Journal

meterstick

WHAT TO DO

1. Fill the plastic squeeze bottle with water.

2. Insert the rubber stopper into the top of the bottle. Insert the glass or hard plastic tubing into one hole in the stopper. Insert the flexible tubing into the second hole.

3. Predict whether the hard plastic or flexible plastic tube will allow water to squirt farther when you squeeze the bottle.

4. Lay the bottle on its side with the ends of the tubes at the edge of the pan.

5. Using a meterstick and a catch pan, firmly squeeze the plastic bottle one time. Observe

how far the water squirts from each tube. Measure this distance in centimeters and record it.

6. Refill the bottle and repeat Steps 5 and 6 two more times, using the same amount of force each time.

7. Calculate the average distance that water squirted from each tube (add the three distances and divide the total by three). Record the answer.

CONCLUSIONS

1. Infer what body organ the plastic bottle represents. What does the water represent?

2. Compare your prediction with your observations.

3. Which tube was under higher pressure? Lower pressure?

ASKING NEW QUESTIONS

1. Artery walls are more muscular, but can be less elastic or flexible, than veins. Which tube represents an artery, and which represents a vein?

2. Based on your answer to the previous question, compare blood pressure in arteries and veins.

SCIENTIFIC METHODS SELF CHECK

✔ Did I **predict** how far the water would travel?

✔ Did I **observe** how far the water squirted for each tube?

✔ Did I **interpret the data** I collected?

The Digestive System

Find Out

- How food is broken down
- How food is digested in your body
- How digested food is moved to cells in the body

Vocabulary

digestion
enzymes
esophagus
stomach
pancreas
liver
gallbladder
villi

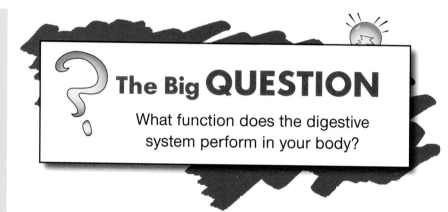

The Big QUESTION

What function does the digestive system perform in your body?

*H*ave you ever wondered how your body breaks down the food you eat? How does your body use food? Your lunch—in fact, all of the food you eat—travels through a complex set of organs that work together to transform the food you eat into usable substances.

The Breakdown of Food

When you eat food, it enters your body in a form that cannot be used by the cells in your body. The changing of food into a usable form is called **digestion.** Food must be broken down into a form that body cells can use to perform their life processes. All cells need food for energy, growth, and repair. The body changes food into usable forms by moving it through the digestive system.

Your digestive tract is a long tube that runs through your body. The tube is narrow in some places and wide in others. Throughout this tube food undergoes changes that allow it to be used by the body.

Food is broken down in the digestive system in two ways. The food you eat changes both physically and chemically. These processes start in the mouth and continue all along the digestive tract.

A physical change occurs when large pieces of food are broken down into smaller pieces. Your bites of food are cut, chopped, and finally ground by your teeth into smaller particles. While your bite of food still has the same chemical properties as when it entered your mouth, the size and shape have changed. When food is ground and mixed along your digestive tract, the food is also physically changed.

A chemical change occurs when the chemical properties of the food you eat change. Chemical changes help turn food into a form that cells can use. Your digestive system has parts that make chemicals that help with these chemical changes. These chemicals are added to food as it moves through the organs of your digestive system. Now, let's look at how and where these chemical and physical changes take place in your digestive system.

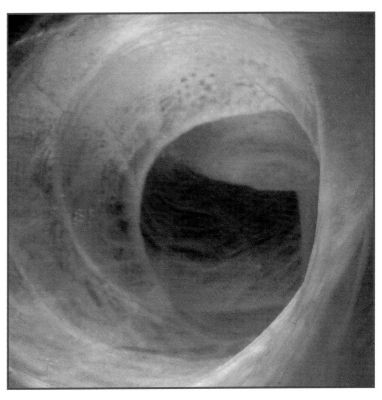

In the digestive system, physical and chemical changes break down food into a form that can be used by cells. Many of these chemical changes take place inside the small intestines.

Digestion in Your Body

Although most of the digestive processes take place in organs located within your body, digestion begins in your mouth.

Imagine you are having lunch in the school cafeteria, eating a turkey sandwich with mayonnaise. When you take a bite of your sandwich, your teeth chew and grind the pieces of bread and turkey into small particles. Your teeth cause a physical change in the food by making it into a size that you will be able to swallow.

In the digestive system, food undergoes physical and chemical changes that allow it to be used by the body.

Teeth
physical change

Saliva
chemical change (starch)

Stomach
physical change
chemical change (proteins)

Small intestine
physical change
chemical change
(fats, proteins, carbohydrates)

As you chew, the food becomes mixed with a clear liquid called saliva (sə lī′ və). Saliva is made in your salivary (sal′ ə vâr ē) glands, which are located under your tongue and behind your jaw. Saliva contains **enzymes** (en′ zīmz), chemicals that help speed up the digestive process. Enzymes and other chemicals that aid digestion are often called digestive juices. The enzymes chemically change the starches in the food you eat. In this case, the bread of your sandwich is changed into a simple sugar called glucose that can be easily used by your cells.

After your bite of sandwich has been thoroughly chewed, your tongue helps push the food to the back of your mouth and into your esophagus. Your **esophagus** (i sôf′ ə gəs) is a muscular tube connecting your mouth to your stomach.

After your food leaves your mouth, it travels down the esophagus and into your stomach, where digestion continues. The **stomach** is a baglike, muscular organ that mixes food and chemically changes protein. It can expand to hold about one liter of food and drink. The cells in the lining of your stomach make two chemicals that break down the protein from the turkey in your sandwich. One of the chemicals is an enzyme. The other is a type of acid called hydrochloric (hī drə klor′ ik) acid, which is usually referred to as stomach acid.

The muscles in the walls of your stomach spend about four hours mixing and churning the food around as the digestive juices work to change the food into usable forms. Your stomach, however, absorbs very little of this broken down food. Instead, it acts as more of a holding place for the food you eat until the food is ready to go through the next step of digestion.

After your stomach has finished mixing and churning your sandwich with the digestive juices, it passes the churned-up mixture on to your small intestine, a hollow tube that coils around for several meters.

Inside the small intestine, chemicals from the liver, pancreas, and gallbladder are added to the food mixture. Although food does not move through these organs, the chemicals they release into the small intestine help to break down food.

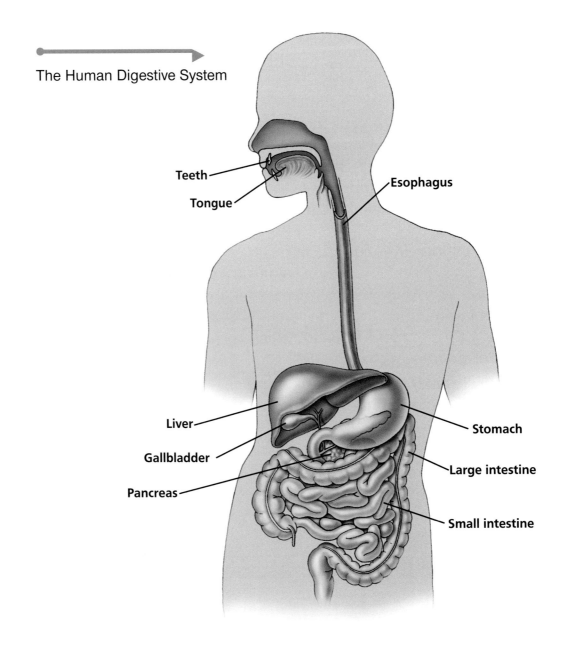

The Human Digestive System

Teeth

Tongue

Esophagus

Liver

Gallbladder

Pancreas

Stomach

Large intestine

Small intestine

The **pancreas** (pan′ krē əs) is a soft, oblong organ that makes three different enzymes that are released through a small tube into the small intestine. One enzyme breaks down fat, one breaks down protein, and one further breaks down carbohydrates. These enzymes speed up the chemical changes that help to complete the breakdown of fats, proteins, and carbohydrates.

The **liver** is a large, soft organ that lies just under your diaphragm. Although the liver performs many functions for the body, it helps in digestion by producing a chemical called bile. Bile is a greenish liquid that causes a physical change to occur in fats. Bile makes large fat droplets, like those from the mayonnaise and turkey, become smaller. The liver constantly produces bile, which collects in the **gallbladder.** The gallbladder stores bile until the fats enter the small intestine.

When the sandwich is fully broken down, it can be absorbed by the small intestine. The inner layer of the small intestine is lined with millions of tiny fingerlike projections called **villi.** The villi contain many kilometers of capillaries ready to absorb the broken-down food.

The several-meter length of the small intestine is where usable parts of the sandwich are absorbed. But some parts of the sandwich are too big or too complex to be broken down. This undigested food moves on to the large intestine.

The large intestine is a hollow tube like your small intestine but larger in diameter. The large intestine's main job is to absorb and recycle water from undigested food. Its walls absorb water from the waste that passes through it. By the time food has reached the end of the large intestine, most of the water has been absorbed from the waste material. The remaining waste material then passes out of your body.

Moving Digested Food to Body Cells

You learned that the small intestine is the site where digestion is completed and nutrients are absorbed by the blood. To get from the small intestine to cells in the body, nutrients are carried by blood.

Nutrients move out of the small intestine and into blood through the villi that line the inside of the small intestine. The villi contain many capillaries. The nutrients diffuse into the blood through the thin walls of the capillaries. Once inside the blood, nutrients are moved to all of the cells in your body.

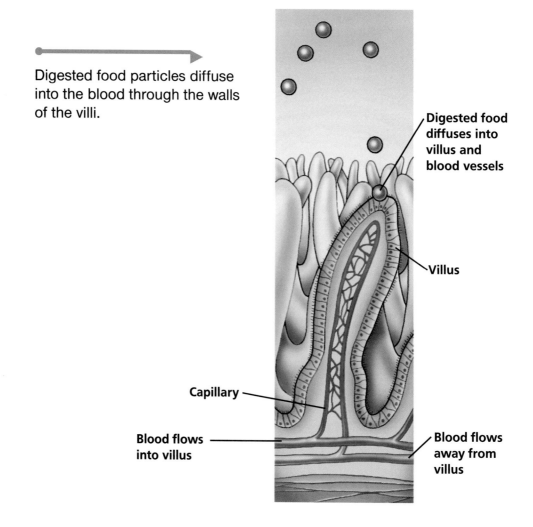

Digested food particles diffuse into the blood through the walls of the villi.

Digested food diffuses into villus and blood vessels

Villus

Capillary

Blood flows into villus

Blood flows away from villus

Did you know that villi allow your small intestine to absorb more digested food than if your small intestine were smooth? Remember that the villi are shaped like little fingers and stick out from the walls of your small intestine. In order for digested food to be absorbed, it must come close to a capillary so the food can diffuse into the blood. By having millions of little projections that stick out into digested food, more intestinal surface comes into contact with the digested food. This means more food can be absorbed than if the small intestine had a smooth inner surface.

Your digestive system performs many functions that physically and chemically change the food you eat into a form that can be used by the cells in your body. There are many parts that must work together in order for your body to change the food you eat for lunch into the food that cells can use. The food that is absorbed during digestion provides your body with the energy it needs to live and grow.

The surface area for absorbing food is increased by the four to five million villi that line the small intestine.

CHECKPOINT

1. Name the two ways in which food is broken down.

2. Describe three parts of your digestive system and discuss the function of each.

3. How is digested food moved to cells in the body?

 What function does the digestive system perform in your body?

ACTIVITY

Investigating Absorption

Find Out

Do this activity to learn how villi aid in the absorption of food.

Process Skills

Measuring
Communicating
Hypothesizing
Experimenting
Controlling Variables
Using Numbers
Interpreting Data
Inferring

WHAT YOU NEED

graduated cylinder

masking tape

four 250-mL beakers

water

ten paper towels

grease pencil

Activity Journal

WHAT TO DO

1. Label the four beakers "A," "B," "C," and "D" with the grease pencil.

2. Measure 150 mL of water in the graduated cylinder.

3. Fill each beaker with 150 mL of water. Record the amount of water in each beaker.

4. Roll each paper towel into a tube. Use the masking tape to hold each of the paper towels in a roll.

5. Put one rolled paper towel by beaker A, two by beaker B, three by beaker C, and four by beaker D.

6. Make a **hypothesis** by telling in which beaker the most water will be absorbed and why. **Record** your hypothesis.

7. Place the towels into their respective beakers.

8. Wait five minutes and **observe** each of the beakers. **Record** your observations. Remove the paper towels and **record** the amount of water that remains in each of the beakers.

9. **Subtract** the amount of water that remains in each beaker from the amount that each beaker began with. **Record** the difference as the amount of water absorbed for each of your beakers.

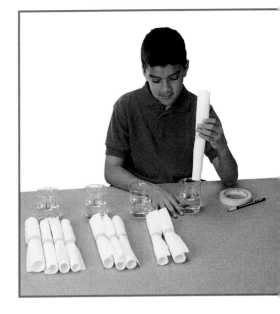

CONCLUSIONS

1. Compare your hypothesis with your results.

2. Explain why some beakers absorbed more water than others.

3. In what ways are the paper towels like villi in your small intestine?

ASKING NEW QUESTIONS

1. How would a beaker that had five paper towels in it compare with those that you observed in the activity?

2. Based on the results of your activity, infer how the number of villi in your small intestine increases the surface area of your small intestine and allows more food to be absorbed.

SCIENTIFIC METHODS SELF CHECK

✔ Did I make a **hypothesis** telling in which beaker the most water would be absorbed?

✔ Did I **calculate** the amount of water absorbed in each beaker?

✔ Did I **interpret the data** I collected?

The Excretory System

Find Out

- How the body removes wastes
- What parts make up the excretory system and how each functions
- How the kidneys filter blood

Vocabulary

excretion
urea
kidneys
ureter
bladder
urethra
nephrons
Bowman's capsule

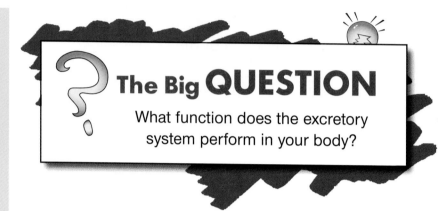

The Big QUESTION

What function does the excretory system perform in your body?

Did you know that the water from a faucet in your home has been purified? The drinking water in most communities is purified before it comes out of the faucet in your kitchen. Filters strain out large materials. Settling basins remove materials that float, and chemicals kill bacteria and other organisms that might cause disease. Your body has a system that works in a way that is similar to the equipment that purifies water. Your excretory system has parts that help remove the wastes from your body.

How Wastes Are Removed

To understand how wastes are removed from your body, you can think of your body as a large factory that takes in the raw materials that it needs to perform its life functions. The materials are transported to different areas in the factory where they will be changed into a form that is useful.

These changes in raw materials are much like the changes that take place in your digestive system, where the food you eat is changed into a form that your body's cells can use.

To change the raw materials into a useful form, the factory must use energy. In your body, all cells use energy to perform the jobs that the body needs them to do. When a factory produces a new product from the raw materials, some wastes are produced or left over. These wastes are not needed by the factory and will be taken away. Similarly, when food is digested or when cells use energy to perform their life processes, wastes are produced that the body does not need. It is the job of the excretory system to remove many of these wastes from your body.

Your blood contains many kinds of wastes from all of the activities that take place in your body. These wastes are chemicals that are not needed by the body and are harmful if they are not removed. Your body's process of getting rid of some of these wastes is called **excretion.** The excretory system is made up of those organs that remove some of these wastes from your body.

The organs of your excretory system filter blood and remove wastes, much like the way harmful substances are filtered out of the water you drink.

The wastes that your body eliminates in a liquid form are removed by the organs that make up your excretory system. Like the water that comes out of your faucet, the blood in your body is filtered. The excretory organs filter your blood and remove wastes from your body.

How the Excretory System Works

You now know that your body produces many chemical wastes and that the job of the excretory system is to remove wastes from your body. One of the chemical wastes that your body produces is urea. **Urea** (yoo rē′ ə) is a waste that results from the breakdown of proteins. If urea is not removed from the body, it can act as a poison to the cells in your body and can keep them from functioning properly. Urea is picked up from body cells by the blood and is carried to the kidneys, where urea is removed.

The **kidneys** are the main organs in the excretory system that filter blood. You have two kidneys and each is about as big as your fist. You might think of the kidneys as blood filters. In the same way that large or harmful substances are filtered out of drinking water, the kidneys filter blood and remove harmful wastes. During one day, your kidneys can filter as much as 200 L of blood.

In one day, your kidneys can filter 200 L of blood. That is like filtering the liquid in one hundred 2-L bottles like this one.

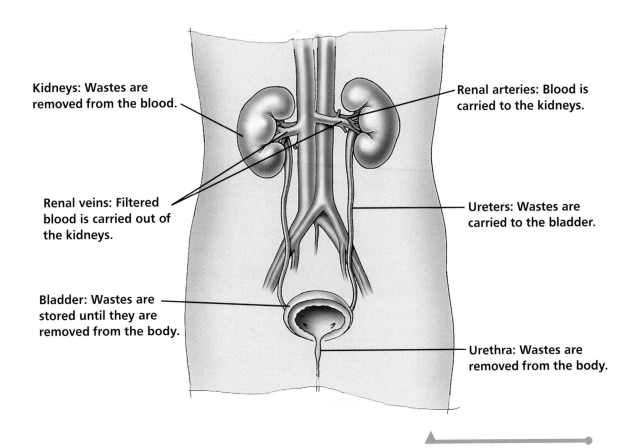

Kidneys: Wastes are removed from the blood.

Renal arteries: Blood is carried to the kidneys.

Renal veins: Filtered blood is carried out of the kidneys.

Ureters: Wastes are carried to the bladder.

Bladder: Wastes are stored until they are removed from the body.

Urethra: Wastes are removed from the body.

The excretory system filters blood and removes the wastes from the body.

For kidneys and other excretory organs to perform their jobs of removing wastes, they must work together to perform many functions. The work of the excretory system begins when blood that is carrying wastes moves through the body's arteries. The arteries that go to the kidneys are called the renal arteries. The renal arteries come directly from the aorta, the largest artery in the body.

Inside the kidneys, blood is filtered and urea is removed from the blood. The blood that leaves the kidneys is free of urea. This filtered blood is carried through a vein out of each kidney, called the renal vein. Then it goes to the heart where it is pumped back to the cells to deliver a new load of raw materials and again pick up wastes.

After wastes have been removed from blood, they are eliminated from the body. Wastes removed from blood leave each kidney through a ureter. A **ureter** (yo͞or′ ət ər) is a tube that carries wastes from each kidney to the urinary bladder.

The **bladder** is a sac that stores wastes removed by the kidneys. The urinary bladder acts as a kind of holding tank for wastes until the body is ready to eliminate them. When the bladder receives a message from the brain telling it to eliminate the wastes, the wastes move out of the body through a tube called the urethra. The **urethra** (yo͞o rē′ thrə) is the tube that carries wastes from the bladder to the outside of the body.

Your kidneys remove wastes from the blood as blood moves away from the heart. Once the wastes are removed from the blood, they are carried to the bladder through the ureters.

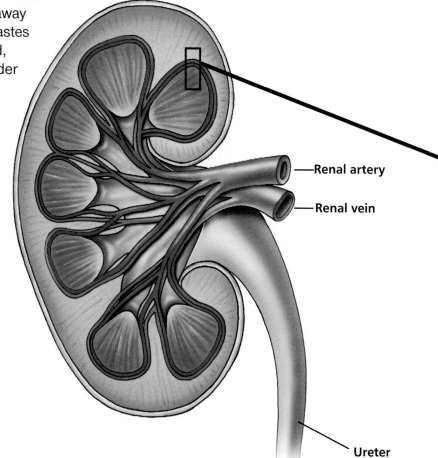

Renal artery

Renal vein

Ureter

The Kidneys Filter Blood

Now that you know how the organs in the excretory system work to remove some of the wastes in blood, let's take a closer look at how blood is filtered in the kidneys.

There are many complex structures that make up the kidneys so that blood in your body can be filtered. You know that blood enters the kidney through the renal artery that comes from the aorta. The blood from the renal artery moves into the kidney, which has many tiny filters inside of it.

Each kidney has about one million **nephrons** (nef′ rônz), the tiny filtering units of the kidney. Each nephron is made up of a cuplike structure called the **Bowman's capsule.** In the center of each Bowman's capsule, there is a mass of capillaries. When the blood moves into the kidney through the renal artery, it continues through smaller and smaller arteries. The blood finally enters the mass of capillaries.

The kidneys in your body are made up of about one million nephrons. Nephrons like the one shown here filter the blood with the structures that are shown.

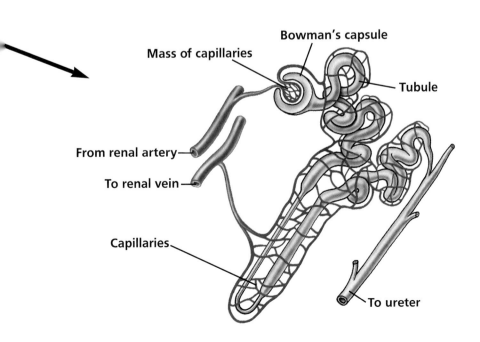

Mass of capillaries

Bowman's capsule

Tubule

From renal artery

To renal vein

Capillaries

To ureter

The first step of the process takes place as the blood pressure forces most of the water, sugar, salts, and wastes out of your capillaries and into the cup portion of the Bowman's capsule. The constant flow of blood into the kidneys forces the liquid out of the cup portion of the capsule and into a narrow tubule.

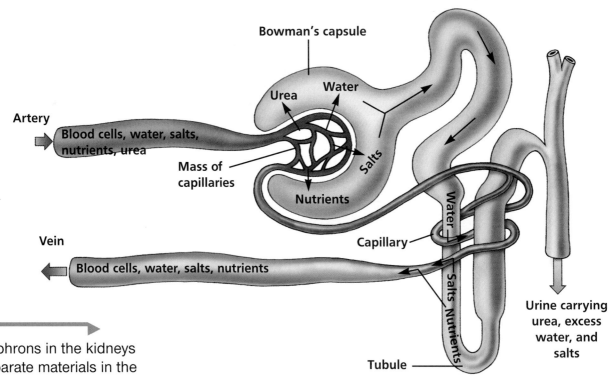

Nephrons in the kidneys separate materials in the blood and then return nutrients, water, and salts to the blood. Urea, excess water, and excess salt are removed from the nephron and sent through the ureter to the bladder as urine.

The second step of the process is where the wastes are removed from the blood. Certain cells that line the tubule move needed materials, such as food molecules and some salts, back into the capillaries. In addition, some of the water travels by osmosis out of the tubules and back into the capillaries. The blood, now put back together and cleaned, makes its way out of the kidneys through the renal vein. The renal vein then returns the cleaned blood to be circulated throughout the body. The remaining waste will be excreted.

The liquid that is squeezed into the narrow tubules in the nephrons is called urine. Urine is the liquid waste that contains excess salts, water, urea, and other wastes. The urine in each collecting tubule drains into the ureters and moves on to the bladder. It is this liquid waste that leaves the body through your urethra.

The excretory system is made up of many parts that function to filter blood and remove the wastes from your body. You already learned that the digestive system removes certain solid wastes from your body. You also know that the circulatory and respiratory systems remove some of the gaseous wastes, such as carbon dioxide, from your body. Now you know that it is the organs that make up the excretory system that filter blood and eliminate wastes in a liquid form from your body.

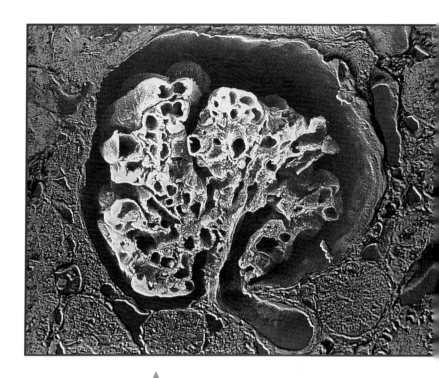

This color-enhanced photo image is of a nephron under very high magnification. The mass that appears yellow in the image is the mass of capillaries, and the Bowman's capsule is the pink-colored area surrounding it.

CHECKPOINT

1. How are wastes eliminated in a liquid form removed from the blood and body?

2. What parts make up the excretory system and how does each function?

3. How do the kidneys filter blood?

 What function does the excretory system perform in your body?

ACTIVITY

Filtering a Mixture

Find Out

Do this activity to model how wastes are removed from the blood.

Process Skills

Measuring
Predicting
Observing
Communicating
Interpreting Data
Constructing Models

WHAT YOU NEED

two 250-mL beakers

funnel

two pieces of crushed chalk

water

red food coloring

filter paper

Activity Journal

WHAT TO DO

1. Measure 125 mL of water and pour it into one beaker. Add three drops of red food coloring.

   Safety! *Handle glassware carefully. Wear safety glasses. Wipe up any spills immediately.*

2. Add two pieces of crushed chalk to the colored water.

3. Line the funnel with the filter paper. Place the funnel in the empty beaker.

4. **Predict** what will happen as the water and crushed-chalk mixture is poured through the filter.

5. Slowly pour the water and crushed-chalk mixture through the filter paper into the beaker.

6. **Observe** the filter paper and **record** your observations.

CONCLUSIONS

1. Compare your prediction with your observations.

2. What happened when the mixture was poured through the filter paper?

3. Describe how this filtering process compares to the kidneys' filtering process.

ASKING NEW QUESTIONS

1. What would happen if you kept adding larger particles of chalk to the mixture? What kinds of further information would be helpful to support your conclusion or to answer new questions that you have?

2. Describe how this activity could be changed to make it more like the filter system in your kidneys.

SCIENTIFIC METHODS SELF CHECK

✔ Did I **predict** what would happen when the water and crushed-chalk mixture was poured into the filter?

✔ Did I **observe** what happened when the mixture was filtered?

✔ Did I **record** my observations?

Review

Reviewing Vocabulary and Concepts

Write the letter of the answer that completes each sentence.

1. Flaps in the heart that keep blood flowing in one direction are ___.
   - **a.** skin
   - **b.** veins
   - **c.** valves
   - **d.** doors

2. Capillaries are the smallest type of ___, with walls one cell thick.
   - **a.** organ
   - **b.** blood vessel
   - **c.** cell
   - **d.** blood cell

3. ___ are chemicals that help speed up the process of digestion.
   - **a.** Nutrients
   - **b.** Enzymes
   - **c.** Water
   - **d.** Blood vessels

4. Your body's process of getting rid of wastes eliminated in a liquid form is called ___.
   - **a.** excretion
   - **b.** digestion
   - **c.** respiration
   - **d.** movement

5. The ___ is a sac that stores wastes from the kidneys.
   - **a.** stomach
   - **b.** bladder
   - **c.** heart
   - **d.** lungs

Match each definition on the left with the correct term.

6. chambers in the heart that pump blood to the lungs and body cells
   - **a.** arteries

7. blood vessels that carry blood away from the heart
   - **b.** bronchi

8. two short tubes that carry air from the trachea to the lungs
   - **c.** ventricles

9. waste that results from the breakdown of proteins
   - **d.** ureters

10. the tubes that carry wastes from the kidneys to the bladder
    - **e.** urea

Understanding What You Learned

1. How does the circulatory system move blood through your body?

2. How are gases exchanged in your body?

3. How is food digested in your body?

4. How does digested food move from the digestive tract to the cells?

5. Describe the function of the excretory system.

Applying What You Learned

1. What might happen if the valves in your heart didn't close properly?

2. Imagine that you are in a movie theater and smell popcorn. Describe how the smell of popcorn in the air is taken into your nose and lungs.

3. How do enzymes help in digestion?

4. What would happen if urea was not removed from the body?

 5. How do the systems in the human body work together to perform necessary life functions?

For Your **Portfolio**

Think of three different activities that you do or might like to do. Write down these three activities and list what body systems affect your ability to do each activity. Pick one activity and act it out. Have other students guess what the activity is and what systems are important to that activity.

CHAPTER

2

Exercise and Physical Fitness

Building a healthy body is important to building a healthy life. Physical fitness is a state of health that allows your body to perform many activities. Being physically fit does not mean that you have to be a star athlete or train for the Olympics. By developing the body to its individual potential, everyone can achieve physical fitness.

Developing physical fitness takes exercise, energy, and time. To exercise safely, it's important to know how your body is supported and moves. It is also important to understand how food and energy are important to physical fitness. By understanding your body and the importance of physical fitness, you can better understand the benefits of exercise.

The Big IDEA

Exercise helps to make the body healthy and physically fit.

SCIENCE INVESTIGATION

CHAPTER

Doing activities affects your level of physical fitness. Find out how in your *Activity Journal.*

Support and Movement

Find Out

- What the skeletal system does for your body
- How your joints affect the movement of your body
- How muscles move your body

Vocabulary

spongy bone
compact bone
bone marrow
joints
involuntary muscles
voluntary muscles
tendons

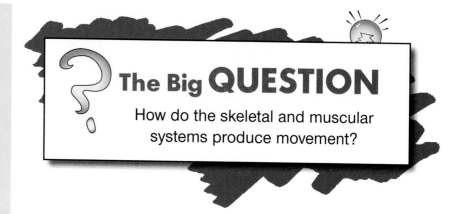

The Big QUESTION

How do the skeletal and muscular systems produce movement?

Your body is constantly in motion. Whether you are diving, snowboarding, or just sitting in a chair, your bones and muscles are working together to support and move your body. The many ways in which your body moves are due to the skeletal and muscular systems that work together in your body.

The Skeletal System

When you walk to school, play a sport, or do your homework, parts of your body must work together to produce the movement involved in each of these activities. To understand how your body moves, you must first understand the framework that supports the body.

The skeletal system is made up of the many bones in your body. The skeletal system has five main functions that it performs. The skeleton provides shape and support for your body. Your skeletal bones also protect many of the organs that are inside you, such as the heart, the lungs, and the brain. Another function that the skeleton performs is the storage of the body's supply of calcium and phosphorus. Finally, the skeletal system produces your body's supply of blood.

The skeletal and muscular systems work together to support and move your body.

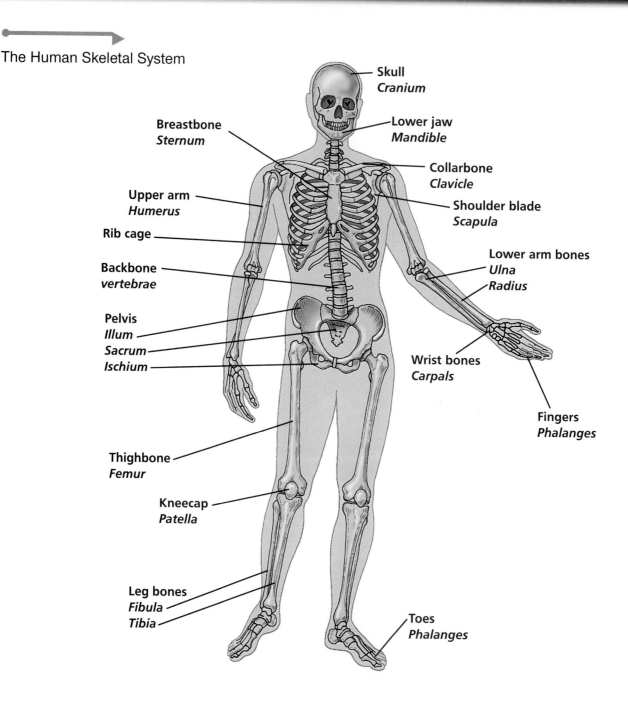

Skull
Cranium

Lower jaw
Mandible

Collarbone
Clavicle

Shoulder blade
Scapula

Breastbone
Sternum

Upper arm
Humerus

Rib cage

Backbone
vertebrae

Pelvis
Illum
Sacrum
Ischium

Lower arm bones
Ulna
Radius

Wrist bones
Carpals

Fingers
Phalanges

Thighbone
Femur

Kneecap
Patella

Leg bones
Fibula
Tibia

Toes
Phalanges

Your skeleton is composed of approximately 206 bones of many different sizes and shapes that together perform these many functions. Many of the major bones in your body are shown in the above diagram. Notice that the common name of a bone is usually different from the medical name. Your body has more bones than this diagram can show. For example, the skull, or cranium, you see in the diagram is made up of approximately 22 different bones.

Every bone in your body is alive. Like the other organs in your body, each bone is made up of cells that take in food and perform respiration. Bone cells have the same requirements for food and oxygen as the other cells in your body. Because bone cells are living, they can reproduce and make more bone. This results in bone growth. You know your bones grow because you are taller now than when you were younger.

Unlike the organs that make up the systems you studied in the last chapter, the bones that make up your skeletal system have living and nonliving parts. Living parts of bones include the many blood vessels in bone, the bone cells, and the nerve cells. The nonliving parts of bone are the calcium, phosphorus, and other minerals that are stored in bone. These nonliving minerals are what make your bones strong and hard.

Let's take a look at the parts that make up bone. Spongy bone, compact bone, and bone marrow can be found in most of the bones in your body. Each part has its own particular structure and function in bone.

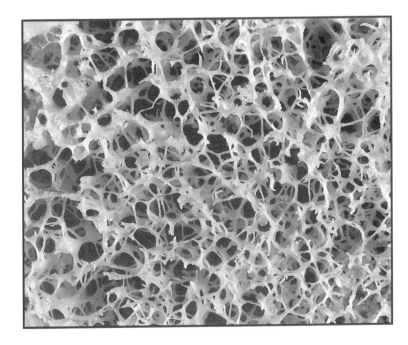

Spongy bone has many tiny openings that protect small blood vessels that run along the end of bones.

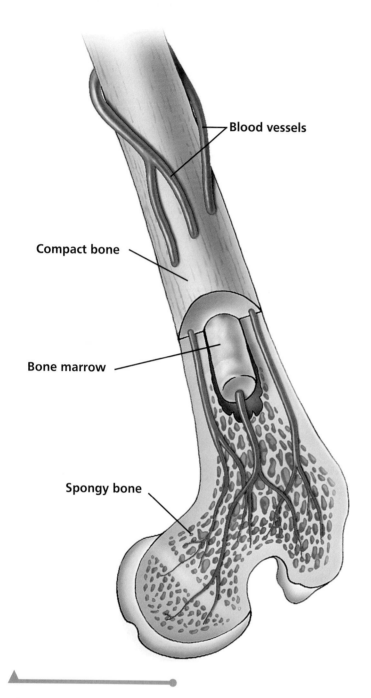

Like the many openings that hold water in sponges, the **spongy bone** in your body also has many openings. Spongy bone is found near the end of many bones. Unlike a sponge, spongy bone is hard. The many tiny openings in spongy bone help to protect the capillaries that run inside the ends of these bones.

Bones are also made up of **compact bone,** which is a thick outer layer filled with compounds of calcium and phosphorus. In addition to minerals, compact bone also contains living bone material, such as blood vessels, bone cells, and nerves. Compact bone has a dense, sturdy structure that contains elastic fibers, which keep bones flexible enough to withstand resistance without breaking.

Many bones have a hollow area, or cavity, inside of them. This space, as well as the spaces in spongy bone, is filled with a dark, gel-like substance called **bone marrow.** Bone marrow is a living part of the bone that makes blood cells. These cells are sent from your bones into the circulatory system to replenish your body's supply of blood.

Healthy bones are both hard and flexible. The arrangement of minerals and fibers in your bones gives them great strength. Your bones must be strong enough to withstand the forces

Most bones in your body have spongy bone, compact bone, and bone marrow. Each of these types of bone tissues have a particular structure and function in each bone.

that act on them. Think of how much force is exerted on your bones when you jump. When you jump upward, you must push against the ground with enough force to overcome the pull of gravity and lift your body weight. Your bones must be strong enough to enable this movement.

When landing from a jump, you hit the ground with a considerable force. What characteristics of your bones and your skeletal system make them able to absorb the forces of jumping and landing without breaking?

The minerals in your bones help to make them strong. However, your bones must also be lightweight enough for you to move. The arrangement of materials and spaces in spongy bone help keep your skeleton lightweight.

The spongy nature of the ends of bone helps you in another way. The ends of bone act as shock absorbers that spread the impact over a larger area. Running shoes with cushioned soles work like spongy bone to absorb shock.

Bones in your skeleton must be strong enough to keep from breaking due to the forces exerted upon them, such as the forces that your bones encounter when you jump and land from a jump.

Joints and Body Movement

Other areas of your skeletal system that absorb shock are **joints,** places where two or more bones meet or are held together. Forces that act on your body are concentrated in joints. There are many different kinds of joints in your body. Some joints allow movement and some do not. Look at the basketball player below to find out how many different kinds of joints are in your body.

Match the different types of joints with the examples on the basketball player.

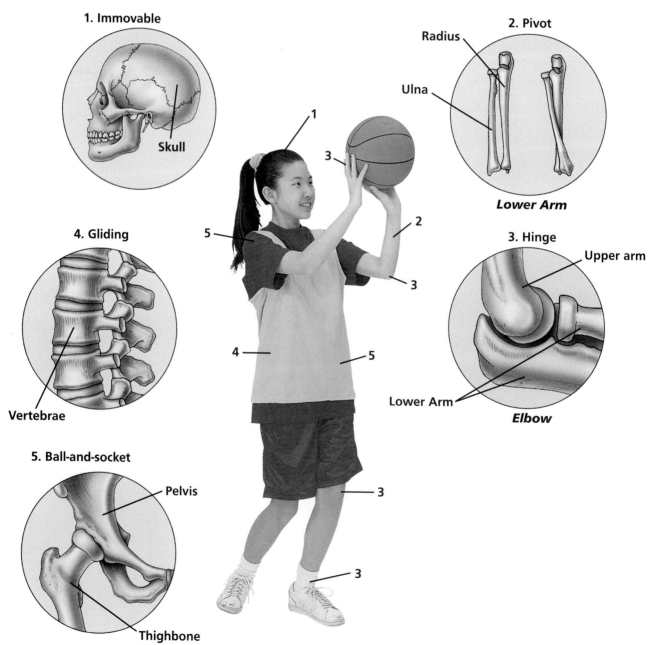

1. Immovable

Skull

2. Pivot

Radius

Ulna

Lower Arm

4. Gliding

Vertebrae

3. Hinge

Upper arm

Lower Arm

Elbow

5. Ball-and-socket

Pelvis

Thighbone

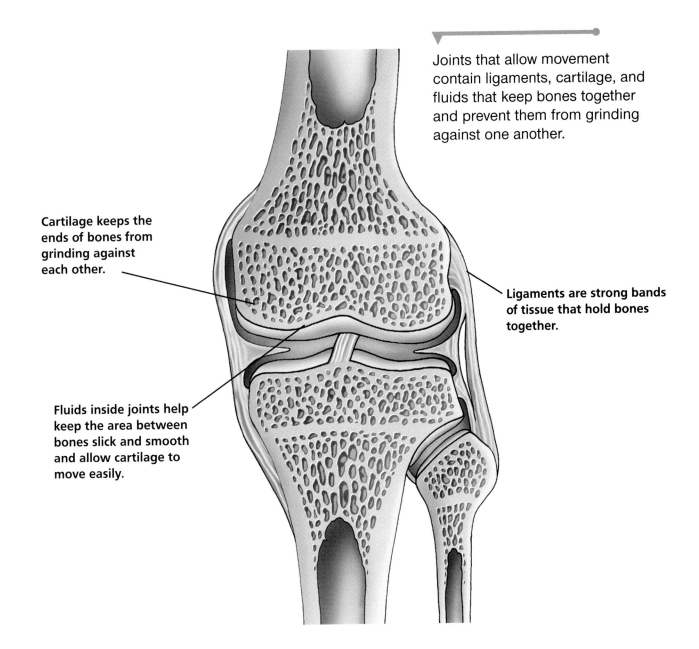

Joints that allow movement contain ligaments, cartilage, and fluids that keep bones together and prevent them from grinding against one another.

Cartilage keeps the ends of bones from grinding against each other.

Ligaments are strong bands of tissue that hold bones together.

Fluids inside joints help keep the area between bones slick and smooth and allow cartilage to move easily.

When you jump in the air, what keeps your bones from separating or bumping against one another? Bones in movable joints are held together with strong bands of tissue called ligaments. A thin layer of cartilage, a soft, flexible material, also can be found between bones. Cartilage keeps the ends of bones from grinding against each other. Joints also contain fluid that keeps the area between bones slick and smooth, and allows cartilage covering the ends of bones to move easily.

D47

Muscles Move Your Body

Your bones and muscles work together for movement in joints. Bones have no power to move by themselves. They need muscles to move them.

Skeletal Muscle

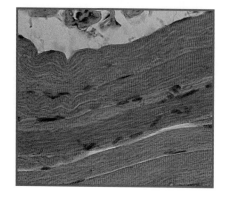

Cardiac Muscle

Smooth Muscle

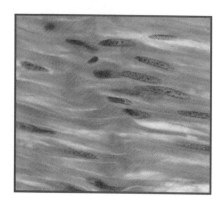

Arm

Heart

Intestine

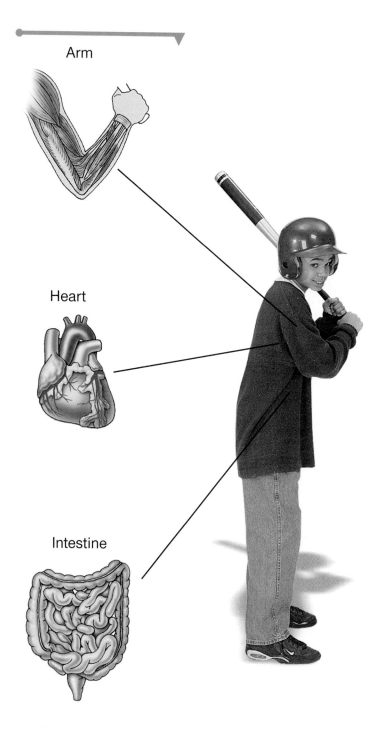

Muscle is a body tissue that changes its length and shape to cause movement. The kinds of movements muscles carry out depend on where the muscles are located.

The muscular system is made up of all the muscles in your body. Your muscular system is composed of three types of muscle: smooth, cardiac, and skeletal. Each type performs different functions in the body in different places.

The smooth muscle makes up the intestines, arteries, and many other body organs. Smooth muscle is involuntary muscle. **Involuntary muscles** are muscles you cannot control. You have no control over the working of your intestines or blood vessels. The cells of smooth muscle are longer and more spindle-shaped than the cells in other types of muscles.

The heart is the only organ in the body made up of cardiac muscle. Cardiac muscle is an involuntary muscle and is made of bundles of fibers. This muscle type looks striped. The cells in it form a tight weave that make this muscle very strong.

The skeletal muscles are voluntary muscles that move the bones of the skeleton. All external body movements are caused by skeletal muscles.

Voluntary muscles are those muscles you can control. If you decide to sit down, go for a walk, or jump rope, you are deciding what you want your skeletal muscles to do. The skeletal muscles are made of bundles of fibers and make up the majority of muscles in your body.

As the man pitches the ball, he and the boy on the opposite page have some muscles that can be controlled, called voluntary muscles. Some muscles, called involuntary muscles, are not controlled by the baseball players in the photos.

In tug-of-war, your biceps muscle is relaxed before you pull the rope and is contracted as you pull the rope. The triceps muscle is contracted before you pull and is relaxed as the rope is pulled.

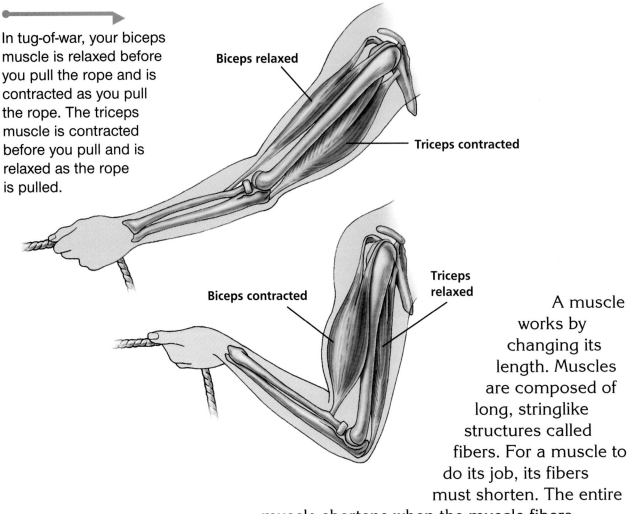

Biceps relaxed

Triceps contracted

Biceps contracted

Triceps relaxed

A muscle works by changing its length. Muscles are composed of long, stringlike structures called fibers. For a muscle to do its job, its fibers must shorten. The entire muscle shortens when the muscle fibers contract. The contraction of muscles allows you to move the bones that make up your skeleton. Muscles can only pull bones. They cannot push a bone into action.

In addition, skeletal muscles do not pull directly on the bones that they move. Rather, they are connected to bones by tendons. **Tendons** (ten′ dənz) are tough, connective tissues that attach muscles to bone. The tendons cause the bone to be pulled when the muscle contracts.

Let's look at how skeletal muscles work. Imagine you are playing tug-of-war. Look at the arm in the diagram above. Before you begin to pull on the rope, the muscles in your upper arm are relaxed. These muscle fibers have not yet contracted.

When your muscle fibers are working they contract. The bulging you see when a muscle is working is due to the thickening of muscle fibers as they shorten when they contract.

Because muscles can only shorten, it takes a pair of skeletal muscles working opposite of each other to move bones back and forth. When one muscle contracts, the opposite muscle relaxes. Look at the pair of skeletal muscles that you used in tug-of-war. As the muscle on the top of your arm—the biceps—contracts, the muscle on the back of your arm—the triceps—relaxes. Similarly, when the triceps contracts, the biceps relaxes. In order for your arm to pull in the game of tug-of-war, both of these muscles must work together to produce the movement needed for the game. Like these muscles, many of the muscles in your body work in pairs to produce movement.

The muscles, joints, and bones that make up your body work together in many ways to produce movement. Each of the many parts that make up your muscular and skeletal systems has its own unique structure and function that allows your body to move.

CHECKPOINT

1. What does the skeletal system do for your body?
2. How do your joints affect the movement of your body?
3. How do muscles move your body?
 How do the skeletal and muscular systems produce movement?

ACTIVITY

Investigating Muscles and Bones

Find Out

Do this activity to learn how muscles move bones.

Process Skills

Predicting
Observing
Communicating
Classifying
Inferring

WHAT YOU NEED

cooked chicken leg and thigh

forceps

waxed paper

plastic knife

hand lens

Activity Journal

WHAT TO DO

1. Predict what parts of the muscular and skeletal systems you will see in the chicken leg and thigh.

2. Place the cooked chicken leg on the waxed paper. Carefully remove the skin with the plastic knife and forceps.

3. Use the forceps to locate and observe muscles and bones in the leg and thigh. Notice how these parts are connected to each other.

4. Draw and label what you see.

5. Bend and straighten the leg and thigh at the joint. Observe what happens to the muscles.

6. Use the knife to cut the muscle away from the bone. Locate and observe the bones, joints, ligaments, and cartilage.

7. Draw and label these parts.

8. Classify the parts that you observed by recording which were part of the skeletal system and which were part of the muscular system.

9. Wash your hands.

CONCLUSIONS

1. What kind of joint did you find between the thigh bone and the lower leg of the chicken?

2. What parts did you find around the joints of the bones? How do these parts function?

ASKING NEW QUESTIONS

1. Identify which muscles contract and relax when a chicken lifts its leg to walk.

2. Infer how your leg is similar to a chicken leg in the way it moves.

SCIENTIFIC METHODS SELF CHECK

✔ Did I **predict** what parts of the muscular and skeletal systems I would find?

✔ Did I **observe** the muscles and bones in the chicken leg and thigh?

✔ Did I **classify** the parts of the chicken leg and thigh?

Physical Fitness

Find Out

- How exercise helps your body stay healthy
- How exercise increases strength and endurance
- What you should do to exercise safely

Vocabulary

physical fitness
exercise
strength
endurance
cardiovascular exercise
flexibility

The Big QUESTION

How does exercise help you achieve physical fitness?

What does "being fit" really mean? What characteristics would you use to describe someone who is physically fit? What characteristics would you use to describe someone who is not? Everyone can develop physical fitness.

Physical Fitness and Exercise

Your body performs many functions that allow you to live and grow. To maintain a healthy body, it is important for your body to get enough exercise, sleep, rest, and nutrients from a well-balanced diet. In the next chapter, we will explore how to maintain a well-balanced diet. In this lesson, we will explore how exercise helps maintain a healthy body.

You have learned that your muscular system produces movement by using your body's muscles. How does this movement help you to become physically fit?

There is no one way to become physically fit. **Physical fitness** is the level of health at which you have muscular endurance, flexibility, a well-conditioned heart, strength, and the right amount of body fat. Healthy muscles can assist your body in achieving this level of health.

Exercise is a regular series of movements that conditions your muscles. By exercising frequently, your body can achieve physical fitness. Regular exercise can increase your body's ability to do work. Exercise can prevent you from feeling tired, sore, or weak when you run or play hard. Sitting, standing, and walking are easier if your muscles are strong from regular exercise. Exercise can also help to strengthen your heart and lungs.

Exercise is a regular series of movements that conditions your muscles.

Strength and Endurance

You are building strength when your muscles exert a force at one time.

Endurance is your muscles' ability to exert force over time.

Strength is the ability of your muscles to exert a force. The greater your ability to exert a force, the stronger your muscles are. This force can be lifting an object or pushing against something. Muscle strength is the measure of how much force you can exert at a single time. Pushing or pulling against a force helps you develop muscle strength. When you row a boat, you use muscles to push the oars against the force of water. When you lift weights, you are pushing against gravity to lift an object from the floor or a stand. Whenever you ask your muscles to work as hard as they can at one time, you are building strength. Can you think of any other exercises that would help you build strength?

Endurance is a measure of the ability of your muscles to exert a force over a period of time. For example, doing one push-up may show that you have strength in your arm and shoulder muscles. Doing 50 push-ups one after the other shows that you have endurance as well as muscle strength.

Have you ever watched 100-m sprinters run? The starting pistol goes off, and they run as fast as they can for 100 m. They are asking their leg muscles to work hard so the runner can cross the set distance in the shortest time. They are asking their muscles to exert a great deal of force at one time.

Now compare this to something like an 800-m race. Long-distance runners must be fast but also able to keep running for a longer period of time than the sprinter. A long-distance runner must have endurance to keep running over a long period of time.

Endurance can also be considered as a level of fitness achieved by your heart and lungs. Do you recall how it feels to run so hard you were out of breath? Your heart was probably beating very fast and you were breathing rapidly. Your heart and lungs were trying to get oxygen to the parts of your body that needed it. Endurance for your heart and lungs refers to how quickly they can get oxygen to your body and then slow down to your normal heart and breathing rate after exercising.

Cardiovascular exercise is important in building endurance. **Cardiovascular exercise** is exercise that increases your heart and breathing rate for an extended period of time. For example, going up and down stairs for 20 minutes requires that your lungs get more oxygen and that your heart pump more blood and oxygen to your muscles. The more physically fit you are, the quicker your heartbeat and breathing rate return to their normal resting rate after exercising.

Did you know that simply walking up stairs instead of taking an elevator will help you improve your cardiovascular fitness? So will walking instead of taking the bus. Remember that exercise is the key to improving your cardiovascular endurance. The first step is to decide which type of endurance-building exercise you want to do. If improved endurance is your goal, then it is important to choose something you like to do. The best exercises are those that are enjoyable, build endurance, increase muscle strength, and improve flexibility all at the same time.

Cross-country skiing is a cardiovascular exercise that can increase your heart and breathing rate for an extended period of time.

Exercise Safety

Flexibility describes the ability of muscles and joints to move in their full range of motion. How do jumping jacks help increase your flexibility?

One way to avoid injury while exercising is by increasing your flexibility. **Flexibility** (fleks′ i bil′ ə tē) describes the ability of your muscles and joints to move within a full range of motion. When a person feels stiff, he or she could be feeling the result of poor flexibility. Stretching exercises help you to keep your muscles and joints flexible.

Flexibility helps you avoid injury while exercising. When you stretch the muscles in particular parts of your body, you are causing movement in some joints. For example, reaching toward the ceiling causes the joints in your shoulders to work. By causing slow, controlled movement in your joints and muscles, your body will slowly warm up. By warming up your joints and muscles before exercise, they will be less likely to tear or be strained by activity.

In addition to stretching, you also can achieve flexibility by exercising muscles in their full range of motion. When you are at home, pick up a can from your kitchen. Starting with your hand by your side, raise the can very slowly above your head while keeping your arm straight. Now slowly move your arm in the largest, widest circle you can make. By moving the can in your arm's widest circle, you exercised your arm's full range of motion.

By strengthening muscles in their full range of motion, your body will be able to move well in many different ways. For example, if the only exercise your arm muscles received was picking up your school bag in the morning, then you probably wouldn't be able to lift that same school bag high above your head without risking injury. By exercising your muscles in their full range of motion, you can avoid injury when you do activities that you do not normally do.

Exercise involves many parts of your body. To avoid injury, start your exercise routine by warming up and end it by cooling down.

Warming up is an important part of any vigorous exercise routine. To warm up, slowly move and stretch those muscles that you will be using. This allows your muscles to get used to an increased flow of blood and a greater demand of work. Basically, warming up is a short period of mild exercise. Once you have stretched your muscles and engaged them in mild activity, you can begin exercising.

Warming up prepares muscles and joints for exercise and can prevent injury.

The workout period is the time for you to increase your heart rate and breathing rate. To build cardiovascular and muscular endurance, exercise your body until your muscles feel tired. If you are just beginning to exercise, ten minutes may be enough.

Have your legs ever been so tired that they were wobbly? Your muscles were probably overworked and became too tired to perform properly. Although your muscles might be strong, muscular fatigue occurs when muscles cannot keep up the level of activity demanded of them. You should exercise your muscles so that they are tired but not fatigued.

Cooling down after exercising is important because it helps your body return to its normal level of activity. When you start to exercise, an increased amount of blood travels to the cells in your muscles. If you do not cool down, the muscles may tighten due to the abrupt change in the muscles' blood flow.

Your workout should increase your heart and breathing rate but should not fatigue your muscles.

Another way of avoiding injury is by exercising regularly. You should not set out on a 5-km race the first time that you exercise. You could injure yourself if you try to do too much without exercising regularly and preparing your body for what you want it to do.

Exercise is not something you do for a few months then stop. Regular exercise is important enough to your health that it should be a part of your normal routine. If you don't enjoy the exercise you choose, it will be harder to make it a part of your daily routine. The first step is to choose something active that you like to do. For instance, if you have a young dog that likes to run, maybe brisk walking or running with your dog is the form of exercise for you.

If you decide that running or brisk walking outdoors is the type of exercise you would like to start doing, there are some important safety tips you need to remember.

1. Exercise with a friend or family member. Do not walk or run by yourself.

2. Avoid walking or running when it is dark. If you do walk or run after dark, wear reflective clothing and take a flashlight.

3. Always tell someone where you are going, and pay attention to the time you are supposed to be back.

4. Carry a card with your name, address, and phone number and some spare change for phone calls.

No matter what type of exercise you decide to do, it is important to keep safety in mind. Exercise is supposed to help, not hurt you. Preparing your body for exercise by stretching, warming up, and cooling down is important in avoiding injury. The above safety tips can help to keep you safe outdoors, but there are also other factors that affect your safety as you exercise.

Whenever you exercise, your body will lose fluids as you sweat. Sweating is a way that the body helps to cool itself down. It is important to drink enough fluids, particularly water, to replace the fluids that you lose during exercise through perspiration. If your body does not have enough fluids to cool itself, your body could overheat and cause serious physical problems to occur.

Environmental conditions are also important to consider when exercising safely. If it is hot, drink more fluids. If it is cold, layers of clothing can keep your body warm, but allow for some layers to be removed if you get hot while exercising.

Finally, the proper equipment is also important to your safety. Proper-fitting protective gear designed for your activity should be worn, such as helmets, guards, and padding, to prevent injury. Some activities require special footwear and good footwear can prevent many leg or knee injuries. The most expensive shoes are not always the best. Shoes should be appropriate for the activity, fit well, and provide cushioning and support.

Exercise can greatly increase your level of physical fitness, but the benefits of exercise can be lost if injury occurs. By exercising safely, you can increase your body's strength, endurance, flexibility, and overall health.

Always remember to replace fluids lost during exercise.

CHECKPOINT

1. How does exercise help your body stay healthy?

2. How does exercise increase muscle strength and endurance?

3. What should you do to exercise safely?

 How does exercise help you achieve physical fitness?

ACTIVITY
Investigating Strength and Endurance

Find Out

Do this activity to learn how strength is different from endurance.

Process Skills

Measuring
Using Numbers
Communicating
Interpreting Data
Hypothesizing
Designing Investigations
Experimenting
Controlling Variables

WHAT YOU NEED

an empty plastic milk jug with a handle and lid

a watch or clock

balance

marker

600-mL beaker

water

funnel

Activity Journal

Activity Journal

WHAT TO DO

1. Measure 500 mL of water in the beaker and pour it through the funnel into the plastic jug.

2. With the marker, draw a line at the water level on the jug and mark it "500 mL." Repeat this process seven times. **Record** the amount of water that the jug now contains.

3. Hold the jug in one hand and rest your arm by your side. Try and lift the jug by bending your arm at your elbow. If the jug is too heavy, remove 500 mL and try again. If it is still too heavy, remove 500 mL more until you can lift the jug.

4. Record the amount of water that you were able to lift and record the **mass** of the jug with this amount of water.

5. Using this same jug and quantity of water, see if you can lift the jug above your head while keeping your arm straight. If you cannot, continue removing 500 mL of water until you can.

6. Record the amount of water and the **mass** of the jug that you were able to lift above your head.

7. Using this quantity of water, lift the jug as you did in Step 3 as many times as you can in two minutes or until your muscle feels tired.

8. Record the number of times you could lift the jug.

CONCLUSIONS

1. How was your muscle's endurance investigated?

2. How was your muscle's full range of motion used?

3. How did the amount of weight that you could lift change as you explored strength, flexibility, and endurance?

ASKING NEW QUESTIONS

1. Develop a testable question. Plan and conduct a simple investigation based on this question and write instructions that others can follow to carry out the procedure.

2. Identify the dependent and controlled variables in the investigation.

3. Prepare a report of your investigation that includes the tests conducted, data collected, or evidence examined, and the conclusions drawn.

SCIENTIFIC METHODS SELF CHECK

✔ Did I determine the **mass** of the jug?

✔ Did I **record** the amount of water in the jug?

Energy in Your Body

Find Out

- How your body converts and uses energy in performing its life processes
- How muscles convert and use energy for motion
- How homeostasis is affected by exercise

Vocabulary

potential energy
kinetic energy
metabolism
feedback
homeostasis

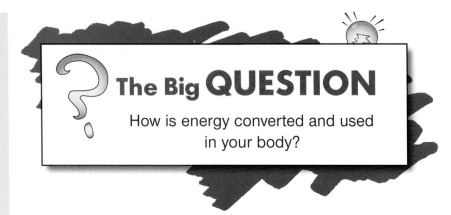

The Big QUESTION

How is energy converted and used in your body?

Your body needs continuous energy to work properly. Some activities require more energy than others. Even when you sleep, your body uses energy to keep itself functioning. Where does your body get energy? How is energy used?

Energy in Your Body

Have you ever watched a candle burn? Do you know what is needed in order for a candle to burn? A candle flame needs wax for fuel in order to burn. When the wax is gone, the flame goes out. The candle also needs oxygen in order for it to burn. Have you ever put out a candle flame by covering it? When you cover a candle, you eliminate its supply of oxygen. Once all of the oxygen inside the cover is used in the burning process, the flame goes out.

The cells in your body are similar to the candle in that they need fuel and oxygen. The fuel that your body uses is food. The food you digest in your small intestine is the fuel that is used by all the cells in your body. In order to burn this fuel, your cells need oxygen. Oxygen is taken into the body by the lungs and sent to all of your body's cells by the blood.

When oxygen is used to burn fuel, the energy in the fuel changes forms. Remember that the food that your body cells use is called glucose. The energy in glucose is stored as chemical energy. Oxygen burns glucose in respiration. When this happens, the chemical energy stored in glucose is converted into mechanical energy, which cells use to perform their life processes. For instance, muscle cells use this mechanical energy to contract the muscle. Thermal energy given off in the form of heat is also produced when glucose is burned in your body.

This process of converting chemical energy into mechanical energy must be present in living things in order for them to perform life processes. Respiration is important to all the parts of your body. Without respiration, the cells, tissues, and organs that make up your body would not be able to do the activities your body needs them to do.

Like a candle flame, the cells in your body use oxygen to burn fuel.

Muscles Convert and Use Energy

These sprinters on the blocks before the race have more potential chemical energy than while they are running.

When the sprinters run, their bodies use kinetic mechanical energy to contract their muscles for movement.

In the first chapter of this book, you learned that the different parts of cells in your body perform different functions that allow them to live and grow. You learned that mitochondria are the parts of cells responsible for performing the process of respiration.

Mitochondria are the powerhouses of the cells in your body. They are able to break down glucose and convert its chemical energy into energy the cells can use for their life processes.

The different kinds of cells that make up the tissues of your body have different numbers of mitochondria in them. Can you guess what type of cells have the greatest number of mitochondria? If you guessed the cells that make up muscle tissues, you were right! The number of mitochondria that can be found in a cell usually depends on the amount of energy that the cell needs to perform its job in your body.

The cells that make up your muscles need a great deal of energy to perform their job. Your muscles are responsible for all of your body's movement. In order to have enough energy to move your body, your muscle cells need many mitochondria. Some muscle cells have as many as one thousand mitochondria in one cell.

Your muscles need energy whenever they contract. For example, when you straighten your leg, your muscle uses energy. Muscles use the mechanical energy from respiration to contract. When the supply of glucose is used up in respiration, muscles can become tired and need to rest.

Before your muscles contract, glucose is stored as chemical potential energy. **Potential energy** is the energy stored in an object, such as the relaxed muscles in your leg. When your muscles contract, they use the energy that was stored as glucose. When your body converts glucose from chemical energy into mechanical energy, it transforms the potential energy into kinetic energy. **Kinetic energy** is the energy of objects in motion, in this case, the muscles and bones in your leg.

When muscles contract, such as when a ball is kicked, energy is needed. This energy comes from the mitochondria in muscle cells that perform cellular respiration.

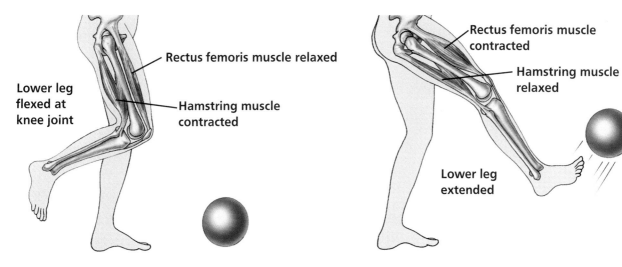

Lower leg flexed at knee joint

Rectus femoris muscle relaxed

Hamstring muscle contracted

Rectus femoris muscle contracted

Hamstring muscle relaxed

Lower leg extended

Muscles also produce thermal energy when they contract. The heat produced by respiration helps keep your body temperature constant. When your muscles work hard, your body temperature rises. Then your skin produces sweat that helps to cool your body down.

Your body is made up of many different muscles. The amount of energy that is required for each set of muscles to contract depends on many factors. These factors include the difficulty of the job that the muscle must perform and the fitness of the muscle that is being used. For example, your biceps uses more energy when it contracts to carry a bag of groceries than when it contracts to touch your nose. The more difficult the job, the more energy your muscles will use.

Muscular fitness also affects how much energy your body uses to perform an activity. For example, someone with fit biceps may be able to pick up a heavy bag of groceries with one hand. Another person of about the same body size may not be able to lift the bag of groceries because the biceps in that person's arm are not as strong. The person who was not able to lift the bag of groceries might have used more energy in trying to lift the bag than the person who could lift it easily with one hand. The person with physically fit biceps used less energy to lift the bag because that person's muscles are stronger. The amount of energy required for the biceps to contract is different for each of these two people, even though they both are using the same kind of muscle.

Did you know that you have more than 600 muscles in your body? Just a few of these muscles are shown in the diagram. The muscles that are shown are those that are often used in daily exercise. Look at the muscles in the diagram. What would affect how much energy these muscles need to perform their function? What processes provide these muscles with the energy they need to perform certain functions? How might you exercise these muscles?

Muscles in the Human Body

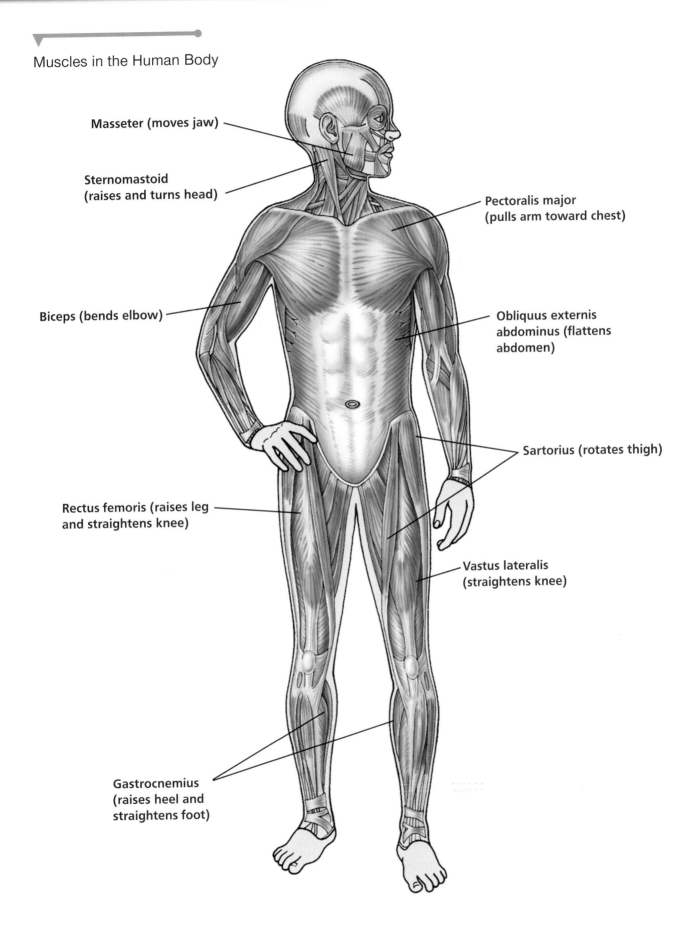

Masseter (moves jaw)

Sternomastoid
(raises and turns head)

Pectoralis major
(pulls arm toward chest)

Biceps (bends elbow)

Obliquus externis
abdominus (flattens
abdomen)

Sartorius (rotates thigh)

Rectus femoris (raises leg
and straightens knee)

Vastus lateralis
(straightens knee)

Gastrocnemius
(raises heel and
straightens foot)

Exercise and Homeostasis

Respiration is just one of the many types of chemical changes that occur in your body. You also learned that enzymes in your digestive tract speed up chemical changes that digest food. **Metabolism** is the total of all the activities of an organism that enable it to stay alive, grow, and reproduce. When your body goes through a growth spurt, your metabolic rate is usually very high. When you are resting or asleep, your rate of metabolism is lower than when you are active.

Systems of **feedback** regulate the metabolism in your body. You might know about some mechanical systems of feedback. One is the thermostat that controls the temperature of your home or school. If a room is too cold, the thermostat will turn on the heater. When the temperature in the room reaches a desired temperature, the heater will turn off. Feedback is a signal to a device that controls an activity. Sensors in the room send feedback to the thermostat to turn the heater off or on.

Your body regulates your temperature due to feedback it receives from the body. Sweat helps to cool the body down when its temperature increases.

In your body, feedback is a signal to increase, decrease, or maintain certain activities. When you exercise, your muscles use oxygen faster. Sensors in your body test the amounts of oxygen and carbon dioxide in your blood. Signals from these sensors are sent to your brain, which sends a message to the lungs directing them to breathe faster.

Feedback allows you to maintain a balanced state. **Homeostasis** (hṓ mē ō stā́ sis) is the tendency of an organism to adjust itself to maintain a balanced state. When your lungs are directed to breathe in more air or when your heart is told to beat faster, your body is working to achieve homeostasis.

Homeostasis is affected by muscular activity. If your body becomes too warm from exercise, your sweat glands are directed to release sweat. Sweat then moves out onto the skin and cools your body down. This process balances the heat produced by a greater amount of exercise to keep your body temperature at a normal level.

CHECKPOINT

1. How does your body convert and use energy to perform its life processes?
2. How do muscles convert and use energy for motion?
3. How is homeostasis affected by exercise?
   How is energy converted and used in your body?

ACTIVITY

Converting Energy

Find Out

Do this activity to learn how potential chemical energy can be converted to kinetic mechanical energy.

Process Skills

Measuring
Observing
Communicating
Inferring
Interpreting Data

WHAT YOU NEED

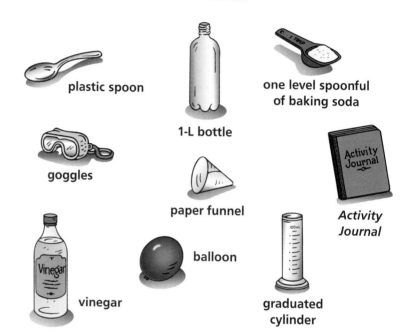

plastic spoon

1-L bottle

one level spoonful of baking soda

goggles

paper funnel

Activity Journal

vinegar

balloon

graduated cylinder

WHAT TO DO

1. Put on safety goggles.

2. Measure 60 mL of vinegar and pour it in the 1-L bottle.

3. Make a paper funnel and use it to put the baking soda inside the balloon. To keep the baking soda from dropping into the bottle, have another student pinch the middle of the balloon while you place the neck of the balloon around the bottle neck.

4. Lift the balloon up and shake the baking soda down into the vinegar.

5. Observe what happens and record your observations.

CONCLUSIONS

1. Infer where the potential chemical energy was stored.
2. What object did the kinetic mechanical energy move?

ASKING NEW QUESTIONS

1. How was the energy conversion in the activity like the energy conversion that takes place in your muscles?
2. What activity do all cells perform that converts potential chemical energy into kinetic mechanical energy?

SCIENTIFIC METHODS SELF CHECK

✔ Did I accurately **measure** the vinegar and baking soda?

✔ Did I **infer** where the potential chemical energy was stored?

✔ Did I **interpret the data** I collected?

CHAPTER
2

Review

Reviewing Vocabulary and Concepts

Write the letter of the answer that completes each sentence.

1. Places where two or more bones meet are ___.
   a. tendons
   b. potential energy
   c. spongy bone
   d. joints

2. ___ is a body tissue that can cause movement by changing its length and shape.
   a. Muscle
   b. Endurance
   c. Compact bone
   d. Metabolism

3. The ability of your muscles and joints to move within their normal range of motion is ___.
   a. flexibility
   b. exercise
   c. endurance
   d. homeostasis

4. The tendency of an organism to adjust itself to maintain a balanced state is ___.
   a. voluntary muscle
   b. flexibility
   c. kinetic energy
   d. homeostasis

Match each definition on the left with the correct term.

5. type of bone with many tiny openings that is usually found near the ends of many bones

6. a gel-like substance inside of bones

7. a tough, connective tissue that attaches muscles to bone

8. a regular series of movements that strengthen your body

9. the energy of objects in motion

10. the total of all the activities of an organism that enable it to stay alive, grow, and reproduce

a. metabolism

b. tendon

c. kinetic energy

d. spongy bone

e. exercise

f. bone marrow

Understanding What You Learned

1. What are the five main functions of the skeletal system?

2. What characteristics of your bones and skeletal system help them absorb impact?

3. What are the three types of muscle in your muscular system?

4. Why are warming up and cooling down important parts of exercise?

5. What does the contraction of muscles allow your body to do?

Applying What You Learned

1. Which joints are you using when you kick a ball?

2. If you twist your knee, which parts of your knee could you have damaged?

3. You're riding your bike down the street and a squirrel runs in front of you. When you brake to avoid the squirrel, are you using voluntary or involuntary muscles?

4. Running is a good exercise because it works so many parts of the body. What body parts do you use to run?

 5. How does exercise help to make the body healthy and physically fit?

For Your **Portfolio**

Imagine that you are planning a three-week bicycling trip across the United States. Because the trip is physically demanding, design a training program. Discuss which activities in your training increase muscle strength, flexibility, and endurance. Also include what equipment you need and what safety precautions you should follow.

CHAPTER 3

Nutrition and Health

Everyone has different eating habits and enjoys different kinds of foods. Each of these foods provides energy for your body. It is important to provide your body with enough energy for your cells to perform their life functions.

You must also supply your body with the right kinds of foods in the right amounts. Food contains many substances that your body needs. If these substances are not in your diet, your body may not function properly. Many different kinds of foods can make up a healthful diet as long as they provide your body with the energy and nutrients that it needs to function properly.

The Big IDEA

Nutritious food is important for growth and health.

CHAPTER SCIENCE INVESTIGATION

Learn why nutrients are important in a healthy diet. Find out how in your *Activity Journal.*

Nutrition

Find Out

- What nutrients in food your body needs
- What nutrients do for your body
- How the energy in food is measured

Vocabulary

nutrition
nutrients
carbohydrates
proteins
fats
vitamins
minerals
Calorie

The Big QUESTION

What makes up a healthful diet?

A car needs fuel to keep running. Like a car, your body also needs fuel to keep running. You and the motor in a car need the right amount of fuel and oxygen to keep working properly. Without the proper balance of these substances, your body and the motor would slow down or stop. Food is the fuel that keeps your body running.

Nutrients and Your Body

To keep your body cells running properly, you must provide them with the substances they need for growth and repair. Your cells also need materials that will provide the energy for their life processes. Most of these materials are supplied to your cells in the food you eat. The study of food and its use by the body is called **nutrition** (nσσ trish′ ən). The chemicals in food that are needed by cells are called **nutrients** (nσσ′ trē ənts). There are about 50 nutrients that your body needs.

Many of the nutrients your body needs are made within your body. There are six classes of nutrients, however, that are needed from the food you eat. It is not only important to get these nutrients, but it is also important to get them in the right amounts.

A healthy body needs the right amounts of six nutrients daily. These nutrients are proteins, carbohydrates, fats, vitamins, minerals, and water. Getting a balance of nutrients is important. If even one nutrient class is missing, your body will not function as it should. Yet getting too much of any one could also cause problems.

You can use the United States Department of Agriculture (USDA) Food Guide Pyramid as a guide for getting the right balance of nutrients. Such a diet would be made up largely of foods from the bottom of the pyramid like bread, cereal, rice, potatoes, and pasta. These carbohydrates give your body much of the energy it needs. The diet would also include many vegetables and fruits for vitamins as well as carbohydrates and fiber.

Use the Food Guide Pyramid as a guide to healthful eating. The amount of food you need from each group decreases as you move up the pyramid.

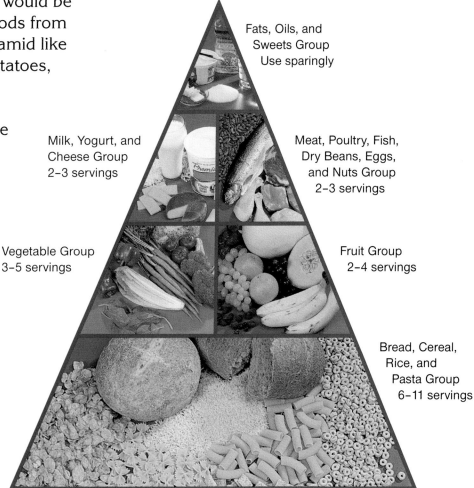

Fats, Oils, and Sweets Group Use sparingly

Milk, Yogurt, and Cheese Group 2–3 servings

Meat, Poultry, Fish, Dry Beans, Eggs, and Nuts Group 2–3 servings

Vegetable Group 3–5 servings

Fruit Group 2–4 servings

Bread, Cereal, Rice, and Pasta Group 6–11 servings

As you move up the pyramid, notice that you need smaller amounts of protein. Your body does not store protein, so it is important to eat protein-rich food every day. Milk and milk products, like cheese and yogurt, also give your body protein. You need the least amount of fats. Extra fats and sugar are stored in the body as fat.

If the proper amounts of foods and the right nutrients are consumed, your body will likely have more energy available for activities over a longer period of time. Just because foods are eaten together does not mean your body will use them at the same time. That is because some nutrients take longer to digest than others.

Sugar, vitamins, and water change very little as they pass through the digestive system. Complex carbohydrates, such as bread and pasta, take a little longer because they must be broken down into starches, then into sugars. Meats containing large amounts of proteins take even longer to digest than carbohydrates. Fats are digested very slowly. Because foods digest at different rates, a balanced meal will keep you feeling energetic for a long time. Sugar from fruits will give you a quick jolt of energy, whereas meat with fat and protein might still be churning in your stomach. By the time the quick energy is used up, the energy from fats is available.

Because foods digest at different rates, a balanced meal will keep you feeling energetic for a long time.

What Nutrients Do

Each nutrient does a special job in your body. **Carbohydrates** (kar bō hī′ drāts) give your body most of its "quick" energy. Sugar and starch are two kinds of carbohydrates. The supply of carbohydrates is the first to be used up when your body needs energy.

Proteins are nutrients that build and repair body parts. Proteins also make up large parts of tissues, such as bone, muscle, and skin. Foods such as meat, eggs, beans, and nuts supply your body with protein.

Fat is another nutrient that provides large amounts of energy in your body. **Fats** are nutrients that carry vitamins A, D, E, and K throughout the body, can be used by the body to build nerves, and can be stored under the skin as a supply of energy.

Although water does not provide material for growth or energy, you need more of it than any other nutrient. Most of your body is made of water. Water also distributes nutrients throughout your body.

Vitamins are chemical compounds needed in small amounts for cellular respiration. **Minerals** are nutrients needed in small amounts that help regulate chemical reactions in your body. Minerals and vitamins are necessary for survival.

Each vitamin and mineral does a different job. For example, vitamin D strengthens bones and teeth. Iron makes your red blood cells healthy. Vitamins also help to release energy from carbohydrates, fats, and proteins. Without vitamins, the body cannot fully use other nutrients. Take a look at the sources and functions of some vitamins and minerals in the charts that follow.

Carbohydrates

Proteins

Fats

Vitamins and minerals

Food Sources and Functions of Vitamins

Name	Sources	Function	Daily Value
vitamin A	milk, butter, margarine, eggs, liver, leafy green and yellow vegetables	normal growth in children, good vision, healthy skin and hair	5000 I.U.*
vitamin B_1 (thiamine)	cereals, fish, lean meat, liver, milk, poultry, green vegetables	proper function of heart and nervous system, prevents beriberi	1.5 mg
vitamin B_2	eggs, bread, cereals, leafy green vegetables, lean meat, liver, dried yeast, milk	healthy skin, prevents sensitivity of eyes to light, building and maintaining tissues	1.7 mg
vitamin B_6 (pyridoxine, pyridoxamine)	wheat germ, vegetables, dried yeast, meat, whole grain cereals	healthy teeth, blood vessels, red blood cells, and nervous system	2 mg
niacin (B_3) (niacinamide)	lean meat, liver, dried yeast, cereals and bread, eggs, green vegetables	prevents pellagra and appetite loss, aids nervous system and food conversion to energy	20 mg
vitamin C (ascorbic acid)	citrus fruits, berries, tomatoes, cabbage, green vegetables	prevents scurvy, builds strong body cells and blood vessels	60 mg
vitamin D (includes D_2, D_3, and D_4)	vitamin D fortified milk, cod liver oil, salmon, tuna, egg yolk	prevents rickets, aids use of calcium and phosphorus	400 I.U.
vitamin E (tocopherols)	vegetable oils, whole grain cereals	prevents damage to red blood cells	30 I.U.

* International Unit

Some Minerals Needed by the Human Body

Mineral	Some sources	Some functions	Daily Value
calcium	milk and milk products, leafy green vegetables, cheese, sardines, peanuts, dried beans	maintains strong bones and teeth; important for nerves, muscles, and blood; aids nervous system	800–1200 mg
chlorine	table salt, cheese, cured meats, kelp, olives	helps form stomach acid used in digestion; helps blood carry carbon dioxide to lungs	No Daily Value
iodine	iodized table salt, seafood	used to make thyroid hormones; promotes growth	80–150 mg
iron	liver, lean meats, raisins, beans and peas, whole grain products, egg yolk	carries oxygen as part of hemoglobin in blood; promotes resistance to disease	10–18 mg
magnesium	grapefruit, lemons, nuts, seeds, dark green vegetables	helps regulate body temperature; helps regulate muscles, nerves, and blood; may help fight depression	300–400 mg
phosphorus	foods in meat group, milk, cheese, whole grain products	needed for strong bones and teeth; used in muscle functions and cell wall formation	800–1200 mg
potassium	bananas, avocados, orange juice, leafy vegetables	helps maintain fluid levels in cells; needed for nerve impulses; aids in elimination of wastes	3500 mg
sodium	table salt, cheese, other foods with added salt, bacon, carrots	helps regulate fluid levels in body; needed for nerve impulses	2400 mg
sulfur	meats, milk, eggs, beans and peas, fish, cabbage	used in synthesis of some amino acids; fights bacterial infections	No Daily Value
zinc	seafoods, meats, cereals, nuts, vegetables	used to make certain enzymes; needed for growth of tissues; helps in healing wounds	15 mg

Energy in Food Can Be Measured

All the energy you have comes from food. Your body needs energy for all its activities. Even when you aren't moving, your heart is pumping, your lungs are inhaling and exhaling, your digestive system is breaking down foods, and new cells are forming. Your digestive system is constantly changing food into a form your body can use.

A **Calorie** is a measure of the energy in food. Foods differ in the amount of energy, or Calories, they contain. Foods high in Calories provide a lot of energy. Low-Calorie foods provide less energy.

Your body needs a certain amount of Calories each day to provide your body cells with enough energy to perform their life processes. How many Calories do you need a day? The answer to this question is not a simple one. Your age, body size, gender, and daily activities are all important in determining how many Calories your body needs. The easiest way to receive enough Calories is to eat different kinds of healthful foods in the quantities recommended on the Food Guide Pyramid.

The kinds of activities and lifestyle you have also affect the amount of Calories you need each day. If you walk to school each day, you will need more Calories than if you ride a bus. The greater the amount of energy your body uses in activities, the more Calories you will need.

When the number of Calories taken in equals the number of Calories used, your body weight will remain about the same. If you take

Your body needs energy for all its activities.

Activity	Calories used per hour
Basketball	500
Bicycling	210–660
Golfing	150–360
Football	500
Housework	180–240
Jogging	500–800
Lawn mowing	250–480
Raking leaves	300–360
Sitting	100
Cross-country skiing	600–660
Snow shoveling	420–480
Swimming	500–700
Tennis	420–480
Volleyball	350
Walking	150–480

in more Calories than you use, you will gain weight. The extra Calories will be stored in your body as fat. If you take in fewer Calories than you use, you will lose weight.

The best way to reach the ideal body weight for you is to exercise regularly and eat healthful, balanced meals that provide your body with the nutrients it needs.

CHECKPOINT

1. What nutrients in food does your body need?

2. What do nutrients do for your body?

3. How is energy in food measured?

 What makes up a healthful diet?

ACTIVITY

Investigating Protein in Milk

Find Out

Do this activity to learn how much protein is in milk.

Process Skills

Measuring
Observing
Communicating
Interpreting Data
Using Numbers
Inferring

WHAT YOU NEED

skim milk

vinegar

graduated cylinder

two 250-mL beakers

dropper

cheesecloth

Activity Journal

stirring rod or plastic straw

funnel

WHAT TO DO

1. Measure 100 mL of warm skim milk in the graduated cylinder. Pour the milk into a beaker. Observe and record the amount of milk.

2. Add 20 drops of vinegar to the milk. Mix the milk and vinegar with a stirring rod or plastic straw.

3. Stir until the milk separates into a solid white part and a liquid part.

4. Line a funnel with a single layer of wet cheesecloth. Place the funnel so that the second beaker is below it.

5. Pour the milk into the funnel and wait until all the liquid has drained through the cheesecloth.

6. **Measure** the volume of the liquid in the graduated cylinder. **Record** the volume.

7. The solid material in the cheesecloth is protein. **Observe** its color and texture. **Record** your observations.

CONCLUSIONS

1. What do you think caused the milk to separate?

2. How much protein was in your sample of milk? Determine the percentage of protein in your milk sample by dividing the volume of protein by the volume of milk in your sample.

ASKING NEW QUESTIONS

1. How is protein important in your diet?

2. **Infer** what type of mixture milk is.

SCIENTIFIC METHODS SELF CHECK

✔ Did I **record** my observations?

✔ Did I **interpret the data** I collected?

✔ Did I **calculate** the percentage of protein in milk?

Growth and Changing Dietary Needs

Find Out

- How your dietary needs change as you grow older
- Why some people might need nutritional supplements
- How your bones grow and change as you grow older

Vocabulary

dietary needs
nutritional deficiency
nutritional supplement
vegetarian

The Big QUESTION

How does growth affect the human body?

By eating a variety of healthful foods, just about everyone can get all of the nutrients the body needs. But that doesn't mean everyone needs the same foods in the same amounts. People of different ages have different dietary needs. How will your dietary needs change as you get older?

Changing Dietary Needs

Your body changes constantly. While you are growing, more and more cells are added to those you already have. Food provides the nutrients that the billions of cells in your body need to live and grow. You have many more cells now than you did when you were a baby.

Growth is not just a matter of size. As a baby, you may not have had any hair. You couldn't sit up or stand or talk. You couldn't digest most foods. As your cells multiplied, they combined and developed in different ways to build the person you are today.

And you are not finished yet. You will grow taller. You will gain weight. You will look different, be different, and be able to do different things at different ages. It is not surprising, then, that your dietary needs will change, too. **Dietary needs** are the nutritional needs of the body that allow it to perform its life processes and maintain good health.

Dietary needs change as your body grows, changes, and matures.

Babies need many nutrients so that their bodies can grow and develop properly.

Knowing the dietary needs of different age groups will help you make better choices about what you eat as you grow older. What you eat at each age will affect your health for the rest of your life.

All the nutrients new babies need are usually supplied in milk from their mothers or special infant formulas sold in stores. Babies need many nutrients so that their bodies can grow and develop properly. During the early stages of growth, nutrients are particularly important to brain and bone development. At about six months, some babies start to eat iron-fortified cereals and strained fruits and vegetables in addition to formula or milk.

For toddlers and preschoolers, fats continue to be important for brain development. Milk is an important source of calcium and vitamin D. Both are needed for proper bone growth.

As with all people, toddlers and preschoolers need a balanced diet, one with about four servings of breads and cereals, four or five

Toddlers and preschoolers need a balanced diet for their bodies to grow and develop properly. At this age, many more foods can be digested compared to those that babies can digest.

servings of fruits and vegetables, and one or two servings of meat or another protein source.

School-aged children also need a balanced diet with two or three servings of meat or another protein source, four servings of bread and cereal, and four or five servings of fruits and vegetables daily. They can also switch to low-fat milk. They can get the fats they need from meat and other protein sources. Two eight-ounce glasses of milk a day can provide minerals for their growing bones.

Like infants, teenagers and young adults need a lot of milk because they are growing very fast. They need about four glasses a day. Because their bodies are larger and growing quickly, they need larger portions of proteins than they did when they were ten years old and younger.

Adults need a balanced, low-fat, high-fiber diet. That means they need to eat plenty of fruits, vegetables, and whole grains. They need smaller amounts of meat or other protein sources. Women who become pregnant especially need to make sure they are getting the vitamins and minerals they need. A deficiency in certain vitamins and minerals can interfere with an unborn baby's development. A **nutritional deficiency** is a shortage of a nutrient that the body needs in your diet.

School-aged children need a balanced diet that provides lots of energy for activities.

Teenagers need to provide the right amount of nutrients for their quickly growing bodies.

Adults need a balanced, low-fat, high-fiber diet.

Nutritional Supplements

Getting a daily dose of vitamins is critical to your health, no matter how old you are. Does that mean you should be taking a nutritional supplement, or vitamin and mineral pill? Probably not. A **nutritional supplement** is an amount of vitamins or minerals that is taken as a liquid or pill in addition to the food in a person's diet. If you are eating a balanced diet, taking extra vitamins and minerals won't necessarily make you stronger or healthier.

Nutritional supplements only help when you have a nutritional deficiency or shortage of a nutrient in your diet. If you do not eat balanced meals, have a restricted diet, have a food allergy, or are a **vegetarian,** that is, someone who does not eat meat or animal products, you may need a supplement. Your doctor will tell you if you do.

Bone Growth in Humans

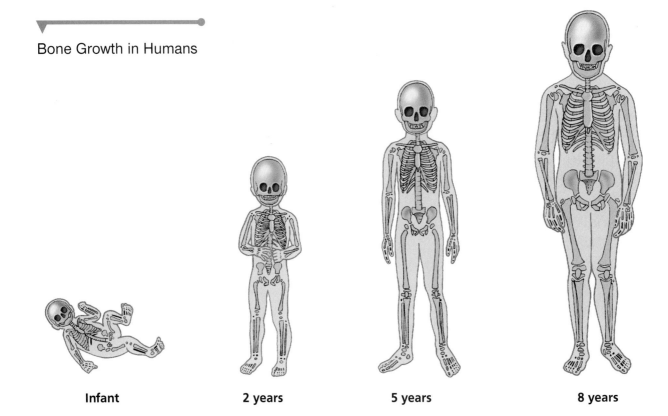

| Infant | 2 years | 5 years | 8 years |

Bone Development

Throughout your life, the bones that make up your skeleton change in many ways. You now know that the dietary needs of some age groups are different from others. You might have noticed that some of these dietary needs were different because of the bone growth that normally takes place during certain times in a human's life.

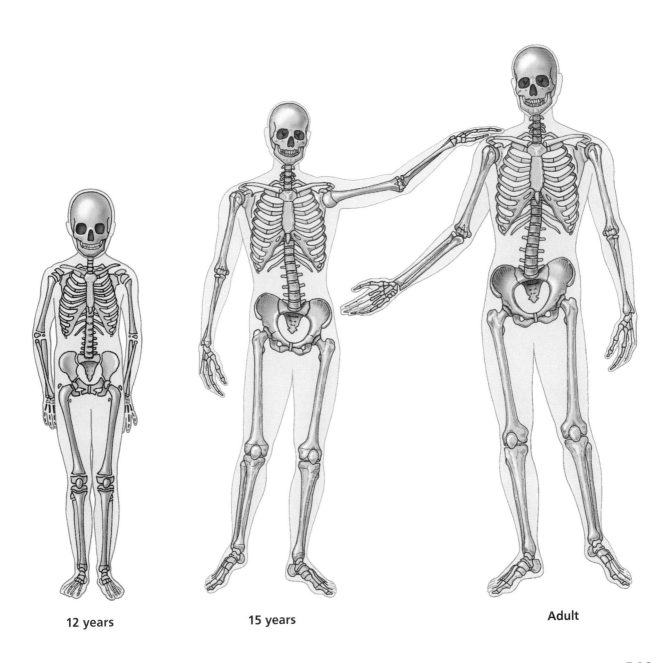

12 years   15 years   Adult

Bone tissue, like other tissues in your body, is made up of living cells. When bone cells reproduce and make more bone, bone growth can occur. The growth of your bones allows you to move in ways that you could not when you were an infant. Bone growth also changes your shape and allows you to grow taller than you were as a baby.

Not only does the size of your bones change as you grow, but the hardness of some bones can also change. The X-ray photos on this page show the way that cartilage in the hand is gradually replaced by bone as people age.

All bone begins as a tough, rubbery substance called cartilage. As a person ages, most of his or her cartilage is gradually

The X-ray images of human hands show that cartilage is gradually replaced by bone.

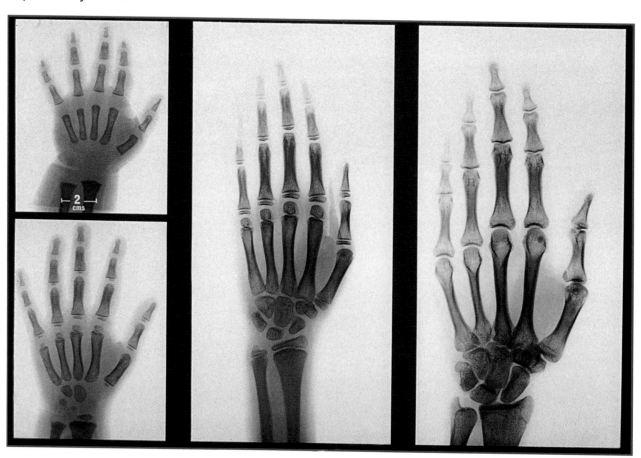

replaced by hard bone. If you look from left to right across the X-ray photos, you can notice that many of the bones in the hand look more defined in the adult compared to the bones in the small children. This is due to the replacement of cartilage with bone as a child becomes an adult.

There are many different ways that your body grows and changes as you get older. Throughout your entire life, changes take place in your body. The changes that one person may experience as he or she grows may be somewhat different from the changes that take place in another person of the same age and gender.

It is important to remember that there are many different body types that people can have. Some people are taller than others. Some people have a bigger bone structure than other people. These characteristics, along with many others, make every person unique.

CHECKPOINT

1. How do your dietary needs change as you grow older?

2. When might you need a nutritional supplement?

3. How do your bones grow and change as you age?

 How does growth affect the human body?

ACTIVITY

Identifying Vitamin C Content

Find Out

Do this activity to learn which kinds of juices contain vitamin C.

Process Skills

Measuring
Predicting
Controlling Variables
Observing
Communicating
Experimenting

WHAT YOU NEED

indophenol solution

dropper

ten test tubes

test tube rack

graduated cylinder

masking tape and pen

ten bottles or jars containing water, orange juice, pineapple juice, apple juice, tomato juice, cranberry juice, lime juice, lemon juice, carrot juice, and grapefruit juice

Activity Journal

WHAT TO DO

1. Using the masking tape and pen, label the test tubes 1 through 10.

2. Measure 5 mL of indophenol solution into each test tube. Indophenol is a blue liquid that turns colorless when vitamin C is present. The more vitamin C in a juice, the less juice is required to change the color of the indophenol solution.

 Safety! *Wear goggles. Do not eat or drink the solution.*

D96

3. **Predict** which juices contain vitamin C and which juices you think will have the most vitamin C. **Record** your predictions.

4. Add 20 drops of water to test tube 1. **Record** your observations.

5. Begin adding orange juice, one drop at a time, to test tube 2. **Record** the number of drops needed to change the color of the indophenol solution.

6. Using the remaining test tubes, repeat Step 5 for the other juices. For each juice, **record** the number of drops needed to turn the indophenol colorless.

CONCLUSIONS

1. How did your predictions compare to your observations?

2. Which juices appear to contain vitamin C? How do you know?

3. Which juices do not contain vitamin C? How do you know?

ASKING NEW QUESTIONS

1. Why do you think the amount of vitamin C varies in some fruit juices?

2. What might be a good way to get vitamin C in your diet without taking vitamin supplements?

SCIENTIFIC METHODS SELF CHECK

✔ Did I **predict** which juices contain vitamin C?

✔ Did I accurately **record** my observations?

✔ Did I **experiment** to find out which juices contain vitamin C?

LESSON 3

Nutrition-Related Diseases

Find Out

- Why nutrients are important
- What diseases are related to nutrition
- What some health problems related to food or digestion are

Vocabulary

malnutrition
deficiency disease
rickets
beriberi
goiter
iron deficiency anemia
heart disease
diabetes
hypoglycemia

The Big QUESTION
How can nutrition affect health?

Years ago, some sailors on long voyages would become very ill. Some sailors became extremely weak with gums that bled, teeth that fell out, and skin that bruised easily. Many sailors died from this mysterious illness. Eventually the cause and cure of this terrible disease called scurvy were discovered. The sailors suffering from scurvy were missing an important nutrient that their bodies needed to perform properly.

Nutrients Are Important for Health

In the last two lessons, you have learned that nutrients are used by your body to perform important functions and that some of your dietary needs change. Without certain nutrients your body will not work properly. **Malnutrition** is the result of not getting enough nutrients for the body to function properly.

There are many factors that can cause malnutrition. Some people suffer from malnutrition because they cannot get enough nourishing food or cannot get the proper balance of foods. Some individuals have illnesses or other physical problems that prevent their bodies from digesting or using nutrients properly. For other people, the cause of malnutrition is due to poverty. For still others, malnutrition is caused by poor eating habits. Regardless of the reason, the results are the same: the body does not get the nutrients it needs to function properly. Your body needs a balanced diet of different foods that, together, provide the right amounts of all the essential nutrients.

Labels today can inform people of the nutrients found in food they buy. The nutrients are listed in terms of Daily Value. Daily Value is the maximum daily intake of nutrients recommended for a 2000-Calorie-per-day diet. The percent Daily Value on a food label shows how much of the Daily Value one serving of the food contains. This is the amount for an average person, not necessarily what your individual body needs. But this information, along with a listing of ingredients on packages, can help you learn what nutrients different foods contain or do not contain.

Shoppers who take time to read labels can find out about the nutritional value of foods they buy.

Serving Size ¾ cup (30g)
Servings Per Container About 11

Amount Per Serving	Whole Grain Total	with ½ cup skim milk
Calories	110	150
Calories from Fat	10	10
	% Daily Value**	
Total Fat 1g*	1%	1%
Saturated Fat 0g	0%	0%
Polyunsaturated Fat 0g		
Monounsaturated Fat 0g		
Cholesterol 0mg	0%	1%
Sodium 190mg	8%	11%
Potassium 100mg	3%	9%
Total Carbohydrate 24g	8%	10%
Dietary Fiber 3g	11%	11%
Sugars 5g		
Other Carbohydrate 16g		
Protein 3g		
Vitamin A	10%	15%
Vitamin C	25%	25%
Calcium	25%	40%
Iron	100%	100%
Vitamin D	10%	25%
Vitamin E	100%	100%
Thiamin	100%	100%
Riboflavin	100%	110%
Niacin	100%	100%
Vitamin B₆	100%	100%
Folic Acid	100%	100%
Vitamin B₁₂	100%	110%
Pantothenic Acid	100%	100%
Phosphorus	8%	20%
Magnesium	6%	10%
Zinc	100%	100%
Copper	4%	4%

* Amount in Cereal. A serving of cereal plus skim milk provides 1g total fat, less than 5mg cholesterol, 260mg sodium, 300mg potassium, 30g total carbohydrate (11g sugars) and 7g protein.
** Percent Daily Values are based on a 2,000 calorie diet. Your daily values may be higher or lower depending on your calorie needs:

	Calories:	2,000	2,500
Total Fat	Less than	65g	80g
Sat Fat	Less than	20g	25g
Cholesterol	Less than	300mg	300mg
Sodium	Less than	2,400mg	2,400mg
Potassium		3,500mg	3,500mg
Total Carbohydrate		300g	375g
Dietary Fiber		25g	30g

Deficiency Diseases

When your body does not get the nutrients it needs for a long period of time, a **deficiency disease** can develop. The lack of just one nutrient can seriously affect your health. Deficiency diseases have been discovered for 26 of the nutrients your body needs. Each of these diseases can be cured by providing adequate amounts of the nutrient in the diet.

More than 100 years ago, many children worked in factories all day. Some of these children suffered from rickets because they did not get enough sunlight or vitamin D in their diets.

Some deficiency diseases are caused by the lack of a certain vitamin. In the case of early sailors, a lack of vitamin C was the cause of scurvy—the illness that devastated crews on long voyages. In about 1740, a ship's doctor discovered that sailors who visited tropical islands and ate citrus fruits didn't get scurvy. After that, sailors packed oranges, lemons, and limes on long voyages. In 1928, another doctor discovered that the lack of vitamin C was the cause of scurvy.

Rickets is a vitamin D deficiency disease that causes the bones to become soft and misshapen. Your body gets vitamin D from some foods but mostly from exposing the skin to sunlight. Vitamin D enables your body to store calcium. Without vitamin D the bones become soft and misshapen.

In Asia, thousands of people once suffered from **beriberi,** a disease that can leave you weak and partially paralyzed and can eventually lead to heart failure. In 1912, two doctors discovered that the cause of this disease was a shortage of thiamine, one of the B vitamins.

The absence of another B vitamin, niacin, causes the disease pellagra (pə la′ grə). Its symptoms include thick, rough blisters on the hands, feet, and face and a sore mouth and tongue. The disease can also affect the digestive and nervous systems.

A shortage of vitamin A causes night blindness, or the loss of ability to see in dim light. Someone with a vitamin A deficiency may also find seeing different shades of gray very difficult.

Goiter is an iodine-deficiency disease that causes a bump or swelling to form on the neck.

Deficiency diseases may also result from not getting the minerals you need in your diet. **Goiter** (goi′ tər), an iodine-deficiency disease, was once a widespread problem for people living far from oceans, where the soil and seafood contain iodine. Without iodine, the thyroid gland becomes overactive and enlarged, causing a swelling or bump to form on the neck. Today, most table salt has been supplemented with enough iodine that people can avoid this deficiency.

Iron deficiency anemia (ə nē′ mē ə) is the most common nutritional deficiency in America today. Iron, an important mineral in the body, is necessary for red blood cells to carry oxygen to body cells. People with iron anemia often feel weak and tired because their bodies' cells are not getting enough oxygen.

As nutritionists learn more about deficiency diseases, an effort is being made to add essential nutrients to food. For example, vitamin D is added to milk and niacin to enriched breads.

Health Problems Related to Food and Digestion

Some health problems are due to eating too much of certain types of food. Most Americans eat more salt, fats, and sugar than they need. A high-fat diet is not a healthful diet. Meats and fried foods contain large amounts of fat. While an adequate amount of fat is important to your diet, excess fat can build up in your arteries and block the flow of blood. Too much fat has also been linked with types of cancer in the body.

Another problem of excess is too much salt. Salt also can cause a person to retain fluids, which can result in high blood pressure. Nutritionists advise you not to add salt to foods. Many processed foods already contain salt and some foods naturally contain sodium, one nutrient found in salt.

A more common problem is too much sugar. Today the average American eats about 60 kg of sugar a year. Most of it comes from soft drinks and sweets and snacks like candy, baked goods, jams, jellies, presweetened cereals, and desserts. You can discover sugar "hidden" in your food by reading labels and looking for words like *sucrose, corn syrup, fructose, honey,* and, of course, *sugar.* Even vegetables and meat dishes often include sugar.

Too much sugar can cause tooth decay and weight gain. People who are extremely overweight may have a greater risk of suffering from heart disease or high blood pressure.

Nutrition Facts

Serving Size 1 egg (34g)
Servings Per Container 4

Amount Per Serving

Calories 170   Calories from Fat 90

	% Daily Value**
Total Fat 10g	15%
Saturated Fat 5g	25%
Cholesterol 5mg	2%
Sodium 60mg	3%
Total Carbohydrate 20g	7%
Dietary Fiber 1g	4%
Sugars 18g	
Protein 2g	

Vitamin A *	•	Vitamin C *	
Calcium 4%	•	Iron *	

*Contains less than 2% of the Daily Value of these nutrients.

**Percent Daily Values are based on a 2,000 calorie diet. Your daily values may be higher or lower depending on your calorie needs:

	Calories:	2,000	2,500
Total Fat	Less than	65g	80g
Sat. Fat	Less than	20g	25g
Cholesterol	Less than	300mg	300mg
Sodium	Less than	2,400mg	2,400mg
Total Carbohydrate		300g	375g
Dietary Fiber		25g	30g

MILK CHOCOLATE (SUGAR, COCOA BUTTER, CHOCOLATE, LACTOSE, SKIM MILK, MILKFAT, SOY LECITHIN, ARTIFICIAL FLAVOR), PEANUTS, SUGAR, CORN SYRUP, INVERT SUGAR, PARTIALLY HYDROGENATED PALM KERNEL OIL, SKIM MILK, LESS THAN 2% - COCONUT OIL, BUTTER, COCOA BUTTER, MILKFAT, CREAM, LACTOSE, SALT, WHEY, MONO AND DIGLYCERIDES, SOY LECITHIN, VANILLA, POTASSIUM SORBATE TO MAINTAIN FRESHNESS, ARTIFICIAL FLAVOR.

DISTRIBUTED BY
DIVISION OF
HACKETTSTOWN, NJ 07840-1503 USA

By looking at food labels, you might find sugar "hidden" in foods you would not expect to have a great deal of sugar.

These are some of the most common foods associated with food allergies.

Heart disease, the number one cause of death in America, can be prevented in many cases by eating a healthful diet, exercising, and avoiding tobacco, alcohol, and stress. The best diet for the heart is one that is high in fiber and low in salt, fat, and cholesterol, a fatty, white substance found mostly in meat. This diet can be achieved by following the recommendations listed on the Food Guide Pyramid.

Some people have food allergies (al′ ər jēz) that prevent them from eating foods they need. Food allergies might cause you to get headaches, diarrhea, nausea, sniffles, or skin rashes when you eat certain foods.

The foods that most commonly cause allergic reactions are seafood, berries, nuts, milk, wheat, corn, tomatoes, oranges, grapefruits, eggs, and chocolate. Chemicals added to foods for flavor or to preserve them can also cause allergic reactions in some people.

In many cases, you can outgrow a food allergy. A food that caused trouble for you as a toddler may not do so today. Many teenagers leave their food allergies behind. On the other hand, a food allergy can develop at any age.

Some diseases prevent the body from converting food to energy. Consequently, the bodies of people suffering from these types of diseases are affected in many of the same ways as those of people with nutritional deficiencies.

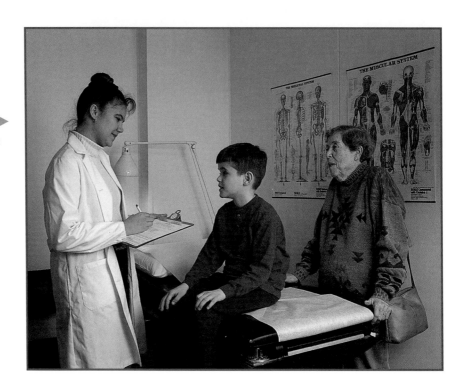

Doctors can help people with diabetes learn to control their illness so that they can lead an active life.

More than 12 million Americans have diabetes. **Diabetes** (dī ə bē′ tēz) is a disease that results from problems in the body's production of insulin. Insulin is a hormone that helps cells take in glucose, a sugar that results from the breakdown of food. Because glucose is the body's main fuel, diabetes can cause serious problems if glucose cannot be used for energy. The symptoms of diabetes include excess thirst, excess hunger, weight loss, lack of energy, excess production of urine, shortness of breath, and dry skin.

There are two types of diabetes: Type I, called insulin-dependent diabetes, and Type II. About one million people in the United States suffer from Type I diabetes. These people must take insulin through daily injections.

Most people with diabetes have Type II, a form of the disease that results from either the production of too little insulin or the body's inability to use it. This type of diabetes can be controlled with prescription medication. However, many people are able to control Type II diabetes through a restricted diet and regular exercise.

Hypoglycemia (hī pō glī sē′ mē ə) is a condition that occurs when the amount of glucose in your body cells drops too low to fuel the body's activity. This can happen when the pancreas produces an excess of insulin, which reduces the glucose in the body to dangerously low levels. Hypoglycemia can also result from inadequate food intake or poor timing of snacks and meals. A person with hypoglycemia will feel weak, drowsy, sometimes confused, hungry, and dizzy. Other symptoms include paleness, headache, irritability, trembling, sweating, rapid heartbeat, and a cold, clammy feeling. With an increased knowledge of their illnesses, people with diabetes and hypoglycemia can manage their diets and live healthy, active lives.

CHECKPOINT

1. Why are nutrients important to your health?
2. What diseases are related to nutrition?
3. What are some health problems related to food or digestion?

 How can nutrition affect health?

ACTIVITY

Investigating Sugar Content in Foods

Find Out

Do this activity to see what foods contain sugar.

Process Skills

Hypothesizing
Observing
Communicating
Interpreting Data

WHAT YOU NEED

sugar test paper

slides

water

plastic knife

droppers

sweet potato and other food samples for sugar test

Activity Journal

honey

WHAT TO DO

1. Look at the foods you are going to test for sugar. Write a hypothesis that predicts which foods will contain sugar and which will not.

2. Using the dropper, put a drop of honey on the slide. Touch a piece of sugar test paper to the honey. Wait one minute.

3. Observe the color of the test paper. If the test paper turns green, sugar is present. If no green color shows, sugar is not present. Record the color of the test paper.

4. Using the plastic knife, cut a small slice of sweet potato and touch a piece of sugar test paper to the inside of the slice for one minute.

5. Observe and record the color of the test paper.

6. Repeat Steps 2 and 3 for any other liquid foods you are testing. Repeat Steps 4 and 5 for any other solid foods you are testing. Record your observations for each food.

CONCLUSIONS

1. Compare your hypothesis with your data.
2. Which foods contained sugar?
3. Which foods did not contain sugar?

ASKING NEW QUESTIONS

1. Why is it important to test water for sugar in this activity?
2. What diseases are associated with sugar intake?

SCIENTIFIC METHODS SELF CHECK

✔ Did I make a **hypothesis** about which foods contained sugar and which did not?

✔ Did I **observe** the sugar test paper when testing different foods?

✔ Did I **record** my observations?

Review

Reviewing Vocabulary and Concepts

Write the letter of the answer that completes each sentence.

1. Chemical compounds needed in small amounts for cellular respiration are ___.
   a. vitamins   **b.** starches
   c. sugars   **d.** carbohydrates

2. A measure of the energy in food is a ___.
   a. nutrient   **b.** Calorie
   c. fat   **d.** protein

3. A shortage of a necessary nutrient can lead to ___.
   a. healthy bones   **b.** cartilage growth
   c. a balanced diet   **d.** a nutritional deficiency

4. A shortage of vitamin D can cause ___.
   a. rickets   **b.** hypoglycemia
   c. beriberi   **d.** blisters

5. An iodine deficiency that leads to a swelling in the neck is called ___.
   a. high blood pressure   **b.** goiter
   c. pellagra   **d.** iron deficiency anemia

Match each definition on the left with the correct term.

6. these nutrients help regulate chemical reactions in your body
   a. malnutrition

7. a measure of the energy in food
   b. heart disease

8. the result of not getting enough nutrients
   c. minerals

9. the number one cause of death in the United States
   d. Calorie

10. a disease resulting in problems with the body's production of insulin
   e. diabetes

Understanding What You Learned

1. How do we get the nutrients we need to stay healthy?

2. What are the six classes of nutrients we need and why is each important?

3. Why is a balanced diet important?

4. What are nutritional supplements? Who might need a nutritional supplement?

5. What are some causes of malnutrition?

Applying What You Learned

1. Why do people have to be careful when they take vitamin supplements?

2. What could happen to an infant who does not receive enough milk or formula in the first six months of life?

3. What are some important foods people your age should be eating every day?

4. What foods do people your age eat that may not be part of a healthful balanced diet?

 5. How is nutritious food important for growth and health?

For Your Portfolio

Use photographs from newspapers and magazines of the foods you eat and drink on a regular basis to construct your own food pyramid showing the foods according to amounts of each that you consume. Compare your food pyramid with the one on page D79 and identify nutrients that are lacking in your diet.

Unit Review

Concept Review

1. How do the systems in the body work together to perform functions necessary for life?

2. How does exercise help to make the body healthy and physically fit?

3. How is nutritious food important to growth and health?

Problem Solving

1. If every so often your heart began to beat irregularly, and you became faint of breath, what body systems would you want to get checked by a doctor?

2. Create an exercise program for yourself that changes with the seasons. List the benefits of each activity to your specific body parts and overall health. For example, if ice skating is your winter activity, benefits would be strengthening your leg muscles and improving your cardiovascular health.

3. Think about some of the causes of malnutrition. Suggest a solution for one of the causes.

Something to Do

Working in a group of three, pick an example of a movement that would show strength, endurance, and flexibility. Draw an example of a food that would be high in protein, one that would be high in fat, and one that would be high in carbohydrates. Each group will take a turn acting out the three movements and displaying their pictures of food for the class. Each student will have a movement and picture to present. The class will guess what the movements and pictures show.

Reference

Diversity of Living Things

The living things that inhabit Earth are similar in some ways but are very different in others. All living things are similar because all are made up of one or more cells. However, the structure of living things as well as the way that those cells function to perform the life processes of each organism can vary greatly from one living thing to the next. Look at some of the differences that can be found among living things.

Life Processes

Heart Rate

Some animals have different heart rates than other animals. The smaller the animal, the faster the heart rate will usually be.

Mammal	Heart beats per minute
Elephant	25
Human	70
Small dog	120
Mouse	600-700

House mouse

Holding Their Breath

The length of time that various animals can hold their breath varies. The following are some mammals and the average length of time each can hold its breath.

Mammal	Average time in minutes
Human	1
Sea otter	5
Platypus	10
Hippopotamus	15
Beaver	20
Seal	15-28
Greenland whale	60
Bottlenose whale	120

Platypus

Redwood tree

Diversity in Size

The Tallest Trees

Tree	Height in meters
Eucalyptus	132
Douglas fir	125
Redwood	113

Gecko

The Largest and Smallest Animals

Animal type	Animals	Size
Sea mammal		
Largest	**Blue whale**	30.5-33.5 meters long
Smallest	**Commerson's dolphin**	23-32 kilograms
Land mammal		
Largest	**African elephant**	3.2 meters tall at shoulder
Smallest	**Bumblebee bat**	2.54 cm long; 1.6-2 grams
Bird		
Largest	**North American ostrich**	2.4-2.7 meters tall; 156.5 kilograms
Smallest	**Bee hummingbird**	5.7 cm long; 4.6 grams
Fish		
Largest	**Whale shark**	12.5 meters long; 16.5 metric tons;
Smallest	**Dwarf pygmy goby**	8.9 millimeters long
Reptile		
Largest	**Salt water crocodile**	4.3-4.9 meters long; 408-680 kilograms
Smallest	**Gecko**	1.7 centimeters long

Populations Sharing Earth

The natural resources found on or in Earth's surface support a vast amount of living things. Some resources, such as fossil fuels, are used exclusively by humans. Other resources, such as water, are used by nearly all living things.

The changes that humans can cause in ecosystems can affect availability of resources as well as the survival of many plant and animal populations. As humans, we need to be aware of the impact that our actions can have on the world in which we live.

Endangered Species

Each year, an estimated 27,000 species of animals, plants, fungi, and microorganisms become extinct.

There are 157 threatened species and 504 endangered species in just the United States.

In the United States, six species have been removed from the federal endangered and threatened species list since 1973 because they have recovered and seven species have been removed because they have become extinct.

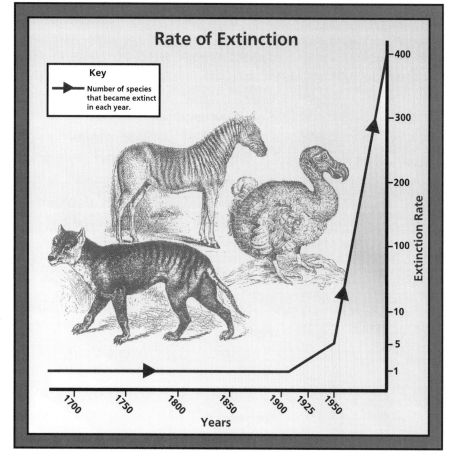

Rate of Extinction

Key
→ Number of species that became extinct in each year.

Extinction Rate

Years
1700 1750 1800 1850 1900 1925 1950

Human Population

According to the Population Division of the United Nations, by the middle of the twenty-first century, about 7.3-10.7 billion people will populate Earth. In 1950, the human population was 2.5 billion and by 2050, about three to four times as many people will be living on Earth.

In the United States

- The average American generates 52 metric tons of garbage by the age of 75.
- Fifty percent of the wetland, 90% of the northwestern old-growth forests, and 99% of the tall-grass prairie have been destroyed in the last 200 years.
- Americans constitute 5% of the world's population but consume 24% of the world's energy.

In the world:

- More than 1 out of 5 people in the world do not get enough to eat.
- An estimated 1.7 billion people lack access to clean drinking water.
- Every year over three million metric tons of oil contaminates the oceans.

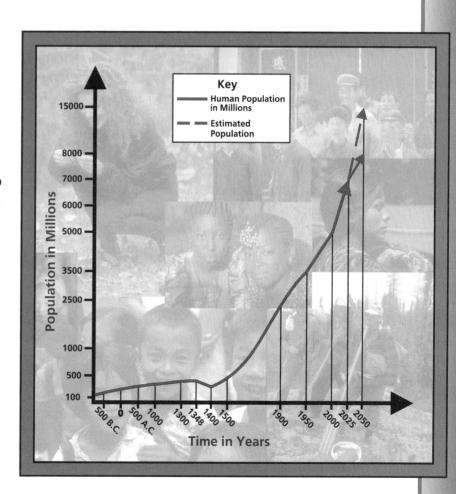

Earth's Diverse Surface

Earth's surface is not the same from place to place. If you were to travel around the globe, you would find many different kinds of climates, ecosystems, and surface features. The varieties of land features and water sources, as well as the altitude and climate, have made many parts of Earth's surface and the organisms living on it very different across the world.

Physical Characteristics of Earth

Mass and Density

Earth is estimated to have a mass of 5,970,000,000,000,000,000,000,000 kilograms and a density more than 5.5 times that of water.

Surface Features

Land and Water Ratio

Approximately 30 percent of Earth's surface is land. This is about 148,300,000 square kilometers. The area of Earth's water surface is approximately 361,800,000 square kilometers, or about 70 percent of Earth's surface.

Highest and Lowest Points on Earth

The highest point of land is 8,848 meters above sea level, plus or minus 3 meters because of snow. This point is at the top of Mt. Everest, which is in the Himalayas on the Nepal-Tibet border.

Mt. Everest

The lowest point on land is the Dead Sea, which lies between Israel and Jordan and is 399 meters below sea level. The lowest point on Earth's surface is thought to be in the Marianas Trench in the western Pacific Ocean extending from southeast of Guam to northwest of the Marianas Islands. It has been measured as 11,034 meters below sea level.

Water Sources

Depth of the Ocean

The average depth of the ocean floor is 4,000 meters.

Deepest Lake

Lake Baikal, located in southeast Siberia, is 1,620 meters deep at its maximum depth, making it the deepest lake in the world.

Lake Baikal

Highest and Lowest Temperatures

The highest temperature on Earth was recorded as 58 °C at Al Aziziyah, Libya, on September 13, 1922. The highest temperature in the United States was 56.7 °C in Death Valley, California.

Death Valley

The lowest temperature recorded on Earth was –89.6 °C at Vostok Station in Antarctica on July 21, 1983. The lowest temperature recorded in the United States was –62.1 °C on January 23, 1971, in Prospect Creek, Alaska.

The Solar System

The sun and the planets that are in our solar system have unique physical and chemical characteristics that make the sun and the planets very different from each other. The solar system is also made up of asteroids, comets, and meteors. The many objects found in our solar system have many different sizes, shapes, and compositions.

The Sun

Temperature of the Sun

The center of the sun is about 15,000,000°C. The photosphere, or surface, of the sun is about 5,500 °C.

Light from the Sun

Sunlight takes about 8 minutes and 20 seconds to reach Earth, traveling at 299,792 kilometers per second.

Asteroids and Meteorites

Asteroids

Asteroids are smaller than any of the nine major planets in the solar system and are not satellites of any planet. The first and largest asteroid to be discovered has a diameter of 936 kilometers. Over 18,000 asteroids have been identified and astronomers have recognized the orbits of about 5000.

Meteorites

The largest meteorite found on Earth is located in Namibia and has a mass of 66,100 kilograms.

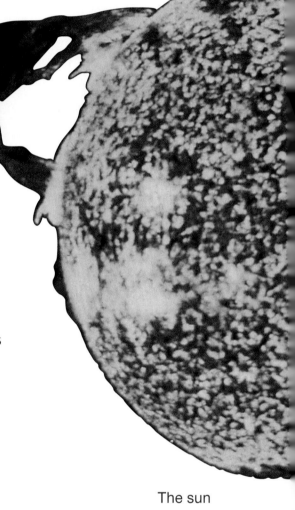

The sun

The Solar System

Gravitational Force

If the gravitational force on Earth is taken as 1, the comparative gravitational forces of the sun and planets are as follows:

Sun	27.9	**Moon**	0.16	**Uranus**	0.93
Mercury	0.37	**Mars**	0.38	**Neptune**	1.22
Venus	0.88	**Jupiter**	2.64	**Pluto**	0.06
Earth	1.00	**Saturn**	1.15		

Weight comparisons can be made by using this table. For example, if a person weighed 80 kilograms on Earth, then by multiplying that number by the comparative gravitational force of Mercury, 0.37, you will discover that the same person would weigh 29.6 kilograms on Mercury (80 × 0.37 = 29.6).

	Average distance from sun (km)	Colors of Planets	Diameters (km)
Mercury	57,909,100	Orange	4,878
Venus	108,208,600	Yellow	12,104
Earth	149,598,000	Blue, brown, green	12,756
Mars	227,939,200	Red	6,794
Jupiter	788,298,400	Yellow, red, brown, white	142,984
Saturn	1,427,010,000	Yellow	120,538
Uranus	2,869,600,000	Green	51,118
Neptune	4,496,700,000	Blue	50,530
Pluto	3,666,000,000	Yellow	2,290

Diversity of Elements

Given the vast amount of space that can be found in the universe, it might almost seem surprising that all things in it are made up of a little over 100 elements. Some elements have physical and chemical properties similar to other elements, but each element is unique from any other. The elements that make up our universe can combine in many ways. The results of many of these combinations can be seen in the great diversity of living and nonliving things on Earth.

Elements

There are 94 naturally occurring elements. Over 6.8 million chemical compounds have been produced from these elements, and over 65,000 of these are in common use.

Liquid Elements

The elements mercury (Hg) and bromine (Br) are liquid at room temperature, 20 ° to 25 °C. Gallium (Ga), with a melting point of 29.8 °C and cesium (Cs) with a melting point of 28.4 °C, are liquids slightly above room temperature.

Most Abundant Element

The most abundant, or common, element in the universe is hydrogen. Hydrogen (H) makes up about 75 percent of the mass of the universe. It is estimated that more than 90 percent of all atoms in the universe are hydrogen atoms.

Mercury

Most Abundant Element on Earth

The most abundant element on Earth is oxygen (O). Oxygen is the most abundant element in Earth's crust, waters, and atmosphere. It composes 49.5% of the total mass of these compounds.

Tantalum

Uses of Some Elements

Tantalum (Ta)— A rare, pale gray metal, used in electric lamp filaments and alloys. Tantalum is also used in surgery to replace parts of the body, such as in skull plates and wire connecting the ends of nerves.

Tungsten (W)—A hard, gray metal that is resistant to corrosion. It is used in alloys to make tools and lamp filaments.

Cobalt (Co)—A hard, silvery-white, magnetic metal found combined with sulfur and arsenic. It is used in alloys, such as with iron to make magnets. Cobalt chloride is used to test for water. Cobalt also produces a blue color in glass and ceramics.

Cobalt

Chromium (Cr)—A hard, white metal found as chrome iron ore. It is used as a corrosion-resistant coating on steel objects and in stainless steel. Chromium plating is used on car parts, bicycle handlebars and cutlery.

Tungsten

Chromium

Electricity

Electricity is the energy of moving electrons. There are many diverse sources that can be used to generate electricity, but in order for electricity to be produced, all sources rely on the movement of electrons. Electrons are in action in every atom of every element and compound that make up our world. The energy of moving electrons is all around us, in animals, in the sky, and in the home.

Lightning

Lightning is the sudden flow of electricity from a cloud that has become charged due to the rubbing together of different particles, such as water droplets and ice crystals. This rubbing can cause static electricity. Positive charges build up at the top of a cloud, and negative ones at the bottom. The ground has a positive charge. When the difference between the charges gets bigger, lightning sparks across the gap.

- The temperature of the air around a bolt of lightning is about 30,000 °C, which is about six times hotter than the surface of the sun.

- The sudden increase in the temperature of the air causes the air to expand very quickly. Thunder is the sound of the hot air expanding.

- Lightning can strike in the same place twice. Tall buildings, such as

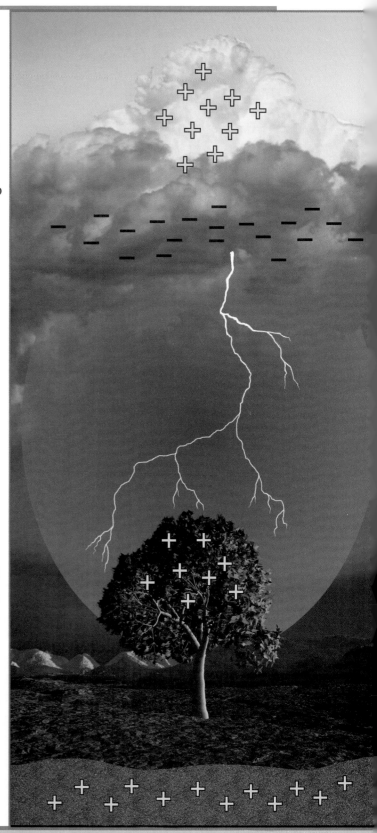

the Empire State Building in New York City, can be struck several times during the same storm. During one storm, lightning struck the Empire State Building 12 times.

- A stroke of lightning discharges from 10 to 100 million volts of electricity. An average stroke has 30,000 amperes.

Energy for Electrical Appliances

Following is the estimated annual energy consumption for various household electrical products.

Appliance	Estimated kilowatt-hours
Clock	17
Clothes dryer	993
Clothes washer	103
Computer	25–400
Freezer	1820
Radio	86
Television	502
Videocassette recorder (VCR)	10–70
Water heater	4219

Utility Meters

A utility meter shows the amount of energy used in a particular house, apartment, or building. On older electric and gas meters, a series of four or five dials show the amount of energy being consumed. The dials are read left to right, and if the pointer falls between two numbers, the lower number is recorded. In the electric meter shown, the dial registers 13,644 kilowatt hours. Gas meters are set to read hundreds of cubic feet. New meter models have digital displays.

Electric Eel

An electric eel has current-producing organs made up of electric plates on both sides of its vertebral column running almost its entire body length. The electrical charge is released by the central nervous system as a defense mechanism. On average, the charge is 350 volts. The most powerful electric eel produces a shock of 400 to 650 volts.

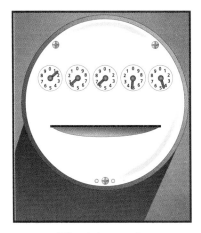

Electric meter

The Human Body

The human body is a unified structure that is made up of many diverse parts that work together. In order for these parts to work together properly, the body must have the substances it needs to perform its life processes. The human body is composed of many different chemicals that are necessary for its survival. These chemicals, in combination with proper functioning of its cells, tissues, and organs, make the human body strong and healthy.

Major Elements in the Human Body

Elements	Percentage	Function
Oxygen	65.0	Part of all major nutrients of tissues; vital to energy production
Carbon	18.5	Essential life element of proteins, carbo-hydrates, and fats; building blocks of cells
Hydrogen	9.5	Part of major nutrients; building blocks of cells
Nitrogen	3.3	Essential part of proteins; essential to most body functions
Calcium	1.5	Forms nonliving bone parts; a messenger between cells
Phosphorus	1.0	Important to bone building; essential to cell energy

Bones in the Human Body

Babies are born with about 300 to 350 bones, but many of these join together between birth and maturity. The average adult has a total of 206 bones.

Location	Number
Skull	22
Ears (pair)	6
Vertebrae	26
Sternum	3
Throat	1
Pectoral girdle	4
Arms (pair)	60
Hip bones	2
Legs (pair)	58
Total	206

Organs

Largest Organ in the Human Body

The largest and heaviest organ is the skin, with a total surface area of about 1.9 square meters for an average-sized person. The skin weighs 2.7 kilograms on an average person.

The Heart

The heart squeezes out about 70.8 grams of blood every beat. It pumps about 9450 liters of blood a day.

Skin and Hair

Hairs on Your Head

- The amount of hair covering a human's head varies from one person to the next. An average person has about 100,000 hairs on his or her scalp.
- Most people shed between 50 to 100 hairs daily.
- Each hair grows about 12.7 centimeters every year.

Goose bumps

The puckering of the skin, or goose bumps, is the result of contracting muscle fibers in the skin. This muscular activity will produce more heat and raise the temperature of the body. Sweating will cool off a body and reduce the heat, causing the body temperature to lower.

The human body

Glossary

A

absolute magnitude the amount of light a star gives off

abyssal plain the flat bottom of the ocean floor on which sediment has fallen

acids substances that usually react with metals and contain hydrogen

active transport the movement of materials by living cells from areas of lower concentration to areas of higher concentration

adaptation a trait that helps an organism survive in a particular ecosystem

air a mixture of gases that makes up Earth's atmosphere

air pressure the force of air pushing against something, such as Earth's surface

alloys mixtures of pure metals

alveoli the tiny air sacs in the lungs

anemometer an instrument that measures the speed of wind

anthracite a hard coal that burns more cleanly than bituminous coal

apparent magnitude the brightness of a star as viewed from Earth

arteries the blood vessels that carry blood away from the heart

asteroids rocky fragments ranging in size from tiny dust particles to more than 1000 km in diameter; many are found in the asteroid belt between Mars and Jupiter

atmosphere a mixture of gases that surrounds a planet

atoms the smallest pieces of an element that still have the properties of that element

atomic number the number of protons in an atom's nucleus

B

barometer an instrument that records air pressure

bases substances that contain hydroxide and can neutralize an acid

Beaufort scale a scale that labels winds by speed and force

behavior the way an organism acts toward its ecosystem

beriberi a disease caused by a thiamine deficiency that could lead to weakness, paralysis, and heart failure

biomass a source of energy, consisting of matter that is or was living

bituminous coal a coal that produces many pollutants when burned; it is often called soft coal

bladder a sac that stores waste removed from the kidneys before it is eliminated

Glossary

boiling point the point at which a substance changes from a liquid to a gas

bone marrow a gel-like substance that fills the cavity inside a bone; the bone marrow is a living part of the bone where blood cells are made

Bowman's capsule the cuplike structure in each nephron where blood is filtered

breakwater a structure built with concrete or rock to protect the shore from erosion

bronchi two short tubes that carry air from the trachea to the lungs

C

caldera a bowl-shaped depression, which can be caused by a volcanic eruption

Calorie a measure of the energy in food

capillaries the smallest type of blood vessels, with walls that are only 1 cell thick

carbohydrates nutrients that are the first to be used up when your body needs energy

carbon cycle a cycle in which carbon moves through an ecosystem

cardiovascular exercise exercise that increases one's heart and breathing rate for an extended period of time

carrying capacity the maximum population size in an area that the resources can support

cell the smallest unit of living matter that can perform life functions

cell membrane the very thin covering that surrounds a cell and allows certain substances to move into and out of the cell

cell theory a theory that states that all organisms are made up of one or more cells, that cells are the basic units of structure and function in all living things, and that all cells come from cells that already exist

cell wall the rigid structure outside the cell membrane that supports and protects the plant cell

chemical change when two or more substances react and new substances are formed

chemical energy energy stored in matter when atoms join together

chemical property how a substance reacts with other substances

chemical reaction activity that occurs during a chemical change

chemical symbol the symbol that represents an element's name

chloroplasts small oval- or disk-shaped structures that contain chlorophyll, which allows plants to make their own food

Glossary

cilia hairlike extensions on the surface of a cell

circulatory system a system that moves nutrients and oxygen through an animal's body and removes waste products

cirrus high and wispy clouds, usually made up of ice crystals

climate the patterns of weather over many years

coal a sedimentary rock made up mostly of carbon and hydrogen

cold front when a cold air mass moves into a region of warm air, forcing the warm air quickly upward along the front

colloid a heterogeneous mixture containing particles that stay evenly distributed throughout the mixture

comet mass of dust, ice, frozen gas, and rock particles orbiting the sun

community all of the populations that live in an ecosystem

compact bone the thick outer layer of bones

compound a substance made of two or more elements chemically combined

compound microscope a microscope that increases magnification by using more than one lens

condensation the process by which a gas changes to a liquid

connective tissue in animals that is made up of strong, elastic cells that hold muscles together and keep parts of the body in place

continental shelf the ocean floor along a coast that slopes gently

convection current the movement of a fluid, such as a liquid or a gas, caused when it is unevenly heated so that some parts become less dense and other parts become more dense

corona a star's outermost layer that is made of super-hot gases

craters large depressions in the ground

cumulus a billowy kind of cloud that is associated with good weather

cytoplasm the gel-like substance inside the cell membrane

D

deficiency disease a disease that develops when the body does not receive the nutrients it needs for a long period of time

density the mass of an object divided by its volume

dermal the outermost tissue layer on a plant's roots, leaves, and stems

Glossary

dew point the temperature at which condensation occurs

diabetes a disease that results from problems in the body's production of insulin

dietary needs the nutritional needs of the body that allow it to perform its life processes and maintain good health

diffusion the movement of particles from an area where they are more concentrated to an area where they are less concentrated

digestion the process of changing food into a usable form

dome the result of magma forcing Earth's crust upward, much like a bubble, causing a mountain to form

E

ecosystem all the living and nonliving things within a particular area and their relationship to each other

efficiency the percentage of energy converted to a usable form

electric current the movement of electrons along a path or circuit

electrical energy the form of energy caused by the presence or movement of electrons

electrons negatively charged particles surrounding the nucleus of an atom

electron cloud model a model in which electrons form a cloud around the atom's nucleus where an electron's charge will be found

element a substance made up of only one kind of atom

endurance a measure of the ability of your muscles to exert a force over a period of time

energy the ability to make things happen, cause change, and do work

energy pyramid a model that shows the amount of energy flowing from one organism to the next in a food chain

energy transfer a flow of energy from one place to another

enzymes chemicals that help speed up the process of digestion

epiglottis the flap that covers the windpipe during swallowing

epithelial a kind of tissue in animals that is made up of tightly packed cells that cover the body and make up the internal lining of some animals

esophagus a muscular tube connecting the mouth and the stomach

eukaryotic cells cells with a nucleus

Glossary

evaporation the process in which liquid water changes to water vapor

excretion the body's process of getting rid of wastes

exercise a regular series of movements that conditions your muscles

exosphere the uppermost layer of Earth's atmosphere; beyond it is outer space

F

families the columns of elements in the periodic table; they are also called groups

fats nutrients that carry A, D, E, and K, can be used by the body to build nerves, and can be stored under the skin as an energy supply

faults weak areas in Earth's crust along which energy can be released in the form of earthquakes

faulting the formation of cracks in Earth's surface due to pressure that forces Earth's crust to slip down or to thrust upward along the cracks

feedback the systems that regulate metabolism in the body

flagellum a long, whiplike structure that extends from a cell and moves the cell through water

flexibility the ability of muscles and joints to move within a full range of motion

folding the process by which Earth's crust responds to pressures, resulting in a surface that has folds; the Appalachian Mountains were formed by folding

food chain the transfer of energy as organisms feed on other organisms

food web a network of interrelated food chains

fossil fuels substances, such as coal, oil, and natural gas, formed from organisms that lived on Earth millions of years ago

freshwater water that has a low enough mineral content to be used by people and land animals

friction the force that opposes motion, causing heat to be given off as two surfaces rub together

G

gallbladder an organ that stores bile until it is needed in the small intestine

geothermal energy energy that comes from Earth

glaciers huge masses of ice that move over land

goiter an iodine-deficiency disease that causes thyroid problems

gravity the attraction between two objects based upon the mass of each object and the distance between them

Glossary

ground plant tissue that may perform photosynthesis, store sugars and nutrients, and provide support

groundwater water that is stored in porous rock or large pockets between rocks underground

H

habitat where a population lives and meets its needs

heart organ that pumps blood throughout the body of some animals

heart disease a term referring to the many heart conditions resulting from poor diet, lack of exercise, and other lifestyle choices

heat thermal energy that is being transferred between objects at different temperatures

heterogeneous mixture a mixture in which components are spread unevenly throughout the mixture and sometimes can be separated easily

homeostasis the tendency of an organism to adjust itself to maintain a balanced state

homogeneous mixtures mixtures that are composed of ingredients that are evenly spread throughout the mixtures; also called solutions

humidity the amount of water vapor in the air

hurricane a severe storm that begins at sea, moves in a circular pattern, can become up to 800 km across, and can generate winds as fast as 360 km/h; hurricanes can cause great damage to ships, buildings, and vegetation

hydroelectric electricity generated by falling or flowing water

hydrosphere Earth's large bodies of water, like the Great Lakes and the oceans

hypoglycemia a condition that occurs when the amount of glucose in your body drops too low to fuel the body's activity

I

icebergs large masses of floating ice

indicators chemicals that are used to test for acids and bases

inexhaustible resources resources that are constantly being used and recycled

innate behavior a behavior that an animal is born with and that is passed on from generation to generation

insoluble a substance that cannot be dissolved in a given substance

intestine a long tube below the stomach that helps process the food an animal consumes so that it can be used by cells in the body

Glossary

involuntary muscles muscles that function without one's control

ionosphere an electrically conductive region at the top of the mesosphere that can reflect radio waves

iron deficiency anemia a deficiency caused by a lack of iron in the diet, leading to feelings of weakness and tiredness

J

jetties barriers usually built in pairs that extend from both sides of the mouth of a river into an ocean or lake

joints where two or more bones meet or are held together

Jovian the gas-giant planets in the solar system, which are Jupiter, Saturn, Uranus, and Neptune; they are much larger and less dense than terrestrial planets

K

kidneys the main organs in the excretory system that filter blood

kinetic energy the energy of objects in motion dependent upon an object's mass and how fast the object is moving

L

lava the hot, melted rock that erupts from a volcano

leaves plant organs that perform the majority of photosynthesis in plants

learned behavior behavior that is taught and can change as a result of experience and training

lignite a soft, dark-brown coal often having a woody texture

limiting factor any condition that influences the growth or survival of an organism or species

lithosphere the outer layer of Earth's surface

liver a soft organ, which is found beneath the diaphragm, that makes bile

lungs the breathing organs of mammals, birds, and reptiles

M

magma extremely hot, molten rock

malnutrition condition resulting from not getting enough nutrients for the body to grow or function properly

mass the quantity of matter in a material

mass number the number of protons and neutrons in the nucleus of an atom

Glossary

mass wasting the movement of rock, snow, mud, or soil down a slope

mechanical energy the energy of moving parts; a result of kinetic energy and gravitation

melting point point at which a substance changes from a solid to a liquid state

mesosphere the layer of Earth's atmosphere above the stratosphere extending between 50 and 80 km above Earth's surface

metabolism all of the chemical changes that occur in an organism

metals elements that are usually shiny, good conductors of heat and electricity, and exist as solids at room temperature

metalloids elements that have some properties of both metals and nonmetals

meteoroids small fragments of material that are falling through space

Mid-ocean ridges continuous chains of mountains that run down the center of every major ocean

minerals nutrients needed to help regulate chemical reactions in the body

mitochondria organelles in which energy is released from a cell's food

mixture a substance that is formed when two or more substances are physically combined

molecule two or more atoms that are joined together

monsoons seasonal winds that bring heavy rains

multicellular organisms organisms that are made up of more than one cell

muscle a kind of tissue in animals that is made up of cells that contract, get shorter, and relax, allowing the body to move

N

natural gas fossil fuel in the form of a gas

neap tides the lowest tides that occur when the sun and the moon are at right angles to each other and their combined gravitational attraction acts on the water in the ocean

nephrons the tiny filtering units of the kidneys; the kidneys are made of about one million nephrons

nerve a type of animal tissue that relays messages between the brain and the rest of the body

nervous system the system that controls the activities of all the other systems in the body of an animal; in many animals, it is made up of the brain, spinal cord, and nerve tissue that branches off the spinal cord

Glossary

neutron an uncharged, or neutral, particle in the nucleus of an atom

niche the role or function of an organism in its community

nitrogen cycle the cycle by which nitrogen moves through the ecosystem

nonmetals elements that do not conduct electricity or heat well; at room temperature they are usually gases or hard, brittle solids

nonrenewable energy energy sources that cannot be renewed by natural means in less than 30 years

nuclear energy the potential energy stored in the nucleus, or center of atoms

nucleus 1. a cellular structure that directs the activities of a cell 2. the tiny, dense center of an atom

nutrients the chemicals in food that are needed by cells

nutrition the study of food and its use by the body

nutritional deficiency a shortage of a nutrient that the body needs

nutritional supplement an amount of vitamins and minerals that is consumed in addition to the food in a diet

O

ocean current a sustained, long-lasting movement of ocean water caused by differences in density of water

ocean trenches long, narrow depressions that are some of the deepest places in the ocean where active volcanoes and earthquakes are common

ocean waves movements caused by the passage of energy through water

oceanography the study of Earth's seas and oceans

oceans the bodies of salt water that cover three quarters of Earth

ores rock and mineral deposits that are large enough to make them worth mining

organ a structure made up of several different types of tissue that all work together to do a particular job in an organism

organ system a group of organs that work together to perform a specific job in living things

organelles structures within the cytoplasm of a eukaryotic cell

osmosis the diffusion of water through a membrane

ozone a gas found in the atmosphere that filters much of the sun's ultraviolet rays

Glossary

P

pancreas an organ that produces three enzymes to break down fat, protein, and carbohydrates

peat a mixture of water and plant materials that will eventually, under the right conditions, form coal

periodic table a table that organizes the elements and their properties

periods the horizontal rows of elements in the periodic table

petroleum the most widely used fossil fuel; it is a liquid and is also called oil

photosphere a star's surface

photosynthesis the process by which plants use energy from light to produce food

physical change a change that takes place when a substance keeps the same chemical properties, but changes form

physical fitness the level of health at which you have muscular endurance, flexibility, a well-conditioned heart, strength, and the right amount of body fat

physical property a characteristic of matter that can be observed without changing the chemical composition of the substance

population all the organisms of the same species that live in an area

population density the number of individuals per unit of living space in an ecosystem

potential energy the energy stored in an object or the energy an object has due to its position

precipitation water in liquid (rain) or solid form (snow, sleet, or hail) that falls toward Earth's surface

predation when one organism hunts and eats another

products substances that are formed during a chemical reaction

prokaryotic cells cells that do not have a nucleus

proteins nutrients that build and repair body parts

proton a positively charged particle in the nucleus of an atom

pseudopod an extension of the inside fluid of the cell that allows for the movement of some unicellular organisms

R

radiant energy energy, such as light, that travels in waves

radiation the energy Earth receives from the sun

reactants substances that undergo change during a chemical reaction

reactivity how a substance chemically changes with another substance

Glossary

red dwarf relatively small and cool stars that have extremely long lives

red giant a star that near the end of its life has a greatly expanded surface

reflecting telescope a telescope that uses mirrors to magnify an image of a distant object

refracting telescope a telescope that uses glass lenses to gather light and magnify the images of distant objects

relative humidity the ratio of water vapor in the air to the amount of water vapor the air can hold at its present temperature

renewable energy sources that can be replaced by natural means in less than 30 years

respiration the process by which cells release energy from food

response the action of an organism as the result of a stimulus

rickets a disease caused by a deficiency of vitamin D, leading to soft and misshapen bones

rift valley a long, narrow depression with steep walls caused by the pulling apart of Earth's crust; rift valleys are found on land and under the sea

rift zones regions of the ocean floor that are spreading

roots plant organs that may anchor the plant in the soil, absorb the water and minerals a plant needs to grow, and store food for the plant

runoff water that flows across the surface of the ground

S

salt water water found in Earth's oceans; its salinity is so great that people and land animals cannot consume it

seawalls structures built just behind the shoreline to help keep the ocean away from the shore

skeletal system the system that provides shape and support in the bodies of some animals; in most animals, it is made up of bone

solar cells devices able to convert solar energy directly into electricity

solar system the sun, the nine planets, and other objects that orbit the sun

soluble a substance that can be dissolved in a given substance

sonar scientific equipment that uses sound waves to locate objects and measure the depth of the ocean

spongy bone hard bone filled with many openings; it is found near the end of many bones

spring tides the highest tides that occur when the sun, the moon, and Earth are all in alignment and

Glossary

their gravitational attraction acts on the water in the ocean

stems plant organs that may support plant leaves and move water and nutrients throughout a plant

stimulus anything that causes an organism to react

stomach a baglike, muscular organ that mixes food and chemically changes protein

stratosphere the layer of atmosphere above the troposphere; it extends from about 10 to 50 km above Earth's surface and contains the ozone layer

stratus layers of clouds that are associated with wind and rain or snow

strength the ability of the muscles to exert a force

suspension a type of heterogeneous mixture in which something is mixed in a gas or liquid and it does not dissolve but will eventually separate

symbiosis a specific interaction between two species over a long period of time

T

tendons tough, connective tissues that attach muscle to bone

terrestrial planets the inner planets in the solar system— Mercury, Venus, Earth, and Mars; they have solid cores and are made mostly of rock

thermal energy the energy of the random movement of atoms in matter

thermosphere the layer of atmosphere above the mesosphere; it extends between 80 and 480 km above Earth

tissues groups of similar cells in plants and animals that work together to perform a particular function in an organism

tornado a dangerous, funnel-shaped column of air that occurs when winds near the top of a thunderhead rotate, causing an updraft of air

trachea a tube that carries air to two shorter tubes leading to the lungs

transport system the system by which the leaves, stems, and roots move water, nutrients, and minerals throughout a plant

tropism plant response that involves a change of position by growing toward or away from a stimulus

troposphere the part of the atmosphere closest to Earth's surface; it is about 10 km thick; where all of our weather occurs

Glossary

U

unicellular organisms organisms that are made of only one cell

urea a waste that results from the breakdown of proteins

ureter a tube that carries wastes from the kidney to the bladder

urethra a tube that carries liquid wastes from the bladder to the outside of the body

V

vacuoles storage areas found in some eukaryotic cells that can store food, water, and waste

valves flaps in the heart that keep blood flowing in one direction

vascular tissue made up of vessels that move substances throughout a plant

vegetarian someone who does not eat meat

veins the blood vessels that carry blood to the heart

vent an opening or crack in Earth's crust through which lava may reach Earth's surface

villi the millions of tiny, fingerlike projections that line the small intestine and absorb broken-down food

vitamins chemical compounds needed in small amounts for cellular respiration

volume the amount of space something takes up

voluntary muscles muscles that you can control

W

warm front when a warm air mass catches up with a mass of cold air, causing warm air to rise slowly over the cold air

water cycle the continual movement of water from one place to another and from one state of matter to another in an ecosystem

water table the highest level of groundwater

weather the sum of the atmospheric conditions in any particular place on Earth

weight the amount of gravitational force exerted on one object by another

white dwarf the hot star that is formed when a giant star collapses and casts off its outer layers of gas; the final stage of a sunlike star

wind an air mass that moves across Earth's surface due to differences in air pressure

Index

A

Index

Index

Index

Index

Index

Index

Index

Index

prokaryotic cells, A18, A21
prominences, B139
proteins, D79–D81, D86–D87
proton, C41–C42, C60
pseudopod, A12
Ptolemy, B116

R

radiant energy, B28–B29, B34–B35,
   C77, C80
radiation, B21, B28, B63
radio waves, B22
rain, B30–B31, B55, B62, B65
   acid rain, B19
reactants, C18–C19
recycling, B111
red blood cells, B142, D9, D12
red dwarfs, B142
red giants, B142
reflecting telescope, B144
refracting telescope, B143
relative humidity, B66–B67
renal arteries, D29–D32
renal veins, D29–D32
renewable energy sources, C95,
   C100–C101, C103
   biomass, C103
   hydroelectric power, C100–C101
reproductive adaptations, A101–A102
respiration, A34–A37, A90–A91, D65,
   D67, D70
respiratory system, D10–D11
   alveoli, D10–D12
   bronchi, D11
   diaphragm, A56, D11
   epiglottis, D11
   lungs, A56, A62–A63, A104,
      D10–D13
   trachea, D11

response, A99
retrograde, B133
revolve, B118–B120
rickets, D100
rift valley, B91
rift zones, B73
rocks, B105
   igneous, B96, B105
   metamorphic, B96, B105
   sandstone, B105
   sedimentary, B96, B105
roots, A59, A70–A71, A103
rotate, B10–B11, B118, B120–B121
rubber, C17
runoff, B62, B65
rust, C10–C11
Rutherford, Ernest, C40

S

salinity, B54
saliva, D18–D19
salt, D102
salt water, B53–B54, B56–B59
sandstone, B105
satellites, B38, B74
Saturn, B132–B133
scavengers, A89
scurvy, D98, D100
sea breeze, B30
seawalls, B98
sediment, B100–B101
sedimentary rocks, B96, B105
shells (atoms), C41–C42
skeletal muscles, D48–D51, D69
skeletal system, A68–A69, D40–D47
   bone marrow, D43–D44
   bones, A68, D41–D47, D50–D53
   cartilage, A68, D47, D94–D95
   compact bone, D43–D44
   joints, D46–D47
   ligaments, D47

Index

Index

U

ultraviolet (UV) rays, B21
unicellular organisms, A9–A13, A44
universe, B116
Uranus, B132–B133
urea, D28, D32
ureter, D29–D30
urethra, D29–D30, D33
urine, D32–D33

V

vacuoles, A19, A21–A23
valleys, B91, B99
valves, D6–D7
van Leeuwenhoek, Antonie, A6
vascular plants, A49
vascular tissue, A49–A50, A59–A61
vegetarian, D92
veins, D8
    plant, A61
    renal, D29–D32
vent, B86
ventricle, A57, A66–A67, D6–D7
Venus, B130
villi, D21–D23
visible radiation, B139
vitamins, D79–D82, D92, D96–D97,
    D100–D101
vocal chords, B7
volcanic eruptions, B95
volcanoes, B82, B84, B86–B87,
    B90–B91
    caldera, B86, B92–B93
    lava, B86–B87
    magma, B85, B95, B105
    mass wasting, B87
    vent, B86
volume, C5
voluntary muscles, D49

W

warm front, B41
water, B48–B77
    states of, B30, B51, B61–B65
    and weather, B30
water cycle, B60–B69
    condensation, B64–B65, B67
    evaporation, B63
    precipitation, B30, B41, B55, B62,
        B65, B68–B69
water table, B52
water vapor, B30, B53, B63–B64,
    B66–B67, B131
water wheels, C100
waves (earthquake), B88
waves (ocean), B76–B77
weather, B9–B11, B26–B33, B36–B43
    air pressure, B8–B15, B38
    wind, B9–B11, B13, B76, C95–C97
weather balloons, B13, B38
weather forecasting, B36–B43
weathering, B96–B101
weather instruments, B12–B13, B38
    anemometer, B12
    barometer, B12
    thermometer, B12, B38
weather satellites, B13, B38
weight, B119, C5
white blood cells, D9
white dwarf, B142
wind, B9–B11, B13, B76, C95–C97
wind direction, B38
wind energy, C95–C97
wind speed, B12, B38
work, A29, C72

X

xylem, A49, A59, A61

Credits

Photo Credits

Covers, Title Page, Unit Openers, Gary Vestal/Tony Stone Images; **iv (t)**, Dennis Kunkel/PhotoTake NYC, **(b)**, Stephen Dalton/Animals Animals; **v**, ©Stephen Dalton/Photo Researchers, Inc.; **vi (t)**, Michael Glannechini/Photo Researchers, Inc., **(b)**, Douglas Faulkner/Photo Researchers, Inc.; **vii (t)**, Stephanie Dinkins/Photo Researchers, Inc., **(b)**, Art Wolfe/Tony Stone Images; **viii (t)**, Erich Schrempp/Photo Researchers, Inc, **(b)**, David Pollack/The Stock Market; **ix**, David Barnes/The Stock Market; **x (t)**, Tom McHugh/Photo Researchers, Inc., **(b)**, David Madison; **xi**, Felicia Martinez/PhotoEdit; **xii, xiii, xiv, xv**, Matt Meadows; **A2-A3**, Dennis Kunkel/PhotoTake NYC; **A5**, ©Manfred Kage/Peter Arnold, Inc.; **A6**, Corbis/Bettmann; **A7 (t)**, Corbis/Bettmann, **(b)**, Leonard Lessin/Peter Arnold, Inc.; **A8 (l)**, Visuals Unlimited/©R. Calentine, **(r)**, Visuals Unlimited/©Michael Eichelberger; **A9**, C. Allen Morgan/DRK Photo; **A10 (l)**, Visuals Unlimited/©T. E. Adams, **(r)**, ©Michael Abbey/Photo Researchers, Inc.; **A11 (t)**, Visuals Unlimited/©Michael Abbey, **(b)**, Visuals Unlimited/©Karl Auderheide; **A12**, Visuals Unlimited/©Michael Abbey; **A13**, George J. Sanker/DRK Photo; **A14, A15**, Brent Turner/BLT Productions; **A17**, ©Alfred Pasieka/Science Photo Library/Photo Researchers, Inc.; **A18 (t)**, ©Dr. Kari Lounatmaa/Science Photo Library/Photo Researchers, Inc., **(b)**, ©David Phillips/Photo Researchers, Inc.; **A19 (t)**, ©Alfred Pasieka/Science Photo Library/Photo Researchers, Inc., **(b)**, ©BioPhoto Associates/Photo Researchers, Inc.; **A20**, ©Professors P. Motta & T. Naguro/Science Photo Library/Photo Researchers, Inc.; **A21 (t)**, ©Moredun Animal Health Ltd/Science Photo Library/Photo Researchers, Inc., **(c)**, Visuals Unlimited/©David M. Phillips, **(b)**, ©CNRI/Science Photo Library/Photo Researchers, Inc.; **A24 (t)**, Visuals Unlimited/©R. Calentine, **(b)**, ©Dr. Kari Lounatmaa/Science Photo Library/Photo Researchers, Inc.; **A26, A27**, ©Matt Meadows; **A29**, A. & M. Shah/Animals Animals; **A30 (l)**, Jim Nilsen/Tony Stone Images, **(r)**, ©Don Fawcett/Photo Researchers, Inc.; **A31**, ©Matt Meadows; **A33 (t)**, Visuals Unlimited/©Stanley Flegler, **(b)**, Visuals Unlimited/©David M. Phillips; **A34**, Myrleen Ferguson/PhotoEdit; **A36**, Verna R. Johnston/Photo Researchers, Inc.; **A38, A39**, ©Matt Meadows; **A42-A43**, Stephen Dalton/Animals Animals; **A45 (tr)**, Visuals Unlimited/©Don W. Fawcett, **(l)**, ©David Young-Wolff/PhotoEdit, **(br)**, ©Ed Reschke/Peter Arnold, Inc.; **A46 (l)**, ©Boehringer Ingelheim International Gmbh, Photo Lennart Nilsson/Albert Bonniers Forlag AB, THE INCREDIBLE MACHINE, National Geographic Society, **(r)**, ©L & D Klein/Photo Researchers, Inc.; **A47 (t)**, Gerard Lacz/Animals Animals, **(b)**, ©BioPhoto Associates/Photo Researchers, Inc.; **A48 (t)**, ©Tom & Pat Leeson/Photo Researchers, Inc, **(b)**, ©Ed Reschke/Peter Arnold, Inc.; **A49**, R. Packwood/Earth Scenes; **A51**, Ralph A. Reinhold/Animals Animals; **A52, A53**, ©Matt Meadows; **A55**, ©A. & F. Michler/Peter Arnold, Inc.; **A56**, Visuals Unlimited/©Don W. Fawcett; **A57**, ©Luiz C. Marigo/Peter Arnold, Inc.; **A58**, Tom Brakefield/DRK Photo; **A59 (t)**, ©Matt Meadows, **(b)**, Visuals Unlimited/©Stanley Elems; **A60 (t)**, Ray Pfortner/Peter Arnold, Inc., **(b)**, ©Richard Kirby, David Spears Ltd./Science Photo Library/Photo Researchers, Inc.; **A61**, Visuals Unlimited/©David Sieren; **A62, A63**, ©Matt Meadows; **A65**, Stephen Dalton/Animals Animals; **A66**, Visuals Unlimited/©Gerald & Buff Corsi; **A67 (t)**, Wayne Lankinen/DRK Photo, **(b)**, ©John Cancalosi/Peter Arnold, Inc.; **A70**, ©Runk/Schoenberger from Grant Heilman; **A72, A73**, ©Matt Meadows; **A76-A77**, ©Stephen Dalton/Photo Researchers, Inc.; **A79**, Stephen J. Krasemann/DRK Photo; **A80**, ©S. Fried/Photo Researchers, Inc.; **A82**, ©Leonard Lee Rue III/Photo Researchers, Inc.; **A83**, ©Tim Davis/Photo Researchers, Inc.; **A84 (t)**, M. Philip Kahl/DRK Photo, **(b)**, Tom Bean/DRK Photo; **A85**, Robert Lubeck/Earth Scenes; **A87**, ©Matt Meadows; **A89 (t)**, Spencer Grant/PhotoEdit, **(b)**, Mark Stouffer/Animals Animals; **A93 (t)**, ©Adam Jones/Photo Researchers, Inc., **(c)**, Breck P. Kent/Animals Animals, **(b)**, Alan G. Nelson/Animals Animals; **A94 (tl)**, Ralph Reinhold/Animals Animals, **(tc)**, Andy Rouse/DRK Photo, **(tr)**, Leonard Lee Rue III/DRK Photo, **(cl)**, Joe McDonald/Animals Animals, **(cr)**, ©Suzanne & Joseph Collins/Photo Researchers, Inc., **(bl)**, ©E.R. Degginger/Photo Researchers, Inc., **(bc)**, Darrell Gulin/DRK Photo, **(br)**, ©John Mitchell/Photo Researchers, Inc.; **A95 (t)**, C.W. Schwartz/Animals Animals, **(ctl)**, Wayne Lankinen/DRK Photo, **(ctr)**, Sid & Shirley Rucker/DRK Photo, **(cb)**, Bertram G. Murray/Animals Animals, **(b)**, Michael Gadomski/Earth Scenes; **A96** Studiohio; **A99**, Joe McDonald/Animals Animals; **A100**, Jeff Lepore/Photo Researchers, Inc.; **A101 (t)**, James H. Robinson/Animals Animals, **(b)**, Zig Leszczynski/Animals Animals; **A102 (l)**, Barbara Gerlach/DRK Photo, **(r)**, ©Ed Reschke/Peter Arnold, Inc.; **A103 (t)**, Ed Reschke/Peter Arnold, Inc., **(b)**, ©Andrew J. Martinez/Photo Researchers, Inc.; **A104 (t)**, C. Milkins/Animals Animals, **(c)**, Tim David/Photo Researchers, Inc., **(b)**, Jim Zipp/Photo Researchers, Inc.; **A105 (t)**, Lewis S. Trusty/Animals Animals, **(b)**, W. Gregory Brown/Animals Animals; **A106, A107, A111**, ©Matt Meadows; **B2-B3**, ©Michael Glannechini/Photo Researchers, Inc.; **B5, B6**, ©KS Studios; **B12 (t)**, ©Corbis/Paul Seheult, **(b)**, Jules Bucher/Photo Researchers, Inc.; **B14, B15**, ©KS Studios; **B17**, David Marron/Earth Scenes; **B19**, ©Dr. Morley Read/Science Photo Library/Photo Researchers, Inc.; **B24, B25**, ©Matt Meadows; **B27**, Patti McConville/The Image Bank; **B31 (t)**, ©Michael P. Gadomski/Photo Researchers, Inc., **(b)**, ©Michael Lustbader/Photo Researchers, Inc.; **B34, B35**, ©KS Studios; **B37**, ©Frank Schreider/Photo Researchers, Inc.; **B39**, Eastcott/Momatiuk/Earth Scenes; **B42**, E.R. Degginger/Earth Scenes; **B44, B45**, ©Matt Meadows; **B48-B49**, Douglas Faulkner/Photo Researchers, Inc.; **B51 (t)**, Michael Ginnechini/Photo Researchers, Inc., **(b)**, Michael P. Gadomski/Photo Researchers, Inc.; **B52**, Visuals Unlimited/©Mark E. Gibson; **B53**, NASA; **B54**, ©Robert C. Fields/Earth Scenes; **B55**, Roland Seitre/Peter Arnold, Inc.; **B56**, Clyde H. Smith/Peter Arnold, Inc.; **B57**, George Chan/Photo Researchers, Inc.; **B58, B59**, Studiohio; **B61**, Breck P. Kent/Earth Scenes; **B64**, ©Phillip Hayson/Photo Researchers, Inc.; **B65**, Stephen J. Krasemann/Photo Researchers, Inc.; **B66**, Manfred Danegger/Peter Arnold, Inc.; **B68, B69**, ©Matt Meadows; **B74 (t)**, World Ocean Floor/Bruce Heezen & Marie Tharp, **(b)**, US Department of Energy/Photo Researchers, Inc.; **B78, B79**, ©Matt Meadows; **B82-B83**, Stephanie Dinkins/Photo Researchers, Inc.; **B86**, ©Georg Gerster/Photo Researchers, Inc.; **B87**, ©Tom & Pat Leeson/Photo Researchers, Inc.; **B88**, Kevin Schafer/Peter Arnold, Inc.; **B89**, ©Gregory G. Dimijian/Photo Researchers, Inc.; **B90**, ©Tim Davis/Photo Researchers, Inc.; **B92, B93**, ©Matt Meadows; **B96**, Charles Patek/Earth Scenes; **B97**, John Kieffer/Peter Arnold, Inc.; **B98 (t)**, Graham Ewens/Science Photo Library/Photo Researchers, Inc., **(b)**, Breck P. Kent/Earth Scenes; **B99 (t)**, ©Tom Bean/DRK Photo, **(b)**, ©Mark C. Burnett/Photo Researchers, Inc.; **B102**, Platinum Studios; **B103**, Breck P. Kent; **B105 (t)**, George Bernard/Earth Scenes, **(c)**, George Roos/Peter Arnold, Inc., **(b)**, John Cancalbsi/Peter Arnold, Inc.; **B106**, Horst Schafer/Peter Arnold, Inc; **B108**, ©Georg Gerster/Photo Researchers, Inc.; **B110**, Richard W. Brooks/Photo Researchers, Inc.; **B113**, ©Matt Meadows; **B116-B117**, Art Wolfe/Tony Stone Images; **B120**, Myrleen Ferguson/PhotoEdit; **B122**, Corbis; **B123**, Galen Rowell/Peter Arnold, Inc.; **B125**, ©Corbis/Roger Ressmeyer; **B126, B127**, ©Matt Meadows; **B130-B134**, NASA; **B135**, ©Science Photo Library/Photo Researchers, Inc; **B136**, ©Matt Meadows; **B139**, NASA/Peter Arnold, Inc.; **B141**, Celestial Image Co./Science Photo Library/Photo, Researchers, Inc.; **B145**, Zig Leszczynski/Earth Scenes; **B146, B147, B151**, ©Matt Meadows; **C2-C3**, Erich Schrempp/Photo Researchers, Inc; **C5**, Corbis/Richard T. Nowitz; **C6 (t)**, Corbis/Kevin R. Morris, **(b)**, Visuals Unlimited/©Deneve Feigh Bunde; **C7**, Shirley Richards/Photo Researchers, Inc.; **C10**, R.J. Erwin/Photo Researchers, Inc.; **C12, C13**, ©Matt Meadows; **C15**, ©KS Studios; **C16**, First Image; **C17 (t)**, Visuals Unlimited/©G. Prance, **(b)**, Will & Deni McIntyre/Photo Researchers, Inc.; **C21, C23**, ©Matt Meadows; **C25**, ©KS Studios; **C26, C27**, Aaron Haupt; **C28**, Argus Fotoarchiv/Peter Arnold, Inc.; **C29 (t)**, Corbis/Lois Ellen Frank, **(b)**, First Image; **C30**, David Parker/Science Photo Library/Photo Researchers, Inc.; **C32, C33**, ©Matt Meadows; **C36-C37**, David Pollack/The Stock Market; **C43 (t)**, ©Charles D. Winters/Photo Researchers, Inc., **(b)**, ©Russ Lappa/Photo Researchers, Inc.; **C44 (t)**, Lenoard Lessin/Peter Arnold, Inc., **(b)**, Wes Thompson/The Stock Market; **C45**, Charles D. Winters/Photo Researchers, Inc.; **C46, C47**, Studiohio; **C49**, K.D. McGraw/From Rainbow; **C50**, First Image; **C51 (tr)**, Lawrence Migdale/Photo Researchers, Inc., **(bl)**, Manfred Kage/Peter Arnold, Inc., **(br)**, Martyn F. Chillmaid/Science Photo Library/Photo Researchers, Inc.; **C52-C53**, ©Matt Meadows; **C54**, IBM Research/Peter Arnold, Inc; **C55**, Charles Falco/Photo Researchers, Inc.; **C56**, ©Matt Meadows; **C59**, Corbis/Steve Raymer; **C61**, ©First Image; **C66, C67**, ©Matt Meadows; **C70-71**, David Barnes/The Stock Market; **C73**, David Madison; **C75**, Vandystadt/Photo Researchers, Inc.; **C76-C77**, ©David Madison; **C79**, Jeff Lepore/Photo Researchers, Inc.; **C80**, Dan Guravich/Photo Researchers, Inc.; **C82, C83**, ©Matt Meadows; **C90**, Mark Burnett/Photo Researchers, Inc.; **C92, C93**, ©Matt Meadows; **C95**, Tony Craddock/Science Photo Library/Photo Researchers, Inc.; **C97**, Visuals Unlimited/©Doug Sokell; **C98**, Kevin Schafer/Peter Arnold, Inc.; **C99, C102**, ©Franciois Gohier/Photo Researchers, Inc.; **C103**, Warren Gretz/NREL/US Department of Energy/Science Photo Library/Photo Researchers, Inc.; **C104 (t)**, Visuals Unlimited/©Jeff Greenberg, **(b)**, Georg Gerster/Photo Researchers, Inc.; **C105**, Simon Fraser/Science Photo Library/Photo Researchers, Inc.; **C107, C111**, ©Matt Meadows; **D2-D3**, ©Tom McHugh/Photo Researchers, Inc.; **D5**, Ed Reschke/Peter Arnold, Inc.; **D7**, ©KS Studios; **D9 (t)**, ©David Phillips/Photo Researchers, Inc., **(b)**, ©Meckes/Ottawa/Photo Researchers, Inc.; **D14, D15**, ©Matt Meadows; **D17**, Manfred Kage/Peter Arnold, Inc.; **D18**, ©Matt Meadows; **D23**, Visuals Unlimited/©G. Shuh-R. Kessel; **D24, D25**, ©Matt Meadows; **D27**, Bob Daemmrich/The Image Works; **D28**, First Image; **D33**, ©SECCHI-Lecaque/Roussel-UCLAF/CNRI/Science Photo Library/Photo Researchers, Inc.; **D34, D35**, ©Matt Meadows; **D38-D39**, David Madison; **D41**, ©Don Mason/The Stock Market; **D43**, F. & A. Michler/Peter Arnold, Inc.; **D45, D46**, ©KS Studios; **D48 (tl)**, Visuals Unlimited/©Fred Hossler, **(r)**, ©KS Studios, **(cl)**, Manfred Kage/Peter Arnold, Inc., **(bl)**, ©BioPhoto Associates/Photo Researchers, Inc.; **D49**, ©KS Studios; **D53, D53**, ©Matt Meadows; **D55**, David Madison Photography; **D56 (t)**, Bob Daemmrich/Tony Stone Images, **(b)**, ©David Young-Wolff/PhotoEdit; **D57**, David Madison; **D58, D58**, ©KS Studios; **D59 (t)**, David Young-Wolff/PhotoEdit, **(b)**, ©David Madison/Tony Stone Images; **D61**, Michael Newman/PhotoEdit; **D62, D63**, ©Matt Meadows; **D65**, Dan McCoy from Rainbow; **D66, D66**, David Madison; **D70**, David Young-Wolff/PhotoEdit; **D72, D73**, ©Matt Meadows; **D76-D77**, Felicia Martinez/PhotoEdit; **D80**, ©David Young-Wolff/PhotoEdit; **D81**, ©KS Studios; **D84**, Lori Adamski Peek/Tony Stone Images; **D86, D87**, ©Matt Meadows; **D89**, Jennie Woodcock/Tony Stone Images; **D90 (t)**, ©David Young-Wolff/PhotoEdit, **(b)**, Penny Gentieu/Tony Stone Images; **D91 (t)**, Mary Kate Denny/Tony Stone Images, **(c)**, David Sutherland/Tony Stone Images, **(b)**, Bob Daemmrich/Stock Boston; **D94**, BioPhoto Associates/Photo Researchers, Inc.; **D96, D96**, ©Matt Meadows; **D99**, First Image; **D100**, Archive Photos; **D101**, John Paul Kay/Peter Arnold, Inc.; **D102**, First Image; **D103**, ©KS Studios; **D104**, David K. Crow/PhotoEdit; **D106, D107, D111**, ©Matt Meadows; **D79**, ©KS Studios; **R2**, Tom McHugh/Photo Researchers, Inc.; **R3 (l)**, Tony Craddock/Science Photo Library/Photo Researchers, Inc., **(r)**, Marian Bacon/Animals Animals; **R4-R5**, Alan Schein/The Stock Market; **R6**, Dietrich Rose/OKAPIA/Photo Researchers, Inc.; **R7 (t)**, Novosti Press Agency/Science Photo Library/Photo Researchers, Inc, **(b)**, Dan Suzio/Photo Researchers, Inc.; **R8–R9**, Visuals Unlimited; **R10**, ©Esbin-Anderson/The Image Works; **R11 (l)**, Tony Freeman/PhotoEdit, **(r)**, Charles D. Winters/Photo Researchers, Inc., **(b)**, David Barber/PhotoEdit; **R13**, Visuals Unlimited/©Ken Lucas; **R15**, Tim Davis/David Madison Photography.

Art Credits

A22, A23, A25, A32, A35, A36, Precision Graphics; **A50**, Dartmouth Publishing, Inc.; **A56**, Precision Graphics; **A57**, Dartmouth Publishing, Inc.; **A58**, Precision Graphics; **A66, A67**, Dartmouth Publishing, Inc.; **A68, A69**, Chris Higgins/PP/FA; **A91, A92, B7, B8, B10, B18, B22, B28, B29, B31, B32, B33, B72–73, B95, B100, B119, B129, B142**, Precision Graphics; **C9, C18, C1,9 C20, C39, C40, C41, C42, C50, C60, C62–63, C89**, Burmar Technical Corporation; **D6, D8, D12, D20, D22, D29, D30, D31, D32, D42, D44, D46, D47, D48, D50, D67, D69**, Sandra McMahon/McMahon Medical Art; **D82, D83**, Chris Higgins/PP/FA; **D92**, Sandra McMahon/McMahon Medical Art.